"In this book Dr. Martin is squarely facing the serious crisis that is unfolding both in the Church and in the culture. He does so in an honest but fair manner and offers solutions that, if implemented, would do a great deal to restore health and strength to the Church, and allow it to be the light to the world it is meant to be. An important book that should be widely read."

CARDINAL GERHARD L. MÜLLER
Former Prefect of the Congregation for the Doctrine of the Faith

"It is impossible to deny the crisis of division and widespread confusion that characterizes the Church in our day. Nor can anyone who loves the Church ignore the strong theological undercurrents that Dr. Martin identifies, currents that try to separate what cannot be legitimately divided: pastoral charity from revealed truth. This is an important book well worth reading."

BISHOP SCOTT MCCAIG, C.C.
Military Ordinary of Canada

"This book is a massive achievement. Ralph Martin is one of the most reliable analysts of the state of the Church. He is brave and bold, outspoken but never snarky or alarmist. Some of his chapters, such as that on culpability, shed fresh light on some of the most debilitating confusions of our age. This book will be the go-to book for those who want a comprehensive view of the crisis in the Church today."

JANET SMITH
Author of Self-Gift: Humanae Vitae and the Thought of John Paul II

"Ralph Martin's new book is the clear blast of a trumpet, a bright light in the midst of a fog of confusion and apathy. Its analysis of the present crisis in the Church is profoundly sobering, but not dispiriting. No, God himself is at work to purify and renew his Church, and this book will inspire both clergy and laity to collaborate in that work through soul-searching, repentance, courage, zeal for holiness, and a renewed hope in the victory of the risen Lord."

MARY HEALY
Member of the Pontifical Biblical Commission and Co-Editor of the Catholic Commentary on Sacred Scripture

"Ralph Martin's remarkable book provides an extraordinary opportunity to engage in a self-examination of our 'own faithfulness to Christ's will for the Church and accordingly to undertake with vigor the task of renewal and reform' (Vatican II, *Unitatis Redintegratio* 4).... His book simply could not have come at a better time."

EDUARDO J. ECHEVERRIA
Professor of Philosophy and Systematic Theology,
Sacred Heart Major Seminary

"The Catholic Church is in deep crisis. It doesn't take a genius to see that. However, to present an accurate and synthetic picture of the crisis, to identify its roots, and to indicate the path forward takes more than a genius: it takes a man filled with the Spirit of God. Ralph Martin is just such a person, and his new book is fire alarm, tonic and fresh air all wrapped into one."

MSGR. ANDREW MCLEAN CUMMINGS
Director of Spiritual Formation,
Mount Saint Mary's Seminary

"The crisis of truth is back. An unblinking analysis of these toxic threats to the Church is once again desperately needed, but while many have provided elements of such an analysis, few have proffered so sweeping an evaluation while retaining admirable balance and evincing heartfelt love for the Church. Yet Dr. Martin goes further still in this book, which I do not hesitate to call prophetic. He points the way forward by holding fast to Scripture, rejecting the rationalization of sin and the false security of universalism, and recommending the proven remedies of repentance and reliance on the power of the Holy Spirit."

Fr. Peter Ryan, S.J.

Professor of Theology, Director of Spiritual Formation,
Sacred Heart Major Seminary, Former Executive Director of the
USCCB Committee on Doctrine

A CHURCH
IN CRISIS

A CHURCH IN CRISIS

PATHWAYS FORWARD

RALPH MARTIN

EMMAUS
ROAD
PUBLISHING

Steubenville, Ohio
www.emmausroad.org

Emmaus Road Publishing
1468 Parkview Circle
Steubenville, Ohio 43952

Library of Congress Control Number: 2020945074
ISBN 978-1-64585-048-9 (hardcover) 978-1-64585-049-6 (paperback)
978-1-949013-75-7 (ebook)

Cover design and layout by Emily Demary
Cover image: "Topshot-France-Fire-Notre Dame."
Photo by: HUBERT HITIER/AFP via Getty Images

DEDICATION

TO MY WIFE ANNE, whose steadfast and sacrificial love for fifty-two years has been a pillar of strength and a powerful impetus to keep saying yes to the Lord in whatever mission he assigned us; most of what I've done would never have happened without her; to Fr. Michael Scanlan, whose God-sent friendship helped me to carry out the original *A Crisis of Truth* mission, and who continues to help me with the mission of this book from "the other side"; and to Peter Herbeck, my partner in mission for the last thirty years, with whom I've discussed virtually every idea in this book and who could have written it himself, another God-sent friend who came at the needed time. And to Deacon Daniel Foley, a longtime friend who succeeded Bishop Sam Jacobs as the Chairman of the US Board of Renewal Ministries and who has been a special support all these years. Deacon Dan's laborious proofreading of *Will Many Be Saved?* and this book has greatly improved the final products.

ACKNOWLEDGEMENTS

BESIDES THOSE I've mentioned in the dedication, I want to thank Pete Burak, the leader of our young adult ministry, who also shares in the overall leadership of Renewal Ministries and who, after reading the original *A Crisis of Truth* a few years ago, urged me to consider reprinting it with some minor revisions as he found it amazingly relevant to our current situation. I ended up doing virtually an entirely new book, but his encouragement was important. And Jack Lynch, the leader of our TV and Radio ministries and a donor to Renewal Ministries for many years before "retiring" and joining the team, urged the same. Jack remembers more of what I've said and done over the years, including the whole message of *A Crisis of Truth* than I do. He's the one who found the original high-quality video recordings of *A Crisis of Truth* in the Bentley Historical Library at the University of Michigan and put them in usable form for TV and DVD use. He, with Pete, strongly encouraged me to do a revision of the original book, as did Heather Schultz, our newsletter editor and social media director. And I want to thank Heather and her daughter, Meghan, for getting the text of the original book into workable electronic form so we can make it available on our website for those who want to compare this version with the original. The "revision" amounted to virtually a new book, and without their encouragement and help, I may not have given it serious consideration.

And I want to thank all the board members of Renewal Ministries, of both the United States and Canada, and friends and donors of Renewal Ministries who have made possible forty years of preaching the Gospel and serving God's people all over the world. And I am grateful for our whole team of twenty truly wonderful people here in Ann Arbor (with a special mention of Sr. Ann Shields, part of the spiritual heart of this ministry for many years), and many friends, partners in ministry, and Country Coordinators throughout the world. And special thanks also to Ave Maria Radio and Eternal Word Television Network, who have carried our TV and radio programs for many years and are true partners in preaching the Gospel. And special thanks to Sacred Heart Major Seminary, which has entrusted me with the privilege of teaching seminarians and priests these past twenty years, giving me the opportunity to contribute to our present and future leaders. A very healthy seminary. Thanks to all the bishops, rectors, and academic deans during this time for supporting me in this mission.

I want to thank my friends and colleagues, most especially Fr. Peter Ryan, who has given me important input on this book, and also Dr. Mary Healy, Francisco Gavrilides, Dr. Janet Smith, and Dr. Peter Williamson, who took valuable time away from their own important projects to read some, if not all, of this book and give valuable input. The book is far better because of their input.

And finally, I am grateful for the whole team at Emmaus Road Publishing: Scott Hahn, Ken Baldwin, Chris Erickson, Rob Corzine, Anthony Puorro and all their staff who played such a critical role in bringing this book to publication.

TABLE OF CONTENTS

INTRODUCTION		1
PART I	*A Church in Crisis*	13
CHAPTER 1	*A Time of Confusion and Division*	15
CHAPTER 2	*Is There a Solid Place to Stand?*	45
CHAPTER 3	*Is It All a Game? The Fog of Universalism*	67
CHAPTER 4	*The Revolution Continues*	97
CHAPTER 5	*How Long Will You Straddle the Issue?*	147
CHAPTER 6	*Is Anyone Responsible?*	201
PART II	*Pathways Forward*	231
CHAPTER 7	*Seeing and Not Seeing*	233
CHAPTER 8	*Powers, Principalities, and Organizations*	251
CHAPTER 9	*Pastoral Passivity: Good Shepherds and Bad*	297
CHAPTER 10	*The Signs of the Times: Pointing toward Judgment*	337
CHAPTER 11	*A Time for Repentance*	357
CHAPTER 12	*A Time for Action*	385
CHAPTER 13	*The Inexhaustible Riches of Jesus: Participating in the Prophetic Mission of Jesus*	413
ENDNOTES		441

INTRODUCTION

MY FAMILY AND I were still living in Belgium when I flew from Brussels to Minneapolis–St. Paul to deliver five talks entitled "A Crisis of Truth." The year was 1980.

During the four years we lived in Belgium, I had become increasingly aware that there were an emerging number of texts being published by theologians and popular Catholic writers that were not only seriously departing from the faith but were also influencing many ordinary Catholics to do the same. A widespread skepticism about the reliability and authority of Sacred Scripture was pervading the worldwide Church. More and more real evangelization was being dismissed in favor of what was considered really meaningful: human development and social justice. There was a virtual assault on traditional sexual morality. And in the midst of it all was a widespread episcopal silence, with occasional indirect nods in the direction of "Well, this is what the Church teaches, but follow your own conscience." Many interpreted this feeble teaching as permission to do what they wanted to do.

In many dioceses and many countries, this undermining of faith, morality, and mission was tolerated or even actively advanced by something like a fifth column within the Church. Leading purveyors of the confusion were being appointed and protected in key positions on seminary and university theological faculties.

I must say that when I traveled back to the United States to give these "Crisis of Truth" talks, I felt that I was being commissioned by the Lord to do so. I realized that besides my own study and observation, I was being assisted by the Holy Spirit to identify and communicate issues that were really important for the salvation of souls and the true renewal of the Church. I thought that if I could just successfully complete this mission—and deliver these five talks—perhaps my mission in life would have been accomplished. The very strong response to the talks and the subsequent initiatives that many took to make sure this message was promulgated widely made me think that my mission was indeed accomplished. Somewhat to my surprise, it wasn't! And a lot has happened over the past forty years! And still is.

When we moved back to the States in June of 1980, I sent a letter to a small group of friends asking if they could financially help make this possible. They responded generously and what eventually became Renewal Ministries[1] was born. Our first mission was to make sure the message of the crisis of truth was as widely distributed as possible. The talks were recorded and taped in a professional setting. A small group of people in South Bend, IN, devoted themselves to arranging for the videotaped talks to be shown in parishes and other settings, with teams of people organizing and being present for them. Hundreds of people showed up in venues all across the United States and Canada to view the talks and lead responses to them in discussion groups, with many discerning what actions they could take to implement the message they were hearing.

Someone sent Mother Angelica the audio version of the talks, and she asked me to come down to EWTN in Alabama to record some TV programs with her on the crisis of truth. Then she invited me to develop a weekly TV program to pursue these and other themes out of which *The Choices We Face* was born. It is now the longest-running weekly Catholic TV program in the world, thirty-five years and counting.[2] Then people encouraged me to put the teachings into book form, which I did.

In 1982, the book form of my five talks, *A Crisis of Truth: The Attack on Faith, Morality, and Mission in the Catholic Church*,[3] was published by Servant Books and immediately became a bestseller. To this day, I still run into people who tell me that reading that book saved their faith or, for many priests, saved their vocations. I am profoundly grateful to God that the *A Crisis of Truth* project helped so many people in really significant ways.

At a certain point, I received a very important telephone call. It was from Fr. Michael Scanlan, T.O.R., at that time in his early years as president of Franciscan University of Steubenville. He had just listened to the audio version of the talks in his car. He pulled off to the side of the road and called me. He told me he had a strong experience of the Holy Spirit while listening to the talks and felt that the Holy Spirit had told him that he was to "stand with me" as I continued to deliver this message. He thought this message was really from the Lord and was very much needed in the Church. Fr. Mike felt that the Lord was calling him to do all he could to help me. He thought I would be severely attacked by people who were undermining the faith or by those who were permitting this undermining to happen, and that he was supposed to offer the protection of his position and credentials to vouch for the academic soundness of what I was saying.

The fact was that I had no credentials to do what I was doing. I was a "self-taught" theologian with no theology degrees. I had graduated from the University of Notre Dame with a major in philosophy and had indeed won the philosophy award the year I graduated.

I had gone off to Princeton to begin a doctorate program in philosophy but, after the first year, felt called to a very different mission than the academic life.[4] Just before I graduated from Notre Dame, I had experienced a profound conversion through the Cursillo movement, and at the end of my first year at Princeton, my friend Steve Clark and I spent a summer at a monastery in upstate New York opening our futures to the Lord. At the end of the summer, we felt the Lord was calling us to give up our fellowships for graduate study in order to begin to more directly preach the Gospel, which we did, first in the context of the Cursillo Movement and later in the context of the Catholic Charismatic Renewal. It was the desire to have the international office for the Catholic Charismatic Renewal in a more international location that led us to move to Belgium and establish the office there.

In that roadside telephone call, Fr. Mike told me, "I have a law degree from Harvard Law School, I have years of philosophy and theology studies and a theology degree,[5] I've been rector of a Major Seminary, and I'm president of a Catholic University. I want to put those credentials at your service. I want to literally stand next to you as you preach and teach this message and vouch for its soundness and its importance."

I can't tell you how loved I felt or how overwhelmed with gratitude I was. I can't tell you how thankful I am to Fr. Mike Scanlan and to the Lord, who inspired him to do this. He knew what I would face, and he knew the support I would need to proceed with confidence. He cleared his schedule and traveled all over the world with me for years, literally standing next to me, introducing me before I gave each of the talks and commenting afterwards on what I had said.

As I write this, I have just recently returned from a long trip to Australia, where I gave ten talks to hundreds of young people, including seminarians and priests, on evangelization and holiness. One of the highlights of the trip was reuniting with a bishop I had met years ago in Rome who is now an archbishop in a major Australian city, Archbishop Julian Porteous of Hobart, Tasmania. He reminded me, and later said so publicly in one of his talks, that we had actually met back in the eighties when I was doing a weekend of teaching on *A Crisis of Truth* in Brisbane with Fr. Mike, when the bishop was just a newly ordained priest. He said the weekend made a big impact on him, and he quoted several times things I said that have stuck with him all these years.

Msgr. Charles Pope from Washington, D.C., who publishes one of the best blogs in the Church today[6] and also writes a column for *Our Sunday Visitor*, has appeared several times on our weekly TV programs and has said several times that reading *A Crisis of Truth* was very important for him as a young man in keeping his head clear about the truth and inoculating him against the pervasive corruption of the time.

This past summer, Dr. Scott Hahn, who has done more to reestablish the Sacred Scriptures as indeed *Sacred* Scriptures, told me, while we were together at his summer conference for priests, that he used *A Crisis of Truth* as a text in one of his first college teaching assignments, and one of his first students who was deeply touched by it is now the head of the Augustine Institute.[7]

When the book was published, a number of key people saw its significance and offered endorsements:

> "If one book can serve to provide the information and insights necessary to bring about the cure of the malady afflicting the church today, *A Crisis of Truth* is it." (Msgr. George Kelly, Director, Institute for Advanced Studies in Catholic Doctrine, St. John's University, New York)

"Ralph Martin's *A Crisis of Truth* is an important, responsible look at where we are now with advice on how we can correct the situation—with God's help." (Ralph McInerny, University of Notre Dame)

"I hope this book will be read and discussed and acted on by seminarians, teachers, religious, priests, bishops—indeed, by every mature Catholic." (Germain Grisez, Flynn Professor of Christian Ethics, Matt. St. Mary's College and Seminary)

"Ralph Martin's *A Crisis of Truth* is an astute and penetrating analysis of the present plight of our faith. I hope both his analysis and his proposals are heeded before it is too late." (James Hitchcock, Professor of History, Saint Louis University)

While there was strong support for the message, there was also strong opposition. Speaking invitations were mysteriously rescinded. Some people awkwardly told me that they would like me to deliver this message in their dioceses but that they couldn't invite me. In at least three dioceses that I know of, a blanket ban on my speaking was communicated to diocesan officials and lay leaders by the bishop. I later discovered that one of these dioceses was being governed by an archbishop who was later discovered to be in an active homosexual relationship and was being blackmailed by his "lover."

Under the leadership of Pope John Paul II, working closely with Cardinal Joseph Ratzinger, many efforts were made to address this deadly crisis of truth. One by one, dissenting theologians were asked to retract unsound teachings or no longer call themselves Catholic theologians. One after another, clarifying documents were published addressing various confusions.

What was at stake in many cases was the authentic interpretation of Vatican II. Many were appealing to the "spirit" of Vatican II by claiming that while Vatican II was a good start, it didn't go far enough and more change was needed. And there were a smaller number of people claiming that Vatican II was a rupture with Catholic tradition and was flawed, either as a whole or at least in some of its documents. The schism initiated by the French Archbishop Marcel Lefebvre, founder of the Society of Saint Pius X, was a result of this suspicious view of Vatican II and the beginnings of what has become an influential "traditionalist" movement that, in some of its expressions today, has taken radical and extreme forms.

Under the leadership of John Paul II and Cardinal Ratzinger, a worldwide Synod of Bishops was called on the twenty-fifth anniversary of Vatican II to try to settle its authentic interpretation. At the synod, it was affirmed that when there was possible ambiguity in the meaning of the teachings of Vatican II, difficulties had to be resolved and interpreted in light of the Catholic tradition. This became known as the "hermeneutic of continuity."

This authentic interpretation of Vatican II continued to be advanced during the pontificate of Benedict XVI. By the time he resigned in 2013, it seemed like what I had called a "crisis of truth" had been largely resolved and the Church was on a sound footing as regards faith, morality, and mission.

But quite surprisingly, for many of us, since Benedict resigned in 2013, it seems that many of the same problems that I addressed in my work on *A Crisis of Truth* are back, in very similar forms as before—but with some disturbing new features as well. But before we begin to analyze the situation in detail, let me explain when I first became aware that something disturbing was stirring again. At the time, I didn't fully understand some of the unusual features of the event, but as time went on, I understood more fully its significance as a harbinger of what was to come.

I was invited to present an academic paper at a conference that Georgetown University was holding to commemorate the fiftieth anniversary of Vatican II. Some students of a professor at Louvain University in Belgium were citing one of my books on the interpretation of Vatican II in their seminars and papers, and the professor, one of the organizers of the Georgetown conference, was convinced by his students to invite me. I was asked to give a presentation on what Vatican II teaches on the possibility of people who haven't heard the Gospel being saved. What amazed me when I arrived at Georgetown was the atmosphere surrounding the conference. I can only describe it as the "hermeneutic of rupture" on full display, as if happy days were here again, now that Pope Benedict, through his resignation, had also retired the "hermeneutic of continuity."

What also amazed me was who some of my co-presenters were. Fr. Charles Curran, a very famous dissenter from *Humanae Vitae*, was there. Fr. Roger Haight, whose work on Christology, world religions, and related topics had been examined by the Vatican and found deficient, was there. Cardinal Walter Kasper, the main influence on the Synods of the Family and its subsequent document, *Amoris Laetitia*, and its famous footnote (promoting the "merciful" approach to divorce and remarriage without annulment) was the keynote speaker. Paulist Press proudly announced they were going to publish all his writings here in the United States. Many other dissenters were there as well.

Another speaker of note was Cardinal Antonio Tagle from Manila, recently appointed as the head of the Congregation for the Evangelization of Peoples, whose responsibility is the hundreds of missionary dioceses in the world. He is known to follow the progressive "Bologna" school of interpretation of Vatican II rather than the Ratzinger "hermeneutic of continuity" school. Tagle is rumored to be Pope Francis's choice to succeed him, which is why many think he was brought from Manila to Rome and given the powerful position of overseeing so many of the world's dioceses and bishops, controlling their grants and funding. On the other hand, solid priests and bishops who know him well say that just because he is associated with the Bologna school of interpretation doesn't mean he is committed to all their positions. I was actually in Cardinal Tagle's "small group" at the Synod on New Evangelization in 2012, during which it was announced that Benedict XVI had named him as a cardinal.

In my own section of the conference, I was one of three presenters. It was a good opportunity to present my research on the correct interpretation of Vatican II's teaching on the possibility of being saved without hearing the Gospel to a decidedly more progressive audience than I normally would have been able to address. After the session, I was able to have a good dialogue with some well-known theologians whose fame, in part, consisted in having been corrected by the Vatican. Another speaker in my section of the conference was a young Dominican priest from Canada who is in charge of the Canadian Dominicans' office of New Evangelization. Quite surprisingly, his main point ended up being that we should place a moratorium on evangelization and focus on interreligious dialogue. I still find myself puzzling over that.

The point in sharing this is that a lot of people at this high-level conference—theologians and cardinals—obviously knew something about the agenda of Pope Francis that the rest of us didn't. It also became clear that many influential theologians, bishops, and cardinals had persisted in holding positions closer to the "hermeneutic of rupture" in their interpretation of Vatican II than I had ever imagined to be the case. It makes me give some credence to the comments of Cardinal Godfried Danneels that the election of Pope Francis was planned for and lobbied for years in advance by the

"Saint Gallen mafia," which included Cardinal Carlo Maria Martini and Cardinal Kasper among their numbers. These comments are repeated in both Cardinal Danneels's authorized biography and in Austen Ivereigh's book on the election of Pope Francis,[8] as well as in numerous news articles and interviews with the principals.[9] The fact that Cardinal Danneels appeared next to Pope Francis on the balcony overlooking St. Peter's Square the evening he was elected pope and that he was appointed to the important Synods on the Family even though he was eighty-five years old and there were two other Belgians appointed, are indications of special papal favor.[10]

Many people have strongly suggested to me, as I noted in the Acknowledgements, that we should republish *A Crisis of Truth*. People who both remember it and have reread it have recently told me that almost all of it is still extremely relevant. I have reread it now myself and agree that its main points are still very relevant, and we have decided to "republish" it in digital form online, and we do think people who read it today in light of what is happening will find it amazingly relevant.[11]

But after some consideration, I've decided that revising it wouldn't be the best way to address the current manifestation of the crisis, and so this new book. It will treat of many of the same topics from *A Crisis of Truth* but in the context of their manifestation to-day. It will also draw on deeper studies I've done over the years on issues related to the undermining of faith, morality, and mission. (Fr. Mike is no longer physically with us and I now have theological credentials, but I still value even more his support from where he is now). My hope—and prayer—is that this book will be able to do for many today what *A Crisis of Truth* did years ago: deliver its readers from confusion and discouragement and re-center them on the rock who is Jesus—the same yesterday, today, and forever—inspiring them to an even greater dedication to holiness and mission and a commitment to tell people everything Jesus asks us to tell them in order to be saved.

In Part I of *A Church in Crisis*, I will analyze the confusion and division we are currently experiencing. Chapter 1 will survey the problems that will be examined in more detail in later chapters. Chapter 2 will reaffirm the reliability of Scripture, tradition, and the authentic magisterium as expressed in the *Catechism of the Catholic Church* as the rock on which we can stand. Chapter 3 will examine the fog of universalism that is spreading throughout the Church and how it undermines holiness, evangelization, and vocations. Chapter 4 will examine how the sexual revolution is aggressively pressing on to its ultimate victory, where nothing will be considered established by nature or God and we can will ourselves to be whatever we want, the ultimate rebellion of the creature. Chapter 5 will examine the religious fervor that is surrounding various secular causes, how the Church is dangerously allied with these causes, and how this distorts its message and actions. Chapter 6 will consider the dominant mentality that hardly anyone is likely meaningfully culpable for what the Church continues to call mortal sin. Part II of the book will examine what we need to understand and do to open pathways to genuine renewal.

We're going to be analyzing some very troubling developments in the Church today, and I want to share my deepest conviction, right up front: Despite the grave problems we examine, the Church that Christ founded is the Catholic Church. And despite its current poverty, and even sometimes corruption, the Catholic Church is still the only church where the fullness of the means of salvation can be found. May none of us make the mistake of throwing out the baby with the bathwater! Yes, let's get rid of the dirty bathwater so the precious gift of Jesus, the real treasure of the Church, can be more easily seen, believed in, loved, and followed than ever before.

Part I

A Church in Crisis

Chapter 1

A TIME OF CONFUSION AND DIVISION

IT'S CLEAR that we are living in a time of confusion and division, both in the Church and in the world. I am not qualified to evaluate whether this is the worst confusion the Church has seen or not—we have been through some pretty bad times over the centuries—but it is serious. And it is our time and our confusion, so it is something we must deal with.

The world is always beset by confusion and division, but it is certainly intensifying throughout the world as hostility to the Church and its teachings grows. Many human rights groups who track the persecution of Christians worldwide claim that even more Christians are being persecuted and killed for their faith today than in the early centuries of the Church when Christianity was illegal in the Roman Empire.[12]

CONFUSION IN THE CHURCH

Fortunately, none of us reading this have had to live through the terrible centuries and decades where there were corrupt popes engaging in immorality, selling church offices, and carrying out military adventures. We have been blessed in our lifetimes by solid popes, some of whom have been canonized. We are not, then, a generation dealing with profligate popes, but we are dealing with serious confusion in the Church over doctrinal and moral matters of the utmost importance. This confusion sometimes seems to be emanating now also from Rome. It isn't that heretical doctrine is being formally taught, but confusing and ambiguous documents, informal comments, and perplexing events and actions seem to regularly muddy the waters on what exactly the pope or a particular synod of bishops might actually be attempting to communicate and what we are still supposed to believe as Catholics. This has left national bishops' conferences and individual cardinals and bishops openly disagreeing, sometimes in very disagreeable ways, about how to interpret these documents, comments, and actions. Along with these confusing statements and actions, there is good solid teaching that is clearly in continuity with the Deposit of Faith, but how to put the two streams together is often quite a puzzle.

Here I need to say something about my approach to evaluating the role of Pope Francis in analyzing the widespread confusion and ambiguity. Like many people, when Pope Francis was first elected, I was thrilled by his fresh approach to the trappings of the papacy. I loved that he decided to live in the Vatican guesthouse, that he dressed simply and even used inexpensive cars to travel in. I even responded positively to his repeated exhortations about not being afraid "to make a mess." I, for the most part, really liked *Evangelii Gaudium*, his apostolic exhortation following upon the 2012 Synod of Bishops on the New Evangelization, even though it was rather silent on the eternal consequences of unrepented serious sin. I had been appointed by Pope Benedict as a theological consultant to that synod and was there for its entirety. Even though his apostolic exhortation *Evangelii Gaudium* broke with tradition and wasn't really an elaboration of the final approved propositions from the synod (Pope Francis wasn't at the synod), it had many wonderful things in it, and I assign it and teach it in my classes at the seminary.

However, as time went on, and particularly after the intense battles at the two Synods on the Family and the publication of *Amoris Laetitia*, it became clear that there was a serious ambiguity in the document that many thought opened a pathway for divorced and remarried people to be allowed to "move beyond" their first marriage(s) and receive communion in good faith, without submitting the opinion of whether their first marriage(s) were valid or not to the judgment of the Church by petitioning for an annulment.[13]

This put me in the difficult place in which I presently find myself. Despite some of the extreme attacks on Pope Francis, he is clearly the legitimately elected successor of St. Peter and deserves the respect due to a pope. Catholics who think they are defending the faith by calling the pope an apostate or heretic are doing a great disservice to the Church and sowing fear and suspicion among not an inconsiderable number of the faithful. In attacking the pope in such an extreme way in the name of preserving the Catholic faith, such critics are themselves drifting into a sectarian mentality or even informal schism. I am alarmed by how many concerned Catholics I meet in countries all over the world who are living in fear and doubt because of some of the more extreme attacks on the pope. It needs to be said that Pope Francis, in many of the things he teaches officially and says informally, conveys clearly orthodox and inspiring things. He is certainly not officially teaching heresy, and it is important to keep in mind that he says he believes everything in the *Catechism of the Catholic Church*.

But he clearly says and does things that seem to contradict or put into question other admirable things he has said and done. For a long period of time, Pope Francis continued to give interviews to the atheist Italian journalist, Eugenio Scalfari, who regularly published his accounts of their conversations. After each interview or conversation, Scalfari published his account of it. Scalfari had claimed at various times that the pope has, among other things, denied the divinity of Christ and doesn't believe in hell but rather believes that souls, instead of going to hell, are annihilated.[14] The pope himself has never responded publicly to these interpretations of his interviews. Vatican press people deny that these are accurate accounts of the interviews, which seems somewhat of a feeble response.

The net effect of this is that a rather intense polarization has occurred in the Church. When I give talks now and quote Pope Francis favorably, people come up to me mad and wonder why I am ignorant of what one or another website or blog has said about how evil the pope is. At other times, during the question and answer session after a talk, when someone inevitably asks me about Pope Francis, I answer like this: "There are many wonderful things the pope says and does, but there are also some confusing and troubling things. And who can deny that there is an objective confusion that has been engendered that he doesn't seem eager to clear up." This usually causes pro-Francis people in the audience to accuse me of not respecting the pope. I imagine the same responses may occur as people read this book. Because I'm underlining a rather unusual confusion and division, even among the highest leadership of the Church, that has occurred under Francis's pontificate, I need to talk about his role in dealing with it or not dealing with it, since "the buck" does stop there. I do so with total confidence that he is the true pope and deserves our respect and says and does many good things. You'd have to sit in on my classes on the New Evangelization as we discuss *Evangelii Gaudium* to hear all the positive things, but since the focus of this book is the problems that have emerged during his pontificate, I will necessarily have to speak about his role in them more frequently than I might wish.

I must also say that the doctrinal, moral, and pastoral problems that have emerged during Francis's pontificate are not unique to him or this time.

Commenting on a symposium held at Boston College with such prominent leaders as Cardinal Blase Cupich from Chicago, Cardinal Joseph Tobin from Newark, Cardinal Reinhard Marx from Germany, Bishop John Stowe from Kentucky, and Bishop Robert McElroy from San Diego, *Catholic World Report* headlined: "Symposium on priesthood 'renews' failed revolution of the Sixties and Seventies."[15] Whether this is a fair judgment of this symposium or not I have not taken the time to research. The point I want to make, though, is that some people are perceiving that issues we thought were settled a long time ago are now reappearing in rather aggressive form at the highest levels of the Church.

The number of bishops openly proposing teachings contrary to those established by the Church seems to be growing. A number of the prominent hierarchy in attendance at the symposium on priesthood have promoted a "welcoming" attitude toward LGBTQ people but notably omit a call to repentance that has always been central to Church teaching on human sexuality. Some are also known for resisting the guidelines set forth by the Congregation for the Doctrine of the Faith—and the majority opinion of the American bishops that abortion has a certain priority among social issues today and should weigh heavily as a primary factor in voting decisions. One bishop at the symposium, Bishop McElroy, has proposed that since it is likely that in the long run more people will die from "climate change" than from abortion, climate change also has a claim on priority. "The death toll from abortion is more immediate, but the long-term death toll from unchecked climate change is larger and threatens the very future of humanity," he also said. Making note of the competing claims of these, and other, issues, he said that "the drive to label a single issue preeminent distorts the call to authentic discipleship in voting rather than advancing it."[16]

Whatever the intention of people who claim this, the net effect is to provide a rationale so Catholics can feel free to vote for pro-abortion candidates and still claim to be faithful Catholics. Not long ago, my wife and I attended the local Jesuit parish in our city, and the whole sermon was devoted to reading Bishop McElroy's comments on the equal, or even superior, priority of climate change; the priest's intent was obviously to give permission to vote for pro-abortion candidates.

It's understandable that these issues are resurfacing, although many of us really did think they were settled by John Paul II and Pope Benedict! The underlying structures of the confusions and infidelities are rooted in the human heart and go back to the garden where we were first tempted: "You will not die . . . you will be like God" (Gen 3:4–5). The temptation is to disbelieve in the Word of God, in his goodness, his power, his truthfulness—and become gods ourselves—arbiters of good and evil, life and death. The powers and principalities behind the current confusion have long experience in moving the human race, and now the Church, in this direction. Even if a new pope were elected tomorrow, these underlying structures of unbelief and infidelity that have already become so successful in luring millions of Catholics away from the faith would still be poisoning the Church. In many places, they are gaining strength and even taking control.

The "modernist" controversy, rooted in the desire to accommodate Revelation to the culture or to prevailing philosophies historicizing and relativizing the entire faith, resurfaces time and time again. Discussion about the legitimate concepts of "living tradition" or of "development of doctrine," while legitimate concepts, can sometimes cloak efforts to depart from the tradition or to change doctrine.

The homily Cardinal Ratzinger gave on April 19, 2005, before the opening of the Conclave in which he was elected pope, remains significant today. In it, Ratzinger described the challenges we are currently facing. In commenting on one of the texts for the day, Paul's warning about being "tossed about to and fro and carried about with every wind of doctrine" (Eph 4:14), Ratzinger said:

> How many winds of doctrine have we known in these last decades, how many ideological currents, how many fashions of thought? The small boat of thought of many Christians has often remained agitated by the waves, tossed from one extreme to the other: from Marxism to liberalism, to libertinism; from collectivism to radical individualism; from atheism to a vague religious mysticism; from agnosticism to syncretism, etc. . . . To have a clear faith, according to the creed of the Church, is often labeled as fundamentalism. While relativism, that is, allowing oneself to be carried about with every wind of "doctrine," seems to be the only attitude that is fashionable. A dictatorship of relativism is being constituted that recognizes nothing as absolute and which only leaves the "I" and its whims as the ultimate measure. . . . We have another measure: the Son of God, true man. He is the measure of true humanism. . . . Adult and mature is a faith profoundly rooted in friendship with Christ. This friendship opens us to all that

is good and gives us the measure to discern between what is true and what is false, between deceit and truth.[17]

Underneath the surface of our culture, steadily working away to destroy the faith, is a demonic intellectual and cultural rebellion that many trace to the "Enlightenment" but which has deep roots in Eden and has been at work ever since. The immediate intellectual transmitters of the virus which have injected massive sickness into the culture have been identified by Catholic scholar Henri de Lubac as Auguste Comte (1798–1857), Ludwig Feuerbach (1804–1872), Karl Marx (1818–1883), and Friedrich Nietzsche (1844–1900).[18]

Comte's goal was to "replace Christianity in Europe . . . to discover a man with no trace of God in him,"[19] by passing through the stages of theology to metaphysics and finally to the maturity of science. He believed that once all God talk was banished, society would become harmonious and perfected. De Lubac believed that the Church was complicit in allowing this virus to enter by pretending there was a compatibility between Comte's "Positivism" and the Church when there wasn't at all.

Feuerbach asserted that "God is only the sum of the attributes that make up the greatness of man. . . . It is the essence of man that is the supreme being."[20] One of Feuerbach's greatest disciples, Karl Marx, took the theory even further, applying the coming liberation to economic forces and class warfare and releasing the horror of communism on the world. He wrote, "The religion of the workers has no God . . . because it seeks to restore the divinity of man."[21]

Nietzsche saw deeply what the extreme consequences of the "death of God" would be: a deed which he thought had already been accomplished, the foundations of Christian culture having been cut off at the roots by open and hidden unbelief without most people recognizing it yet. He saw the spiritual crisis and hypocrisy of modernity and was willing to follow their nihilistic underpinnings to their terrifying conclusions. When God is dead, the only thing that is left is the will to power and the totally ungrounded longing for the rise of the superman who is beyond good and evil.

These are just a sampling of the forces that continue to bubble underneath the surface of our secularized culture and that are becoming more explicit all the time. And now the same forces are bubbling up within the Church.

THE CURRENT CONFUSION

It probably all began with the famous response of Pope Francis to the question of why a bishop with a rumored homosexual history was being appointed to a Vatican position: "Who am I to judge?"[22] This was a bellwether moment. This statement was promulgated far and wide and led LGBTQ groups to hail what they perceived as Francis's more accepting approach to homosexuality.[23] He was recognized as "man of the year" by the leading English language homosexual publication, *The Advocate.*

Pope Francis later informally clarified his meaning, that he was referring to someone who perhaps had a homosexual past but was now trying to seek God and deserved our mercy and, implicitly, a "second chance." Whether it was wise to appoint someone in that situation to a prominent Vatican position is another question. Although he has spoken out against ordaining homosexual men to the priesthood, Pope Francis has extremely rarely, if ever, identified the active practice of homosexuality as a grave sin that could exclude someone from the kingdom of God if not repented of before death. The impression strongly remains that he is "soft" on homosexuality, and he is encouraging that attitude in the wider Church. When he received Fr. James Martin, S.J., a well-known advocate for a more "welcoming" approach to the gay community, whom he had previously appointed as an official Consultor to the Vatican Department of Communications, in a relatively lengthy private audience, the impression was solidified. Receiving him in a private audience happened shortly after Archbishop Chaput and other American bishops warned the faithful of Fr. Martin's specious reasoning concerning the "welcoming" of active homosexuals into our church communities without mentioning the need for repentance. The audience with the pope was widely seen, and publicly announced by Fr. Martin, as an endorsement of his approach and a rebuke to Archbishop Chaput. When a group of American bishops visited with the pope subsequently on their *ad limina* visit, conflicting interpretations were publicly aired by several bishops about whether Pope Francis expressed dismay about Fr. Martin publicizing the meeting or not.[24]

As we will see many times over in this book, it is not unusual that what Pope Francis says or does is subject to a variety of interpretations, often leading to open conflicts among bishops or cardinals about what he really means. Apart from the question of determining what Pope Francis may really mean in a particular situation, the undeniable fact is that ambiguity and confusion often is the result, an ambiguity and confusion that he seems very reluctant to dispel.

The next events that caused massive confusion and division were the two Synods on the Family. The working documents for both synods were widely criticized for being doctrinally deficient, and the final fruit of the two synods, Pope Francis's apostolic exhortation *Amoris Laetitia*, was acknowledged to contain many good things about marriage and family life, but the good things were soon overshadowed by a firestorm of criticism. Critics pointed out certain passages and a particular footnote that seemed to be dangerously ambiguous, perhaps intentionally so, leaving open the possibility of those divorced and civilly remarried being able to receive Communion as a result of "pastoral accompaniment" rather than an actual objective judgment on the validity of the first marriage. Unfortunately, there is also ample documentation that there was a "shadow synod" conducted shortly before the official synods that clearly intended to advance theological positions that departed from the clear and perennial teaching of the Church and to influence the upcoming official synods; namely, that there are indeed truly intrinsically evil actions that are objectively gravely sinful.[25] The intrinsically evil actions that this theological pressure was intended to question were most particularly in the area of sexual morality.

Various national bishops' conferences and individual bishops offered widely varying interpretations of the document, in a way reminiscent of the varied episcopal responses to Pope St. Paul VI's *Humanae Vitae*. The German bishops seemed to feel it was a vindication of their approach to updating their Church's approach to sexual morality to take into account recent "better understandings" of human sexuality that could apply not just to the matter of divorced and remarried couples but also to those in homosexual relationships and premarital sexual relationships. The majority of German bishops now appear to be in favor of blessing homosexual unions. The hugely wealthy German Church is still getting billions of dollars each year as a result of the church tax that the state collects for them—despite dwindling numbers of those practicing their faith. The German Church is one of the biggest employers in Germany and employs many Catholics and non-Catholics in openly immoral sexual relationships, both heterosexual and homosexual, many of whom oppose Church teaching and even refer for abortions.[26]

On the other side of the German/Polish border, the Polish bishops have issued statements saying that any ambiguity in *Amoris*

Laetitia needs to be interpreted in harmony with the Catholic tradition and can't contradict the firmly held biblical and traditional understanding of Jesus's teaching on the indissolubility of Catholic marriage;[27] namely, that unless it was determined by an objective evaluation conducted by Church authority that a first marriage was not a true marriage, to divorce and remarry would be to put oneself in a state of adultery, an objectively grave sin.

This raises very serious questions. Pope Francis spoke in *Evangelii Gaudium* of the importance of a "healthy decentralization" in the Church. The multiplicity of regional interpretations certainly doesn't qualify as healthy decentralization. How can there be regional differences on serious moral matters about whether something is a grave sin or not? There are universal moral absolutes, and they are the same the world over. As Jesus said, a house divided against itself cannot stand. How can divorced and remarried people without annulments and active homosexuals in one town be admitted to Communion while a few meters away, people in such situations are being called to repentance and amendment of life before they can be admitted to Communion? This is a confusion that can't be accepted as a legitimate diversity of opinions. It must be resolved.

Cardinal Gerhard Mueller, who served for five years as head of the Congregation for the Doctrine of the Faith but whose term was not renewed by Pope Francis, has published wonderfully comprehensive accounts of the history of Catholic teaching on marriage and divorce and tried to bring clarity to the muddy waters. He has also published a truly excellent "Manifesto of Faith" that has clarified other important areas of doctrinal and moral truth that are being called into question today. The Manifesto begins:

> In the face of growing confusion about the doctrine of the Faith, many bishops, priests, religious and lay people of the Catholic Church have requested that I make a public tes-

timony about the truth of revelation. It is the shepherds' very own task to guide those entrusted to them on the path of salvation. This can only succeed if they know this way and follow it themselves. The words of the Apostle here apply: "For above all I have delivered unto you what I have received" (1 Cor. 15:3). Today, many Christians are no longer even aware of the basic teachings of the Faith, so there is a growing danger of missing the path to eternal life. However, it remains the very purpose of the Church to lead humanity to Jesus Christ, the light of the nations (see LG 1). In this situation, the question of orientation arises. According to John Paul II, the Catechism of the Catholic Church is a "safe standard for the doctrine of the faith" (*Fidei Depositum* IV). It was written with the aim of strengthening the Faith of the brothers and sisters whose belief has been massively questioned by the "dictatorship of relativism."[28]

The cardinal went on to reaffirm basic Christian truths which are currently in question, including the reality of grave sin, the obligation to form one's conscience, the need to be free of mortal sin before receiving Communion, the need for faith and repentance for salvation, the reality of hell and eternal punishment, and the deception of the Antichrist, all of which, he points out, are clearly taught in the *Catechism of the Catholic Church*.

This reminded me of a text that John Paul II wrote in his 1984 *Reconciliatio et Paenitentia* document:

> Nor can the church omit, without serious mutilation of her essential message, a constant catechesis on what the traditional Christian language calls the four last things of man: death, judgment (universal and particular), hell and heav-

en. In a culture which tends to imprison man in the earthly life at which he is more or less successful, the pastors of the church are asked to provide a catechesis which will reveal and illustrate with the certainties of faith what comes after the present life: beyond the mysterious gates of death, an eternity of joy in communion with God or the punishment of separation from him. Only in this eschatological vision can one realize the exact nature of sin and feel decisively moved to penance and reconciliation.[29]

Cardinal Walter Kasper, the main driver of the effort to make it possible for divorced and remarried couples to be admitted to the Eucharist without an annulment, reacted strongly to Cardinal Mueller's Manifesto. Accusing it of causing confusion and division in the Church, he said that he was "totally horrified" at Mueller's statement that failing to teach the truths of the Catholic faith "is the fraud of Antichrist." He claimed that Mueller is somehow disloyal to the pope by publishing the Manifesto and that this could "unhinge the Catholic Church."[30]

Cardinal Willem Eijk, Archbishop of Utrecht, the Netherlands, recently raised the question of the "final trial" that the Church must undergo before the Lord returns and the "religious deception" that the *Catechism* speaks of in §675 as being present today. He said this in response to Pope Francis's refusal to reaffirm what the *Catechism* and Canon Law teach about the impossibility of intercommunion with Protestants in a meeting with German bishops, as well as in response to two cardinals calling for the blessing of homosexual unions and the still-unresolved conflicting interpretations of *Amoris Laetitia*:

> Observing that the bishops and, above all, the Successor of Peter fail to maintain and transmit faithfully and in unity

the deposit of faith contained in Sacred Tradition and Sacred Scripture, I cannot help but think of Article 675 of the Catechism of the Catholic Church:

"The Church's ultimate trial

Before Christ's second coming the Church must pass through a final trial that will shake the faith of many believers. The persecution that accompanies her pilgrimage on earth will unveil the 'mystery of iniquity' in the form of a religious deception offering men an apparent solution to their problems at the price of apostasy from the truth."[31]

Cardinal Eijk has now added his grave concerns to those raised by Cardinals Carlo Caffarra, Joachim Meisner, Raymond Burke, Gerhard Mueller, Robert Sarah, Paul Josef Cordes, Walter Brandmüller, Joseph Zen, and many other bishops and scholars, men of substance who love the Church and are deeply concerned enough to speak out. Many others I know share the same concerns in personal conversations but are hesitant to speak out for various reasons. When one considers the growing numbers of faithful theologians, bishops, and cardinals raising very grave concerns, publicly and privately, about the confusion emanating from Rome and from entire episcopates such as in Germany, it does seem like the unity of the Church and the unity of the cardinals and bishops is being destroyed—unhinged even—by the lack of clear leadership addressing the competing interpretations of documents, comments, actions, and appointments.

But it wasn't until the Synod on the Amazon that much wider circles in the Church became aware of how deep the confusion had penetrated the Church.

They say a picture is worth a thousand words. The photo that was seen by millions around the world of a group of Catholics from the Amazon, including a Franciscan priest, prostrating themselves in the Vatican gardens, in the presence of Pope Francis, before small wooden statues carved to resemble naked pregnant women, triggered the writing of many hundreds of thousands of words (see chapter 5).

All the recent synods have been manifestly engineered to reach specific outcomes. The majority of those invited as delegates were chosen because of their sympathy to what the synod organizers wanted to accomplish.

George Weigel's assessment of the manipulation at the Amazon Synod is worth noting.

> The roster of synod participants reflected a narrow band-width of Catholic opinion. Some will remember the rather stifling atmosphere within the Synod Hall, which reinforced the impression created by the synod's managers that (to vary Orwell) some viewpoints were more equal than other viewpoints. Some will remember the extraordinary things that were said in the synod assembly and in the synod's press conferences—including the boast by a venerable missionary bishop that he hadn't baptized an indigenous person in 35 years. Still others will remember that Rome in October 2019 was awash in German money and full of German-financed non-governmental organizations, which functioned more like political lobbies (or theatrical companies) than ecclesial communities.[32]

But it isn't just the events and predetermined outcomes that have increased confusion about what the Church actually still believes today. Pope Francis's appointments have also signaled in this direction. There are numerous examples, but let's consider the bishop Weigel referenced above. As a main organizer and theological/pastoral source for the synod, Austrian Bishop Erwin Kräutler bragged that he had never baptized a single convert in all his years working in the Amazon. What kind of signal his significant influence on the synod is supposed to give concerning the urgent call to evangelization is rather unclear—or maybe not, as we will see later. A significant number of bishops spoke of the need for the "indigenous" peoples to teach us and for us to learn from them. Others spoke of the need to listen to the cries of "mother earth" and make care of the environment and preservation of the ecosystem of the Amazon a main focus of the Church today.

While Pope Francis has spoken eloquently about the importance of evangelization, particularly in his first years as pope, more recently he has spoken harshly against what he calls "proselytism," which he has never clearly defined. He seems more and more to be calling for Catholics only to give silent witness and not preach and teach the Gospel. We will examine this issue in more detail later.

There seems to be a regularly recurring ambiguity in what is being said from Rome. Lots of good statements and initiatives are not infrequently countered by statements and initiatives that seem to contradict or call into question the good. Some have speculated that perhaps what we are seeing is a purposeful "gaslighting" strategy in which contradictory developments keep people confused but still able to point to the "good." But a certain direction, whether intentional or not, can be discerned through appointments and what interpretations of his documents that the pope or his closest advisors say he favors.[33]

Another example of confusion that yet again seems to undermine the unique claims of Christ and the need to evangelize was the 2019 signing of a joint statement by the pope and a prominent Muslim leader, the grand imam of al-Azhar, Sheik Ahmad el-Tayeb. The document includes the assertion that "the pluralism and the diversity of religions, colour, sex, race and language are willed by God in His wisdom, through which He created human beings."[34] Bishop Athanasius Schneider, in an audience with the pope, asked him to clarify what he meant. Pope Francis replied that he meant world religions were only "permitted by God," not positively willed. Bishop Schneider asked if the pope would please make this clear publicly, but so far Pope Francis has not done so, just as he has not responded to the requests of prominent cardinals and theologians to clarify if the teaching of John Paul II in *Veritatis Splendor* needs to be taken into account in interpreting Pope Francis's teaching in *Amoris Laetitia.*

In that particular case, questions were submitted to Pope Francis by four distinguished cardinals, who were concerned that the teaching of *Amoris Laetitia* raised questions about whether previous teaching on important matters is still binding. They asked, among other things, whether the teaching of *Familiaris Consortio* §84, that the divorced and civilly remarried may not be admitted to Holy Communion unless they renounce adultery, is still binding, and whether the teaching of *Veritatis Splendor* §79, that there are absolute moral norms that exclude intrinsically evil acts without exception, is still binding.[35] *Amoris Laetitia* contains many citations from *Familiaris Consortio* but, shockingly, omits the texts that would bring clarity to the current confusion. In *Familiaris Consortio*, after calling for mercy and pastoral care to be extended to the divorced and civilly remarried, St. John Paul II reaffirms the constant teaching of the Church:

> However, the Church reaffirms her practice, which is based upon Sacred Scripture, of not admitting to Eucharistic Communion divorced persons who have remarried. They are unable to be admitted thereto from the fact that their state and condition of life objectively contradict that

union of love between Christ and the Church which is signified and effected by the Eucharist. Besides this, there is another special pastoral reason: if these people were admitted to the Eucharist, the faithful would be led into error and confusion regarding the Church's teaching about the indissolubility of marriage.

Reconciliation in the sacrament of Penance which would open the way to the Eucharist, can only be granted to those who, repenting of having broken the sign of the Covenant and of fidelity to Christ, are sincerely ready to undertake a way of life that is no longer in contradiction to the indissolubility of marriage. This means, in practice, that when, for serious reasons, such as for example the children's upbringing, a man and a woman cannot satisfy the obligation to separate, they "take on themselves the duty to live in complete continence, that is, by abstinence from the acts proper to married couples."

Similarly, the respect due to the sacrament of Matrimony, to the couples themselves and their families, and also to the community of the faithful, forbids any pastor, for whatever reason or pretext even of a pastoral nature, to perform ceremonies of any kind for divorced people who remarry. Such ceremonies would give the impression of the celebration of a new sacramentally valid marriage, and would thus lead people into error concerning the indissolubility of a validly contracted marriage.

By acting in this way, the Church professes her own fidelity to Christ and to His truth. At the same time she shows motherly concern for these children of hers, especially those who, through no fault of their own, have been abandoned by their legitimate partner.

With firm confidence she believes that those who have rejected the Lord's command and are still living in this state will be able to obtain from God the grace of conversion and salvation, provided that they have persevered in prayer, penance and charity.[36]

The concerned cardinals asked for a private meeting with Pope Francis to discuss these issues. Pope Francis refused to meet with them and never responded to their concerns. He has not answered these important questions, and he apparently has no intention of doing so, for they were submitted in September of 2016. In bringing up this matter, I do not mean to signal agreement or disagreement with those cardinals on other issues, nor is it my concern to address the question of whether or not it was appropriate for the cardinals to publicize their concerns, but the questions were in fact asked and indeed were on the minds of many people throughout the Church. The question inevitably arises as to why Pope Francis is unwilling to respond to these questions in the affirmative, as he necessarily would have to in order to accord with our tradition; this would certainly settle a lot of the confusion and disunity unfolding in the Church concerning these critical issues. Unfortunately, some make the case that he has responded to them in an indirect way and has answered in the negative by claiming to place the interpretation of the Argentina bishops on the level of a magisterial teaching, claiming it is the "only interpretation." (We will examine the teaching of the Argentinian bishops on this issue in a later chapter). If those who claim that Pope Francis has responded to the dubia in the negative are correct, and that his response is that *Amoris Laetitia* shouldn't be interpreted in light of *Familiaris Consortio* and *Veritatis Splendor*, we are in serious trouble indeed.

If the pope really wanted the teachings of *Familiaris Consortio* and *Veritatis Splendor* to hold sway, one would expect him to respond in a way that would make that clear, either directly to the cardinals or in some other way that he found suitable. If, however, Pope Francis does not want that, one can understand why he would simply not respond rather than state clearly that the teachings of *Familiaris Consortio* and *Veritatis Splendor* are not binding. The latter course of action might well provoke a schism, but not responding gives the impression that he does not consider the teachings binding without actually saying so, and, indeed, is of a piece with the impression that *Amoris Laetitia* itself gives on the same points of controversy. In both cases, the impression is given, without any clear teaching, that the divorced and remarried who lack annulments may receive Holy Communion in certain circumstances and that acts that the Church has consistently taught to be always and everywhere gravely wrong admit of exceptions after all. This ambiguity almost seems to be a hallmark of Pope Francis's approach to issues and unfortunately only permits confusion and division to increase.

As puzzling as the multitude of these actions and statements has been, they all in some manner could be interpreted in a way that is in harmony with Scripture and tradition, even though it would take quite some effort. Cardinal Mueller is heroically trying to do so, but his frustration is becoming apparent. What is not a matter of puzzled interpretation, though, is what Pope Francis allowed to happen (or ordered to happen?) with the John Paul II Pontifical Theological Institute for Marriage and Family Sciences. John Paul II established the Institute in 1982 to deepen the understanding and acceptance of the foundational Catholic teachings on marriage, sexuality, and the family. It has branch institutes in various countries and has been an important source of training for orthodox theologians. Under Pope Francis, the founders and key leaders of the Institute who were experts in the teaching of John Paul II were removed from teaching their classes, and two professors were appointed to the faculty despite being known to be public dissenters on Catholic teaching on marriage and family life, including an openness to homosexual relations as possibly being good in some circumstances.[37] The archbishop who was appointed to preside over this "renewal" of the Institute, the Italian Archbishop Vincenzo Paglia, is notorious for commissioning a mural in his cathedral by a homosexual artist depicting the archbishop in an embrace with a man ascending into heaven. Many who have seen the mural describe it as unmistakably "homoerotic."[38]

As George Weigel put it:

> An exercise in raw intellectual vandalism has been underway in Rome since July 23: what was originally known as the Pontifical John Paul II Institute for Marriage and the Family has been peremptorily but systematically stripped of its most distinguished faculty, and its core courses in fundamental moral theology have been cancelled. Concurrently, academics known to be opposed to the teaching of *Humanae Vitae* on the appropriate means of regulating fertility and the teaching of *Veritatis Splendor* on intrinsically evil acts are being appointed to teach at the reconfigured Institute, which is housed at the Pontifical Lateran University—the pope's own institution of higher learning. Sixteen hundred nine years after the first Vandal sack of Rome, they're at it again, although this time the chief vandal wears an archbishop's *zucchetto*.[39]

And then there was the shock felt around the world: the Cardinal Theodore McCarrick scandal. One of the most influential American cardinals and a close advisor to Pope Francis, McCarrick was discovered to have sexually harassed seminarians and even young boys for many years and was nevertheless continually promoted despite the fact that his nefarious behavior was an open secret. The clergy sex abuse crisis had already shaken the faith of millions of Catholics. What the McCarrick case broke open was the reality that the cover-up by bishops was almost official policy until recently, and that the silence of the hierarchy was supposedly to protect the reputation of the Church. When the Pennsylvania attorney general published his detailed report about exactly what these homosexual predatory clergy did to their victims, the shock and disgust further deepened.[40]

And then the bombshell. A well-connected Italian archbishop, Carlo Maria Viganò, who had been nuncio to the United States from 2011 to 2016 and held key Vatican positions before that, published a letter claiming that there was a homosexual network in the Vatican and that key American bishops and cardinals had known of Cardinal McCarrick's pattern of predatory behavior and ignored it. He further claimed that Benedict XVI had ordered Cardinal McCarrick to stop traveling and live a quiet life. But even after Cardinal McCarrick retired, Pope Francis continued to consult him about episcopal appointments in the United States and sent him on important missions—McCarrick was involved in negotiations to make a deal with China on the appointment of bishops, which many see as a sellout to China and a betrayal of the persecuted Church. Archbishop Viganò further claimed that he told Pope Francis about Cardinal McCarrick's predatory behavior but that Pope Francis continued to consult and work with him. While the McCarrick issue is very important, even more important are Viganò's claims that there is a homosexual network in the Church and that an absence of an unambiguous papal reaffirmation of the grave wrong of homosexual activity is muddying the waters.[41]

When confronted with the Viganò letter by journalists, Pope Francis said he wasn't going to say anything in response to it. Eventually, under pressure, he promised to do an investigation into the McCarrick matter and publish the results. As of this writing, it has been almost two years, and no results have been published.[42] The Cardinal Secretary of State said that the report was complete and on the pope's desk, but that was many months ago. And once it is published, if it is, what credibility will it have? No outside auditors have been allowed to review the documents, presuming that they haven't been altered or destroyed. There is not much confidence left in bishops investigating bishops.

What once was called an "American problem" is now being acknowledged as a worldwide problem in the Catholic Church. Clergy abuse cases and the parallel cover-up by bishops, some of whom have been exposed as abusers themselves, have now come to light in many other countries.

Sometimes, even when horrendous corruption has been revealed, such as in the case of the founder of the Legionaries of Christ, Fr. Marcial Maciel, the cardinal commissioned by Pope Benedict XVI to oversee the reform of the order refused to look into who was responsible for aiding and abetting Maciel, most of whom remained in leadership positions in the order. The cardinal charged with reform looked only at the documents and tried to improve them, which he did, but ignored the deeply rooted culture of the order that needed thorough reform and in-depth investigation into what really happened and who knew what when. Since then, it has been revealed that thirty-three priests and seventy-one seminarians sexually abused hundreds of minors from the 1940s to today. The founder of the Legionaries himself abused sixty minors, some as young as eleven, fathered children, and sodomized two of his sons. Eleven of the priestly abusers were themselves victims of their founder, while others were abused by some of his other victims. The cover-up continued even when an investigation and reform had supposedly been completed, either through naiveté, incompetence, or worse.[43]

Ironically, the head of Pope Francis's special council of cardinals tasked with cleaning up and reorganizing the Vatican, Cardinal Óscar Rodríguez Maradiaga, who has been called the "vice-pope," has been accused by many of his seminarians of covering up a homosexual network in his archdiocesan seminary in Honduras. Cardinal Maradiaga's hand-picked auxiliary bishop has been forced to resign because of homosexual activity and financial impropriety.[44] Cardinal Maradiaga has called the testimony of his seminarians "gossip" and claims that the pope has commiserated with him about all the "evil being done against you."[45] Another of Pope Francis's "group of nine" advisors, the Chilean cardinal, Francisco Javier Errázuriz, has been implicated in covering up abuse in Chile and has had to return to Chile for the investigation.

But it isn't just sexual disorder and cover-ups that are plaguing the Church, including the Vatican, but also widespread financial impropriety. The two often go together.

If it weren't so tragic, financial impropriety at the Vatican could almost be considered an unbelievable comedy of errors. Embezzlement, money laundering, investments in movies that undermine Catholic values, misusing Peter's Pence,[46] bailing out corrupt enterprises, firing outside auditors when they get too close to cardinals' malfeasance, cardinals "misappropriating funds," elaborate self-enrichment schemes, mysterious arrests without explanation—all are "current events."[47]

The growing deficits of the Vatican finances may force reform, but who knows? As the veteran Vatican commentator John Allen puts it:

Bottom line: Like any company, or any family, facing deep and mounting debt, the Vatican can't go on like it has. Change is coming. The drama pivots on what sort of change it will be—and on that front, and with apologies for the Econ 101 pun, demand for answers at the moment significantly exceeds supply.[48]

But financial wrongdoing and incompetent or nonexistent oversight is not limited to Rome. It exists in many dioceses and has often been covered up. It is not uncommon for clergy in immoral relationships to embezzle money from their parishes to buy condos in Florida for themselves and their lovers.[49]

Cardinal George Pell, in his first interview with Australian national television after being acquitted of sexual abuse charges, was asked whether it's possible that enemies in Rome colluded with Australian enemies of the cardinal to try to remove him from his financial oversight role by encouraging false charges to be lodged against him. His answer: "Most of the senior people in Rome who are in any way sympathetic to financial reform believe that they are connected." He added, though, that he didn't have any evidence of that.

Asked how high up in the hierarchy financial corruption goes, Cardinal Pell replied: "Who knows? It's a little bit like anti-Catholicism in Victoria, you're not quite sure where the vein runs, how thick and broad it is, and how high it goes."[50] The cardinal said that Pope Francis supported his efforts at reform, but obviously very highly placed officials are blocking the reform.

I remember once visiting a cardinal in Rome who was from outside Italy, and he told me how officials in his office were being imposed on him by powerful Italians in the curia and he couldn't choose his own collaborators. He said regional loyalties are extremely strong in Italy, and officials from the same region protect each other in what seems to be a code of clan loyalty that enables them to keep control of the levers of power.

What kind of response are we seeing to this whirlwind of events? While virtually everyone condemns the abuse of children, there is a noticeable silence concerning sexual immorality among "consenting adults," including clergy involved in such relationships. There is a clear desire to avoid the issue of homosexual networks among bishops and clergy and keep the focus on condemning abuse of children. There is also a tendency to propose that the bishops handle this problem themselves, perhaps with lay boards having some involvement. Unfortunately, the history of these situations shows that there really is something like an "old boy network," where seminary classmates and mentors who help advance each other's careers are rather loath to blow the whistle on each other. I was speaking with one bishop, who in many ways is a really good bishop, about an egregious case of homosexual activity on the part of a prominent pastor. The bishop only reluctantly removed this priest, after the problem was evident for a long time, but refused to identify the nature of the problem when announcing the pastor's leave of absence. When I asked him why he didn't tell the truth about the situation, he said he didn't want to upset the older gay priests in his diocese and make them feel bad.

For every priest or bishop exposed for wrongdoing, there are many more that have not yet come to light, and perhaps never will. A bishop accused of sexual abuse and financial wrongdoing in Argentina, including abuse of seminarians, Gustavo Zanchetta, was invited by Pope Francis to accept a position in the Vatican overseeing finances, where he still serves to this day while awaiting trial in Argentina. Zanchetta worked closely with Pope Francis when he was archbishop of Buenos Aires and was one of the first bishops that the pope ordained. When the public criticism became so great, he was put on leave, but is back again at his job:

In Argentina, Zanchetta is facing charges of defrauding the state and "aggravated continuous sexual abuse," with two former seminarians having filed a criminal complaint against him. Public records show that Zanchetta received over one million pesos, close to $250,000 at the time, from the provincial government for the restoration of a parish rectory and for a series of lectures in the local seminary that never took place.[51]

When the pope published a document on how to handle accusations against bishops, *Vox Estis*, it called for accusations to be investigated by the head of the ecclesiastical province and then referred to Rome, and Rome was supposed to respond within thirty days. The allegations of corrupt behavior of the former archbishop of Minneapolis–St. Paul, Archbishop John Nienstedt, were found by the current archbishop to be credible and forwarded to Rome, but more than a year later, there is no response.

While the authority belongs with the bishops, it is necessary to assure a just handling of cases involving bishops and clergy with significant qualified, competent, lay involvement. The sickness in the Church will not be cured by avoiding this significant problem, whether it be homosexual or heterosexual relationships involving clergy or immoral behavior by bishops or bishops covering for clergy or each other. It is encouraging to see, in my home diocese of Lansing, that a committee including professional lay members has been set up to handle issues of sexual immorality involving clergy with adults. Hopefully, it will have the freedom and authority to follow the evidence wherever it may lead.

On the doctrinal and moral issues, we are seeing a polarization that seems to be getting worse. On the one hand are those who celebrate the softening of sexual morality, the truth about Jesus's uniqueness, and the reality of hell, and are glad to see "the spirit of Vatican II" back again. On the other hand, in reaction to this blurring of doctrine and morality and also liturgical abuses, we are seeing an aggressive "traditionalist" resurgence, advocating a return to the Tridentine liturgy as a touchstone of real orthodoxy. Often, unfortunately, this movement brings with it an attack on the legitimacy of the *Novus Ordo* and those who frequent it—namely, the vast majority of practicing Catholics. Sometimes, the traditionalist resurgence is combined with vicious attacks on the pope and false and rash judgments labeling him a heretic, an apostate, or even the Antichrist.

Is there a way forward that avoids these polarizing extremes without compromising the truth in any way? I believe there is. It's the path that Pope St. John Paul II and Pope Benedict XVI tried to guide us on during the many years of their pontificates: the authentic interpretation of Vatican II, the challenging way of the Gospel, of the real Jesus, as revealed to us in Scripture and tradition and articulated for us today in the *Catechism of the Catholic Church*. But it is not enough to just point to these sources of light and truth. We must specify what truths must be recovered today in light of what is being attacked and bring clarity where the confusion is greatest.

As we begin to address specific issues and hopefully bring the truth and light of the Gospel to them, it is important to remember that all this confusion and division is happening under the providential hand of God. He is permitting the confusion, the ambiguity, the division, and he has a plan to bring good out of it. It is clear that the Church is in need of a deep purification. God is permitting the darkness to be exposed so that the deep wounds of sin and infidelity may be healed, that profound repentance may take place, and the light of Christ shine forth ever more brightly.

Chapter 2

Is There a Solid Place
to Stand?

In the midst of the confusion and polarization, is there a solid place to stand and not be buffeted by every wind of the culture, every alarming event in the Church, and as Scripture says, "every wind of doctrine" (Eph 4:14)? Is there a solid place to stand and not be deceived by the many false teachers and prophets that Jesus and the Apostles warn us will certainly be present? How can we find the narrow way that leads to life and not be swept away through the wide door that leads to destruction (see Matt 7:13–14)?

It all comes down to the question of revelation. Has God revealed himself? If so, how can we have access to what he reveals? If we can have access to what he reveals, how can we be sure that we correctly understand it? How can we discern true "development" from false development in our understanding of the truths of the faith?

It begins with Scripture. Is Scripture a reliable witness to who God is and what his will is? Are the Apostles credible witnesses[52] to the real Jesus and what he said and did? How are we, as Catholics, to approach the interpretation of Scripture?

After years of corrosive Scripture scholarship that has eroded many Catholics' confidence in the reliability and relevance of the

Sacred Scriptures, we are seeing a wonderful resurgence of solid Scripture scholarship. This is exemplified in many ways by Pope Benedict XVI[53] and hundreds of scholars, including many young ones, who are approaching the interpretation of Scripture not only with solid scientific and philosophical credentials but also with an eye to the hermeneutic of faith, in harmony with our tradition's approach to Scripture.[54]

Despite this resurgence of solid biblical scholarship and theology, there is a persistent underground stream of corrosive approaches to the Scriptures that destroys them as a source of certain truth and as reliable guidance for our lives. These approaches enable an unguided and spurious "development of doctrine" that attempts to reverse revealed truths in the name of progress.

As one Vatican commentator assessed Pope Benedict's contribution to restoring confidence to readers of the Scripture:

> Benedict XVI went even further—beyond the historical-critical discussion common to theology, as it interpreted and sometimes manipulated texts so that the Bible could say everything and nothing at once. With his three books on Jesus of Nazareth, Benedict showed a new way, a theological discussion based on the assumption of the Gospel's historical veracity.
>
> Today, the Church is back to the earlier, historical-critical discussion, and not by chance the German theologians, marginalized in the 90s for their daring positions, are back on the stage. On stage with these theologians are also issues such as the horizontal Church (non-hierarchical) and other similar positions from the 80s that corresponded at the time to the Media Council, the definition of which is one of the most important legacies of Benedict XVI's pontificate.[55]

This stream of skepticism is alive and well in the Church and not afraid to reassert itself in the highest places. A shocking example of this is the recent comments by the Superior General of the Jesuits, Fr. Arturo Marcelino Sosa, who casually commented, in relationship to the divorce and remarriage question, "No one was there with a tape recorder so do we really know what Jesus said?" The text of the whole interview is even more disturbing. It's clear that his "flexible" approach to Scripture and doctrine allows "developing" interpretations that, under the final authority of "conscience," can actually overturn the teaching of Jesus while claiming to be faithful to its contemporary understanding of it. When asked if it's possible to question the blanket statement of Jesus, that "What therefore God has joined together, let not man put asunder" (Matt 19:6), Fr. Sosa replied: "I go along with what Pope Francis says. One does not bring into doubt, one brings into discernment." He further stated, "True discernment cannot dispense with doctrine." And when the interviewer asked if it can reach conclusions different from doctrine, Fr. Sosa answered, "That is so."[56] He went on to say that the devil is not a personal agent of evil but merely a symbol.[57] The demythologizing thrust of skeptical German scholarship of the seventies and eighties that widely penetrated the Church at that time, and that I wrote about in the original *A Crisis of Truth*, is unfortunately still alive and well in very high places.

Another example of sly unbelief in the authority and inspiration of Sacred Scripture came from Fr. James Martin, S.J., who continues to campaign for a welcome to be extended to the LGBTQ community, without any mention of repentance or submission to God's Word on sexuality. On his Twitter account on October 23, 2019, Fr. Martin retweeted Fr. Richard Rohr's post endorsing a quote from a Methodist biblical scholar and activist:

> "Interesting": Where the Bible mentions [same-sex sexual] behavior at all, it clearly condemns it. I freely grant that. The issue is precisely whether the biblical judgment is correct. The Bible sanctioned slavery as well and nowhere attacked it as unjust. Are we prepared to argue today that slavery is biblically justified?[58]

Slavery is a grossly unjust social structure that was part of the culture of Rome and many ancient (and modern) societies. The New Testament never approves of slavery but in fact subverts it by teaching the radical equality of those who are Christians, including slaves and masters (see Paul's Letter to Philemon). This prepared the way for the Church to condemn slavery when it was no longer a persecuted minority just getting its footing in a pagan empire.[59] The biblical teaching on homosexual activity we find in the Old Testament is explicitly affirmed as important moral teaching in the New Testament and has always been taught as such throughout the history of the Church and by all the Christian churches up until very recent times, as it is to this day in the *Catechism of the Catholic Church*.[60] Just in the last fifty years or so have we seen the mainline Protestant churches, who are leading the way in a profoundly mistaken strategy to become relevant and stop their radically declining memberships, concede to the sexual revolution and start to hang LGBTQ banners and flags outside their churches in a futile effort to stop the decline. Unfortunately, the Catholic Church is now being besieged as the last significant holdout to being on the "right side of history," regarding what is now called the "greatest civil rights issue of our time." The pressure is coming from both within and without. We will examine this more closely in a later chapter. Fr. James Martin's sly questioning of Scripture is just the tip of the iceberg.

Besides the questioning of Scripture such as we see in the superior of the Jesuits and Fr. Martin, there is an observable discomfort in the life of the Church today when it comes to continuing to preach and teach truths of the faith that are in direct conflict with powerful pressures from the culture. When the important biblical texts on sexual morality appear in the regular cycle of lectionary readings, many priests and homilists now skip over them and choose another text to preach on. There is a growing discomfort when the Word of God conflicts with the culture, since we know that many in our congregations have already accepted the lies of the culture and would be upset if we challenged them with the real Jesus and what the real Jesus says. The "bracketing of Scripture" is sometimes an example of this. The practice of bracketing parts of the Scripture goes back to the mists of post-Vatican II liturgical developments, ostensibly in the effort to shorten longer readings, making it easier for people to pay attention. Sometimes though, the bracketing seems to be influenced by an effort to put in brackets parts of parables and other readings that would challenge or upset people. For example, when the punch line of a parable speaks about "wailing and gnashing of teeth" in the "outer darkness," or eternal punishment, even when the reading is rather short, those parts often get bracketed. For example, in one of the readings for the second Sunday of Lent of Year C, the reading from Philippians 3:17–4:1 brackets out this: "For many, of whom I have often told you and now tell you even with tears, live as enemies of the cross of Christ. Their end is destruction, their god is the belly, and they glory in their shame, with minds set on earthly things." This completely "neuters" the assigned reading, which wasn't at all overly long. Even when the reading is longer, the part chosen to be omitted is often the one with the most pointed and relevant section that speaks of eternal consequences. The Gospel reading for the sixteenth Sunday in Ordinary Time of Year A was Matthew 13:24–43, and the part left out was Jesus's explanation of the parable, which one would think would be the most important section!

The bracketed-out part:

He who sows the good seed is the Son of man; the field is the world, and the good seed means the sons of the kingdom; the weeds are the sons of the evil one, and the enemy who sowed them is the devil; the harvest is the close of the age, and the reapers are angels. Just as the weeds are gathered and burned with fire, so will it be at the close of the age. The Son of man will send his angels, and they will gather out of his kingdom all causes of sin and all evildoers, and throw them into the furnace of fire; there men will weep and gnash their teeth. Then the righteous will shine like the sun in the kingdom of their Father. He who has ears, let him hear. (Matt 13:37–43)

On another Sunday the Gospel reading which contained three of Jesus's parables was reduced to just two, which took up one sentence each. The third parable, the parable of the net that brings up good and bad fish, was bracketed out as was Jesus's very important explanation of this parable (Matt 13:44–52).

"So will it be at the close of the age. The angels will come out and separate the evil from the righteous, and throw them into the furnace of fire; there men will weep and gnash their teeth. Have you understood this?" (Matt 13:49–51).

How can we understand these things when we hardly ever hear them and almost never hear an explanation of the importance of these very serious warnings of Jesus? The virus of universalism, covering over the reality of final judgment, is penetrating the Church.

One time, I asked a scholarly and orthodox archbishop what he thought about the bracketing, and he said he thought that sometimes the bracketing was out of a concern for shortening lengthy passages (e.g., the genealogies) but sometimes, unfortunately, they indeed seemed influenced by actual discomfort with aspects of the Gospel and of Jesus himself.

Sometimes, we find this in the Office of Readings in the Liturgy of the Hours as well. For example, in the reading for the Wednesday of the Second Week in Ordinary Time, the text from *Lumen Gentium* §16, which speaks of the possibility of people being saved who haven't heard the Gospel, is cut off after talking about this possibility and doesn't include the essential last three lines, which speak of how difficult it is to be saved without hearing the Gospel and how "very often" human beings fall prey to the world, the flesh, and the devil and desperately need to hear the Gospel since their salvation is at great risk.

Liturgical scholars have told me this "bracketing" goes back at least to the early 1970s, when undercurrents of what Paul calls "blushing for the Gospel" (see 2 Tim 1:8) were strongly abroad in the land. On the advice of liturgical scholars, Pope Paul VI decided to omit about 120 verses from the psalms that are commonly called imprecatory psalms, which wish that punishment be inflicted on the enemies of God and his people. The introduction to the revised Liturgy of the Hours says that these were removed because these psalms could cause "psychological difficulty." This ignores the entire tradition of the Church (and the fact that these psalms are sometimes carried forward in the prayer of the New Testament, e.g., Rev 6:10). Our tradition contains a rich reflection on how to apply these psalms in light of the New Testament.[61] The grave danger here is that once you begin editing the Word of God on the basis of "psychological difficulty," you have fundamentally undermined it. And as each generation increases in their "psychological difficulty" in accepting the Word of God where it conflicts with the current modern mentality or cultural presuppositions, where will it stop? Already, even when challenging passages are not already bracketed, priests and deacons, feeling the "psychological difficulty" of their people, and perhaps their own, with texts that conflict with the culture, readily ignore the challenging ones. What this is cloaking, unfortunately, is often the acceptance of "another gospel"—a supposedly more compassionate and modern one—that still uses the words of the Gospel in selective ways. Many of our priests and people are conflicted—wanting to continue to be Catholics but, at the same time, accepting a different gospel, one which is extremely uncomfortable with some of the most important and clearly understood words of Jesus and the Apostles. This can eventually grow to the point where so-called Catholics no longer believe the revealed word of God but have committed themselves to what is really another gospel, a false religion, a perversion of true Catholic faith. In such cases, the way back to the true path is to repent of such disastrous unbelief. To tamper with revelation, to not obey Jesus, to change his Word, and to not believe in it is a grave sin.

The softening of the Revelation of the one true God and his Word to the human race continues almost on a daily basis. In response to the coronavirus pandemic in 2020, the Vatican issued a new Mass for a time of pandemic, which omits texts from the original votive Mass for "times of pestilence" that speak of God's wrath and chastisement for sins.[62] I think of J. B. Phillips's translation of the Scripture years ago titled *Your God Is Too Small*. I think we are reaching a point where, ignoring the justice and holiness of God, someone could rightly say, "Your God is too nice." Being faithful to what God reveals to us of his nature, while challenging, is necessary, otherwise we will construct a God in our own image who agrees with our presuppositions rather than challenging them. Paul urges us to "note . . . the kindness and the severity of God" (Rom 11:22), his justice and his mercy. And God often severely judges, even in history, stubborn unfaithfulness. Consider the lament of Azariah,

one of the three young men thrown into the furnace, living in exile
for persistent refusal to heed the prophet's call for Israel to repent:

> You have executed true judgments in all that you have
>> brought upon us
>> and upon Jerusalem, the holy city of our fathers,
>>> for in truth and justice you have brought all this upon
>>> us because of our sins.
> For we have sinfully and lawlessly departed from you,
>> and have sinned in all things and have not obeyed your
>> commandments;
> we have not observed them or done them,
>> as you have commanded us that it might go well with us.
> So all that you have brought upon us,
>> and all that you have done to us,
>> you have done in true judgment.
> You have given us into the hands of lawless enemies, most
>> hateful rebels,
>> and to an unjust king, the most wicked in all the world.
> And now we cannot open our mouths;
>> shame and disgrace have befallen your servants and
>> worshipers.
> For your name's sake do not give us up utterly,
>> and do not break your covenant,
>> and do not withdraw your mercy from us,
> for the sake of Abraham your beloved
>> and for the sake of Isaac your servant
>> and Israel your holy one,
> to whom you did promise
>> to make their descendants as many as the stars of heaven
>> and as the sand on the shore of the sea.
> For we, O Lord, have become fewer than any nation,

and are brought low this day in all the world because of
our sins.

And at this time there is no prince, or prophet, or leader,
no burnt offering, or sacrifice, or oblation, or incense,
no place to make an offering before you or to find mercy.

Yet with a contrite heart and a humble spirit may we be
accepted,
as though it were with burnt offerings of rams and bulls,
and with tens of thousands of fat lambs;
such may our sacrifice be in your sight this day,
and may we wholly follow you,
for there will be no shame for those who trust in you.

And now with all our heart we follow you,
we fear you and seek your face. (Dan 3:5–18)

Unfortunately, this pressure from the culture and from corrosive scholarship is present at the highest level of the Church,
including the Pontifical Biblical Commission. The commission is
composed of distinguished biblical scholars from around the world.
It recently published a three-hundred-page study addressing the
question "What is man?" In such a long document, there are many
twists and turns, but it is disappointing to find in Chapter III what
appears to be waffling concerning the sin of homosexual acts:

In conclusion, our exegetical examination of the texts of
the Old and of the New Testaments has brought to light
elements that must be considered for an evaluation of
homosexuality in its ethical implications. Certain formulations of biblical authors, as well as the disciplinary
directives of Leviticus, require an intelligent interpretation that safeguards the values that the sacred text intends to promote, thus avoiding repetition to the letter

that which carries with it cultural traits of that time. The contribution provided by science, together with the reflections of theologians and moralists, will be indispensable for an adequate exposition of the problem that is only sketched out in this Document. In addition, pastoral care will be required, particularly with regard to individual persons, in order to realize the service to the good that the Church has to assume in her mission for mankind.[63]

While considering the disparate interpretations of biblical texts that condemn same-sex relationships and the cultural influences on them, the document stops short of affirming unambiguously the Church's unbroken tradition of understanding these texts as definitively condemning homosexual acts. Statements like this from such a distinguished source can only confirm priests and bishops in their reluctance to preach clearly about sexual sin and, in particular, about the issue that is at the cutting edge of the sexual revolution at this time, the active practice of homosexuality. It's a clear sign to many that highly placed officials in the Church are wavering in their belief in God's Word on this very important issue, and others as well. Very disappointing, very damaging, and very serious.

Paul, speaking of how many of Jesus's own people rejected him and were cut off, warns:

> They were broken off because of their unbelief, but you stand fast only through faith. So do not become proud, but stand in awe. For if God did not spare the natural branches, neither will he spare you. Note then the kindness and the severity of God: severity toward those who have fallen, but God's kindness to you, provided you continue in his kindness; otherwise you too will be cut off. (Rom 11:20–22)

If we continue to edit the Word of God because of "psychological difficulty," we are in danger of ourselves being cut off for not obeying Jesus's command to teach everything he has revealed to us (see Matt 28:20), and the blood of the people to whom we were responsible for teaching "the whole counsel of God," and didn't, will be on our hands: "Therefore I testify to you this day that I am innocent of the blood of all of you, for I did not shrink from declaring to you the whole counsel of God" (Acts 20:26–27).

St. John Paul II, in *Catechesi Tradendae*, underlined how important it is to pass on to our people everything that Jesus revealed to us:

> A disciple of Christ has the right to receive "the word of faith" not in mutilated, falsified or diminished form but whole and entire, in all its rigor and vigor. . . . This is why, when a person first becomes aware of "the surpassing worth of knowing Christ Jesus," . . . there is no valid pretext for refusing Him any part whatever of that knowledge.[64]

At the beginning of the World Synod of Bishops on the New Evangelization, in 2012, one of the presiding cardinals began the synod by saying, "Our number one priority as a Church today is to recover our confidence in the truth of the faith."[65] I would add that this must begin with our approach to Scripture. We need to recover our confidence in the truthfulness and reliability of Sacred Scripture.

In Chapter 28 of Jeremiah, in the context of a strong condemnation of false shepherds, who in fact scatter the flock; false prophets, who tell God's people lies; and false priests, who mislead the people, the Lord proclaims:

> Is not my word like fire . . . like a hammer which breaks the rock in pieces? (Jer 23:29)

Thomas Aquinas, commenting on the epistle to the Hebrews, says this about the power of the word of God:

> As it says in Hebrews 4:12, "For the word of God is living and active, sharper than any two-edged sword, and piercing through to the division between soul and spirit, joints and marrow; discerning the purposes and thoughts of the heart." Thus preaching is called the sword of the Spirit because it cannot reach the human spirit unless it is wielded by the Holy Spirit: "It will not be you speaking but the Spirit of your Father who is speaking in you" (Matt 10:20). . . . Thus we have weapons for fighting the demons themselves, namely, the sword of the Spirit which is the word of God. This happens frequently in sermons in which the word of God, penetrating the hearts of sinners, drives out the tangled mass of sins and demons.[66]

Yes, we need the word of God to be taught and preached in the power of the Holy Spirit so God's people may be freed from the tangled mass of sins and demons affecting their thinking, acting, and their entire lives.

A beautiful reading from the Book of Wisdom, used in the Christmas season to speak of the Incarnation, almost always leaves off the challenging concluding verses, with resonances of the destroying angel of the Book of Exodus, sent to punish evil in Egypt, and later the infidelity of the Jews in the desert, struck down by a plague (see Exod 12:23):

> Thy all-powerful word leaped from heaven, from the royal throne, into the midst of the land that was doomed, a stern warrior carrying the sharp sword of thy authentic command, and stood and filled all things with death, and touched heaven while standing on the earth. (Wis 18:15–16)

Does God's word in Scripture really have this power? Yes, if it is preached and taught with conviction, faith, authority, and the anointing of the Holy Spirit and if we have confidence in its truthfulness and reliability. But for many Catholics, this is not the case.

How would I characterize many Catholics' approach to Scripture? Food for thought? Material for meditation? One opinion among many? Outdated myths? Can't take it literally? Needs to be adjusted to fit the times? Out of date? Not consonant with modern knowledge? Boring? We're not fundamentalists! We need to eat the meat but spit out the bones! The Church's teaching is changing; listen to the pope!

Of course, as faithful Catholics, we know that there is a very proper role for the various critical biblical disciplines that help us discern what kind of biblical literature we are dealing with as a guide to its proper interpretation. But these disciplines are intended to help us "receive" the Word that is being communicated in whatever literary form it may be, not having it "veiled" from us.[67]

As Cardinal Robert Sarah expressed it:

> Today, Scripture is considered nothing more than a set of ancient documents, fascinating of course, but devoid of supernatural importance, the understanding of which is no longer possible except for specialists. . . . Every Catholic must have the audacity to believe that his faith, in communion with the faith of the Church, is above any new magisterium of experts and intellectuals.[68]

How sad that God's Word has been veiled from so many! It is a fire, a rock, a power, a lifeline, an urgent warning, a privileged communication, a source of life-saving knowledge, the key to happiness, and a profound love letter! And while there are some parts of Scripture genuinely difficult to interpret, as Mark Twain said on one occasion, "It is not those parts of scripture that are hard to understand that most disturb me, but those parts that are so clear!" In his days on earth, Jesus encountered the same "veiling" present among the religious authorities of the time and responded with sadness, anger, and joy! "You search the scriptures, because you think that in them you have eternal life; and it is they that bear witness to me; yet you refuse to come to me that you may have life" (John 5:39–40).

As Fr. Francis Martin, a biblical scholar, pointed out time and time again: the written Word leads us into relationship with the Living Word, Jesus himself, and all the heavenly realities. "[Jesus] rejoiced in the Holy Spirit and said, 'I thank thee, Father, Lord of heaven and earth, that thou hast hidden these things from the wise and understanding and revealed them to babes; yea, Father, for such was thy gracious will" (Luke 10:21).

We should "devour" and treasure God's Word as our most precious possession. "Thy words were found, and I ate them, and thy words became to me a joy and the delight of my heart" (Jer 15:16).

The Catholic Church, while acknowledging the role of linguistic studies, historical-critical studies, literary analysis, redaction criticism, and cultural and archaeological research, nevertheless clearly teaches in its important document on Sacred Revelation from Vatican II, *Dei Verbum*, that Scripture, while fully a human word, is at the same time a Divine Word, inspired by the Spirit and without error:

> Therefore, since everything asserted by the inspired authors or sacred writers must be held to be asserted by the Holy Spirit, it follows that the books of Scripture must be acknowledged as teaching solidly, faithfully and without error that truth which God wanted put into sacred writings for the sake of salvation.[69]

As Cardinal Ratzinger put it, "The Catholic tradition ... trusts the evangelists; it believes what they say."[70]

Does this have implications for life? It certainly does. Consider, for example, a very relevant text for the confusion of our times in the area of sexual morality and its clear implications for our lives:

> Do you not know that the unrighteous will not inherit the kingdom of God? Do not be deceived; neither the immoral, nor idolaters, nor adulterers, nor homosexuals, nor thieves, nor the greedy nor drunkards, nor revilers, nor robbers will inherit the kingdom of God. (1 Cor 6:9–10)[71]

These and many other texts have to do with our eternal salvation, heaven or hell. There is no other knowledge with greater personal and practical relevance than what is revealed to us in Sacred Scripture for the sake of our salvation. In Scripture, we find a revelation of the purpose of creation, the horror of sin and rebellion against God, the reason for suffering and death, the awe-inspiring plan of God for the salvation of the human race, a plan which raises us to a place of unimaginable dignity and glory through an act of sacrificial love that will never be praised or adored enough. And most importantly of all, what we must do in order to be saved!

Is any knowledge of greater value?

Of course, the whole notion of salvation, of heaven and hell, has come under attack either directly or by gradual fogginess, and we will consider this confusion in a later chapter as well.

As Cardinal Sarah put it:

> Man does not feel that he is in danger. Many in the Church no longer dare to teach the reality of salvation and eternal life. In homilies there is a strange silence concerning the last things. Preachers avoid speaking about original sin. That appears to be archaic. The sense of sin seems to have

disappeared. Good and evil no longer exist. Relativism, that terribly effective bleach, has wiped out everything in its path. Doctrinal and moral confusion is reaching its height. Evil is good, good is evil. Man no longer feels any need to be saved. The loss of the sense of salvation is the consequence of the loss of the transcendence of God.

We do not seem to be worried about what will happen to us when we have left this earth. From this perspective, we prefer to think that the devil no longer exists. Some bishops even say that he is only a symbolic image. Jesus Christ is supposedly lying, therefore, when he claims that he is quite real, that he was tempted several times by him, the Prince of this World![72]

But how do we know we are interpreting these passages concerning fundamental truths correctly, even though they seem to be clear assertions? Here is where the Church and our tradition comes in. Many heresies throughout the ages have come and gone and have forced the Church to clarify her teaching and the correct understanding of key verses. Other truths have never been seriously challenged but have been continually affirmed and reaffirmed in document after document, in catechism after catechism, and come to us today in a reliable form in the current *Catechism of the Catholic Church*. Just as many people in the Church today are ignorant of Scripture, so are many ignorant of our tradition as it is embodied in contemporary language and sensibility in the relatively recent *Catechism of the Catholic Church*, which we will have occasion to refer to periodically throughout this book. Everything I say in this chapter, indeed in the book as a whole, concerning doctrine or morality or missiology is based on the clarity of God's Word as it comes to us in Scripture, tradition, and the *Catechism of the Catholic Church*.

The *Catechism*, developed under the oversight of John Paul II, is an authoritative and irreplaceable guide to what the Catholic Church actually believes and teaches. A monumental achievement. Recent attempts to "amend" the *Catechism* are troublesome.

Before we can proceed to specific truths that are under attack, we need to consider the notion of development of doctrine. Advocates of "catching up with the times" pin their hopes on this notion. Cardinal Carlo Maria Martini, deceased archbishop of Milan and a leader of the forces that were pushing for the Church to "catch up with the times," said shortly before he died that "the Church is two centuries behind, and needs to catch up."[73] Pope Francis repeated Cardinal Martini's remark in a talk he gave to the Curia shortly before Christmas, 2019.[74]

Catching up with the times or scurrying to accommodate the culture so we can allegedly be "on the right side of history" is a recipe for disaster unless it is guided by sure knowledge of the deposit of faith and its reliable restatement in the *Catechism of the Catholic Church*. Understanding what true development of doctrine is remains essential for this discernment.

Commenting on the pope's endorsement of Cardinal Martini's plea that we catch up with the times, George Weigel asked:

> Is there a single example, anywhere, of a local Church where a frantic effort to catch up with 21st-century secularism and its worship of the new trinity (Me, Myself, and I) has led to an evangelical renaissance—to a wave of conversions to Christ?[75]

What is the truth about development of doctrine? We can grow in our understanding of a doctrine by understanding better the historical context in which it was formulated, by understanding better the intent of its authors, by understanding how it has been applied throughout the ages and received by the Church, and by more deeply penetrating its meaning and implications by theological reflection. St. John Henry Newman[76] is well known for attempting to articulate how we can discern a true development of doctrine from a distortion or reversal of doctrine.[77] But the first one to offer guidance on this issue is a fourth-century monk, St. Vincent of Lérins, who articulated a rule of thumb for discerning true development that in its clarity has never been surpassed.

My colleague at Sacred Heart Major Seminary in the Archdiocese of Detroit, Eduardo Echeverria, has done extensive work in studying the truths concerning development of doctrine and has written extensively on this subject. I am indebted to him and grateful for his clarity of thought and deep historical and doctrinal knowledge.[78] He sums up Vincent's teaching:

> Furthermore, there is a crucial difference for Vincent between change and development (progress). He asks, "Is there then to be no progress of religion in the Church of Christ? There is certainly, and very great. For who is he that is so envious toward men, so hostile toward God, as to endeavor to hinder it? But it [progress] must be such as may be truly a *progress* of the faith, not a *change*; for when each thing is improved in itself, that is progress; but when a thing is turned out of one thing into another, that is *change*." To be distinguished from change, then, development must occur within the "proper limits, i.e., within the same dogma, the same meaning, the same judgment [*in eodem scilicet dogmate, eodem sensu eademque sententia*].[79]

Some of the undermining of Catholic truth that we will analyze in subsequent chapters invokes a nebulous understanding of "development" that seeks to weaken the clarity and certainty of revealed truth, leading in some cases to an actual reversal of the explicit teaching of Jesus as it has been understood in the Church for almost two thousand years.[80]

A truly shocking example concerns a very influential priest, Fr. Thomas Rosica, who was the main English-language spokesperson for the Vatican during the important Synods on the Family:

> Pope Francis breaks Catholic traditions whenever he wants
> . . . Our Church has indeed entered a new phase: with the advent of this first Jesuit pope, it is openly ruled by an individual rather than by the authority of Scripture alone or even its own dictates of Tradition plus Scripture.[81]

This statement made in a column he wrote for the feast of St. Ignatius of Loyola was actually plagiarized from a Protestant critic of the papacy. Not too long after this, it was discovered that Fr. Rosica regularly plagiarized the writings of others and had to resign from his various positions. Of course, Pope Francis had never said this about himself, but for someone close to the Vatican's inner circle to exult in the pope's freedom from the need to be a servant of Scripture and tradition is troubling indeed.[82]

Once we depart from a truly Catholic understanding of the authority and reliability of Scripture and tradition, there is no longer a foundation to stand on, and Christianity has no defense from the cultural pressures of the time that insist that we accommodate ourselves to them. Where will the liberal Protestant denominations stop as they eagerly reinterpret the faith to allow for whatever popular opinion demands that they accept? If the Catholic Church doesn't remain very clear on what the revealed truths of our faith are, we will be—and are in some ways already—cast adrift in the same sea of relativism and cultural accommodation as they are.

While we are all being exhorted to make sure we are "on the

right side of history," as if history actually had a mind, the culture as a whole is rushing like lemmings madly toward the sea, where they will drown, or to the cliff, which they will hurtle over and perish. One thinks of the vision of St. Faustina:

> One day, I saw two roads. One was broad, covered with sand and flowers, full of joy, music and all sorts of pleasures. People walked along it, dancing and enjoying themselves. They reached the end without realizing it. And at the end of the road there was a horrible precipice; that is, the abyss of hell. The souls fell blindly into it; as they walked, so they fell. And their number was so great that it was impossible to count them. And I saw the other road, or rather, a path, for it was narrow and strewn with thorns and rocks; and the people who walked along it had tears in their eyes, and all kinds of suffering befell them. Some fell down upon the rocks, but stood up immediately and went on. At the end of the road there was a magnificent garden filled with all sorts of happiness, and all these souls entered there. At the very first instant they forgot all their sufferings.[83]

One of the most significant reversals is occurring concerning the most basic of all truths, that concerning salvation. To that we now turn.

Chapter 3

IS IT ALL A GAME? THE FOG OF UNIVERSALISM

IF I WERE TO DESCRIBE how many of our fellow Catholics view the world today, I would describe it like this: "Broad and wide is the way that leads to heaven, and almost everybody is going that way; narrow is the door that leads to hell, difficult is the path, and few there are who travel that way."

This, as you will recognize, is the exact opposite of what Jesus himself says about the situation of the human race as he sees it. The default situation of the human race is lost—not saved—and Jesus's warnings about this are to be received with the utmost attention. What does Jesus say?

> Enter by the narrow gate; for the gate is wide and the way is easy, that leads to destruction, and those who enter by it are many. For the gate is narrow and the way is hard, that leads to life, and those who find it are few. . . . Not everyone who says to me, "Lord, Lord," shall enter the kingdom of heaven, but he who does the will of my Father who is in heaven. (Matt 7:13–14, 21)

We Catholics are not fundamentalists, and the interpretation of this passage has to take into account historical context and be interpreted in harmony with other Scripture passages that treat of the same issue, and in light of how this passage has been received and understood in the history of the Church and how it has been reflected on by our most reliable theologians.

One consideration that might arise is wondering if Jesus's words are primarily applicable to the people of his own time and city, the Jewish people in his day, and not necessarily to us. Is Jesus just speaking about the situation of the Jewish people in his day—most of whom he recognized were heading toward destruction? This destruction was made manifest in the monumental judgment of Jerusalem in AD 70 that Jesus prophesied as the consequences of his people's rejection of him; one million were slaughtered as the Romans destroyed the city and the temple. Or do Jesus's words have wider application to unbelieving cultures of today? Perhaps in some periods in Christian history—maybe in Europe during the High Middle Ages—many were on the broad path heading to salvation, at least in the sense that Christian faith was widespread and was part of the prevailing culture. And even though many people didn't live the faith very well, not many wanted to die without going to confession. But certainly, that is not the case today. Those on the broad way who partake in unbelief and the refusal to acknowledge and repent from serious sin are indeed in danger of judgment, just as those in AD 70 were. The judgment may partially unfold in history, as it did in AD 70, but will certainly take place at the final judgment.

We always need to remember that it is not at all God's will that so many are on the path to destruction and so few are finding and following the way that leads to life. We know from 1 Timothy 2: 3–4 that God wills that the whole human race be saved and come to a knowledge of the truth. But we know that although this is God's "antecedent will," his "consequent will" is that those who do not freely accept the offer of salvation given in his son Jesus will perish.[84] God's respect for human freedom and the extraordinary gift he is ready to bestow on those who humble themselves, repent, and join themselves to his son Jesus require that there be freedom. If there is not freedom to reject as well as to accept the true love and friendship that God extends to the human race, then such love and friendship is not possible. Just like in a human marriage, if there is any force or compulsion, it is not a true marriage and can be annulled. And the end goal of God's offer of salvation is the true marriage of the human race with his son, to be celebrated forever at the wedding feast of the lamb in the eternal kingdom of love. For that freedom is necessary.

We need to also note that the words of Jesus about the "two ways"—the broad way and the narrow way—express one of the most fundamental themes of all of Scripture. God's revelation of himself, as recounted in both the Old and New Testaments, is always an invitation to choose, to choose him or something or someone else. God's revelation is not just abstract knowledge but an urgent invitation to believe, repent, and be saved.

Indeed, one of the most insistent messages of both Testaments is that there are two ways set before the human race: one way leads to life; the other way leads to death. This is not just a theoretical possibility or an empty warning. The witness of the entire Bible—and indeed of all of human history—is to the actual historical realization of choice for and against God.

There are those who choose the way that leads to life and others who choose the way that leads to death, those who choose the blessing and those who choose the curse (see Deut 30:15–20). We see the difference between the wise and the foolish (see Sir 21:11–28), between those who serve God and those who refuse to serve him, between those who fear the Lord and trust in him and those who wickedly defy him and trust in themselves (see Mal 3:16–21), between those who believe and those who refuse to believe, between those who truly know the Father and those who do not, between those who grieve and quench the Spirit and those who do not, between those who worship the one God in Spirit and truth and those who have exchanged the truth of God for a lie and worship the creature, between the city of God and the city of man, between those who love the brethren and those who do not, between the good and the wicked. There are those who are "vessels of mercy" and those who are "vessels of wrath" (Rom 9:22–23), those for whom Christ is the "cornerstone chosen and precious" and those for whom he is a stumbling stone and scandal (see 1 Pet 2:6–8). There are those who eagerly await the return of the Lord and cry out, "Come Lord Jesus!" (Rev 22:20), and there are those who cry out to the mountains, "Fall on us and hide us from the face of him who is seated on the throne, and from the wrath of the Lamb; for the great day of their wrath has come, and who can stand before it?" (Rev 6:16–17). As Aquinas points out, this separation was signaled on the hill of Calvary when one thief humbly turned to Christ with faith, hope, and love, and the other thief bitterly mocked and blasphemed him (see Luke 23:32–43).[85] And Aquinas's sequence for Corpus Christi continues each year to express the perennial faith of the Church:

> Bad and good the feast are sharing,
> Of what divers dooms preparing,
> Endless death, or endless life.
>
> Life to those, to those damnation,
> See how like participation
> Is with unlike issues rife.

This separation which exists even now is finalized, and the eternal reward and punishment appropriate to each individual is carried out definitively on the great Day of Judgment.[86]

Jesus reveals many things, but occasionally he emphasizes, with solemnity, that what he is about to say is of special importance:

Truly, truly, I say to you, the hour is coming, and now is, when the dead will hear the voice of the Son of God, and those who hear will live. For as the Father has life in himself, so he has granted the Son also to have life in himself, and has given him authority to execute judgment, because he is the Son of man. Do not marvel at this; for the hour is coming when all who are in the tombs will hear his voice and come forth, those who have done good, to the resurrection of life, and those who have done evil, to the resurrection of judgment. (John 5:25–29)

Moses starkly put the choice of the two ways to his people:

See, I have set before you this day life and good, death and evil. If you obey the commandments of the your God which I command you this day, by loving the LORD your God, by walking in his ways, and by keeping his commandments and his statutes and his ordinances, then you shall live and multiply, and the LORD your God will bless you in the land which you are entering to take possession of it. But if your heart turns away, and you will not hear, but are drawn away to worship other gods and serve them, I declare to you this day, that you shall perish; you shall not live long in the land which you are going over the Jordan to enter and possess. . . . I have set before you life and death, blessing and curse; therefore choose life, that you and your descendants may live, loving the LORD your God, obeying his voice, and cleaving to him. (Deut 30:15–20)

The psalms continually announce the different fates of the foolish and the wise, the wicked and the righteous. The Book of Psalms opens with this fundamental theme front and center:

Blessed is the man
who walks not in the counsel of the wicked,
nor stands in the way of sinners,
    nor sits in the seat of scoffers;
but his delight is in the law of the LORD,
    and on his law he meditates day and night.
He is like a tree
    planted by streams of water,
that yields its fruit in its season,
    and its leaf does not wither.
In all that he does, he prospers.
The wicked are not so,
    but are like chaff which the wind drives away.
Therefore the wicked will not stand in the judgment,
    nor sinners in the congregation of the righteous;
for the LORD knows the way of the righteous,
    but the way of the wicked will perish. (Ps 1)

The contrast between the just and the wicked and their divergent fates continues throughout the psalms.

The prophets continually prophesy the destruction of those who turn away from the one true God to the worship of idols, to the oppression of the poor, to sexual immorality, to every manner of wickedness and evil.

One of the earliest and most esteemed Christian writings is the Didache, which begins like this: "There are two ways: one of life and one of death, but a great difference between the two ways."[87]

And there are *hundreds* of warnings by Jesus and the Apostles in the sacred writings about the two ways, the two races of men, the two ways to live, the two ultimate destinations. Alongside the multitude of solemn warnings, there are repeated exhortations "not to be deceived" about these matters and the promise that every part of Jesus's words will be fulfilled, even if heaven and earth pass away.

As I write this, we have just completed a staff Bible study for Renewal Ministries on the Gospel of Matthew. We decided to study the Gospel looking for those texts where Jesus spoke about the eternal consequences, either implicitly or explicitly, of refusing to respond to him with faith, repentance, and faithful friendship. We were shocked to discover over sixty of these texts, just in this one Gospel. We are so familiar, for example, with the parables of Jesus that we often fail to notice the severity of what they communicate and the depth of response they demand. Peter Kreeft wrote a book called *Jesus Shock*,[88] and indeed it is shocking to really understand what Jesus repeatedly says.

The weeds and the wheat grow together on this earth but will be eternally separated at the Lord's coming:

> Just as the weeds are gathered and burned with fire, so will it be at the close of the age. The Son of man will send his angels, and they will gather out of his kingdom all causes of sin and all evildoers, and throw them into the furnace of fire; there men will weep and gnash their teeth. Then the righteous will shine like the sun in the kingdom of their Father. He who has ears, let him hear. (Matt 13:40–43)

> Just as good fish are separated from the bad by earthly fishermen,

> So it will be at the close of the age. The angels will come out and separate the evil from the righteous, and throw them

into the furnace of fire; there men will weep and gnash their teeth. (Matt 13:49–50)

And there are wise virgins who are ready for the Lord's return and are able to enter the marriage feast, and there are those who are not ready and cannot enter:

And while they went to buy, the bridegroom came, and those who were ready went in with him to the marriage feast; and the door was shut. Afterward the other maidens came also, saying "Lord, lord, open to us." But he replied, "Truly, I say to you, I do not know you." Watch therefore, for you know neither the day nor the hour. (Matt 25:10–13)

And then there are those who abide in the Lord and stay in close relationship with him and bear fruit and those who don't and are thrown into the fire and burned:

If a man does not abide in me, he is cast forth as a branch and withers; and the branches are gathered, thrown into the fire and burned. (John 15: 6–7)

With such clarity in God's word and with such consistent understanding of these texts throughout the Church's history, one may wonder how we got to this point where most Catholics believe the exact opposite. How did such a massive deception come about?[89]

Cardinal Avery Dulles demonstrated that, up until the middle of the twentieth century, there was an unchallenged consensus among Catholic theologians that Jesus's words are to be interpreted exactly as they are commonly understood, that there really is a heaven and really is a hell, and that faith, repentance, and baptism are necessary for salvation.

Then, with the toxic currents of Scripture scholarship emanating from Germany and the subsequent demythologizing of Scripture, along with the decline of faith in Europe, theological theories began to appear that paved the way for universalism, which is the belief that all or almost all will be saved. The most prominent and most influential of these theologians are Karl Rahner and Hans Urs von Balthasar.

Rahner, writing in the middle part of the last century into the post-conciliar period of the seventies and eighties, elaborated a theory that even though it seemed like there were vast numbers of the world's population that didn't believe in Jesus, they were for the most part "anonymous Christians." By this, Rahner meant that, in their choices for moral action or in their commitment to just principles or in "truly affirming their being," they were in fact saying yes to God. This implicit "yes," Rahner believed, connected them with the salvific grace won by Jesus, even though they didn't know his name or even if they were, in fact, atheists. Rahner's theory has been extensively critiqued[90] but has been widely promulgated and has very much influenced the culture of universalism in the Church.[91]

Even more significant recently has been the work of Hans Urs von Balthasar, who popularized a theory that we are obligated to hope for the salvation of all people and that it may be indeed virtually impossible that human beings can finally resist the grace of God.[92]

And then in the last several decades, there has been a veritable flood of publications advocating universalism. So much so that at one point the Jesuit theologian John Sachs, in a lengthy article in *Theological Studies*, claimed that this was now the new consensus among Catholic theologians, giving credit for this new consensus to Rahner and von Balthasar:

> We have seen that there is a clear consensus among Catholic theologians today in their treatment of the notion of

apocatastasis and the problem of hell. . . . It may not be said that even one person is already or will in fact be damned. All that may and must be believed is that the salvation of the world is a reality already begun and established in Christ. Such a faith expresses itself most consistently in the hope that because of the gracious love of God whose power far surpasses human sin, all men and women will in fact freely and finally surrender to God in love and be saved.

When Balthasar speaks of the duty to hope for the salvation of all, he is articulating the broad consensus of current theologians and the best of the Catholic tradition. Like other theologians, notably Rahner, he intentionally pushes his position to the limit, insisting that such a hope is not merely possible but well founded. . . . I have tried to show that the presumption that human freedom entails a capacity to reject God definitively and eternally seems questionable. And, although this presumption enjoys the weight of the authority of Scripture and tradition, it would seem incorrect to consider this possibility as an object of faith in the same sense that the ability of human freedom in grace to choose God is an object of faith.[93]

While this view may not actually be the consensus of Catholic theologians, it is indisputably hugely influential. And it has become even more influential recently as a new wave of books promoting universalism is being released. The most dramatic of such books is one by David Bentley Hart,[94] which, in inflammatory and often insulting and vituperative language, argues polemically for an empty hell. When one digs down to the foundational stance of people arguing for universalism, one often finds a statement like this: "I can't accept a God who would send anyone to hell."

In the best short treatment of universalism I've seen, Michael McClymond describes Hart's stance:

> Hart charges those who believe in an eternal hell with "moral imbecility." The language of rude dismissal was something of a guilty pleasure when he deployed it against the "New Atheists" more than a decade ago. Now he is denouncing Dante and everyone else who sustains the age-old tradition of the Church. By his reckoning, their view of God should evoke in us "only a kind of remote, vacuous loathing." So much for Augustine, Chrysostom, John of Damascus, Aquinas, Pascal, Newman, Chesterton, C. S. Lewis, and Pope Benedict XVI—not to mention innumerable canonized saints of the Church, the great majority of ancient Greek, Latin, Coptic, and Syriac writers, and such Protestant luminaries as Luther, Melanchthon, Bucer, Calvin, Hooker, and Edwards. Oddly, Hart now sounds very much like Richard Dawkins. No less than the aging atheist, Hart finds the two-thousand-year Christian tradition not just unbelievable but repugnant and inhuman.[95]

Unfortunately, a number of developments in Rome seem to be influenced by this reigning presumption that everyone will be saved in the end. The dominant focus on worldly concerns and the reappearance of a variety of liberation theologies, along with frequent talk about saving the earth, hint at this. Unfortunately, some of Pope Francis's comments seem to lean in this direction as well. In *Amoris Laetitia*, there is the statement: "No one can be condemned for ever, because that is not the logic of the Gospel! Here I am not speaking only of the divorced and remarried, but of everyone, in whatever situation they find themselves."[96] No matter how you wish to interpret the statement, it is difficult to see under any interpretation how what is stated could be true. Is it a reference to people not being excommunicated forever? Well, unless people repent from what caused the excommunication, it is indeed possible for them to be condemned forever. Is it a reference to the divorced and remarried not being denied Communion forever? Well, if their first marriage was valid and they are living in a state of adultery, unless they repent, it is entirely possible that they will be condemned forever. Is it referring to "hell having an end" and eventually everyone being brought to heaven? This would contradict the teaching of Jesus, the Apostles, and the *Catechism of the Catholic Church*.[97]

How to understand what Pope Francis might be saying was perhaps made clearer by his statement about Judas at his daily Mass homily on the Wednesday of Holy Week, 2020. He claimed not to know whether Judas was in hell, even though Jesus said it would have been better if he had never been born,[98] since Jesus kissed him and called him friend.[99]

As a matter of fact, Jesus didn't kiss Judas, but Judas kissed Jesus; this was not a kiss of affection of course, but a kiss of betrayal, a signal to his captors to grab him. Jesus's use of the word "friend" was most probably sorrowful irony. The entire Catholic tradition has always understood Jesus's words about Judas as an indication that he was certainly in hell, even though it has never been "defined."

One of the underlying motivations for universalism is an arrogance that thinks that our understandings of justice, mercy, and love are superior to Scripture and tradition. It is a theory that is attractive to our fallen nature. We can end up judging God. A remarkable example of it comes in the words of John Stuart Mill, a nineteenth-century British philosopher: "I will call no being good, who is not what I mean when I apply that epithet to my fellow creatures."[100] This attitude permeates much of the rationale that universalists give for their turn to universalism.

Universalism is the remarkable rebellion of the human mind against the revealed word of God and the mainstream tradition of the Church. At the same time, the Lord has raised up competent and courageous scholars who have been willing to do the work to trace the origins of universalism and identify its clear departure from Scripture and tradition and even locate its oftentimes occult sources. Among these is Dr. Michael McClymond from Saint Louis University, who has published a definitive two-volume history of the sources and growth of universalism, called *The Devil's Redemption*.[101]

Since Fr. Sach's claim in 1992 that universalism is now the consensus of Catholic theologians, so much so that it is not argued for any more but presumed, the flood of universalistic thought, both explicit and implicit, continues to grow. It is a flood that the Church has not yet countered in an effective way. And it has become more aggressive and self-confident. Dr. McClymond points out that there is a rising generation of scholars who are impatient with the veiled universalism of Rahner and Balthasar and are outrightly proclaiming the certain truth of their theory. As McClymond puts it, in commenting on Hart's book:

> Hart maintains his thesis not as a possible or probable claim, but as indubitably certain. He has no patience for "hopeful universalism"—a view often attributed to Karl Barth and Hans Urs von Balthasar—that remains open to salvation for all but asserts that the matter can't be definitely affirmed or known in advance. Hart's book might be a signal that universalist tentativeness is now out, while assertiveness is in.[102]

The wave of universalist publications and the wide and deep inroads universalism has made into the thinking of ordinary Catholics made me think of the well-known warning of Fr. Frederick

Faber, a highly esteemed priest and spiritual writer who lived in nineteenth-century England:

> The devil's worst and most fatal preparation for the coming of Antichrist is the weakening of men's belief in eternal punishment. Were they the last words I might ever say to you, nothing should I wish to say to you with more emphasis than this; that next to the thought of the Precious Blood (God's merciful suffering for you), there is no thought in all your faith more precious or more needful for you than the thought of Eternal Punishment.[103]

As the Church has turned toward a reemphasis on the need for the Church to evangelize, it has had to counter the presumption of universal salvation in virtually every document it has published on the subject but has not yet effectively done so. Universalism, of course, takes the urgency out of evangelization, but it has not yet been challenged directly enough and clearly enough to be effective in a way that reaches ordinary Catholics, priests, or even theologians.

In every major post-conciliar document on evangelization,[104] explicit reference is made, by both popes and the Congregation for the Doctrine of the Faith (CDF), to the doctrinal confusion that is undermining evangelization. Whether it be Paul VI's 1975 *Evangelii Nuntiandi*, John Paul II's 1990 *Redemptoris Missio*, the CDF's 2000 *Dominus Iesus*, or the CDF's 2007 *Doctrinal Note on Some Aspects of Evangelization*, each attempt by the magisterium to resolve the confusion seems to be met with failure. So much so that we read once again in the 2007 *Doctrinal Note* about this "growing confusion":

> There is today, however, a growing confusion which leads many to leave the missionary command of the Lord unheard and ineffective (cf. Matt 28:19). . . . It is enough, so

they say, to help people to become more human or more faithful to their own religion; it is enough to build communities which strive for justice, freedom, peace and solidarity. Furthermore, some maintain that Christ should not be proclaimed to those who do not know him, nor should joining the Church be promoted, since it would also be possible to be saved without explicit knowledge of Christ and without formal incorporation in the Church.[105]

While the *Doctrinal Note* addresses in a thorough manner the question of whether preaching the Gospel is an imposition on people's freedom, it doesn't thoroughly address the doctrinal confusion lurking around the truth of the possibility for people to be saved without hearing the Gospel and the common temptation to presume such people are saved, as stated in the above quotation.

It was my concern to address this recurring issue that led to my book *Will Many Be Saved? What Vatican II Actually Teaches and Its Implications for the New Evangelization.*[106]

When the seminary where I teach asked me if I would be willing to go to Rome and get a doctorate, I replied that I would if I would be allowed to work on this issue. Fortunately, a senior professor and dean at the Pontifical University of St. Thomas, commonly referred to as the Angelicum, was willing to be my dissertation director on this topic.[107]

Perhaps the best use of this short chapter would be to summarize the argument of the book, which as far as I know, is the most in-depth treatment of this conciliar teaching and which is frequently cited in scholarly studies related to this question.[108] It provides the doctrinal and magisterial underpinning for our interpretation of texts such as "Enter by the narrow gate" (Matt 7:13). This teaching, of course, concerns the Church's mission *ad gentes*, that is, "to the nations." We will also consider, in much briefer form, the application of the teaching to baptized Catholics.

As is clear from my book's title, my main concern is to focus attention on a text from Vatican II that sums up in succinct form, both in the text itself and in its important footnotes, what the Catholic Church actually teaches about the possibility of people being saved without hearing the Gospel and the significant limitations on these conditions.

While clearly affirming the teaching of the Catholic Church, based on Romans 1, Romans 2, and subsequent doctrinal clarifications, that it is indeed possible under certain conditions for people to be saved without hearing the Gospel, I primarily focused on how the Council teaches that "very often" (in Latin, *at saepius* translation) these conditions aren't, in fact, met. Therefore, for the sake of people in this situation and their salvation, the Gospel urgently needs to be preached, not just to "enrich" their lives or "give meaning to their lives" but to save their lives.[109] Of course, my book unreservedly affirms the clear teaching of the Church that since God wills the salvation of the whole human race, each person is given the possibility of being saved in ways known only to God.[110]

Here are the sentences of *Lumen Gentium* (*LG*) §16 in question; first of all, those sentences that affirm the possibility of being saved without hearing the Gospel:

> Those who, through no fault of their own, do not know the Gospel of Christ or his Church, but who nevertheless seek God with a sincere heart, and moved by grace, try in their actions to do his will as they know it through the dictates of their conscience[111]—those too may achieve eternal salvation. Nor shall divine providence deny the assistance necessary for salvation to those who, without any fault of theirs, have not yet arrived at an explicit knowledge of God, and who, not without grace, strive to lead a good life.

Whatever good or truth is found amongst them is considered by the Church to be a preparation for the Gospel[112] and given by him who enlightens all men that they may at length have life.[113]

In many, if not most, cases, those who quote *LG* §16 stop there, but there is one more paragraph that gives an important clarification as to the conditions under which it is possible for someone to be saved without hearing the Gospel: an inculpable ignorance of the Gospel, a sincere seeking of God, and a response to grace that enables one to live in accordance with the dictates of conscience. It is also necessary to pay attention to the very important footnote that references the response of the Holy Office to the Fr. Leonard Feeney case. This doctrinally significant letter makes clear that indeed even an unconscious desire for God and his Church may be salvific, but not just any kind of unconscious desire. The letter makes clear that it is not enough just to simply "believe in God" and "be a good person" in order to be saved, but there must be a personal response to the light of revelation involving a surrender in faith to the person revealing—a supernatural faith—and a change of life that is enabled by an infusion of supernatural charity.

And here are the final three sentences of *LG* §16, which speak about the obstacles to the possibility of salvation being realized without hearing the Gospel:

> But very often [*at saepius*][114], deceived by the Evil One, men have become vain in their reasonings, have exchanged the truth of God for a lie and served the world rather than the Creator (cf. Rom. 1:21, 25). Or else, living and dying in this world without God, they are exposed to ultimate despair. Hence to procure the glory of God and the salvation of all these, the Church, mindful of the Lord's command,

"preach the Gospel to every creature" (Mark 16:16) takes zealous care to foster the missions.

Because sustained attention hasn't been paid recently to the doctrinal truths that the last three sentences of *LG* §16 reaffirm, many Catholics—and Protestants, including a growing number of evangelicals[115]—have made a hugely unwarranted leap from the "possibility" of being saved without hearing the Gospel to the "probability" of being saved and, in some cases, to the presumed certainty of being saved without hearing the Gospel.

Many pastoral leaders, if they are not conscious of being universalists on the theoretical level, have adopted a "practical universalism" that presumes that virtually everybody will be saved, except, perhaps, some exceptionally evil historical figures. What are these doctrinal truths that *LG* §16c reaffirms?

The conciliar text reaffirms the foundational doctrinal truths that we don't live in a neutral environment and that the spiritual realities referred to in the Scripture as the world, the flesh, and the devil present great obstacles to fulfilling the conditions under which it is possible to be saved without the Gospel. Everyone is subject to the weakness of mind and will as a result of original sin, made worse by actual sin; everyone is vulnerable to the "world"—the international secular culture that is aggressively attacking respect for God and his Word and that dominates the media and universities; and everyone without the protection of the "spiritual armor" is subject to the deceptions of the evil one, who sends forth his "fiery darts" (see Eph 6:10–20) multiple times a day.

This is why it's foolish to say, as many people do, that unbelievers are better off not knowing the Gospel because then they are not responsible for living a godly life but are saved through "invincible ignorance." No! This is not true. Those who haven't heard the Gospel have nevertheless been given a revelation from God, who reveals his existence in Creation (see Rom 1:20), a revelation that he expects his creatures to heed. He also reveals his will for human life in the light he gives to each person's conscience and makes clear that each person will be judged on how they have responded to the light they have been given (see Rom 2:4–15). In the very text from Romans 1 that declares that God has revealed himself to everyone, it also declares the unfortunate and common response to this revelation: culpably ignoring it and grievously sinning:

> So they are without excuse; for although they knew God they did not honor him as God or give thanks to him, but they became futile in their thinking and their senseless minds were darkened. Claiming to be wise, they became fools, and exchanged the glory of the immortal God for images resembling mortal man or birds or animals or reptiles. Therefore God gave them up in the lusts of their hearts to impurity, to the dishonoring of their bodies among themselves, because they exchanged the truth about God for a lie and worshiped and served the creature rather than the Creator, who is blessed forever! Amen. (Rom 1:20–25)

Because these sober texts from Vatican II and from Sacred Scripture have been virtually ignored—even by well-known theologians who deal with this issue—a presumption in favor of near universal salvation has permeated the culture of the Church.

Cardinal Dulles explicitly recognizes, in somewhat shocking words, Balthasar's influence in communicating a universalist mentality:

> Hans Urs von Balthasar popularized the idea that we may hope that no one ever goes to hell. Rightly or wrongly, he is often interpreted as though he believed that in the end all men and women attain to the joys of heaven. Priests

and theologians frequently give the impression that the doctrine of hell is a medieval superstition rather than an essential component of the Gospel. In so doing, they may well be doing Satan's work because the fear of hell occupied a central place in the preaching of Jesus.[116]

While Balthasar's hope for universal salvation is perhaps logically possible, it is so only in the sense that it is logically possible that a major league baseball team would win every one of its games in any season. It has never happened, and to use his language, it is "infinitely improbable" that it ever will. Is a theological speculation that is contrary to the weight of Scripture and tradition really well founded? And if it isn't well founded —as I will argue—how pastorally wise and honest is it to teach such a thing?

Cardinal Dulles summarizes the clear consensus of the dogmatic tradition:

> The constant teaching of the Catholic Church supports the idea that there are two classes: the saved and the damned. Three General councils of the Church (Lyons I, 1245; Lyons II, 1274; and Florence, 1439) and Pope Benedict XII's bull *Benedictus Deus* (1336) have taught that everyone who dies in a state of mortal sin goes immediately to suffer the eternal punishments of hell. This belief has perdured without question in the Catholic Church to this day, and is repeated almost verbatim in the *Catechism of the Catholic Church* (CCC 1022, 1035).[117]

The Council of Trent, in teaching carried forward and affirmed by Pope John Paul II in *Veritatis Splendor*, affirms the reality of eternal punishment for unrepented mortal sins:

> It must be asserted, against the subtle modes of thinking

of certain people, who *by fair and flattering words deceive the hearts of the simple-minded* (Rom 16:18), that the grace of justification once received is lost not only by apostasy, by which faith itself is lost, but also by any other mortal sin, though faith is not lost. Thus is defended the teaching of the divine law which excludes from God's kingdom not only unbelievers, but also the faithful if they are guilty of fornication, adultery, wantonness, sodomy, theft, avarice, drunkenness, slander, plundering, and all others who commit mortal sins from which, with the help of divine grace, they can refrain, and because of which they are severed from the grace of Christ. (1 Cor 6: 9–10; 1 Tim 1:9–10).[118]

This section of the Council's teaching on justification ends with the warning that "unless each one faithfully and firmly accepts it, he cannot be justified."[119]

John Paul II reaffirmed this truth clearly:

[The act by which man freely and consciously rejects God] can occur in a direct and formal way, in the sins of idolatry, apostasy and atheism; or in an equivalent way, as in every act of disobedience to God's commandments in a grave matter.[120]

Jesus, John, Matthew, Luke, Mark, James, Peter, Paul, and Jude, in the multiple texts that talk of the final judgment of the human race, are unmistakably declaring that if people persist in unbelief and immorality to the end, they will be eternally lost. To suppose that when the Apostles and sacred writers taught God's will that all men be saved, they thought they were teaching something that wasn't in harmony with their multiple and repeated teachings on the ultimate two outcomes and the specific sins which, if unrepented from before death, will exclude people from the kingdom, lacks all credibility. And for those who say perhaps there are second chances after death, that is not the case. There is nothing in Scripture to indicate that there are second chances after death, but rather, just the opposite.[121] Life is emptied of its meaning if our choices do not end up really mattering for our eternal destinies. And this statement of Cardinal Ratzinger bears repeating: "The Catholic tradition . . . trusts the evangelists; it believes what they say."[122]

As the International Theological Commission's document on eschatology puts it:

> In revealing the Father's secrets to us, Jesus wants to make us his friends (cf. John 15:15). But friendship cannot be forced on us. Friendship with God, like adoption, is an offer, to be freely accepted or rejected. . . . This consummated and freely accepted friendship implies a concrete possibility of rejection. What is freely accepted can be freely rejected. [No one who] thus chooses rejection "has any inheritance in the kingdom of Christ and of God" (Eph 5:5). Eternal damnation has its origin in the free rejection to the very end of God's Love and Mercy. The Church believes that this state consists of deprivation of the sight of God and that the whole "being" of the sinner suffers the repercussion of this loss eternally. . . . This doctrine of faith shows equally the importance of the human capacity of freely rejecting God, and the gravity of such a freely willed rejection.[123]

While we cannot judge the state of anyone's soul and what transpires at the moment of death, it certainly appears—from the view of human resistance to grace, and subsequent judgment, contained in the Scriptures and from empirical observation—that many people persevere to the end in their rejection of God and/or in a life of immorality. Balthasar acknowledges as much but then posits the possible chance(s) after death, for which, as we have already noted, there is no basis in Scripture or the magisterium. He claims that those who take the traditional interpretation of these texts on judgment, following Augustine (but also Aquinas and the entire theological/magisterial mainstream)—that there will be a definitive separation of the human race based on how people have responded to the grace of God—have "transformed" and indeed, "vitiated" the Scriptures which, he claims, only warn of a possibility and do not teach that there will indeed be a division of the human race into the saved and damned. Such an interpretation is strained.

Cardinal Dulles summarizes the meaning of the "two destination" New Testament passages like this:

> As we know from the Gospels, Jesus spoke many times about hell. Throughout his teaching, he holds forth two and only two final possibilities for human existence: the one being everlasting happiness in the presence of God, the other everlasting torment in the absence of God. He describes the fate of the damned under a great variety of metaphors: everlasting fire, outer darkness, tormenting thirst, a gnawing worm, and weeping and gnashing of teeth. . . . Taken in their obvious meaning, passages such as these give the impression that there is a hell, and that many go there; more in fact, than are saved.[124]

Even if one does not want to claim that these passages indisputably reveal that there are people in hell, or that there are more in hell than in heaven, despite the strength of this opinion in the theological tradition, one would at least have to say that from the weight of these Scriptures and the historical testimony of final rejection of God or embrace of immorality, both in Scripture and contemporary history and experience, that it is not just a theoretical possibility but very probable that many end up in hell.[125] Fr. Kevin Flannery, S.J., professor and former Dean of the Philosophy Faculty at the Gregorian, acknowledges that a case can be made that Scripture does not imply with the force of logical necessity that there are people in hell. He argues, though, that the overwhelming weight of Scripture and tradition "approach[s] logical necessity."[126] As Fr. James O'Connor puts it, these passages and how they have been interpreted by the theological tradition and the magisterium lead us to *presume* that there will be many in hell, a presumption that the Holy Spirit who inspired the Scriptures intends us to have, a presumption imparted to us by a God who is utterly truthful and cannot deceive:[127]

> In the light of what it has been given us to know, we must presume that (in numbers completely unknown to us) humans will be included in "the eternal fire prepared for the devil and his angels" (Matt. 25:41), and that we ourselves could be among that number. It is such a presumption that the words of Jesus and the teaching of the Church would appear to have as their own, and better guides in this matter we cannot have. Against such a presumption one cannot have what is properly defined as theological hope, but we can and must have a human hope, a wish which expresses itself in prayer and zealous efforts, for the salvation of all.[128]

This "presumption" which is given to us in Scripture and tradition by a God who is utterly truthful and will not deceive is in opposition to the prevailing "presumption" that everybody or almost everybody will be saved and that finite human freedom is unable to finally resist the grace of God. The current "theological consensus" as Sachs has stated it is precisely the reverse of what has been revealed to us as it has been understood by the Church throughout the ages.[129]

This presents us with a very serious situation. In a sympathetic but critical review of McClymond's work, Roberto De La Noval, a professor of theology at Notre Dame, comes to the startling conclusion that a gap is opening up in the Christian churches between universalists and traditional Christianity and that what we are really facing is a conflict between "two different Gospels,"[130] and that is certainly the case. We can't avoid a choice. And in my opinion, those who choose against the traditional understanding of these matters are choosing a deception that only the devil will benefit from, a pernicious presumption on the mercy of God that will encourage countless souls to happily embark on the "broad way" that only leads to destruction. Painful decisions await many of us. It is time to stop straddling the issue. We have to make a choice, for Scripture and tradition or for a "different Gospel," really, a different, man-made religion. If we have fallen into deception on these matters, we need to repent and embrace again the truth and make reparation for damage we may have done in weakening people's faith, confirming them in lukewarmness, and affirming them in immoral choices.

With this as our doctrinal and magisterial foundation, let's return now to the actual words of Sacred Scripture and one of Jesus's most solemn warnings:

> He went on his way through towns and villages, teaching, and journeying toward Jerusalem. And someone said to him, "Lord, will those who are saved be few?" And he said to them, "Strive to enter by the narrow door; for many, I tell you, will seek to enter and will not be able. When once the householder has risen up and shut the door, you will begin to stand outside and to knock at the door, saying, 'Lord, open to us.' He will answer you, 'I do not know where you

come from.' Then you will begin to say, 'We ate and drank in your presence, and you taught in our streets.' But he will say, 'I tell you, I do not know where you come from; depart from me, all you workers of iniquity!' There you will weep and gnash your teeth, when you see Abraham and Isaac and Jacob and all the prophets in the kingdom of God and you yourselves thrust out. And men will come from east and west, and from north and south, and sit at table in the kingdom of God. And behold, some are last who will be first, and some are first who will be last." (Luke 13:22–30)

It is clear that people were shocked by Jesus's words and thought they were on friendly terms with him and of course should be admitted to his house. Jesus makes clear, though, that familiarity with his teaching, attendance at his teaching and healing sessions, or even eating and drinking with him do not constitute the relationship with him that will admit people to his house. It's clear that faith, repentance, and obedience are necessary; becoming part of Jesus's family before the door closes is essential. Just knowing about Jesus and being positively disposed to him is not enough. It is necessary to enter into relationship with him, obey his teachings, and persevere to the end. It is necessary to "strive" (the underlying Greek word is where we get the English word "agonize") to enter the kingdom of God as the kingdom suffers "violence" and the violent enter it. The violence of conversion, of repentance, of taking up our cross and following Jesus, the violence of crucifying the flesh, of being crucified to the world, falling into the ground and dying, losing our life in abandonment to Jesus so as to truly find it for all eternity in the Father's house.

And now let's take another look at the text from Matthew that we quoted as we began this chapter in its fuller context:

"Enter by the narrow gate; for the gate is wide and the way is easy, that leads to destruction, and those who enter by it are many. For the gate is narrow and the way is hard, that leads to life, and those who find it are few. Beware of false prophets, who come to you in sheep's clothing but inwardly are ravenous wolves. You will know them by their fruits. Are grapes gathered from thorns, or figs from thistles? So, every sound tree bears good fruit, but the bad tree bears evil fruit. A sound tree cannot bear evil fruit, nor can a bad tree bear good fruit. Every tree that does not bear good fruit is cut down and thrown into the fire. Thus you will know them by their fruits. Not everyone who says to me, 'Lord, Lord,' shall enter the kingdom of heaven, but he who does the will of my Father who is in heaven. On that day many will say to me, 'Lord, Lord, did we not prophesy in your name, and cast out demons in your name, and do many mighty works in your name?' And then will I declare to them, 'I never knew you; depart from me, you evildoers.' Every one then who hears these words of mine and does them will be like a wise man who built his house upon the rock; and the rain fell, and the floods came, and the winds blew and beat upon that house, but it did not fall, because it had been founded on the rock. And everyone who hears these words of mine and does not do them will be like a foolish man who built his house upon the sand; and the rain fell, and the floods came, and the winds blew and beat against that house, and it fell; and great was the fall of it." And when Jesus finished these sayings, the crowds were astonished at his teaching, for he taught them as one who had authority, and not as their scribes. (Matt 7:13–29)

The world and Church are full of false prophets who tell us that virtually everyone will be saved or, even more boldly, that everyone will be saved. Denial of the truths connected to Jesus's urgent warnings to enter by the narrow gate or door, in my opinion, has contributed mightily to the accelerating institutional collapse of the Church that we are now experiencing in the developed countries. The whole witness of Scripture is to the two ways, one of which leads home to the Father's house and one of which leads to the "outer darkness" where there is "weeping and gnashing of teeth" (see Matt 8:12). Jesus's clear and urgent warnings are spoken out of love, wanting us all to be in the Father's house and part of his body before the door closes. It's also clear that false prophets and teachers will be severely judged:

> But false prophets also arose among the people, just as there will be false teachers among you, who will secretly bring in destructive heresies, even denying the Master who bought them, bringing upon themselves swift destruction. And many will follow their licentiousness, and because of them the way of truth will be reviled. . . . These are waterless springs and mists driven by a storm; for them the nether gloom of darkness has been reserved. (2 Pet 2:1–2, 17)

The truth of the narrow door is relevant not only for the urgency to preach the Gospel to those who haven't heard it but also for the baptized who aren't living as disciples of Christ, the primary "target audience" of the New Evangelization.

Although it is very important to understand the actual situation of non-Christians in regard to salvation and the necessity of preaching the Gospel, it is also important to understand what the Council (and Scripture!) teaches about the salvation of baptized Catholics. Based on some of the same and similar Scripture passages we have been considering, the Church teaches that it is not enough just to be baptized or even go to Church on Sundays, but that unless we actually obey the teachings of Jesus in thought, word, and deed, not only will we not be saved, but we will be the more severely judged. Vatican II makes this stunningly clear:

> He is not saved, however, who, though part of the body of the Church, does not persevere in charity. He remains indeed in the bosom of the Church, but, as it were, only in a "bodily" manner and not "in his heart." All the Church's children should remember that their exalted status is to be attributed not to their own merits but to the special grace of Christ. If they fail moreover to respond to that grace in thought, word and deed, not only shall they not be saved but they will be the more severely judged.[131]

This text is repeated by St. John Paul II at the end of chapter 1 of *Redemptoris Missio*.

Just like the Jews boasting about having the Temple in their midst was not enough to save them from severe judgment, or the Jews in Jesus's time claiming to be children of Abraham was not enough to save them from condemnation, just claiming we are Catholic is not enough to save any of us from severe judgment. In fact, in Jesus's time, those who were most proud of being "children of Abraham" were so deeply deceived in their prideful presumption that they were blind to the fact that they were, in fact, children of the devil! (see John 8:44). God forbid this would be the case with us because of a diabolical presumption.

May we all take to heart the solemn warnings that Jesus gives us in Luke 13 and in Matthew 7, and in multiple other texts, strive to humble ourselves, and enter through the narrow gate. And may we help others, through our witness, our prayer, and our fasting, to journey with us on the narrow road, the road that leads back to Paradise. May we find ourselves, at journey's end, home in the Father's house, where Jesus has prepared a place for us. The gate to the Father's house is Jesus. The way back to Paradise is Jesus. Jesus's words are the only light in the present darkness—and what a light they are—and we ignore them at our great peril.

Chapter 4

The Revolution Continues

IT CONTINUES. The sexual revolution. What began in the sixties is relentlessly pushing on to its extreme conclusion. What began as a celebration of heterosexual fornication contained in it the seeds of the total overthrow of any relationship sexuality ever had to the natural order and a repudiation of any claim that divine law had on it, and now it pushes on to a mad denial of biological realities. And anyone standing in its way now is considered to be an enemy, a "hater," which justifies any tactic to silence, slander, or destroy. As Lenin said, lies in the service of the revolution are virtuous. A dictatorship must be established before all can be "equal," although it seems that the dictatorship never ends and that some always end up being more equal than others. It's amazing to see the similarity between communist tactics to take power and enforce conformity and the tactics being used to enforce the dictatorship of the sexual revolution. The atheistic materialism that Mary, at Fatima, warned would soon engulf the world if there weren't repentance—and so it did with the scourge of communism—has now engulfed the Western world as well, using different names but similar tactics.[132]

One remarkable revelation of the forces driving second-wave

feminism, abortion, and the sexual revolution of the 1960s and 1970s was published by Sue Ellen Browder, a former writer for the very popular feminist women's magazine *Cosmopolitan*.

Browder said she was attracted to the feminist movement because of her concern for equality in education and jobs, having experienced discrimination in these areas herself. She pointed out that the anti-male and pro-abortion elements that are now deeply embedded in the "women's movement" were not a part of it at the beginning. She gives credit for the connection of the two themes to Helen Gurley Brown, the editor of *Cosmo* for more than thirty years and whom Browder worked under. Brown, author of the book *Sex and the Single Girl*, decided to imitate what *Playboy Magazine* was doing for men by steering her magazine in a similar direction for women. "She gave her writers a printed list of rules to follow, which included instructions about how to make up parts of their stories to sound more convincing."

Some of the rules: "Unless you are a recognized authority on the subject, profound statements must be attributed to somebody appropriate, even if the writer has to invent the authority." And, "Try to locate some of the buildings, restaurants, nightclubs, parks, streets, as well as entire case histories . . . in cities other than New York, even if you deliberately have to plant them elsewhere. Most writers live in New York; 92 percent of our readers do not."

The goal was to give the impression that extravagant affairs were happening all over the country and not just in the corrupt elite of New York, with the goal of normalizing the sexual revolution and spreading it to places like Cleveland and Des Moines.

In her book-length account of how abortion and feminism got connected, *Subverted: How I helped the Sexual Revolution Hijack the Women's Movement*, Browder documents how connecting abortion to the feminist movement met strong resistance but eventually was pushed through. *Cosmo* was "fake news" before "fake news" became a real concern. Browder says that the driving force behind all the propaganda and fake news that *Cosmo* purveyed was money. The magazine preyed on insecure girls, seducing them through glamorous accounts of fake affairs and advertising that promised to make them irresistible if they just had a certain perfume, hair coloring, beautiful clothes, opportunities for traveling solo, casual sex, abortions, and contraception. Browder points to her iPhone and speculates: how truly free can our daughters and granddaughters ever be if they are addicted to the continuing stream of propaganda deluging us day and night?[133]

It is ever more important, in the flood of propaganda and censorship and growing control of what we're allowed to see and say, that we be firmly grounded in the Word of God and in a deep relationship with the Lord that will enable us to distinguish his voice from the voices of our own disordered desires, the pressure of the world, and the lies of the devil. Almost daily, as I'm writing this, I get reports of more Christians being suspended from their social media accounts for violating "community standards," which seem to exclude defense of babies in the womb and the Christian vision of sexuality and marriage. Just today, as I write, a report arrived of a Chaldean Catholic priest in California who had one of his social media accounts suspended because he counseled Christians not to participate in Gay Pride Month celebrations. He, at the same time, indicated our obligation to respect and love those with same-sex attraction, even if we can't support their behavior. He reported being deluged with hate mail and death threats:

> In response to the video, I have received thousands of hateful comments and messages, including death threats and people trying to find me and my family. . . . I will continue to love and pray for all the people doing this. I encourage you all to do the same.[134]

Even non-Christians who refuse to bow down to the latest expression of mob frenzy or dare to raise questions about its wisdom are being banned from social media and more and more frequently being fired from their jobs.

Unfortunately, while the culture is rushing toward destruction, the Church is divided in its response. There are some who are aggressively and sometimes subtly pushing for the Church to accommodate itself to the sexual revolution. Many, perhaps most, are just intimidated and fearful of coming into conflict with the culture, which is now firmly ensconced in the minds and hearts of many even "practicing Catholics." The response of many in the Church is a perplexed, fearful silence. Others are resisting the culture but are worried about whether they will stand alone and are sobered by division within their own families and confusing signals from the Church they look to for support. A well-known and widely published seminary professor was asked by a seminarian whether if he spoke clearly on matters of marriage and sexuality and other serious moral issues after his ordination, would the bishops have his back? The professor's answer: no.

I unfortunately had a personal experience of this when a priest who had been a former student of mine had the difficult task of preaching at the funeral of a teenager who had committed suicide. He tried—in my opinion, very successfully—to balance the truth of God's mercy and yet the objective evil of suicide. And then all hell broke out. The parents protested that it wasn't the sermon they wanted the priest to give and he should have done what they wanted. They went "public" and news feeds all over the world covered the story of the "horribly insensitive" pastor who did such an awful thing. The parents launched a lawsuit against the diocese and demanded that the priest be removed from the priesthood. The diocese, where the priest serves, put their PR machinery into gear in what almost seemed like a panic and profusely apologized for the priest's insensitivity, forbade him to preach at any more funerals, required him to submit his normal Sunday homilies in advance to the diocese for vetting, and told him he needed to get counseling to find out the roots of his insensitivity. I was concerned enough about this situation to contact the priest and show him my support. I also requested an appointment with the diocese and told them my concerns about their outsourcing a teaching moment to the PR department. My concerns were respectfully listened to and, it seemed, even agreed with, but nothing has happened to my knowledge to restore the priest's reputation.[135] Fear of public opinion. Fear of what people will think about us. Fear about loss of reputation. Fear about financial loss. Fear about personal discomfort. It all puts a leash on the Gospel.

It is most unfortunate that just at the moment that the world most needs a clear word of warning from the Church about the consequences of abandoning the natural and divine laws governing human sexuality, the high dignity to which God has raised marriage and sexuality, and other important moral issues such as suicide, the Church seems to be wavering and reluctant to speak clearly.

We've been here before. In the original *A Crisis of Truth*, I gave an account of the theological theories that were being put forward by well-respected Catholic theologians that seemed to indicate that there are no moral absolutes and perhaps, in certain circumstances, actions that were considered intrinsically sinful might not really be so. This current of thought was so insidiously put forth and so widely accepted that a whirlwind of sexual disorder quickly spread, like a virus, in the Church. The revelations of the past several years of the McCarrick predations, the various attorney generals' reports, and the multiple testimonies to the existence of homosexual networks even in high places, give shocking witness to the bankruptcy of such moral theology. And yet, hard as it is to say, it's back. For those interested in how the groundwork was laid for the sexual immorality that spread in the Church, we have available on the Renewal Ministries website the original text of *A Crisis of Truth* that makes shocking reading, even today. It also clearly demonstrates how we got to where we are today.[136]

In order to celebrate the fiftieth anniversary of Vatican II, the *National Catholic Reporter* published an entire issue on the Council, with many of the articles calling for continuing change. One article called for broadening the definition of the magisterium:

> Members of the official magisterium need to listen and to heed—*obedire*—the authentic magisterium of the single, the married and the divorced, the magisterium of parents and children, the magisterium of diversely shaped families, the magisterium of faithful lesbian, gay, bisexual and transgendered Catholics.[137]

Another article, by a theology professor at a Jesuit university, argued that we won't reach the next generation if we don't openly embrace the moral legitimacy of homosexuality:

> The liberalization of Catholicism's staid sexual culture, and the liberation of the pastoral energies of queer Catholics and women, are the last, unfinished pieces of the 1960s reform that hold any interest to the students of this generation. Without them the future of Roman Catholicism looks very shaky . . . Each time I teach liberation theology, I reserve an ever-growing section of the course to questions of gender and sexuality. . . . For many of my students, gay or straight, a Catholic sexual revolution is the rock on which the church of the future will be built—or run aground. [138]

Strange as it may seem, these theories seem to have been given a new lease on life by the ambiguous texts and particular footnote in *Amoris Laetitia* which has been interpreted by individual bishops and cardinals and entire episcopal conferences as allowing divorced and remarried Catholics to be admitted to Communion after consultation with a priest or after a time of "pastoral accompaniment," bypassing the need to seek an objective ruling from the Church about whether the first marriage was a true marriage or not.

A key text in question:

> Because of forms of conditioning and mitigating factors, it is possible that in an objective situation of sin—which may not be subjectively culpable, or fully such—a person can be living in God's grace, can love and can also grow in the life of grace and charity, while receiving the Church's help to this end. Discernment must help to find possible ways of responding to God and growing in the midst of limits. By thinking that everything is black and white, we sometimes close off the way of grace and of growth, and discourage paths of sanctification which give glory to God.[139]

A footnote was appended to this text that added to the controversy:

> In certain cases, this can include the help of the sacraments. Hence, "I want to remind priests that the confessional must not be a torture chamber, but rather an encounter with the Lord's mercy" (Apostolic Exhortation Evangelii Gaudium [24 November 2013], 44: AAS 105 [2013], 1038). I would also point out that the Eucharist "is not a prize for the perfect, but a powerful medicine and nourishment for the weak.[140]

This is not the time to get into a detailed account of the immense amount of controversy that has raged over these texts. We have already discussed some of it. Because of the examples we have already discussed, some are convinced that Pope Francis is reverting to the moral theology of the seventies and treating moral norms as "ideals" rather than "absolutes." If this is the case, it would amount to essentially overturning John Paul II's encyclical on moral theology, *Veritatis Splendor*, which reaffirmed the existence of absolute moral norms and intrinsically evil actions based on the teachings of the Apostles revealed to us in Sacred Scripture.[141] Others claim that he is not doing that and even though he uses the language of moral norms as "ideals," he can be interpreted in an orthodox fashion.

Pope Francis himself has said, as we noted earlier, that the interpretation of the Argentine bishops of *Amoris Laetitia* regarding Communion for the divorced and remarried is the right one. He even entered their interpretation in the official records of papal acts, wanting to elevate the Argentine statement to the level of the magisterium, a claim that has been vigorously disputed.[142]

The Argentine bishops' statement is not without nuance. It is clearly not an invitation for everyone to be admitted to the sacraments without repentance, but it ends up indicating that, in carefully discerned cases, divorced and remarried people without annulments who are unwilling to refrain from sexual relations might be rightly admitted:

> In other, more complex cases, and when a declaration of nullity has not been obtained, the above-mentioned option (not engaging in sexual relationships) may not, in fact, be feasible. Nonetheless, a path of discernment is still possible. If it comes to be recognized that, in a specific case, there are limitations that mitigate responsibility and culpability (cf. 301–302), especially when a person believes

they would incur a subsequent wrong by harming the children of the new union, *Amoris Laetitia* offers the possibility of access to the sacraments of Reconciliation and Eucharist (cf. footnotes 336 and 351).[143]

To make the conversation even more difficult, many commentators have pointed out that while the argument is supposedly about admitting divorced and remarried people to the Eucharist even though they are living in an objective state of adultery, what's at stake is much broader and covers the whole range of sexual sins, including fornication and the practice of homosexuality.

And clearly this is the understanding that many of Francis's supporters have. As Cardinal Cupich made clear, the principles of *Amoris Laetitia* can be extended beyond divorced and remarried people into other moral issues as well, including that of the active practice of homosexuality. Cardinal Cupich bases his understanding on a notion of the primacy of conscience that no longer is seeking to be conformed to the objective, revealed truth but is free to follow subjective considerations.[144] But Cardinal Cupich is not the only one who sees an opening in *Amoris Laetitia* for a greater permissiveness regarding the whole realm of sexual morality. The German bishops cite *Amoris Laetitia* as justification for a "new look" at homosexuality.[145]

When the president of Argentina, along with his mistress, paid an official visit to the pope, besides being warmly received by the pope, he and his mistress were given Communion in St. Peter's Basilica by Bishop Sorondo, head of the Pontifical Academy of Social Sciences, which we will learn more about in the next chapter. Is this an example of the correct interpretation of *Amoris Laetitia*? Bishop Sorondo, under fire for public scandal, defended himself by claiming that canon law required him to give them both Communion. How could the ordinary Catholic not be scandalized—literally, "caused to stumble"—by this?[146]

The bishops of Malta issued an interpretation of *Amoris Laetitia* that was published in the official Vatican newspaper and that basically said that if a person felt at peace about receiving Communion, even if he was divorced and remarried and the case wasn't submitted to the marriage tribunal, the person should feel free to go to Communion.[147] The pope wrote a letter thanking the Maltese bishops for their interpretation of *Amoris Laetitia*.[148]

A huge problem with each person individually deciding about whether they are an exception to a universal moral norm is that no one is a good judge in their own case, and to remove the objective evaluation of the validity of the first marriage from the "discernment process" is to open the door to massive self-deception on the part of those in second or even multiple marriages and to false compassion or intimidation on the part of their chosen pastoral counselors. Especially in a case involving the deep entanglements, emotionally and bodily, that come from a sexual relationship, the pressure to rationalize it as good, life-giving, and truly loving is almost irresistible. The pressure to excuse oneself and minimize or deny culpability and plead that "God will understand my weakness, my need" is powerful. In the case of *Amoris Laetitia*, the "pastoral accompaniment" principle was given its most startling application when the cardinal of the Portuguese diocese where Our Lady of Fatima appeared (!) confirmed that a divorced and remarried couple could receive Communion even though the husband said he was certain that his first marriage was a true marriage.[149] As we have already noted, Jesus's words concerning the holiness of validly contracted marriage are strong and clear and have been understood in this way throughout the centuries by the Church. In response to the Pharisees' question, "Is it lawful to divorce one's wife for any cause?" (Matt 19:3), Jesus responded that this was never God's plan from the beginning and it was time to return to God's purpose for marriage:

> For this reason a man shall leave his father and mother and be joined to his wife, and the two shall become one . . . So they are no longer two but one. What therefore God has joined together, let not man put asunder. . . . And I say to you: whoever divorces his wife, except for unchastity, and marries another, commits adultery; and he who marries a divorced woman, commits adultery. (Matt 19:5–9)[150]

In addition to the theological and pastoral issues in play, about which one can have different interpretations, there is one indisputable fact. There is doctrinal confusion that the pope is not successfully resolving. And the way he seems to be "leaning," if it was made more explicit, would cause even more division, perhaps even a schism. Whole episcopal conferences are disagreeing with each other over these issues. This is just the opposite of the "healthy decentralization" that Pope Francis called for in *Evangelii Gaudium*. It is extremely unhealthy. One article by a seasoned Rome commentator called it "Doctrinal Anarchy."[151]

Many people believe that the focus on divorced and remarried Catholics being able to receive Communion is simply the opening wedge of paving the way for acceptance of homosexual relationships and a general "downgrading" of the notion of serious sexual sin, including fornication, masturbation, and pornography. And of course, this is already happening in many dioceses and parishes, where those in same-sex relationships are being assured that it is licit for them to receive Communion and the call to repentance is never issued.

I happened to run into a Catholic a while back who shared with me that he regularly went to the local Catholic parish in his city run by the Jesuits. As we got talking, he told me about how active he was, how he was the liturgical coordinator for one of the Masses and was also active in the LGBTQ support group. I asked him if those attending were getting good support in living a chaste life, and he replied, "Oh no, we are supported in our relationships. I am married to another male parishioner . . ." I asked whether someone who joined the group and wanted help in remaining chaste would be welcome. He said they would be welcome but wouldn't feel comfortable and someone like that joined a few years back and didn't stay. Unfortunately, many of the LGBTQ ministries in Catholic parishes that are not part of the Courage Network operate very much like this one. Many of the Catholic parishes that are "gay friendly" encourage those plagued by homosexual desires to act on them "responsibly." I communicated this to the bishop of that diocese, and he responded that he would write a letter reminding them to uphold Church teaching. Not effective at all.

And Fr. James Martin, the American Jesuit mentioned earlier, continues to write and speak about the need for the Catholic Church to be more welcoming to the LGBTQ communities and not discriminate against them in any way. Prominent bishops, like Cardinal Tobin of Newark and Cardinal Cupich of Chicago, have endorsed his work, and he is welcome to speak in many American dioceses. He recently spoke to a national gathering of Catholic university presidents.[152] What Fr. Martin never seems to be willing to say is that the Church's welcome needs to include a call to repentance and conversion and the embrace of chastity, and that to act on homosexual desires is a grave sin, just as it is a grave sin to act on heterosexual desires outside of a valid marriage. Archbishop Charles Chaput wrote an article pointing out the significant gaps in what Fr. Martin is teaching, which was very respectfully written but made some essential points:

> A pattern of ambiguity in his teaching tends to undermine
> his stated aims . . . Fr. Martin partners with organizations
> like New Ways Ministry that oppose or ignore the teach-
> ing of the Church, and he endorses events, such as PRIDE

month, that cause confusion for the faithful . . . what is implied or omitted often speaks as loudly as what is actually stated, and in the current climate, incomplete truths do, in fact, present a challenge to faithful Catholic belief.

When people hear that "the Church welcomes gay people" or needs to be more "inclusive and welcoming" without also hearing the conditions of an authentically Christian life set for *all* persons by Jesus Christ and His Church—namely, living a life of chastity—they can easily misunderstand the nature of Christian conversion and discipleship.[153]

Soon after this exchange with Archbishop Chaput, Fr. Martin was given a half-hour private audience with Pope Francis that Fr. Martin emerged from claiming that the pope was supporting his work. Fr. Martin has also been named by Pope Francis as a consultor to the Pontifical Communications Department, again, a move that also seemed to support his ambiguous teaching about "welcoming" without conversion and repentance.[154]

Distressingly, fornication, divorce and remarriage, pornography, and masturbation have become so widely accepted, even among many Catholics, that the real cutting edge of the revolution now is the acceptance of the practice of homosexuality and transgenderism.

In a remarkably short period of time, from being widely viewed as an unfortunate developmental disorder and officially categorized as a psychological problem by the national organizations of psychiatrists and psychologists, homosexual attraction has become widely accepted as a normal variant of sexuality that people have a right to act on. Those who disagree are fiercely persecuted.[155]

Well-funded and aggressive organizations are devoted to driving forward not only tolerance of the "gay lifestyle" but forcing the population to agree that it is a perfectly normal expression of sexuality, and as virtuous as any other form, maybe even more so! More and more jurisdictions—a growing number of US states and a growing number of countries (Canada, Germany, Australia, and Belgium)—are forbidding counselors to assist people who have the inclination to same-sex relationships and want help to live chaste lives. In Canada, a particularly draconian bill has been introduced that threatens with imprisonment those who offer counseling to help people resist homosexual desires and live chaste lives.[156] Pastors who have tried to remain faithful to the preaching and teaching of the Gospel, if they actually communicate what Jesus, the Apostles, and the *Catechism of the Catholic Church* really say about the active practice of homosexuality, have been hauled up before "human rights" tribunals and accused of "hate crimes." Switzerland recently overwhelmingly voted to criminalize what it calls "homophobia," including in it the definition of "hate speech."[157]

J. K. Rowling, the author of the Harry Potter novels, was viciously attacked for supporting an employee in England who lost her job, her termination being upheld by a United Kingdom court, because she posted on social media her view that people can't change their biological sex:

> Forstater's termination was based on the crime of using "offensive and exclusionary" language. In a 26 page judgment Judge James Tayler ruled that Forstater's termination was just. The employment judge concluded from "the totality of the evidence that she is absolutist in her view of sex and it is a core component of her belief that she will refer to a person by the sex she considered appropriate even if it violates their dignity and/or creates an intimidating, hostile, degrading, humiliating or offensive environment. The approach is not worthy of respect in a democratic society."[158]

The international network of LGBTQ activist groups leaps into aggressive action to villainize anyone who dares to question gender ideology. Even well-respected secular feminists who dare to question gender ideology are viciously attacked:

> Gender-critical feminists have suffered professional retaliation and concerted harassment. Such methods are now commonly employed against anyone who questions transgender claims.[159]

The hostility of well-organized pressure groups has not been lost on many Church members, including bishops, priests, and deacons, and whether consciously or unconsciously as we have noted, the topic of sexual morality is almost universally avoided when the Scripture readings on these topics appear during the liturgical year. And yet to remain silent is to consign our people to being evangelized by the culture, which is now demanding total submission on these issues. To remain silent is to turn our people over to the "wolves." We are not being required to offer incense to the emperor now, but we are being required to accept untruths and even myths to anesthetize the consciences of those engaging in such activities.

Anesthetizing consciences is a grave sin. As John Paul II said:

> Modern man experiences the threat of spiritual indifference and even of the death of conscience; and this death is something deeper than sin: it is the killing of the sense of sin. Today, so many factors contribute to killing conscience in the men of our time, and this corresponds to that reality which Christ called "sin against the Holy Spirit.[160]

The words of Sacred Scripture are clear about the seriousness of not only doing these aberrant deeds but, even more so, approving them in others:

They exchanged the truth about God for a lie and worshiped and served the creature rather than the Creator, who is blessed for ever! Amen. For this reason God gave them up to dishonorable passions. Their women exchanged natural relations for unnatural, and the men likewise gave up natural relations with women and were consumed with passion for one another, men committing shameless acts with men and receiving in their own persons the due penalty for their error. And since they did not see fit to acknowledge God, God gave them up to a base mind and to improper conduct. They were filled with all manner of wickedness, evil, covetousness, malice. Full of envy, murder, strife, deceit, malignity, they are gossips, slanderers, haters of God, insolent, haughty, boastful, inventors of evil, disobedient to parents, foolish, faithless, heartless, ruthless. Though they know God's decree that those who do such things deserve to die, they not only do them but approve those who practice them. (Rom 1:25–32)

How many teachers now are being required to use strange pronouns to describe ever-expanding variations of sexuality? At one point, Facebook had more than fifty "gender options" for people to choose from to describe themselves. And now even little children are being given powerful hormones to block their natural sexual development because parents think they are identifying with a nonbiological gender. And yet solid studies have shown that many young children and even adolescents who for a time identify with the opposite sex or feel attraction to the same sex over time grow out of these identifications and attractions and live normal heterosexual lives.

Shockingly, after years of resisting such treatments, surgeons are going along with this rush to treatment and are cutting off perfectly healthy breasts and penises to indulge the fantasy or psychological disorder of those who think, despite their DNA, they are not really a man or a woman. It reminds me of the medical experiments carried out in Nazi Germany. One day, I believe we will look back at this hormonal and surgical treatment of children and call it by its rightful name: child abuse, facilitated by confused adults and "non-judgmental" doctors. Could there also be a financial incentive or a desire to appear "on the cutting edge" in play?

A popular academic book called *The Madness of Crowds*[161] was written by an openly gay commentator who is happy about the widespread acceptance of homosexuality but nevertheless thinks that we are rushing into a catastrophe by a mindless response to so-called gender dysphoria. He states that much of this response is without solid scientific evidence to support the radical treatments that are being more and more frequently performed, with little evidence that those who experience such surgery or hormone treatment are any happier than before. Not only that, but he thinks that well-funded "change" organizations are pushing these changes with a view of destroying the "current order," including marriage and family, deeply influenced by Marxist thought. He claims they don't care about contradictions in their work or in the lack of evidence for what they are pushing. In doing so, they are promoting "the madness of crowds," amplified by technology and immense social pressure. The transformation of Marxism to a broader movement than just "class struggle" aims to include all the "progressive causes"—termed intersectionality—environmentalism, transgenderism, socialism, gender theory, and so on, creating new classes of "exploited minorities," under one umbrella which he terms the "umbrella of the socialist struggle." He documents his claims with extensive references to the main thinkers guiding this movement, who are quite explicit in their desire to destroy marriage and the family and end the "capitalist system." He comments on the likelihood of all the contradictions bringing this movement to a halt and finds it unlikely:

> Yet if the absence of serious discussion and the innate contradictions alone were enough to stop this new religion of social justice, it would hardly have got started. People looking for this movement to wind down because of its inherent contradictions will be waiting a long time. Firstly because they are ignoring the Marxist substructure of much of this movement, and the inherent willingness to rush towards contradiction rather than notice all these nightmarish crashes and wonder whether they aren't telling you something about your choice of journey.[162]

> But the other reason why contradiction is not enough is because nothing about the intersectional, social justice movement suggests that it is really interested in solving any of the problems that it claims to be interested in. The first clue lies in the partial, biased, unrepresentative and unfair depiction of our own societies. Few people think that a country cannot be improved on, but to present it as riddled with bigotry, hatred and oppression is at best a partial and at worst a nakedly hostile prism through which to view society. It is an analysis expressed not in the manner of a critic hoping to improve, but as an enemy eager to destroy. There are signs of this intention everywhere we look.[163]

The riots and protests that took place in Spring and Summer of 2020 added another dimension to the pressure to "get with" the latest social justice focus. All of us were horrified by the death of the African American man which triggered the riots and protests. And hopefully all of us are concerned and troubled by the latent racism that is being exposed in various ways. But then, when we were, in effect, pressured to agree with the organizers' requirement that we adopt the slogan "Black Lives Matter" and kneel to signal our submission to the movement, many of us began to sense another spirit at work than just the spirit of racial justice.

As a matter of fact, it turns out that "Black Lives Matter" is a well-organized, well-funded organization that is dedicated to the overthrow of the family and traditional sexual morality. From their website:

> We are self-reflexive and do the work required to dismantle cisgender privilege and uplift Black trans folk, especially Black trans women who continue to be disproportionately impacted by trans-antagonistic violence.

> We build a space that affirms Black women and is free from sexism, misogyny, and environments in which men are centered.

> We practice empathy. We engage comrades with the intent to learn about and connect with their contexts.

> We disrupt the Western-prescribed nuclear family structure requirement by supporting each other as extended families and "villages" that collectively care for one another, especially our children, to the degree that mothers, parents, and children are comfortable.

> We foster a queer-affirming network. When we gather, we do so with the intention of freeing ourselves from the tight grip of heteronormative thinking, or rather, the belief that all in the world are heterosexual (unless s/he or they disclose otherwise).[164]

Fr. Dwight Longnecker has penned some insightful words about what happens when people no longer have a solid foundation based on truth, reason, evidence, and faith:

> The result of this combination of sentimentality, utilitarianism and propaganda will be irrationality. People will have a very loose grasp of knowledge, will not be able to synthesize information in any coherent way and will paddle around in a shallow pool of emotion, social media opinion, half formed ideas and notions—all of which are coming at them from a whole range of sources of varying authenticity and evidence. So a person's ideas and emotions will be formed from a mishmash of video games, comics, a philosophy course, a book on self-help, a chat show about self-awareness, greeting cards, horror films, yesterday's news and a story their grandpa told them once.
>
> Consequently we will see an increasing number of people who simply have no idea about anything at all responding to world events and their own circumstances like crazed animals—not having any idea of truth, any idea of manners, any idea of good behavior, right thinking or common sense at any level.[165]

Another well-known writer, the late Michael Crichton, a trained anthropologist who wrote the novel *Jurassic Park*, observed that social causes such as environmentalism have for many become something held to with religious fervor that no amount of contradictory science can shake someone out of. He claimed it is one of the most powerful religions in the Western world:

> So that in environmental thinking there is a view that there used to be a sort of Eden and then people came and ruined

that Eden and that we are therefore sort of original sinners because we are destroying this planet and what we can do however is get salvation through sustainability. And if you're a good person, you will seek salvation and if you're a bad person you'll drive SUVs. That is a kind of religious belief. . . . Environmentalism is a kind of fundamentalist religion and that's not a good way to manage the environment. We need a scientific approach.[166]

Dr. Michael McClymond has contributed an insightful chapter in a larger work on "queer theory," which is worth reading for those interested in this topic.[167] I came away from it with a great compassion for those experiencing gender confusion, and after reading a number of the case studies, it became clear to me that abusive experiences and relationships early in life significantly contributed to the confusion that led them to seek to "transition" from one sex to another. Even from a completely secular point of view, it is foolish to think surgery will cure something with deep psychological roots. Competent psychological therapy would seem, even from a completely secular point of view, to be the first line of treatment. And yet the "madness" is pushing for laws to forbid psychological counseling that is willing to help gender-confused people become reconciled to their biological sex or resist homosexual temptations. California has already banned such therapy, and there is a powerful push in Canada, Belgium, Germany, and many other countries to do the same. Pope Francis, thankfully, has been clear that the "transgender" ideology is inimical to Christianity and is a form of "ideological colonization." The diocese of Springfield, Illinois, has published a pastoral guide regarding issues pertaining to gender identity, which is both compassionate and faithful to revealed truth.[168]

How Did We Get Here?

Pressure from the Culture

We have already discussed the immense pressure from the culture that since the sixties has promoted a "sexual freedom" that has now almost become an article of faith. This includes an almost religious obsession with the importance of abortion as a means of assuring that sexual relationships don't have their natural outcome. We are all still trying to come to grips with the fact that one of the major political parties in the United States has now become a party that no longer tolerates anyone who opposes the sexual revolution or abortion or homosexuality. And one of the candidates for the party's nomination for the 2020 presidential election was an openly gay man in a homosexual marriage who claims that it has brought him closer to God and that true Christianity should support it. After failing to obtain his party's nomination, he was hired by the University of Notre Dame.

Msgr. Pope has written an incisive analysis of this perversion of Christianity:

> Again, I must respectfully but firmly say that the god to whom Buttigieg is growing closer through his disordered behavior is not the God who has revealed himself in the Scriptures. It is some other god, perhaps even a demon clothed in the garments of false compassion masquerading as a god. Pretending that God is happy with what he has consistently condemned as sinful is a fantasy. Thus, I respectfully and sincerely warn that his god is imaginary at best and a demon at worst.[169]

I was in a coffee shop the other day and a group of high school students from the local alternative high school were there, and I saw a button on someone's backpack that I had never seen before: "Abortion is normal." Not too long after this, I saw a sign that said, "Abortion is love." It was quite a shock to see these, and it's hard to get them out of my mind. I had never seen such blatant claims about abortion before. It's not normal; it's an abominable crime and a barbaric resurgence of pagan child sacrifice. Sacrificing children through murder to the comfort and convenience of adults is a grave sin. Yes, there can be varying degrees of culpability. Yes, God's mercy is always ready to forgive when we are truly repentant, but we should never forget how awful it is to kill a child in the womb or to encourage or pressure someone to do so.

Moral Theology from the Seventies

One of the most influential works of moral theology published during the 1970s was entitled *Human Sexuality*. Its publication laid the groundwork for much of the widespread moral corruption that has unfolded in recent years. *Human Sexuality* was a joint project of several well-known moral theologians and had actually been commissioned by the Catholic Theological Society.

In Chapter 8 of *A Crisis of Truth*,[170] I wrote:

> A book titled *Human Sexuality* gives striking evidence of how authentic Christian morality is being subverted in the Church today.[171] This study is particularly significant since it was commissioned by the Catholic Theological Society of America and published with its assent, even though the book's contents were not necessarily endorsed by the society as a whole. The authors all held—and still hold—positions of responsibility in Catholic seminaries and theological faculties. After extensive checking, as of this writing, four years after initial publication, I have found no indication that any of the authors have retracted

the substance of their views put forward in this study. The book was published by a Catholic publishing house run by a Catholic religious order. It was translated and published in other countries and continues to be used widely.

The study asserts that the teaching of Scripture, Tradition, and the Church about sexual morality are no longer sufficient guides to moral behavior. The book claims that because modern man faces new situations and now knows much more about sexuality than the scriptural authors did, Scripture becomes just one source of input about moral decisions. The findings of contemporary "experts" in the social sciences are another source. Since Scripture and its authoritative interpretation and clarification in Tradition and contemporary Church teaching are no longer sufficient, the authors claim, modern man needs a new set of principles to judge the morality of sexual behavior.

The authors proceed to formulate such principles.

"We maintain that it is appropriate to ask whether specific sexual behavior realizes certain values that are conducive to creative growth and integration of the human person. Among these values we would single out the following as particularly significant:

(1) Self-liberating. . . .

(2) Other-enriching. . . .

(3) Honest. . . .

(4) Faithful. . . .

(5) Socially responsible. . . .

(6) Life-serving. . . .

(7) Joyous. . . .

Where such qualities prevail, one can be reasonably sure that the sexual behavior that has brought them forth is wholesome and moral. . . . By focusing on the many-splendored values of wholesome sexuality and avoiding absolute categorizations of isolated, individual sexual actions, one can arrive at a much more sensitive and responsible method of evaluating the morality of sexual patterns and expressions."[172]

One immediately suspects that such criteria are not so much "moral principles" as ambiguous slogans employing the jargon of modern social science. Used "creatively" and willfully, such principles can justify virtually any sexual behavior, even behavior that Scripture and Tradition clearly regarded as sinful. Consider, for example, the authors' treatment of adultery. After reviewing the reasons why confessors and counselors may frown on adulterous relationships, the authors say this:

"These facts, however, do not rule out the possibility that there may occasionally arise exceptions, when such relationships can truly be 'creative' and 'integrative' for all involved, and therefore morally acceptable. Extreme caution is imperative in arriving at such conclusions in particular cases."[173]

With this loophole, almost any adulterous relationship can be justified. To be moral, adulterers and their confessors must only exercise "extreme caution."[174]

The Vatican's Congregation for the Doctrine of the Faith published its concerns about the book.[175]

When the German Bishops talk about "reassessing" homosexuality, they cite the need to learn from not only Scripture and tradition but also contemporary experience, new insights from science, and the lived experience of people in same-sex relationships, all with a view to reconsidering the grave moral disorder of active homosexuality, with the goal of blessing same-sex relationships. When Scripture is put in "dialogue" with "contemporary experience," contemporary experience usually wins.

Silence from the Church

Yet pressure from the culture or the corruption of moral theology wouldn't have been enough to ensure the victory of the sexual revolution if it hadn't been aided and abetted by the silence of the Church—and perhaps a lack of faith in the promise of Christ to give the power necessary to live the moral law? The Catholic Church deeply holds that what God commands, he gives the grace to live.

The Western countries that were once deeply informed by the Judeo/Christian tradition have now apostatized to one degree or another. Apostatizing isn't something pagans do—it's something Christians do. To turn away from a faith and a baptism that one once had and repudiate it or "reinterpret it" to accommodate sin is a grave thing indeed. We need to remember the solemn and vivid warnings of Sacred Scripture:

> For if we sin deliberately after receiving the knowledge of the truth, there no longer remains a sacrifice for sins, but a fearful prospect of judgment, and a fury of fire which will consume the adversaries. A man who has violated the law of Moses dies without mercy at the testimony of two or three witnesses. How much worse punishment do you think will

be deserved by the man who has spurned the Son of God, and profaned the blood of the covenant by which he was sanctified, and outraged the Spirit of grace? For we know him who said, "Vengeance is mine, I will repay." And again, "The Lord will judge his people." It is a fearful thing to fall into the hands of the living God. (Heb 10:26–31)

For if, after they have escaped the defilements of the world through the knowledge of our Lord and Savior Jesus Christ, they are again entangled in them and overpowered, the last state has become worse for them than the first. For it would have been better for them never to have known the way of righteousness than after knowing it to turn back from the holy commandment delivered to them. It has happened to them according to the true proverb. The dog turns back to his own vomit, and the sow is washed only to wallow in the mire. (2 Pet 2:20–22)

An even bigger problem than our culture's apostasy is the Church's cowardice and fear. The world is the world, but the Church is supposed to be the Church, a clear voice of truth and love that cries out to the world to believe and repent and so be saved. Where are the voices of the Apostles today crying out with Peter, "Save yourself from this crooked generation" (Acts 2:40)?

Year after year, at the biggest Catholic religious education conference in the world, the Archdiocese of Los Angeles's annual Religious Education Congress, keynote talks and workshops are regularly presented by dissident Catholics. At a recent conference, one of the workshops was titled, "Transgender in Our Schools: One Bread, One Body." The presenters included a female-to-male transsexual; a Catholic mother whose daughter was born a biological female but identifies as male; and Fr. Bryan Massingale, a professor of Theology at Fordham University, who identifies as gay and often speaks on LGBTQ topics, undermining confidence in the teaching of the Church with such comments as, "We certainly need to rethink our Church's official sexual ethics."

The moderator, Arthur Fitzmaurice, is openly gay and serves as resource director for the dissident Catholic Association of Lesbian and Gay Ministries and has signed petitions calling for the Church to change its teaching in the area of sexuality. The goal of the seminar was to increase acceptance of the "trans" identity without addressing the fundamental disorder of denying one's biological gender identity. When asked about little children expressing gender confusion, the speakers said they should be allowed to "tell us who they are" and respect their feelings and let them transition. The speakers at the session commented that they have received many invitations to speak at parishes in the archdiocese as a result of the seminar.[176]

Other speakers at recent Los Angeles conferences included Fr. James Martin, who got a standing ovation; a priest who counseled religious educators to "affirm second and third graders" in their LGBTQ identities; and at the 2020 Congress, a gay priest who painted "the sodomite Christ" was invited to display his artwork.[177] The list could go on and it goes back many years. Many thought that when Archbishop José Gómez, the current president of the United States Conference of Catholic Bishops, came to Los Angeles as archbishop, things would change. They haven't.

R. R. Reno, editor of *First Things*, makes the telling observation:

Ever since the furor over *Humanae Vitae* in 1968, the Church has been in retreat, yielding ground to the sexual revolution. This has been done mostly by making a great show of concern for the human dignity of all people, including homosexuals, while going silent when it comes to specific norms of sexual morality. This has been the way to signal acquiescence, conceding to the sexual revolution its control over the formation of consciences. Fr. James Martin is expert in this tactic.

Germans disdain the Mediterranean hypocrisy that affirms norms, while winking at transgression. . . . In our time, the society wide effort to get everyone to say that sodomy is perfectly normal is the sociological equivalent of the ancient Roman demand that everyone sacrifice to the city's gods. It is the regime's way of destroying resistance and re-directing the loyalty of citizens to its authority.[178]

Remember the awful warning words of Jesus:

You are the salt of the earth; but if salt has lost its taste, how shall its saltiness be restored? It is no longer good for anything except to be thrown out and trodden under foot by men. (Matt 5:13)

Is the rapid decline of the Church in country after country a consequence of the salt losing its savor and now being cast out and trodden down underfoot by her enemies? Is the relentless, never-ending closing of parishes and schools, the bankruptcy of dioceses, and decline in vocations a sign that something is terribly wrong within the Church? Yes, it is. As one person who works closely with the bishops in developing strategies to confront the challenges told me recently, "The Church is on fire."

For a very long time, the immigrant American Church—made up for many years of recently arrived poor immigrants from Ireland, Italy, Germany, and other European countries—wanted to integrate into the wider society and be accepted. I remember when I was a student at Notre Dame, President Theodore Hesburgh proudly declared that we wanted to be the Catholic Harvard. I remember when it was considered a coup to get prominent non-Catholic faculty to come to Notre Dame, and to many other Catholic universities as well. Now, the number of non-Catholic faculty is so sizable at so many Catholic universities and the percentage of believing and practicing Catholic students is so little that there is huge resistance to anything explicitly Catholic in content, and yet such schools still keep the trappings of the "Jesuit tradition," or "Catholic values." At many universities, there is hardly any effort anymore to deal with the culture of alcohol and fornication that is unfortunately prevalent at most Catholic universities.[179] This is indeed, "holding the form of religion but denying the power of it" (2 Tim 3:5).

At all these universities, there are faithful Catholic faculty and students, but the overall environment at many of them now is decidedly rushing headlong into accommodating the culture.

In commenting on the direction that the Church in Germany is taking, R. R. Reno wrote:

> The German Church is not alone. More than 90 percent of Catholic universities in the United States are functionally in accord with the sexual revolution. Most are overtly affirmative; the rest acquiesce quietly. The synodal path toward capitulation has been clearly marked by moral theologians. The majority of those in the West who have earned PhDs in Catholic moral theology during the last fifty years almost certainly agree with the fundamental claims of the sexual revolution and endorse the direction the German Church appears to be taking.[180]

If this is the "green wood" (Catholic universities), imagine what the dry wood (secular universities) is like. The secular private and public universities almost require, in order to survive in the academic world, unquestioned allegiance to a "nonjudgmental" embrace of the sexual revolution and leftist politics. Unfortunately, this is not limited to the universities. Douglas Murray says the fervor of the ideology and its hostility to anyone who opposes it can rightfully be called a "religion." Most American public grade and high schools are now in the hands of an educational elite that see the schools as appropriate vehicles for instilling the "right," "tolerant," "diverse," "welcoming," "globalist" attitudes in children from preschool up. Promoting the supposed fluidity of gender identity is front and center. Even when parents are supposed to be notified about "controversial" topics being presented so they can "opt out" their students, these policies are often ignored, and rare is the parent who can buck the tide in this way. When my children were in the local public high school years ago, I had to fight several times, with the help of the Thomas More Law Center—successfully—to prevent Planned Parenthood "peer educators" from being given access to the school, and I also had to protest a "diversity" day about sexuality where the Christian viewpoint was not allowed to be presented. It's much worse now. The educational establishment thinks they know better than parents about the value of a "diverse," "tolerant," "gender-fluid" education for their children.

It's almost like a pernicious fog is seeping into every area of human life with the view to corrupt children. A number of public libraries and schools are now hosting "drag queen" story hours, where "drag queens" (men dressed up as flamboyant women) read pro-gay children's stories to the children gathered. A Texas teacher who was challenged for inviting "drag queens" into her classroom boldly proclaimed: "Parents should not have the final say. They don't know what is best for their children."[181] One can understand that many hard-pressed parents are now considering the possibility of homeschooling in a way they never thought they would have to.

Even when Catholic schools are better in this regard, they are often financially out of reach of most parents. A massive offensive against the youth of our culture is underway, no less ferocious (and maybe more so because of its "soft power") than the blatant edicts of the Chinese Communist Party that have made it illegal to bring children under eighteen to church.

For many years now, since the sixties actually, there has been such an emphasis on the values of the kingdom—peace, justice, racial equality, human development, and now an overwhelming emphasis on the overriding need to deal with climate change and care for the environment—that the "hierarchy of truths" in these matters has been turned on its head.[182] Along with the emphasis on the issues we share in common with the world, there has been a de-emphasis or silence on those truths that the world most hates us for, particularly in the area of sexuality and the Gospel's call to accept Christ as Lord and Savior. Many generations of Catholics have now heard—from many of its teachers, preachers, and religious educators—that the Church needs to abandon its alleged "fixation" on "bedroom issues" and focus more on the social issues that the world most values. Many generations of Catholics have now heard—from the same teachers, preachers, and religious educators—that God is not so concerned about the little personal issues in the area of sexuality but is instead concerned about the big global issues.

And yes, God is concerned about the big global issues. It is an imperative of Christian charity to be concerned with our common home, with the oppressive injustice of racism, to be concerned with a fair economic system and the provision of basic human needs such as health care and education and a living wage—even though prudential judgments may differ on the best way to meet these needs.

And yet the most personal decisions in the area of sexuality are extremely important for the welfare of both the individual and of society as a whole. The breakdown of marriage and family is exacting a huge cost on society, economically and socially. It is not just "sinful structures" that need to be changed or better funded; it is sinful people. Children being born out of wedlock in huge numbers, often without fathers and without mothers in stable, healthy relationships, are quite understandably "acting out," dropping out of school, and perpetuating a culture of sexual irresponsibility and sometimes drug addiction and violence.

Not only are decisions in the sexual realm important for the individual's well-being in this world and the kind of society we live in, but even more so, they have eternal consequences. What God has revealed about human sexuality clearly links it with our eternal salvation or damnation. Even many orthodox and holy preachers and teachers, who are doing a good job of presenting the positive side of Christianity, avoid, by policy, addressing the sexual issues.

Bishop Robert Barron, who does such a good job presenting the beauty and intelligibility of Catholicism and inspires us with his willingness to engage with deeply secular wellsprings of the culture, is on record as wanting to de-emphasize the sexual issues (if only our culture would allow us to!). In a 2017 book, he expresses agreement with Pope Francis in tactically downplaying the sexual issues in engaging the world and changing the emphasis "to the environment, . . . to the poor, to immigration, and to other parts of our Church."[183]

Vatican II decided on a particular pastoral strategy that in various writings I've described as "accentuate the positive."[184] The pastoral strategy that Pope Francis and Bishop Barron are advocating is a contemporary variation of the operative pastoral strategy of Vatican II and is certainly in the mainstream of the pastoral approach that most of the bishops, priests, and lay leaders use today. But as early as fifteen years after the Council, Pope John Paul II was already saying that the culture had changed and there were new challenges that weren't anticipated at the Council that needed to be considered. An adjustment in pastoral strategy, though, takes nothing away from the enduring doctrinal and spiritual values of the documents of Vatican II, as Pope John Paul II has said:

> With the passing of the years, *the Council documents have lost nothing of their value or brilliance.* They need to be read correctly, to be widely known and taken to heart as important and normative texts of the magisterium within the Church's Tradition. I feel more than ever in duty bound to point to the Council *as the great grace bestowed on the Church in the twentieth century:* there we find a sure compass by which to take our bearings in the century now beginning.[185]

What kind of adjustment am I proposing? A much more direct and powerful preaching of the Gospel, as we see in the preaching of Jesus and the Apostles. With Christendom collapsing and an aggressive, dominating, global secular culture on the ascendency, being "friends with the world" today means almost always becoming an enemy of God. Dialogue is good, finding points of common interest is good, but in the last analysis, if we don't clearly proclaim the radical claims of Jesus to be Savior and Lord and the only way back to the Father's house, we will probably end up denying him. If we don't make clear within some reasonable time frame of leading someone to Christ and the Church that this means obeying Jesus and the Apostles and the Church concerning the truth about sexuality, marriage, and family, we will end up presenting a false gospel.

While there are a wide variety of methods that the Apostles used in attempting to communicate the Gospel (dialogue, debate, personal conversations, public preaching, appeals to the background of those being addressed, looking for points of connection, calling for conversion in the light of supernatural signs and wonders, etc.), the central claim that they were making, that Jesus is Lord and that all human beings are called to repent, believe in him, and change their way of life or be condemned sooner or later because he is returning as judge, was eventually expressed with great power. Their proclamation so directly confronted their listeners that they were frequently met with remarkable conversions, and deep and violent opposition. The hostile reaction to their radical claims about the Lordship of Christ and our immediate need to submit to him frequently included flogging, imprisonment, stoning, expulsion, and ultimately, for almost all of them, martyrdom.

In the final chapter of this book, I will propose what I think needs to be recovered in the preaching of Jesus and the Apostles that is for the most part missing today. Again, by their fruits you will know them (see Matt 7:16). I don't think the pastoral strategy of Vatican II (as distinct from its scriptural, theological, and spiritually excellent documents) and its contemporary variants is today bearing the fruit once hoped for in the developed nations for which the strategy was and is specifically tailored. However we measure success, whether it be in conversions, vocations, zeal for evangelization and holiness of life, church attendance, what Catholics actually believe, or any other measure of church vitality, the radical decline over the last fifty years has been unrelenting and shows no signs of stabilizing. Isn't it time to reconsider our approach? When we emphasize what the world's global elites most value—the environment, immigration, the "poor"—although there is an amazing amount of hypocrisy among them in actually living in accord with their professed values, we are not, in my assessment of the outcomes, winning them to Christ but rather allowing them to congratulate themselves in enlisting the Church into a "chaplaincy" role in pushing their secular agendas. But more on this in our final chapter.

The two issues which I think are most under attack today—the issue of salvation and the issue of sexual morality—I think require us to give clear, truthful answers or to become complicit in affirming our culture in their deceptions and wishful thinking in these areas. It is not loving, kind, or merciful to not tell people the full truth that shows them the path to salvation.

There is particular pressure on the Church and individual Catholics not to speak about the sexual issues, and yet at the same time, these are the issues that our culture is demanding that we be silent on and agree with them on.

One of the main reasons for the growth of the early Church was its emphasis on sexual morality rooted in the believers becoming one body, one spirit with Christ himself. Call it the theology of the body if you will. The difference between the Church and the world on these issues was a prime reason why those pagans of good will could recognize a "higher" way of life that was being lived by Christians in their respect for sexuality, marriage, and family.

Rodney Stark, in one of his major studies on the growth of Christianity,[186] points out that the high sexual morality among Christians (forbidding abortion, infanticide, fornication, adultery, and their openness to life and to children), in stark contrast to that of the surrounding Greco-Roman culture, where sexual promiscuity, homosexuality, abortion, prostitution, and pornography were rampant, was very attractive, particularly to Roman women. It was precisely the high regard that Christianity held sexuality and marriage in that was a major contributor to the spread of the faith, both through evangelization and higher fertility rates.[187]

N. T. Wright, in his studies on St. Paul, points out that holding the Christian community to a high standard of sexual morality was essential for distinguishing the Church from the world and allowing it to give a clear and consistent witness to the "new life in Christ."

He picks out three areas that Paul is eager to stress: sex, money, and the return of the Lord:

> These are issues that were bound to come up precisely because the early Christian worldview was so radically different from anything people had imagined before. . . . Unbridled, crazy, and inflamed lust is a sign *that one does not know God.* Sexual holiness is mandatory, not optional, for followers of Jesus. . . . Sexual holiness isn't just a "rule," an arbitrary commandment. It is part of what it means to turn from idols and serve the true and living God. It is part of being a genuine, image-bearing human being. . . . Clearly Paul often had his work cut out to give pastoral help to people who heard what he said, but found themselves still stuck in long-lasting habits of life. But at the end of the day a clean break had to be made. . . . Sexual purity and financial generosity were to be built into the Christian DNA from the start.[188]

If you'd ask average Catholics what the Church has been emphasizing in recent decades, if they were paying attention at all—and most aren't—they would cite pastoral letters on the economy, on the environment, on education, on racism, on immigration, on voting guides, and so on. Guidance on the social issues and participation as responsible citizens on issues concerning the common good would be most prominent. Even leading bishops and cardinals and, indeed, whole episcopal conferences communicate this mentality and, explicitly or implicitly, communicate a lack of belief in what Sacred Scripture, Sacred tradition, and the *Catechism of the Catholic Church* teach on sexual morality and on the matter of what's necessary to be saved.

One truly egregious example of this is the state of the Catholic

Church in Germany. When Pope Emeritus Benedict XVI published a lengthy analysis of the real causes of the sexual abuse and immorality crisis, reaffirming the clear teachings of Scripture and tradition (most recently stated clearly by John Paul II in the very important encyclical *Veritatis Splendor*), it was met with virulent attacks by leading figures in the German Church. Benedict pointed out that the cultural revolution of the 1960s led to a moral relativism that penetrated Catholic theology and seminaries in which there were already, in his words, "homosexual cliques."[189] This was met with outrage among German moral theologians, who published on the German Bishops' official website and in interviews with Catholic news outlets what can only be called a blatant affirmation of "unbelief" in the truth of the Church's teaching in this area.[190]

Cardinal Gerhard Mueller, former head of the Congregation for the Doctrine of the Faith, characterizes the response of the German theologians to Pope Emeritus Benedict's essay like this: "These are people who neither believe nor think."[191]

Recently, George Weigel changed his opinion on what was going on in the Catholic Church in Germany. He's decided that what we're really seeing there is not just schism—a national Church going off on its own—but actual apostasy, unbelief in what God has revealed.[192]

Our account of many of the issues we have been discussing in this chapter and others as well would not be complete without a further discussion of the role of the German Catholic Church.

THE GERMAN FACTOR

A very significant factor in understanding the influence of the German Church throughout the world is its huge financial prosperity. The German government, like several other European governments, collects a tax from each of its citizens registered as Catholic that is then turned over to the Church. Unless a German Catholic goes through a formal process of de-registering from the Church, the tax is automatically collected. A taxpayer who's registered as a Catholic has 8–9 percent of his income tax given to the Church. More and more German Catholics are de-registering. (While in 2018, 216,078 Catholics formally de-registered and left the Church, the German Church still received 6.64 billion euros that year!) In 2019, 272,771 Catholics de-registered.[193] The penalty for de-registering is no longer being able to receive a Catholic burial, so it takes a fairly significant commitment to de-register, which is why many nonpracticing German Catholics don't de-register.

This means that German Catholic aid agencies have a lot of money that is given out as grants to many poorer countries around the world for things like building churches, buying vehicles, supporting catechists, and so on. Many good initiatives are supported by the German Church. At the same time, there is a natural tendency to want to please donors that you are dependent on, and it seems evident that this sometimes is a factor in voting at events like synods.

At the same time, the great prosperity of the German Church has led to a feeling of security, even invulnerability, as the radical decline in faith, morals, and church attendance doesn't impact the financial situation of the German Church and its ability to employ tens of thousands of people and pay secular-level salaries. The comfort level is significant.

In other Western countries, where there is no state support for the Church, the radical decline in faith and numbers is clearly impacting its financial well-being, and strong actions are being taken to launch a "new evangelization" designed to stop the bleeding. While those efforts have yet to meet with significant success, they are a good sign.

In Germany, however, the response to the growing secularization of its people is rather to "update" the Church and make it more "relevant" to where the culture is.

There is definitely a need to enculturate the Gospel in the various cultures in which it is planted. At the Amazon Synod, there was a lot of talk about enculturating the Gospel more adequately in Amazonian culture. In Germany, the emphasis is on "accommodating" the secularized German culture, particularly in the area of sexual morality.

Several bishops who used to hold traditional positions on the practice of homosexuality have changed to better accommodate the popular consensus. A small number of bishops with orthodox views on these matters, who are attempting to block or slow down this direction, are consistently outvoted,[194] and a very strong majority of the German bishops are clearly in favor of this accommodation to contemporary culture. They say they are motivated by the decline of the Church and the scandal of the sexual abuse crisis, which was also strong in Germany, and want to be more relevant.[195]

Bishop Georg Bätzing of Limburg, who is responsible for the working group on sexuality in preparation for the German Synod, was elected to succeed Cardinal Reinhard Marx as the new president of the German Bishops' Conference. His committee called for drawing on new insights from the social sciences, psychology, and "life experience" to open up our understanding of sexuality from the prohibitions in Church teaching. It specifically called for acknowledging the positive value of masturbation, denied that the practice of homosexuality is intrinsically evil, and called for a consideration of giving blessings to same-sex relationships.[196]

In an Easter Sunday interview, Bishop Bätzing stated that the official Catholic teaching on homosexuality "is something that many people no longer want or can understand. . . . Can we tell them that their relationship is under the blessing of God?" He expressed the hope "that we can come to a statement on this during the Synodal Path. This would be a sign that the public would see as a bridge."[197]

Some of the Austrian bishops have sponsored the publication of a book that includes essays calling for the Church to change her teaching on homosexuality and to bless homosexual relationships. The liturgical scholar, Fr. Ewald Volgger, who contributed an essay to the book, claims that homosexuality "can be not only discussed, but also demanded. . . . There is a considerable number of bishops that would like to see a rethinking in the area of sexual morality for the evaluation of same-sex relationships. . . . Just as marriage between a man and a woman is an image of God's creative love, so is a same-sex relationship an image of God's attention to human beings."[198]

The way for this strategy of "accommodation" has been prepared for by a half century of German theology and Scripture scholarship that has been characterized by a "hermeneutic of suspicion," which has drained Scripture of its authority and opened the way to theological speculation that is not tethered to Scripture and tradition. It is interesting to note that many of the most significant liberation theologians around the world studied in Germany.

The significance of what's going on in Germany now is not just theoretical. It's affecting peoples' lives, not only in Germany, and is spreading like a virus and will impact the whole world. The Polish bishops expressed strong concern that the way *Amoris Laetitia* was being interpreted in Germany was undermining the faith of those in Poland. The Ukrainian bishops expressed the same concern. They further noted that the radical currents in the government, media, and LGBTQ pressure groups were citing the German bishops' approach to these issues in contrast to the "hate-filled" traditionalism of the Ukrainian Church. Their Commission for the Family, with the concurrence of the president and vice president of the Ukrainian bishops' conference, sent a letter to the German bishops' Commission for Marriage and the Family, pleading with them to stop bowing to the LGBTQ lobby and stand firm for the enduring truths of the faith. This "fraternal correction" expressed grave concern that people with homosexual temptations in Ukraine were being discouraged in their efforts to stay chaste by what the German bishops were saying ("homosexuality is normal"), and that couples who were divorced and remarried were justifying their situation by what the German bishops were saying about such situations ("no longer considered as necessarily sinful").[199]

As a spokesman for the Ukrainian bishops put it:

> It seems that the Church in Germany, including its shepherds, is under the strong influence of neo-Marxism. In the Ukraine (I mean also Poland) we have a vaccine against it because we had whole decades when we could see Marxism in its most brutal, totalitarian form. We pray for the Church in Germany, because we've received a lot of material support from their Catholics. Thanks to their support we've been able to build many churches and pastoral houses.

> We haven't forgotten that and apart from our prayers we thanked them for that support in our letter. However, we cannot be silent, because otherwise we'd be guilty of corruption.[200]

The spokesman expressed the hope that other bishops around the world would wake up and not look at what was happening in Germany as an aberration confined to Germany. They are testifying to how the virus of German accommodation to the culture is already affecting believers and bringing government pressure to bear in neighboring countries such as Poland and the Ukraine, and how this virus will affect the whole Church if more voices aren't raised to clearly defend the truth. These concerns and warnings are well founded as German Church officials oftentimes mention that they hope that the German "synodal process" could be a model for other countries, as well as for the Church as a whole.

In my opinion, it is likely that the Germans will stop short of explicitly denying the scriptural, traditional, and current magisterial teaching on sexual sin but will talk about "pastoral accommodations" that, in effect, empty the teaching of its authority and power and call for further study on these matters as our understanding "evolves."

What Should Be Done?

If we don't start teaching clearly and emphatically the truth about human sexuality, the situation—hard to imagine!—will only get worse. More and more of our people will fall into line with the "revolution." More and more lives will be wrecked, marriages will be destroyed or never happen, casual sexual relations will continue to cause deep wounds in mind and body, loneliness and isolation will increase—and many souls will be lost.

As I've mentioned previously, what I consider the two biggest lies of the devil, the two biggest deceptions that have, like a fog, made their way into the Church and are spreading like a virus, are:

- the assumption that almost everyone will be saved because God is so merciful.

- the assumption that sexual sins that were once considered gravely sinful are no longer so in light of "new knowledge" about sexuality.

If no one is going to hell, why make such a fuss over sexual morality? Prominent leaders think and say, "It will only alienate us from the culture. It will only cause unnecessary division in families. It will only make life difficult for priests in marriage preparation and in homilies and teaching," and so on.

But if hell is real and many people go there and if our decisions in the area of sexuality indeed have eternal consequences, then we had better start taking it seriously ourselves and telling people that! There is certainly a crisis of truth, but along with it there is also a crisis of faith. Do we really believe what we teach? Do we really believe the testimony of Jesus and the Apostles about what we must do to be saved?

Let's take a look at some key texts that need to be taught and preached clearly and frequently. We don't have to talk about them "all the time." We don't have to lead with them. We don't have to be insensitive in how we talk about them. We can present them positively! If we just passed on the faith with the same emphases that we see in the teaching of Jesus and the Apostles, we would have a healthy Church. If we just preached clearly and with authority the challenging texts that are given to us in the cycle of readings in the lectionary and did not avoid them, as is regularly done, we'd have a healthy Church. What are some of these texts?

The words of Jesus about God's purpose in creating male and female and God's will concerning marriage and divorce are extremely important to take seriously. They are taught by Jesus with the utmost seriousness.

Even though some controversy has developed about whether Pope Francis is trying to "loosen things up" in the area of sexual morality, and puzzlement grows about why the German bishops and others who openly push the Church in a direction of "loosening up" sexual morality aren't being strongly corrected, we need to take Pope Francis at his word that he believes everything in the *Catechism of the Catholic Church*, and even more so take Jesus and the Apostles at their word that sinning sexually is indeed a serious matter and, unless repented of, will exclude us from the kingdom of God. The Word of God is very clear:

> And Pharisees came up and in order to test him asked, "Is it lawful for a man to divorce his wife?" He answered them, "What did Moses command you?" They said, "Moses allowed a man to write a certificate of divorce, and to put her away." But Jesus said to them, "For your hardness of heart he wrote you this commandment. But from the beginning of creation, 'God made them male and female.' 'For this reason a man shall leave his father and mother and be joined to his wife, and the two shall become one.' So they are no longer two but one. What therefore God has joined together, let not man put asunder." And in the house the disciples asked him again about this matter. And he said to them, "Whoever divorces his wife and marries another, commits adultery against her; and if she divorces her husband and marries another, she commits adultery." (Mark 10:2–12)[201]

But it is not only the act of adultery that is a serious sin: giving in to lustful thoughts about adultery is a serious sin. Jesus is calling us to a higher standard than was previously known in Old Testament times, not a lower standard. And Jesus and his Apostles are consistent in their teaching about the seriousness of sexual immorality:

> You have heard that it was said, "You shall not commit adultery." But I say to you that every one who looks at a woman lustfully has already committed adultery with her in his heart. If your right eye causes you to sin, pluck it out and throw it away; it is better that you lose one of your members than that your whole body be thrown into hell. And if your

right hand causes you to sin, cut it off and throw it away; it is better that you lose one of your members than that your whole body go into hell. (Matt 5:27–30)

Persisting in sexual sin clearly endangers our salvation, and if we don't tell people that clearly and confidently, we ourselves will be liable for judgment (see Ezek 3:16–21; 33:1–9):

Do you not know that the unrighteous will not inherit the kingdom of God? Do not be deceived; neither the immoral, nor idolaters, nor adulterers, nor homosexuals, nor thieves, nor the greedy, nor drunkards, nor revilers, nor robbers will inherit the kingdom of God. (1 Cor 6:9–10)

Jesus loved us too much to avoid speaking difficult truths, and we, too, must speak them.

Sexual sins are not the only serious sins that can exclude us from the kingdom of God but, for those who are baptized, they are singled out as particularly offensive as they are sins against our own body, which is a temple of the Holy Spirit:

Do you not know that your bodies are members of Christ? Shall I therefore take the members of Christ and make them members of a prostitute? Never! . . . Shun immorality. Every other sin which a man commits is outside the body; but the immoral man sins against his own body. Do you not know that your body is a temple of the Holy Spirit within you, which you have from God? You are not your own; you were bought with a price. So glorify God in your body. (1 Cor 6:15–20)

This certainly resonates with what Mary is reported as having said to St. Jacinta on her deathbed, that "more souls go to hell because of sins of impurity than any other."[202]

The Apostles' warnings about the grave danger of engaging in sexual immorality are repeated many times:

> Now the works of the flesh are plain: immorality, impurity, licentiousness, idolatry, sorcery, enmity, strife, jealousy, anger, selfishness, dissension, party spirit, envy, drunkenness, carousing, and the like. I warn you, as I warned you before, that those who do such things shall not inherit the kingdom of God. (Gal 5:19–21)

> But immorality and all impurity or covetousness must not even be named among you, as is fitting among saints. Let there be no filthiness, nor silly talk, nor levity, which are not fitting; but instead let there be thanksgiving. Be sure of this, that no immoral or impure man, or one who is covetous (that is, an idolater), has any inheritance in the kingdom of Christ and of God. Let no one deceive you with empty words, for it is because of these things that the wrath of God comes upon the sons of disobedience. (Eph 5:3–6)

And after the most beautiful description of the final union of God and man, the fate of the unrepentant is revealed:

> But as for the cowardly, the faithless, the polluted, as for murderers, fornicators, sorcerers, idolaters, and all liars, their lot shall be in the lake that burns with fire and brimstone, which is the second death. (Rev 21:8)

As Jesus puts it: "And do not fear those who can kill the body but cannot kill the soul; rather fear him who can destroy both soul and body in hell" (Matt 10:28).[203]

St. Robert Bellarmine expresses the radical priority of putting the issue of salvation front and center in a powerful way:

If you are wise, then, know that you have been created for the glory of God and your own eternal salvation. This is your goal: this is the center of your life; this is the treasure of your heart. If you reach this goal you will find happiness. If you fail to reach it, you will find misery. May you consider truly good whatever leads you to your goal and truly evil whatever makes you fall away from it. Prosperity and adversity, wealth and poverty, health and sickness, honors and humiliations, life and death, in the mind of the wise man, are not be sought for their own sake, nor avoided for their own sake. But if they contribute to the glory of God and your eternal happiness, then they are good and should be sought. If they detract from this, they are evil and must be avoided.[204]

It is in the area of sexual morality today that clear preaching and teaching is most needed, but also most lacking. Fear, cowardice, unbelief, mistaken evangelization strategies, and sometimes bondage to sexual sin very often keep the truly good news of the truth about human sexuality from being communicated clearly and confidently by our clergy.[205]

Our culture, in its most important institutions, has largely abandoned any defense of biblical morality but rather has launched, with all the power that elite institutions can bring to bear, an aggressive effort to enforce a relativism where "anything goes." But as Cardinal Timothy Dolan once said, for the Church it is true that all are welcome, but not that anything goes.

A recovery of zeal for the holiness of God's house and for his glory, a recovery of the prophetic dimension of Jesus's ministry, needs to be based on a recovery of a profound fear of God, love for his people, knowledge of the truth, and faith in the Word of God. Jesus's and the Apostles' teaching about the beauty of Christian marriage and their teaching on sexuality is good news, meant to lead to our fulfillment. We should teach and preach it with joy and confidence, even though we know some will not accept it.

Chapter 5

HOW LONG WILL YOU STRADDLE THE ISSUE?

How long will you straddle the issue? If the LORD is God,
follow him; if Baal, follow him. (I Kgs 18:21, NABRE)

WHEN I WROTE THE ORIGINAL *A Crisis of Truth* back in the
early eighties, the influence of Latin American "liberation theology"
was very strong. Liberation theology was a school of theology that
focused on the liberation of oppressed peoples from the economic,
social, and political forces that were exploiting them. It was inspired
by Marxist analysis and had real imbalances and excesses, but it
certainly pointed to real injustices and structural oppression that
needed to be confronted. It was so strong that both Pope Paul VI
in his apostolic exhortation *Evangelii Nuntiandi* (1975) and Pope
John Paul II in his important encyclical *Redemptoris Missio* (1990),
devoted considerable effort to countering the pressure to focus the
Church's mission primarily on "human development" and the transformation of political and economic "structures of sin." Even more
detailed critiques of liberation theology were issued by the Congregation for the Doctrine of the Faith in two separate documents.[206]

There were many positive elements in liberation theology rooted in a genuine concern for systemic injustice and the oppression of the poor by the ruling elites. There is a very strong stream of prophetic teaching in the Catholic tradition, starting with the Old Testament prophets and running through the New Testament, about the grave offense to God that the oppression of the poor is, oppression that includes withholding from laborers their just wages, not helping people in need through generous almsgiving, and not participating as good citizens in political efforts to "renew the temporal order," as Vatican II puts it. This would certainly include responsible care for the earth. Despoiling the beautiful earth the Lord gave us through pollution or exploitation with no regard for the common good is indeed seriously wrong. There is no doubt that unchecked greed and selfishness or just plain ignorance about the consequences of our actions have gravely damaged parts of the earth, and this needs to stop.

Nevertheless, there were very grave deficiencies in liberation theology. There was a strong tendency to collapse the mission of the Church into simply working for justice in this world with sometimes an explicit, but almost always an implicit, dismissal of the importance of the evil of personal sin, the need for repentance and conversion on a personal level, and the need for an explicit evangelization which calls people to faith in Christ and repentance. A widespread silence about the significance of sexual sin and an open toleration in various places of clerical concubinage and a lax approach to sexual morality characterized many cultures in South America and elsewhere. There was also a very strong and explicit acceptance of many Marxist categories, which favored class warfare and even justified violence in the cause of revolution. Certain priests took up arms and became heroes in the struggle. Scripture passages that talked about redemption were often interpreted to mean redemption from unjust social structures, an understanding that considerably collapsed the meaning of these passages. A good number of priest-theologians published significant liberation theology texts, and when asked to correct errors in their interpretation of Scripture and theology, refused to do so. Sometimes they were allowed to carry on with their work protected by sympathetic bishops; at other times, they left the priesthood. One of the most famous and influential of these priest-theologians was Leonardo Boff, an ex-Franciscan priest who now writes liberation theology as a layperson and claims to be an advisor to Pope Francis.

With the collapse of the Soviet Union in 1989–1991, the enthusiasm for liberation theology quickly abated. At the same time, certain religious orders, like the Jesuits, greatly influenced by liberation theology, had adopted working for justice in this world as a guideline for their apostolic work and continued this emphasis in what was often a one-sided way, as did many other religious orders. Most tragically of all, many of the once-thriving missionary orders who adopted this approach soon experienced a radical decline in numbers and influence.

A few years ago, I was talking to a priest in Rome from one of the Church's most esteemed missionary orders, who was telling me about their latest General Chapter, which promulgated a new mission statement for the order. It established as the new priorities of the order working for human development, care for the environment, and women's rights. All of these, of course, can be very good things, but how sad to see the total omission of the priority of bringing people to know Jesus Christ, to repent of their sins, to be joined to the Church, and to persevere to the end, for the sake of their salvation! This order at the time had no novices, and the average age of the remaining priests was over sixty-five. No wonder. Why sacrifice marriage and family and native country to work as a missionary in a far-off place when you can do something similar, without much of the sacrifice, as a "human development specialist" for the United Nations or any of a number of international aid agencies?

The emphasis of liberation theology on the improvement of "this world" has reappeared in new forms in recent years, often under the banner of "caring for the earth" in an aggressive "environmentalism." A 2014 headline even proclaimed, "Liberation theology is back,"[207] and Leonardo Boff has been widely credited with being a "theologian of reference" for the Amazon Synod. Boff claimed:

> [Pope Francis is] one of us. He has turned Liberation Theology into a common property of the Church. And he has widened it. . . . The whole earth cries. Also, says the pope—and he thus quotes one of the titles of one of my books—we have to hear simultaneously the cry of the poor and the cry of the earth . . . The Pope asked me for material for the sake of *Laudato Si*. I have given him my counsel and sent to him some of what I have written. Which he has also used. Some people told me they were thinking while reading: "Wait, that is Boff!"[208]

Whether Boff was indeed quite the source he claims is impossible to determine, but it is certainly true that themes that he frequently writes about found their way into the encyclical.

Boff also wrote an article for a Brazilian publication that claims that the coronavirus pandemic is "Gaia's" (mother earth's) retaliation for ecological sins. And that while she may continue to spin through the solar system, she may no longer want us on the planet since we are guilty of ecocide and geo-cide.[209] Pope Francis has repeated, on more than one occasion, this mantra: "God always forgives, man sometimes forgives, but nature never forgives."

One of the recurring subtexts of "integral environmentalism" is that human beings are the problem and that the population must be severely reduced. To see the Vatican, the United Nations, and population control secularists like Jeffrey Sachs and George Soros aligning together to "save the planet" is troubling indeed. An alien ideology is being smuggled into the Church under the cover of noble sentiments, still using Christian words but working for a very different agenda.

Edward Pentin, assessing the influence of the UN on the Vatican, or vice versa, interviewed Vatican spokespeople, who acknowledged that the relationship was indeed close but that progress was being made for the common good and Catholic faith and morality were not being compromised. Other voices were not so reassuring. Professor Stefano Fontana, director of the Cardinal Van Thuan International Observatory on the Social Doctrine of the Church, sees instead "a subtle and general surrender to the UN mindset." He pointed out that previously the Vatican wouldn't be a party to UN language that spoke about "reproductive health" since the UN understanding always understood that to include contraception, abortion, and sex education—hallmarks of a secularist worldview—but now they accepted such language, although not intending to mean by it what the UN clearly means. Fontana sees the prestige of the pope and the Vatican being used to promote a "secular religion . . . a multireligious society, ecological religion and planned migration . . . a flattening of ideas that removes metaphysical structures and doctrinal absoluteness." Critics point out particularly that the UN organized the "World Day of Human Fraternity," which grew out of the controversial joint statement that Pope Francis signed with the Imam of Al-Azhar. Critics also see the upcoming events, "The Economy of Francesco" and the "Global Alliance on Education," which the Pope hopes will lead to a new "humanism," as contributing to "globalist ends that are anything but Catholic."[210]

We can't talk about this transmutation of liberation theology into a primary focus of the Church's mission without talking about the pivotal role of the activities and publications that have happened under the leadership of Pope Francis. And it's important to note that while Pope Francis has played a key role in the focus on environmentalism, the forces moving the Church in this direction are much bigger than a particular pope and will remain strong forces even after the next pope is elected. The reappearance of a new form of liberation theology shows that there is a current of "this world" thinking that persists as a perennial temptation of the human mind that has become blind, in many ways, to the revelation of Jesus Christ and the stark message of the Word of God. The eternal perspective of the Gospel is always threatened to be submerged by those whose focus is on this world, on accommodating the culture, on pleasing the "smart people," and on being admired by the experts and by prestigious human institutions such as the United Nations. The "unspiritual man" can never understand the wisdom of God, only the "spiritual man" can (see 1 Cor 2:14–15). There is too much "unspiritual" thinking in the Church today, too much eagerness to receive this "unspiritual" "wisdom of the world" into the Church. As we used to say, Pope John XXIII opened the windows of the Church, but it wasn't only the Holy Spirit who came in.

While Pope John Paul II and Pope Benedict XVI periodically emphasized the need to care for the environment, it never became a primary focus of their preaching and teaching. Yet, when people attempt to identify the main contributions of Pope Francis, they almost always mention his emphasis on care for the environment. He devoted a whole encyclical to care for the environment, *Laudato Si*. And a major emphasis on care for the environment has continued to play a significant role in Pope Francis's pontificate. As I write this, we are in the "Year of *Laudato Si*," in which many events are scheduled to emphasize its teaching and mandate its implementation. The preparatory document (in previous synods called the *lineamenta*), the working document (also called the *instrumentum laboris*), and the final document for the Amazon Synod, as well as the post-synodal apostolic exhortation on the Amazon, *Querida Amazonia*, have all heavily focused on care for the environment. At the same time, multiple conferences, sponsored by the Pontifical Academy of Social Sciences under the guidance of Bishop Marcelo Sánchez Sorondo, its chancellor, have placed heavy emphasis on climate change and the environment. Bishop Sorondo continues to hold conferences with key speakers who are prominent members of the secular population control lobby. He continues to rely on Jeffrey Sachs, an American economist and supporter of population control who is working to link Pope Francis's "Global Education Pact" to create a "new humanism" with wealthy secular private and public foundations that are part of the population control and climate-change movement. As an advisor to Pope Francis on sustainable development, Bishop Sorondo also has promised to bring prominent rock stars and celebrities, such as Greta Thunberg and other activists, to support the "Global Education" initiative for a "new humanism" which Pope Francis has called for.[211] Pope Francis was the first signatory on a document that endorsed the United Nations Sustainable Development Goals, hidden within which is the population control agenda with all its opposition to Catholic truth about the human person.[212]

Bishop Sorondo is the same bishop who returned from a visit to the People's Republic of China claiming, unbelievably, that they are implementing Catholic social teaching better than anywhere else: "At this moment, those who best realize the social doctrine of the Church are the Chinese."[213]

In the meantime, of course, the Catholic Church in China is being systematically corrupted through government control, with all resistance crushed. Is there a whiff of Marxism in the air in the Vatican these days? Cardinal Reinhard Marx, the German bishop who is on the nine-person Council of Cardinals to advise Pope Francis on Vatican reforms, has recently admitted his admiration for Karl Marx.[214] He was also, until recently, the president of the German Bishops' Conference, which is embarking, as we have seen, on a "synodal process" to reexamine the Church's approach to sexual morality, the ordination of women, and other issues, which they hope will bring them into greater harmony with the culture. Let's examine these issues and influences in greater detail now.

THE EXPERTS

Bishop Sorondo seems to have been given free rein to bring in experts at Vatican-sponsored conferences to advise the Church on social and economic issues, experts dedicated to population control and abortion. One of the most prominent of these experts and one of the most frequently invited speakers is Jeffrey Sachs. Photos of these conferences often feature Bishop Sorondo and Jeffrey Sachs sitting side by side, smiling.

For the fourth consecutive year, as a side conference to the Youth Synod in 2019, Bishop Sorondo and Jeffrey Sachs hosted an October 16 Youth Symposium at the Pontifical Academy of Sciences, cosponsored by the Vatican and the Sustainable Development Solutions Network (SDSN), directed by Jeffery Sachs. Titled "Intergenerational Leadership: *Laudato Si* and The Sustainable Development Goals," the symposium had the purpose of enlisting Catholic youth in the effort to enact these goals. Goals 3.7 and 5.6 are devoted to assuring, by 2030, universal access to "sexual and reproductive health services, including for family planning, information and education, and the integration of reproductive health into national strategies and programmes." Throughout the world, the language of "reproductive health" is always interpreted to mean contraception and abortion. At the end of the conference, the Catholic youth held up signs, each endorsing one of the goals, including the two just mentioned.[215]

In February of 2020, at another Vatican conference, Jeffrey Sachs promised that he would bring huge financial resources (twenty-six billion dollars a year) and the resources of the United Nations, the Bill and Melinda Gates Foundation, the International Monetary Fund, and some of the world's leading billionaires, to support Pope Francis's "Global Education Pact" to create a "new humanism."[216] He also attacked the United States for standing in the way of a new global humanism.[217] He was scheduled to be a speaker at a conference to take place in Assisi in March of 2020 entitled "The Economy of Francesco," but it was postponed because of the coronavirus pandemic.[218] Many voices have warned against what often happens in these kinds of collaborations with groups so opposed to the Catholic Church on fundamental moral issues.

As evidence of this, there seems to be a never-ending river of scandals concerning the Church's collaboration with non-Catholic aid agencies. Year after year, there seems to be complaints that the US Bishops' Catholic Campaign for Human Development (CCHD) continues to fund pro-abortion and pro-homosexual groups and radical leftist causes. The same is often the case with the international aid agencies, such as Catholic Relief Services, which have multiple investigative reports documenting how they are implicated in providing contraception devices and abortion information through their various secular partnerships. Since many of the people who work for these nominally Catholic agencies aren't even Catholics, it is no wonder that Catholic sensitivity is often lacking.[219]

Philip Lawler, an excellent journalist and knowledgeable Catholic, has written time and time again, year after year, about the scandalous partnerships and giving history of the CCHD, and yet every year it seems there are fresh scandals. The bishops promise to "clean it up," but somehow it never seems to stay clean. Now well-documented reports are coming out which show how many organizations the Church is funding that are demanding that the police be defunded.[220]

This is similar to what seems to be the never-ending Vatican financial scandals.[221] Despite promising, year after year, to stop the corruption and lack of accountability, there never seems to be an end to it. There must be people in both systems who simply don't care, or even worse, simply don't believe.[222] Bishop Joseph Strickland, a brave voice among the American bishops, has called for a public response to the investigative reports about such serious matters, but other than bland reassurances that the programs have the "confidence" of the bishops, no response to the specific charges has been made.[223] I am happy to say that my own bishop, Earl Boyea, of the Diocese of Lansing, has decided this year not to support the annual collection for the CCHD because of the never-ending scandals.

WHO IS JEFFREY SACHS?

Jeffrey Sachs is a US citizen who has had a long career advising governments and major governmental agencies and non-profits on issues concerning climate change, "green" economic policies, population control, and reproductive "rights." He has been significantly funded by George Soros, who has devoted billions of dollars to aggressive secular causes hostile to Christ and the Church. Sachs received fifty million dollars from George Soros for his previous global initiatives project. Sachs has frequently called for making contraception and abortion available in developing countries to slow down population growth.[224] Bernie Sanders wrote the foreword to Sach's 2017 book on economics, and Sanders was invited to a Vatican conference by Bishop Sorondo, during which Sanders claimed that he and Pope Francis were on the same page concerning economics.[225] When Bishop Sorondo was interviewed and asked why such an outspoken advocate of contraception and abortion as Jeffrey Sachs was so frequently invited to Vatican events and consulted on important initiatives of the pope, Bishop Sorondo said that since he doesn't say those things while he is here, it's fine.

Who Is George Soros?

George Soros is a Hungarian who immigrated to New York and ran one of the most significant investment firms of all time, amassing billions of dollars. When he was once criticized in a *60 Minutes* interview for how his investment policies were harming people and even whole nations, he replied:

> I don't feel guilty because I am engaged in an amoral activity which is not meant to have anything to do with guilt. I cannot and do not look at the social consequences of what I do.[226]

At a certain point, Soros decided he had enough money and began to deploy it to accomplish his political, economic, and social goals. His lead foundation, Open Society Foundations, has more than $19.5 billion in assets and an operating budget of $1.2 billion for 2020. Through a whole network of foundations and international organizations, Soros is active in more than 120 countries, giving thousands of grants to promote his goals. He has already spent more than $32 billion in furthering his objectives. In January of 2020, at the World Economic Forum in Davos, he announced "the most important and enduring project of [his] life"[227]—the Open Society University Network, whose goal is to influence teaching and research in existing universities all over the world in order to, among other things, fight "dictatorship." When asked how to determine who is and who is not a dictator, he replied "a perfect way to tell a dictator or a would-be dictator is if he identifies me as an enemy."[228]

What are Soros's goals? They overlap significantly with those of his close collaborator and advisor, Jeffrey Sachs, such as climate change, but with a particular emphasis on open borders and a global approach to solving problems through utilizing international organizations run by a global, secular elite rather than nation-states. He also invests heavily in influencing journalism schools and training "thought leaders" at universities. The website of his lead foundation has rather sanitized language about its goals, but as you drill down, you find things like promoting acceptance of "same-sex relationships" and the usual concern for health care, which always emphasizes "reproductive health care"—and this always includes contraception, abortion, and an acceptance of the sexual revolution.[229]

Soros sees the United States as an obstacle in accomplishing his global, progressive, socialist, diminishment-of-the-nation-state goals. He contributes a great deal of money to support candidates who then support his global goals and support open borders even in very local elections, including American elections. Recently, the US Attorney General warned that Soros was putting money behind radical left candidates running in state elections to become prosecuting attorneys, who will support open borders and turn from traditional law enforcement to support "inclusive" social change. Some of these radical left prosecuting attorneys have been successfully elected and are now refusing to prosecute the violence and mayhem that has accompanied recent riots in the United States and are instead prosecuting police and others trying to defend life and property from destruction. He gives heavily to Planned Parenthood and the American Civil Liberties Union. He is actively involved in influencing the direction of culture, education, and politics in countries all over the world, but he sees the United States, under its current leadership, as the biggest obstacle to a new "global humanism."

When the coronavirus pandemic broke out, he saw it as a once-in-a-lifetime opportunity to accomplish his revolutionary goals:

> This is the crisis of my lifetime. Even before the pandemic hit, I realized that we were in a revolutionary moment where what would be impossible or even inconceivable in normal times had become not only possible, but probably absolutely necessary. And then came COVID-19, which has totally disrupted people's lives and required very different behavior. It is an unprecedented event that probably has never occurred in this combination. And it really endangers the survival of our civilization.[230]

With the disruption of the coronavirus favoring his revolutionary plans, the emergence of the Black Lives Matter movement added fuel to the fire. A few months after the Black Lives Matter movement came to prominence, Soros's foundation committed 220 million dollars to "progressive" black-led organizations and another 70 million dollars to organizations working to change policing and to train young political activists. Patrick Gaspard, the president of the Open Society Foundations, said now was the time for them to "double down" on their investment in social and political change; this was "the moment we've been investing in for the last 25 years. So it's time to double down. And we understood we can place a bet on these activists—Black and white—who see this as a moment of not just incrementalism, but whole-scale reform."[231]

It is Soros and his money and his own global, educational network that Jeffrey Sachs promises to bring on board in support of Pope Francis's own global education initiatives for a "new humanism."

There's More

But Sachs isn't the only public advocate of positions contrary to the faith who is invited to participate in key Vatican undertakings or who significantly influences the documents or funds the initiatives that are coming from Rome. Professor Hans Joachim Schellnhuber was one of the three people chosen to introduce Pope Francis's encyclical on the environment, *Laudato Si*, to the world at a Vatican press conference on June 18, 2015. When someone who is not a cleric is chosen in this way, it is often a sign that he had a significant role in contributing to the encyclical and is best equipped to answer questions about it. Professor Schellnhuber has been a longtime member of the Club of Rome, an organization that since 1968 has been issuing dire warnings about the catastrophic effects of the world population growing, warnings that have never come to pass but then are revised to predict another dire event. Its goal is reducing the world's population utilizing contraception and abortion. But Professor Schellnhuber is also known for telling government officials that they should obey the scientists and help their citizens "even with coercion" to overcome their resistance to change.[232]

A whole jubilee year was designated (May 2020–May 2021) to celebrate and implement *Laudato Si*, including numerous events with the kind of collaboration that we have already seen in great abundance, with secular and interreligious entities.[233] The unspoken arguments for one world government hinted at by those who make the direst predictions about climate change and population growth sometimes become explicit, as they did when the British political leader and former United Kingdom Prime Minister Gordon Brown called for such. He currently serves as United Nations Special Envoy for Global Education. It is likely that we will see him involved in connection with Pope Francis's global education initiative for a "new humanism."[234] The same seems to be happening with the coronavirus pandemic. It certainly is a serious threat, but as Hillary Clinton openly counseled her followers to "never waste a good crisis,"[235] one wonders to what degree fear, panic, and economic ruin is being welcomed as a chance to impose socialist agendas. In a statement put out by a group of concerned cardinals, bishops, and scholars, including Cardinal Mueller, they warned:

> There are powers interested in creating panic among the world's population with the sole aim of permanently imposing unacceptable forms of restriction on freedoms, of controlling people and of tracking their movements. The imposition of these illiberal measures is a disturbing prelude to the realization of a world government beyond all control.[236]

As one historian put it:

> Liberalism is giving way to some yet unnamed technocratic state-corporation that merges social, economic, and political power even as our society abandons the vestiges of cultural Christianity.[237]

And recently a Harvard professor expressed grave concern about how children are being indoctrinated into "narrow views" through homeschooling. She called for a "presumptive ban" on homeschooling and pointed out that 90 percent of those who do it are conservative Christians. The desire to coerce "recalcitrant" citizens into conformity with secular ideology is barely being restrained.[238]

All it needs now is to gain controlling political power.

When one considers the views of the "elite," coupled with the aggressive removal from social media sites of content that is deemed "offensive" to social peace, a totalitarian control of even the United States is no longer out of the question.

Recently, Facebook established something like a "supreme court" to definitively rule on what posts should be admitted onto Facebook and which should not be.[239]

R. R. Reno raises the question about whether we are moving in the same direction as China in establishing a surveillance state:

> Are we sliding in the same direction? China has instituted a "social credit" score to control behavior. In the United States, nobody working in management for a Fortune 500 company can speak frankly of his reservations about gay marriage or transgenderism without suffering professionally. University students tell me that the first thing you learn as a freshman is *Never say out loud what you are actually thinking.* Twitter mobs enforce progressive orthodoxies. We have a ruthless cultural regime that minutely monitors people's speech, even their thoughts.[240]

Michael McClymond, the professor from Saint Louis University who has written the monumental two-volume study of universalism that we considered in some detail in Chapter 3, has raised the alarm about the connection between the fast-spreading virus of universalism and the coming together of global environmental agencies and the Vatican. He sees it as strengthening the forces that are wanting to combine religion and environmental concern into something like a "religion" of secular humanism or, as he puts it, a "religion of humanity." The focus is on downplaying the differences between religions so they can be enlisted in a new earth-centered religion of humanity. While universalism acknowledges that Jesus was crucified, it wants to take off his "rough edges," where he says that he has not come to bring peace but a sword (see Matt 10:34) so he can be integrated into a new "global humanism." McClymond writes:

> A little more than a century ago, a largely forgotten group of prerevolutionary Russian thinkers pursued a project known as "God-Building." These writers were socialists who—unlike Lenin—viewed religion not as an intractable foe but as a potential ally in the quest for human solidarity. But religion—and God—had to be changed so as to downplay the unique and absolute claims of Christ. A character in a Russian novel gave voice to this desire: "We have got to change our God. . . . It is necessary . . . to invent a new faith; it is necessary to create a God for all."

When McClymond is asked why he believes in the unique claims of Christ and the reality of a final judgment and of heaven and hell he says:

> My answer must be not only "Because this is what the Bible teaches" and "Because church teaching confirms it," but also "Because I have eyes to see." I don't need to hypothesize a world in which human pride and stubbornness cause people to turn away from God's gracious offer of mercy in Jesus Christ. This is the world I live in. This is what I see happening every day. This is what I read in the news. It was also what I am told by the Church: Jesus was crucified. Perfect love appeared in history—and observe what man did in response. . . . Universalism is hopefulness run amok, the opiate of the theologians.[241]

THE AMAZON SYNOD

In 2015, in perhaps what was to presage the even more striking events at the Amazon Synod, the Vatican sponsored a very strange light show on the façade of St. Peter's Basilica.

Its creators "practiced" for the Vatican light show on August 1, 2015, by projecting it on the Empire State Building in New York City and specifically mentioned the purpose of the show was to communicate the message that man-made climate change was destroying the planet, including many animal species. In the NYC "warm-up" act, they also included pagan goddesses such as Gaia (a Greek Mother Earth goddess), Aya (a Babylonian mother goddess associated with the sun and with sexual love), and Mother Earth herself. The creator of the show, Andrew Jones, who calls himself an "android," acknowledged that he used psychedelic substances to help him portray the occult deities accurately. He claimed that the "deities are actively involved, enrolled, and contributing in guiding his hand"[242] as he created the light show. In the NYC show, he also included the Hindu goddess of death and destruction, Kali, who promises wealth to those who worship her by satiating her lust for blood by human sacrifice. New Age spirituality has appropriated her as a kind of Mother Earth goddess.

For the Vatican light show, the explicit images of the goddesses were removed, but the strange images of lizards crawling on the façade of St. Peter's, the ambiguous symbols and images, the single "eye," which features prominently in New Age spirituality, and New Age music with strange sounds, breathing, and ethereal tones, left many in shock or just confused. Michael O'Brien, the Catholic novelist and artist, notes that it was particularly offensive that the light show was planned for the Feast of the Immaculate Conception, where the true Mother should have been honored instead of the implicit bow in the direction of the Mother Earth goddesses.

The vibe was "save the planet," not the salvation brought by Jesus Christ through the fiat of Mary. The organizers praised the Vatican for their full cooperation with the project and claimed that Pope Francis specifically gave the go-ahead.[243] It's amazing how things are occurring in our day that Old Testament prophets warned about thousands of years ago. The following passage from Ezekiel seems especially apropos:

> And he said to me, "Son of man, do you see what they are doing, the great abominations that the house of Israel are committing here, to drive me far from my sanctuary?" . . . And he said to me, "Go in, and see the vile abominations that they are committing here." So I went in and saw; and there, portrayed upon the wall round about, were all kinds of creeping things, and loathsome beasts, and all the idols of the house of Israel. . . . Each had his censer in his hand, and the smoke of the cloud of incense went up. Then he said to me, "Son of man, have you seen what the elders of the house of Israel are doing in the dark, every man in his room of pictures? For they say, 'The LORD does not see us, the LORD has forsaken the land.'" He said also to me, "You will see still greater abominations which they commit." Then he brought me to the entrance of the north gate of the house of the LORD; and behold, there sat women weeping for Tammuz. Then he said to me, "Have you seen this, O son of man? You will see still greater abominations than these." And he brought me into the inner court of the house of the LORD; and behold, at the door of the temple of the LORD, between the porch and the altar, were about twenty-five men, with their backs to the temple of the LORD, and their faces toward the east, worshiping the sun toward the east. Then he said to me, "Have you seen

this, O son of man? Is it too slight a thing for the house of Judah to commit the abominations which they commit here, that they should fill the land with violence, and provoke me further to anger? Lo, they put the branch to their nose. Therefore I will deal in wrath; my eye will not spare, nor will I have pity; and though they cry in my ears with a loud voice, I will not hear them." (Ezek 8:6–18)

At about the same time, an exhibition celebrating the ancient city of Carthage was launched at the Colosseum, featuring a huge statue of the god Moloch, who was known for demanding child sacrifice.[244]

We've already discussed the role that the two Synods on the Family played in opening the door to a more permissive approach to sexual morality. The series of documents,[245] the meetings, the synod itself, its final report, and its post-synodal apostolic exhortation *Querida Amazonia* have served a similar role in moving our understanding of the Church's mission further away from the eternal salvation of human beings to what, for some, has now become its primary mission, caring for the environment, including the "human environment," and a concern for social and economic justice. The language of "preferential option," which featured prominently in the liberation theology of the eighties, reappears, this time as a "preferential option for the indigenous people."[246] While not neglecting an occasional mention of the need to preach the Gospel, the documents are overwhelmingly focused on "saving the Amazon." And "saving the Amazon" is seen as having universal relevance for the worldwide mission of the Church.

Cardinal Michael Czerny, who was intimately involved in guiding the synod and who was appointed as the "Special Secretary of the Synod for the Amazon," was the one chosen to present Pope Francis's post-synodal apostolic exhortation to the world. The Vatican news service featured his comments in this headline: "Cardinal Czerny: Love the Amazon and its people to save the planet." His exact words were these:

> The destiny of the Amazon affects us all, because everything is connected and the salvation of this region and its original peoples is fundamental for the whole world.[247]

There are many more calls for an "integral ecological conversion" than to any explicit conversion to Jesus Christ. And when Christ is mentioned, it is not at all clear that whether we respond to him or not, whether we believe and repent or not, has any eternal consequences or is just meant to enrich what the indigenous peoples, and the documents, call "good living." While preaching the Gospel is not neglected entirely,[248] the predominant, and indeed incessant, message is to "listen to the cries of the earth" or the cries of the "indigenous peoples," with exhortations to listen to their wisdom. At the same time, an absolutely devastating picture is presented about the actual lives of the inhabitants of the Amazon beset by the depopulation of the rural areas and the flight to the cities, which usually means the outlying slums, beset by crime and alcohol and drug addiction, the breakdown of family life, and all the ills associated with that.

Delegates to the synod were selected from the nations bordering the Amazon and prelates from around the world, many of whom were known to be sympathetic to its planned agenda. Retired Archbishop of São Paulo, Brazil, Cardinal Cláudio Hummes, was chosen as Relator General of the Synod. He is widely known for his sympathy for liberation theology and advocacy of ordaining married men and is a leader of the "progressive" wing of the Latin American bishops. A main influence on the synod was a retired Austrian bishop, Erwin Kräutler, who worked in Brazil for many years and was proud of the fact that he never baptized a single person in all his years of missionary work. His books, meetings with the pope, and intimate involvement in the pre-synod planning allowed him to significantly influence the direction of the synod. He was particularly pushing for ordaining married men as priests and women as deacons, and while not successful in obtaining immediate results, his "this world" liberation theology orientation was well represented in the deliberations of the synod.

The synod itself, in its final document, carried forward much of the emphasis of the preparatory documents and indicated that there was a large majority in favor of ordaining married men and considering the diaconate for women.

There was much anticipation for what the pope's response would be in the apostolic exhortation that he published a few months later. There was widespread disappointment among those who noted that the pope didn't say anything about ordaining married men, for or against, and was silent on the issue, as he was on the possible ordination of women. Cardinal Christoph Schönborn, Archbishop of Vienna and a prominent defender of Pope Francis's papacy, publicly expressed his disappointment that Pope Francis didn't do more for the status of women. However, Archbishop Víctor Manuel Fernández, Pope Francis's chief theologian, made it clear in interviews that the pope's silence meant the door was still open and bishops could petition for the right to ordain married men, and that there was a new study group considering the possibility of ordaining women as deacons. He also warned people not to miss the forest for the trees and pointed to the radical social, economic, and political critiques that the pope included in the document and the importance of separating the priesthood from power and promoting a more fully lay-led church.[249] Once again, we encounter an ambiguity which leaves things very much open to interpretation. The pope also took the unusual step of deciding that the final document of the synod should be considered in an ongoing way, along with the apostolic exhortation, as a complete word on the matters under consideration. And then just weeks later, he established a new body of bishops to oversee the implementation of the Amazon Synod and remake the regional Church with an "Amazonian face." He appointed as advisors to this new episcopal body Cardinal Czerny, Cardinal Tagle, and Cardinal Lorenzo Baldisseri, the main organizer of synods during Francis's pontificate. Cardinal Cláudio Hummes, the friend of liberation theology and advocate of married priests, and Bishop Erwin Kräutler, the bishop who brags about never baptizing anyone in many years of missionary work and another strong advocate for a married clergy, will also play significant roles. The executive secretary of the Amazon network REPAM, who played a major role in influencing the direction of the Amazon Synod, said he has "not the slightest doubt that married priests will come."[250]

However, these steps did not satisfy one of Pope Francis's biggest supporters and a leading theological advocate of continuing the "spirit" of Vatican II. Massimo Faggioli, an Italian theologian now teaching at a Catholic university in the United States, Villanova, bemoans Pope Francis's silence on the question of married priests and women as deacons and warns that he is leaving many of his supporters disillusioned.

Faggioli points out many of the things he regards as positive that Pope Francis has done, such as:

> Helped free Catholic moral teaching from its ideological straightjacket . . . opening the sacraments in *Amoris Laetitia* to Catholics in difficult marriage and family situations . . . rehabilitated theologians that were silenced and punished by Rome's post-Vatican II doctrinal policy. He has also guided the Catholic Church into global Catholi-

cism. His focus on socio-economic issues (including those related to the environment, *Laudato Si*), at a time when globalization is in deep crisis, has been prophetic.[251]

But Faggioli expresses deep concern that Francis's important insights aren't being placed in a "clear systematic structure" that can institutionalize change. He claims that the pope has been "much more effective in deconstructing a culturally and historically limited paradigm than in building a new one." He also is concerned that outspoken influential cardinals such as Cardinal Mueller and Cardinal Sarah haven't been reined in by Francis as they clearly restate traditional Catholic doctrine in explicit contrast to Francis's own teaching. His conclusion is that Pope Francis's pontificate "is in crisis."[252]

Faggioli sees some hope on the horizon, however, in the "synodal way" that the German Church is pursuing, in the plenary council currently being prepared for in Australia, and in the actual implementation of the Amazon Synod through the new structures that have been created.[253]

My concern with the whole Amazon Synod process as it pertains to its official written record is not the controversy about ordaining married men as priests or the possible official recognition of women as deacons, which is not to say these aren't important issues. What I am very concerned about is the "horizontal thrust"[254] that was furthered by the documents and the pantheistic overtones that run through the documents when it comes to the elevation of environmentalism and mother earth into quasi-mystical "integral ecological spirituality."[255]

George Weigel described the "project" of those driving the synod like this:

> "The project" was, and is, nothing less than the creation of a New Model Catholicism, in which the Church is con-

ceived primarily as an international non-governmental organization advancing the progressive agenda globally. Various forms of liberation theology, wedded to a certain interpretation of Karl Rahner's notion of the unevangelized as "anonymous Christians," informed the first attempts to realize "the project." The addition of eco-theology to the mix (itself the import of a quasi-religion from Western elites), and a new reverence for indigenous religiosity, seems to have filled out "the project's" understanding of what the Church is, and what the Church is for.[256]

Weigel, in one of the most insightful post-synodal evaluations, identifies what's at stake:

> The cards are now face-up on the table.... And what, precisely is at stake, after this synod and its predecessors during the current pontificate?... At stake is the reality and binding authority of divine revelation as conveyed to us by Scripture and Tradition. Does revelation judge history—including this historical moment and its legitimate concerns about the environment—or does history judge revelation?... At stake is the teaching of the 1993 encyclical *Veritatis Splendor* on the reality of intrinsically evil acts—actions that can never be justified by any calculus of intentions and consequences. ... At stake is the teaching of *Dominus Iesus*, on the unique role of Jesus Christ as Savior.... At stake is the relationship of the universal Church to the local churches: Is Catholicism a federation of national or regional churches, or is Catholicism a universal Church with distinctive local expressions? ... At stake is the realization of the Great Commission of Matthew 28: 19-20: "Go therefore and make disciples of all nations." That is what is at stake.[257]

Perhaps the most authoritative explanation of what the synod was about is best found in Pope Francis's own words. He speaks, toward the beginning of *Querida Amazonia*, about the "four great dreams" he has for the Amazon, which he then explicates in the rest of the document:

> I dream of an Amazon region that fights for the rights of the poor, the original peoples and the least of our brothers and sisters, where their voices can be heard and their dignity advanced.
>
> I dream of an Amazon region that can preserve its distinctive cultural riches, where the beauty of our humanity shines forth in so many varied ways.
>
> I dream of an Amazon region that can jealously preserve its overwhelming natural beauty and the superabundant life teeming in its rivers and forests.
>
> I dream of Christian communities capable of generous commitment, incarnate in the Amazon region, and giving the Church new faces with Amazonian features.[258]

There are many good things said in all the documents. It is right to care for the environment and it is indeed a moral issue. It is right to care for the rights of the poor and to help protect them against policies motivated by greed and not respecting their well-being. But as I read all of them—and they are long!—I kept asking myself, Can you imagine Jesus saying things like this? No. Jesus was laser focused on the salvation of souls, on faith and repentance, on our eternal destinies, and these notes are hardly found in any of the documents. When they are found, they are completely overwhelmed by the very much greater abundance of "this world" concerns.

If I were forced to sum up in a few words my evaluation of the situation, I would say this: There are many good and true things in the Amazon documents, but the overall impression one gets is that there is a greater concern for this world than for the eternal salvation of the inhabitants of the world, which is very sad to see and to say.[259] I think it is also fair to say that either someone is "asleep at the switch" or there are people furthering an impious promotion of syncretism, even idolatry, in allowing what happened with the Pachamama statues.

It seems that a globalist, progressive agenda is making deep inroads into the Vatican, the spearhead of which is Bishop Sorondo and the Pontifical Academy of Social Sciences. During the pontificates of St. John Paul II and Benedict XVI, the Pontifical Academy had perhaps one conference a year. During the pontificate of Pope Francis, the Pontifical Academy is having multiple conferences and other events each year, and Jeffrey Sachs has been invited to speak at more than twenty of them. It is a matter of record that George Soros is a main funder of the Sustainable Development Goals program of the UN, which Pope Francis has endorsed and which Jeffrey Sachs is majorly involved in. It is also a matter of public fact that Pope Francis has supported these initiatives and put his own prestige and the prestige of the Vatican behind them. The globalist, progressive agenda, as a central part of its purpose, is to reduce the world's population through extensive distribution of contraceptives and the wide availability of abortion, along with euthanasia.

Most of the developed nations are contracepting and aborting themselves out of existence, while the Muslim populations, particularly in Europe, keep growing. And now euthanasia is aggressively being pushed and the numbers of those euthanized are growing each year. In just four years, thirteen thousand Canadians have been euthanized, and bills to make it easier are making their way through various governmental units. In 2015, Belgium euthanized over two thousand people, including dozens of mentally disabled patients.[260]

International governmental and nongovernmental agencies continually pressure governments to take strong measures in this direction, and, unfortunately, the United States and other countries, depending on who is in power, have sometimes tied foreign aid to accepting this agenda. Elizabeth Yore, an attorney with a long history of working for major organizations to put an end to human trafficking, shares her shock at attending the first Vatican conference on human trafficking and finding it full of population control experts with nary a pro-lifer in sight. It led her to look into the links between George Soros, Bishop Sorondo, the UN, and Pope Francis's climate teachings and make public her findings. She was General Counsel for the Illinois Department of Children and Family Services; Special Council at Harpo, Inc., Oprah Winfrey's child advocacy organization; and a leader with International Child Advocacy organizations. The account of her experience must be given weight.[261]

But there were other events connected to the Amazon that were extremely significant in what they symbolized and were not written into the documents. Perhaps the event, and the photo that recorded it, that shocked the world was a ceremony in the Vatican gardens, just before the synod began, of a group of indigenous people from the Amazon region, including a Franciscan friar in full habit, in the presence of the pope, prostrating themselves and making offerings to several statues of naked women. Despite repeated requests, the Vatican Press Office refused to indicate what they signified. These figures were brought into St. Peter's Basilica in a canoe to celebrate the beginning of the synod and often appeared in the synod hall under the rostrum where the pope and the presiding cardinals sat.

And then one day, some young men from Austria took the statues from where they were being venerated in a church a few blocks down from the Vatican and threw them into the Tiber. These young men, like many others around the world, thought that it looked for all the world like these statues were being venerated as idols. These men were profoundly offended that the pews in the church where the idols spent the time when they were not at the synod had been rearranged in a circle around the statues so they could be meditated on and venerated. When the statues were recovered, Pope Francis, perhaps inadvertently, revealed what they were when he thanked God and the Italian police that the Pachamama statues were recovered. Who is Pachamama? She is an earth goddess figure venerated in the regions of South America and by other names throughout the world, including Gaia. The two statues of Pachamama reappeared at the end of the synod in a canoe at the front of the synod hall during the concluding session.[262]

In many years of closely following Church documents and discussing these with thousands of seminarians, priests, and bishops throughout the world, I am continually amazed to discover how few Church leaders read them. The ordinary Catholic almost never reads them. And when they are particularly long and repetitious, as are the documents we are currently discussing, and are written in vague, abstract, eco-speech, it is doubly difficult. That's why the casual comments and gestures of the pope are so important and, in many cases, so disturbing.

A letter I recently received from a very sound priest whom I have known for many years, who is heroically laboring in the vineyard, expresses this well. He is not a traditionalist; he is not a "rigid conservative"—he is just a genuinely concerned Catholic priest:

> I don't hear the Gospel of eternal salvation being taught clearly anymore. Our Pope seems to think that there are many other valid ways to get to the Father, besides Jesus.

He gives the impression that what you believe doesn't matter as much as caring for the poor. I witnessed, along with millions of faithful Catholics, the introduction of idols into St. Peter's basilica, with strange accompanying rituals. And now, in the midst of a pandemic which seems to be allowed by God to get our attention, our Holy Father seems to be focusing on the healing of mother earth—perhaps even suggesting that she needs to be appeased in order to stop the worldwide calamities. Where is the outcry over this? Help!

It wasn't just ordinary Catholic priests who were scandalized by the Pachamama events; there was something like a worldwide outcry. Cardinal Mueller warned that photos of the obviously pagan rites would cause hundreds of thousands to leave the Catholic Church.[263] Cardinal Paul Cordes, with whom I worked very closely in Rome in the integration of lay movements into the broader Church, warned of slipping into pantheistic idolatry.[264] And Fr. Mitch Pacwa, the EWTN host, exclaimed to a worldwide audience, "We're not stupid . . . This is an idol!"[265] Fr. Pacwa was especially concerned that the Italian bishops had published a prayer to Pachamama, the "Mother Earth of the Inca peoples":

Pachamama of these places, drink and eat as much as you like of these offerings, so that this earth may be fruitful. Pachamama, good Mother, be propitious! Be propitious! Let the oxen walk well, and let them not get tired.[266]

Fr. Pacwa exclaimed: "Stop! You're talking about making an offering to a goddess!"[267]

It's clear that the virus of undiscerning syncretism and other aberrations is present in many "high places" besides the Vatican, including the Italian Bishops' Conference. The rot is very deep indeed.[268]

However, perhaps it is not as deep as it is in some of what can only be called apostate Protestant denominations. A tweet from Union Theological Seminary in New York City, where Protestant luminaries such as Reinhold Niebuhr and Paul Tillich once taught, shared a prayer that was prayed that day in chapel:

Today in chapel we confessed to plants. Together, we held our grief, joy, regret, hope, guilt and sorrow in prayer; offering them to the beings who sustain us but whose gift we too often fail to honor. What do you confess to the plants in your life?[269]

Msgr. Charles Pope writes movingly of his distress at what was happening in Rome.

I, like many of you, feel overwhelmed by the events of the past month in Rome. Many an evening, late into the night, I have come before the Lord in the rectory chapel in lament for the confusion and chaos in the Church, the Lord's beautiful bride and our mother. . . . Reported from Rome are terrible and seemingly impious things at worst, and confusing and ambiguous things at best. . . . It is clear that the Synod was stacked with liberal—and even radical—members . . . The whole process has been steeped with the jargon and ambiguity that is the hallmark of this papacy. . . . The pope claims that there was no idolatrous intention in prostrating before the carved images . . . but if it isn't an idol of Pachamama (an earth/mother goddess from the Andes), why did the Pope call the image "Pachamama"? How is this not analogous to the "abomination of desolation" that foretold the destruction of Jerusalem (cf. Matt 24: 15)?[270]

Whatever history's judgment of Pope Francis might be and whatever good insights are contained in his writings, the objective reality is that he is causing and passively accepting immense confusion and division in the Church and seems strangely reluctant to resolve it. He is famous for encouraging us to not be afraid of making a mess in our efforts to evangelize, but for a pope to make a mess is really harmful. What is even more disturbing is the possibility that "making a mess" is a strategy for moving the Church in a dangerous direction, where "situation ethics" is back again in a big way, interreligious dialogue is overshadowing evangelization, and vague understandings of "conversion" are the order of the day. Very astute theologians are raising very serious concerns.

Fr. Thomas Weinandy is currently a leading American theologian. He has taught at many universities including Oxford, the Catholic University of America, and the Pontifical Gregorian University in Rome. He was executive director of the American bishops' Committee on Doctrine and also has been a member of the pontifical International Theological Commission. After what he described as profound reflection and serious prayer, he felt he had an obligation to express his very deep concerns about the leadership of Pope Francis in an open letter he wrote to the pope, which an assistant acknowledged had been received and given to the pope but to which the pope never responded. What are some of the concerns Fr. Weinandy raised?

He expressed concern about the "chronic confusion" that seems to mark Francis's pontificate and how his words and actions are often "obscured by ambiguity." He cites Chapter VIII of *Amoris Laetitia* as a prime example of what he says seems to be "intentional ambiguity":

> As you wisely note, pastors should accompany and encourage persons in irregular marriages; but ambiguity persists

about what that "accompaniment" actually means.[271]

Fr. Weinandy also expresses concern about how Pope Francis "calumniates" his distinguished critics by calling them "Pharisaic stone-throwers who embody a merciless rigorism."[272]

He also expresses concern about how Pope Francis regularly demeans the importance of "doctrine," opposing it unfavorably to pastoral compassion when, in fact, pastoral compassion is not compassion if it does not flow from the clear truths of the faith. He also expresses concern about some of the bishops that the pope is appointing, who seem not very deeply rooted in the Catholic tradition and rather interested in accommodation to the culture. Fr. Weinandy also expressed concern about the pope's refusal to correct them when they teach ambiguously or worse, and at the same time, he dismissively demeans his own cardinals and bishops when they ask him for clarifications, simply ignoring them and remaining silent.

Fr. Weinandy finally expresses concern about Pope Francis's approach to "synodality," which seems designed to allow a diversity of moral and doctrinal views to spread in the Church, fundamentally undermining the unity of faith.

When Fr. Weinandy reflects on why the Lord is permitting such confusion, he concludes:

> The only answer that comes to mind is that Jesus wants to manifest just how weak is the faith of many within the Church, even among too many of her bishops. Ironically, your pontificate has given those who hold harmful theological and pastoral views the license and confidence to come into the light and expose their previously hidden darkness. In recognizing this darkness, the Church will humbly need to renew herself, and so continue to grow in holiness. [273]

After writing his letter, Fr. Weinandy was asked to resign from his position as consultor to the American bishops' Committee on Doctrine as a consequence of writing his letter. The previous executive director had also been asked to resign after he privately raised concerns about *Amoris Laetitia* to the Committee.

PROSELYTISM OR EVANGELIZATION?

Just as the emphasis on the environment and hearing the cries of the earth were coming to the forefront, I noticed a shift in how Pope Francis talked about evangelization. Early in his pontificate, especially in his apostolic exhortation after the synod of 2012 on the New Evangelization, *Evangelii Gaudium*, he spoke frequently and fervently about evangelization, understanding by evangelization an invitation to repentance and faith in Jesus Christ. But over the past several years, he has been speaking more and more of the dangers of proselytism and seeming to recommend silent witness of charity rather than proclamation of the Gospel. When he met a woman on his trip to Madagascar, besides urging the Church to "obey the UN," he expressed displeasure when the woman introduced to him two people who had converted to the Catholic Church, calling it proselytism.[274] In his press conference, he made explicit his views:

> Respect for other religions is important. This is why I tell missionaries not to proselytize. Proselytizing is valid for the world of politics, of sport—I root for my team, for yours—not for a faith. But, Holy Father, what does evangelization mean to you? There is a phrase of St Francis that has greatly enlightened me. Francis of Assisi used to say to his brothers: "Bring the Gospel, if it is necessary also with words."[275]

In this regard, it's useful to note that the alleged saying of St. Francis of Assisi that's most quoted in relationship to evangelization and that the pope himself quotes above, is this: "Preach the Gospel and if necessary, use words." It's usually invoked to reassure Catholics that silent "witness" is really all that usually needs to happen.

The problem with invoking this alleged saying is that St. Francis never said it; it's not at all how he went about evangelizing, and it's not at all what Vatican II and the post-conciliar documents on evangelization teach about explicit proclamation. Explicit proclamation is repeatedly urged as a necessary accompaniment to the witness of our lives.

In fact, St. Francis used words—preached the Gospel—all the time! He even went to northern Africa and announced the Gospel of Jesus Christ to Muslims, miraculously living to tell about it.

The basis for the saying may be rooted in something that Francis said in Chapter 17 of the *First Rule* from the year 1221:

> No friar may preach contrary to Church law or without the permission of his minister. The minister, for his part, must be careful not to grant permission indiscriminately. All the friars, however, should preach by their example.

He further elaborates on what he means in Chapter 9 of the *Rule*, written in 1223:

> The friars are forbidden to preach in any diocese, if the bishop objects to it. No friar should dare to preach to the people unless he has been examined and approved by the Minister General of the Order and has received from him the commission to preach.[276]

Others have noticed this as well. My colleague at Renewal Ministries, Peter Burak, who is responsible for our work with "millennials" and is a consultant to the USCCB advisory board on youth ministry, noticed a shift happening in the post-synodal apostolic exhortation that Pope Francis published after the Synod on Youth, *Christus Vivit*. Peter notes:

> I would describe this as a shift to an emphasis on listening, dialogue, accompaniment, and a delayed proclamation of some of the more difficult teachings found in Sacred Scripture and the Catechism. Most would agree that friendship, mutual understanding, and journeying with people are essential elements for evangelization. . . . However, I have noticed a growing trend for leaders to allow a nebulous definition of accompaniment that permits the celebration of the process without requiring the needed conversion. . . . We need to seek and save the lost by preaching a message of love, mercy, joy, and peace but also repentance, forgiveness, and a new way of living. . . . it is easy to promote accompaniment alone to avoid the difficult, awkward, and potentially relationship altering moments of genuine conversion.[277]

It is hard to avoid any longer acknowledging the fact that Pope Francis repeatedly seems to be clearly saying, "be quiet and let your witness be your life, and only if people ask you a question about your life should you tell them the Gospel." It was different in the early years of his papacy; it is what it is now, but who knows what might yet change.

In a short video address to a national meeting of Catholic youth in the United States, Pope Francis encouraged the students to bring Jesus to their environments but then departed from his prepared remarks which he was reading to interject emphatically, "Not with convictions, not to convince, not to proselytize," and then returning to his prepared remarks to say, "but to witness to the tenderness and mercy of Jesus."[278] Confusing? Yes.

Pope Francis, in talking about his own experience growing up in a multicultural and multireligious environment with Muslims and Jews, said he learned that:

> We all are the same, all children of God, and this purifies your gaze, it humanizes it. . . . It never occurred to me (nor should it) to say to a boy or a girl: "You are Jewish, you are Muslim: come, be converted!" . . . We are not living in the time of the Crusades. . . . The last thing I should do is to try to convince an unbeliever. Never. The last thing I should do is speak. (And only if an unbeliever asks.) But listen, the Gospel is never, ever advanced through proselytism.[279]

It seems here that the pope is equating announcing the Gospel, as we are commanded to do by Jesus and as Vatican II and all the post-Vatican II documents on evangelization equally urge, with proselytism.

In his address to the Japanese bishops, Pope Francis made reference to the example of St. Francis Xavier and St. Paul Miki and companions—who of course very directly preached the Gospel and brought converts into the Church, living with a burning conviction of the truth of the faith, the reality of heaven and hell, the shortness of life, and the coming judgment—but only spoke of the Japanese Church's witness to peace and justice, hospitality to foreign workers, and dialogue with non-Christian religions, with no encouragement to directly preach the Gospel.[280] The Church in Japan is not growing, and I doubt it ever will with such a narrowed vision of witness, such a timidity of spirit, such a lack of Pentecostal power.

This, of course, is not a problem just in Japan but throughout Asia as well. There is a strong inclination, policy almost, to "dialogue" rather than "proclaim," despite the Church's repeated urgings to do both.[281] What liberation theology is to Latin America, religious pluralism is to Asia: a silencing of the core of the Gospel. As the former head of the Federation of Asian Bishops' Conferences said:

> Some of us have relatives, parents, spouses or children who are adherents of other religions. We see that these people are good and holy not in spite of but because of the God and religions they believe in. It would therefore be a violation of our conscience to even suggest that baptism is necessary for their salvation.[282]

How different from the ringing call of St. Paul VI:

> There is no true evangelization if the name, the teaching, the life, the promises, the kingdom and the mystery of Jesus of Nazareth, the Son of God are not proclaimed.[283]

Or the many similar words of St. John Paul II:

> The proclamation of the Word of God has *Christian conversion* as its aim: a complete and sincere adherence to Christ and his Gospel through faith. . . . Conversion means accepting, by a personal decision, the saving sovereignty of Christ and becoming his disciple.[284]

And:

> We must rekindle in ourselves the impetus of the beginning and allow ourselves to be filled with the ardor of the apostolic preaching which followed Pentecost. We must revive in ourselves the burning conviction of Paul, who cried out: "Woe to me if I do not preach the Gospel" (1 Cor 9:16). . . . Those who have come into genuine contact

with Christ cannot keep him for themselves, they must proclaim him.[285]

We can count on the power of the same Spirit who was poured out at Pentecost and who impels us still today.[286]

Bishop Robert Barron, who is widely known for his work of evangelization and his admirable willingness to engage contemporary culture to present the beauty of the faith, had also noticed this shift in how Francis talked about evangelization earlier in his pontificate and now seemed to be warning against efforts to convert people by warning against proselytism without defining it and encouraging silent witness. At the *ad limina* visit of the West Coast bishops, Bishop Barron was happy to see one of his fellow bishops ask Pope Francis about this issue, as he too had wondered about what appeared to be a "tension" in the pope's remarks: "I will confess that I have often wondered at some of Francis's rhetoric here and have longed for something like his definition of the term." The pope replied, as reported by Bishop Barron, like this:

> The Holy Father clarified that he, of course, advocates the spreading of the faith, but he is opposed to an aggressive, divisive, numbers-oriented approach to the task.... As he often has in the past, he emphasized with us the centrality of personal witness to the joy of living a life of faith.... In this, of course, he was simply echoing Pope Paul VI, who said that people today listen to teachers precisely in the measure that those teachers are also witnesses.[287] I was particularly gratified to hear him on this point for there have been some in the commentariat who have suggested that engaging in apologetics or theological clarification is tantamount to "proselytizing." Not according to Pope Francis.[288]

Bishop Barron was satisfied by the pope's answer, but I find it less convincing. Yes, we all should share the faith out of a life that's authentically living it. But apologetics and theological clarification or even "teaching" aren't the same as the command to proclaim the Gospel with passion. And what does it mean that evangelization shouldn't be "aggressive" or "divisive" or about "numbers"? Jesus's evangelization was often both aggressive and divisive, and he was concerned about numbers; in fact, he told us it was supposed to be the same with us. The soft, non-offensive Gospel is not the Gospel of Jesus.

Is there anything more aggressive than Jesus's "dialogue" with the Pharisees in John 8:31–59? A small sample: "Why do you not understand what I say? It is because you cannot bear to hear my word. You are of your father the devil, and your will is to do your father's desires" (John 8:43–44).

Jesus was so aggressive and direct that the dialogue concluded by them taking up "stones to throw at him" (John 8:59). Not for the first or last time, either (see John 10:31, et al.)

And numbers? Jesus wept because so many of his own people were rejecting him and he knew what the horrendous consequences would be:

> And when he drew near and saw the city he wept over it, saying, "Would that even today you knew the things that make for peace! But now they are hid from your eyes. For the days shall come upon you, when your enemies will cast up a bank about you and surround you, and hem you in on every side, and dash you to the ground, you and your children within you, and they will not leave one stone upon another in you; because you did not know the time of your visitation." (Luke 19:41–44)

And the Holy Spirit thought it would be good to tell us that three thousand converted on the day of Pentecost (see Acts 2:41). And division?

> Do not think that I have come to bring peace on earth; but a sword. For I have come to set a man against his father, and a daughter against her mother, and a daughter-in-law against her mother-in-law; and a man's foes will be those of his own household. (Matt 10:34–36)

Unfortunately, not long after Bishop Barron's meeting with the pope, Francis urged Chinese Catholics to be "good citizens and not to engage in proselytism."[289] And then, several months later, Pope Francis said in a homily, "In Poland, a university student asked me: 'In university I have many atheist companions. What do I have to tell them to convince them?'—'Nothing, dear, nothing! The last thing you need to do is say something. Start by living, and they, seeing your testimony, will ask you: 'Why do you live like this?'"[290] Is the pope saying that Chinese Catholics, many of whom who have heroically suffered for the faith by preaching the Gospel, shouldn't preach the Gospel? As in many of Pope Francis's statements, we really don't know, but it seems like that is the message that Chinese Catholics will take from his remarks. And comments like this will surely make the Communist Party happy to have someone they may now consider an ally in keeping the Catholic Church under control.

My colleague at Sacred Heart Seminary, Dr. Eduardo Echeverria, has written extensively in a detailed way about the "evolution" of Pope Francis's pronouncements and has identified, with great insight and precision, that Pope Francis's condemnation of "doctrine" and "Pharisaical rigorism" and "rules" has weakened the backbone of the faith, the truths of salvation and of morality out of which pastoral practice needs to flow and be guided.[291] Without clarity about what has been revealed, "pastoral charity" and "pastoral compassion" can quite easily degenerate into approving whatever people want to do. Yes, we need to be a welcoming Church, but we need to be welcoming people to an encounter with Jesus that leads to conversion and a new way of life. Yes, we need to be patiently and compassionately "accompanying" people on their journey, but we need to be leading them to the true food and drink that God has provided for the human race—the Bread that has come down from Heaven, and the water flowing from the heart of Jesus.

As Dr. Echeverria puts it:

> How can we approach the unbeliever without convictions? . . . The message is not content free and empty. . . . Thus, a "personal encounter" with Christ involves a constitutive relation with beliefs, involving an assent of the mind to their truth, beliefs that we come to hold to be true. . . . Francis' view is not that of the *Catechism of the Catholic Church,* where doctrinal beliefs are the actual content of the encounter (CCC 150). . . . Absent in Francis' view is the *truth-oriented dynamic* of evangelical encounter. . . . This absence of the epistemic justification and truth of Christian beliefs is particularly evident in Francis' view of the "dialogue" of religions. His view not only creates confusion, but runs the risk of degenerating into outright religious indifferentism.[292]

From a more pastoral perspective, Fr. Martín Lasarte Topolanski, who is the head of missionary outreach in Africa and Latin America for the Salesian religious order, identifies three pathologies of the approach to mission found in the Amazon and other parts of Latin America. He asks the question, "Why is the Amazon so sterile?"—and the same can be said of much of Latin America in terms of dynamic Catholicism. The first pathology he identifies is the exaggerated respect paid to the "indigenous" cultures that makes the missionaries want to "listen" rather than to preach and to "witness" rather than teach the truth. The second pathology he identifies is what he calls "social moralism." He means by this an almost exclusive focus on providing "services," whether they be health or education or "community development"—what the pope and the Amazon synodal documents describe as being a "Samaritan Church." He points out that the Church's social commitment is important, but not to the extent that it overshadows or even silences the other, more primary missions of the Church: drawing people to repentance and conversion and forming them as disciples of Christ. He reflects, "I visited a diocese, where 95% of the population were Catholics in the early 1980s; today they are 20%. I remember the comment of one of the European missionaries who systematically 'dis-evangelized' the region; 'We do not favor superstition, but human dignity.' That says it all."

The third pathology he identifies is that of the influence of secularism that leads to a silencing of the faith or very timid manifestations of it. In speaking of the lack of indigenous vocations, Fr. Lasarte comments: "No one leaves everything to be a social animator; no one gives his life to an 'opinion'; no one offers the absolute of his life to something relative, but only to the Absolute of God."

He concludes: "There will be authentic priestly vocations only when an authentic, demanding, free and personal relationship is established with the person of Christ. Perhaps it is very simplistic but, in my view, the 'new path' for the evangelization of the Amazon is the novelty of Christ."[293]

Religious Indifferentism

Religious indifferentism seemed to be on display when Pope Francis and a leading Muslim cleric, the Grand Imam of Al-Azhar, a leading

Islamic university, signed the Abu Dhabi declaration (the "Document on Human Fraternity for World Peace and Living Together"), which stated:

> The pluralism and the diversity of religions, color, sex, race and language are willed by God in His wisdom, through which He created human beings.[294]

The document has many positive features, calling for an end to violence in the name of religion, the respect for religious freedom, and working together for peace and justice in the world, but it also calls for avoiding "unproductive discussions," which usually refers to avoiding discussions about the soundness or coherence of various religious systems. In a private audience with Pope Francis, Bishop Athanasius Schneider asked the pope to clarify what he had signed, since it couldn't mean that we were supposed to not evangelize all peoples. The pope then apparently told Bishop Schneider that he meant that it was God's "permissive" will that a diversity of religions existed, not his positive will. Bishop Schneider told the Holy Father that it was important that he share that publicly, as there was a great danger that people would understand what he signed as interreligious dialogue replacing evangelization. One of the most remarkable features of Francis's papacy is the consistent refusal to clarify public statements and actions of his that cause confusion and controversy in the Church.

For example, in an address to the Jesuit-run Pontifical University in Naples, Pope Francis called for a "theology of dialogue and acceptance" in relationship to Jews and Muslims, with not a word about our mission to proclaim Christ. What does the pope mean by "acceptance"? We really don't know, but coupled with all his warnings against proselytism and his strong focus on "this world" improvement, it certainly gives the impression that we shouldn't hope or pray or work for the conversion of Muslims and Jews, despite Jesus's explicit commands.[295]

The pope has never offered a public explanation, despite Bishop Schneider's request.[296] Just as he has never responded to the serious theological clarifications that Cardinal Burke and the other "dubia Cardinals" had asked from him in the midst of the diverse interpretations of *Amoris Laetitia*. Just as he has never responded to the very serious charges that Archbishop Viganò made in his famous manifesto about the pope's complicity in ignoring the discipline that the sexual predator Cardinal McCarrick was under and continuing to consult him as an advisor on American episcopal appointments[297] and as a diplomat in negotiating the infamous China agreement with Beijing. Just as he never gave a reason for ordering Cardinal Mueller to fire three of his most loyal and competent priest assistants at the Congregation for the Doctrine of the Faith. Just as he has never given a really adequate public explanation of the famous "Who am I to judge" statement. When extremely troubling issues arise that seem to implicate Pope Francis directly, he refuses to respond. Rather than "confirming his brethren in the faith" (see Luke 22:32), Pope Francis seems to stir up division and confusion which he refuses to address.

THE CHURCH AND CHINA

For many years, the Catholic Church in China has been in a difficult and divided position. There was that branch of the Church which included a considerable number of bishops and dioceses who accepted the Communist Party's orders to join the official, state-authorized Patriotic Church Association, which was under the control of lay communist officials from the Religious Affairs Bureau and "safe" bishops appointed by the party who were expected to go along with the goals of the party, which included accepting the government's encouragement of contraception and abortion. It also included the demand not to be guided by Rome. The bishops recognized by the Chinese government are expected to be openly subservient. Bishop Fang Xingyao, who is a member of the Standing Committee of the National Committee of the Chinese People's Political Consultative Conference and president of the Chinese Catholic Patriotic Association and vice president of the Council of Chinese Bishops, recently declared at a Communist Party meeting called to discuss religion and the state, "Love for the homeland must be greater than the love for the Church and the law of the country is above canon law."[298]

And then there was the "underground church," which felt like they couldn't be faithful to Christ, the Catholic Church, and in a special way, the pope, if they accepted the Communist Party's control. There were a considerable number of bishops and dioceses in this situation. They suffered greatly and had to carry out ordinations in secret, and the faithful bishops often "disappeared" or spent long years in jail or under house arrest.

And then there was a middle group of bishops and dioceses who, because of reasonably friendly regional and local communist officials, were able to balance between the demands of the government and fidelity to Rome.

That all changed when the Vatican made a secret agreement with the Chinese government that gave the government a role in choosing bishops, with the pope approving them. Right after the agreement was reached, however, the level of persecution ratcheted up. The Chinese government decreed that all churches needed to be engaged in "sinicization," becoming truly Chinese, and support the goals of the party. Depending on the region, churches were bulldozed, crosses were torn down, and young people were forbidden to go to church services, in an attempt to prevent the faith from being passed to the next generation.

On February 1, 2020, a new set of regulations governing religious bodies went into effect that required every gathering and activity of any religious body to have the permission of government officials and required every religion to educate their members to "spread the principles and policies of the Chinese Communist party, implementing the values of socialism." As one Catholic priest in China put it: "In practice, your religion no longer matters. If you are Buddhist, or Taoist, or Muslim or Christian: the only religion allowed is faith in the Chinese Communist Party."[299] Another priest commented: "The CCP's purpose is very clear. It is to change the Catholic Church into a group that belongs to them. These rules will push the Church into serious dangers . . . ever since the rules were introduced, the Christian community in China has been witnessing relentless persecution, with churches being demolished, a ban imposed on online Bible sales, and several hundreds of Christians arrested for inciting subversion of state power."[300] When the churches were allowed limited reopenings after the coronavirus shut them down, new demands were made on churches desiring to reopen: a requirement that churches must now preach on "patriotism" in connection with the liturgy in order to reopen, which is seen by many concerned Chinese Catholics as another attempt to make the churches subservient to the Communist Party and its goals.[301]

Cardinal Zen, former archbishop of Hong Kong, continually warned against the naiveté of making this agreement and to this day opposes it.[302] And, up to now, the secret agreement has not been disclosed even to Cardinal Zen. If you judge a situation not by what is said but by what is done, this agreement has been a disaster. Betrayal of the underground Church may not be too strong a word to describe the outcome of the agreement. There is a relentless crackdown on anyone who resists Chinese Communist Party policies. One brave underground pastor protested the Chinese policy of forced abortions and "disappeared" for quite some time and then was stripped of his rights as a citizen and fined heavily.[303] There are many cases like this. As part of the agreement, the part that we know because it couldn't be hidden, faithful underground bishops were required to resign in favor of government-approved bishops.

What is extremely puzzling is that, in light of the post-agreement acceleration of persecution[304] of the Church in China, the Vatican has remained completely silent, with no defense or voice for those being persecuted. Another instance of what appears to be a policy: ignore criticism, even when it comes from cardinals and leading theologians, and keep moving on with the agenda. As Robert Royal put it:

> How long can the Vatican remain silent about the Chinese repression in Hong Kong and about reports of persecution and re-education camps for religious believers in the rest of China? . . . We cannot allow our desire for better relations—with China, the Muslim world, or the secular forces in our midst—to stop us from speaking some hard truths and acting on them. Anything less will spell further suffering and death to the very people we have the responsibility to protect. . . . To call out the perpetrators and the governments that often enable them would require some tough talk that doesn't just say, sentimentally, that we all seek the same common good and need to practice dialogue.[305]

George Weigel has this to say about both the Vatican agreement with China and a recent letter from Cardinal Re rebuking Cardinal Zen for his continued opposition to the "China agreement":

Perseverance on a difficult but noble path is a virtue. Stubbornness when confronted by irrefutable evidence of a grave mistake is a vice. . . . The bloom is off the Chinese rose just about everywhere in the world. So it is more than disturbing that the Holy See should be doubling down on what everyone (except those directly involved in cutting it) thinks is a very bad deal.[306]

Renewal Ministries has done work in China for many years; I myself have been there and continue to have contact with key people. Our seminary has had seminarians from China for many years, and I believe my account of the situation here is accurate, sad and troubling as it sounds. And even as I write this, numerous reports are being published that indicate an intensified level of persecution. Chinese Christians depending on government aid because of disability or other reasons are being told in many provinces that they must remove Christian images from their homes and replace them with portraits of Chairman Mao and President Xi Jinping.[307]

And it is not only the Christians who are suffering. There have been mass roundups and deportations to "reeducation camps" of ethnic Muslims in the West of China. *The New York Times* obtained secret government documents describing in great detail how to explain to students returning to the region from study in other parts of China or overseas why their relatives and family members were missing. The documents order officials to claim that these are job-training centers meant to counter Islamic extremism. Government officials that resisted were arrested and imprisoned. Disillusioned government officials are suspected as the source of the unprecedented leaks of 403 pages of internal documents directing how to handle the imprisonments and how to explain them publicly, many of them personally signed by President Xi.[308]

CAN'T WE SEE WHERE THIS PATH LEADS?

Are we blind? Can't we see that the accommodation of Christian churches to the incessant demands of the sexual revolution, the secular state, and international governmental organizations has already been tried and has been a catastrophic failure?

Liberal Protestantism, when faced with a growing gap between traditional Christian belief and the rapidly secularizing culture, opted to "reinterpret" Scripture and tradition to make them more acceptable to "modern man," as many in the Church are trying to do today. Up until the 1930s, all the Christian churches, Protestant, Orthodox, and Catholic, strongly upheld the essential link between sexual union in a marriage between one man and one woman, "until death do us part," and the openness to life. All the churches forbade artificial contraception until the Anglican Church changed its position in 1930 and allowed limited use of contraception. The limits soon disappeared. And then the dominos began to fall, not only in the other mainline Protestant churches on this issue, but on other issues as well. Now we've reached the point where the Primate of the Anglican Church, the Archbishop of Canterbury, can't give a straight answer on the moral implications of homosexual activity, and the Anglican Church has now well-established exceptions to justify divorce and remarriage and have de facto accepted the widespread blessings of homosexual unions, including among Anglican clergy. The Episcopal Church in the United States is even further down the road. And the results are all the same: radical decline in numbers, continuing dissolution of any clarity of what the Church stands for, and contrary to Cardinal Dolan's warning that while everyone is welcome, not anything goes, the actual practice and belief of these churches has degenerated to the point of everyone being welcome and anything goes, as long as it's between consenting adults, which is pretty much the only morality we have left as a culture. The world has not embraced the Church as a result of these concessions but has rightly concluded, that "at last, the Church is becoming reasonable and getting on the right side of history." The world will never admire us for our apostasy but will pity us for how long it took for us to do it and congratulate itself on persevering in its pressure until we finally have seen the light. And yet this "light" is the darkness and blindness that Jesus warned about. How pathetic!

Can't we see that a focus on improving this world, with its radical de-emphasis on the eternal perspective of sin and salvation, redemption and judgment, death and resurrection, has already been tried, and with catastrophic results? Are we so blind as to want to follow this path again?

One of the most amazing recent developments is that a number of aggressive atheists are beginning to see the horror of a totally de-Christianized culture and are starting to acknowledge, without themselves claiming to have become believers, that Christianity contributed some great value to our lives and many of the progressive ideals came to birth only as a result of Christianity.

Historian Tom Holland surprised people in a new book, since he is not a Christian but his book "is one of the most ambitious historical defenses of Christianity in a very long time":[309]

> Even the claims of the social justice warriors who despise the faith of their ancestors rest on a foundation of Judeo-Christian values. Those who make arguments based on love, tolerance, and compassion are borrowing fundamentally Christian arguments. If the West had not become Christian, Holland writes, "no one would have gotten woke."[310]

Douglas Murray, author of the book *The Madness of Crowds*, which we have referenced earlier, now calls himself a Christian atheist, acknowledging the great value that the Judeo-Christian reality brought to all of human life. He thinks that society now faces three options: first, reject the idea that all human life is precious. "Another is to work furiously to nail down an atheist version of the sanctity of the individual." And if that doesn't work? "Then there is only one other place to go. Which is back to faith, whether we like it or not."[311]

The author of the article discussing Holland and Murray also quotes Richard Dawkins, Jordan Peterson, Sir Roger Scruton, and Charles Murray, despite their own unbelief or vague belief, in acknowledging the positive influence of Christianity on Western culture. All these figures are delivering a warning to the West:

> Without Christianity, we are heading into a thick and impenetrable darkness. Christianity gave us human rights. It gave us protection for the weak. Compassion rooted in commands to love. Forgiveness for enemies. It revolutionized the world. We are now in the process of undoing that revolution. In fact, we are replacing it with the Sexual Revolution.[312]

The newly emerging forms of the old liberation theology, with its almost exclusive emphasis on "this world" and "the cries of Mother Earth" and so little emphasis on the world to come, will come to the same end that our first attempt to do this did.

When the Latin American Church in its regional assemblies made its "option for the poor," its focus on political and economic improvement with its open acceptance of Marxist influence, the door was open for evangelical and Pentecostal churches to lead people to that encounter with Christ that the human soul most hungers for. As someone put it, while the Catholic Church was opting for the poor, the poor were opting for churches where they could hear the

Gospel preached and worship the one true God in Spirit and truth.

In an article that appeared in the largest secular Argentinian newspaper, there was a blunt and very interesting conversation with a prominent evangelical pastor:

> When your liberation theology appeared, more than 90 percent of Brazilians were Catholic. Now they are at 50 percent and falling. Brazilians, especially the poor, rejected your theo-marxism and ran for the evangelical churches, where they could praise Jesus Christ. . . . We grow because we preach, without timidity and without fear. We preach in the street, on TV, on the radio. We preach to our neighbor. We speak about the love of God to our relatives. . . . When you convert to the evangelical faith, we are stimulated to fulfill the way of Jesus, who said, "Go to all the world and preach the Gospel to every creature." . . . That is why we grow.[313]

The statistics of the decline of membership in the Catholic Church and the rise of evangelical and Pentecostal churches are very similar throughout Central and South America, and even among Hispanics in the United States.[314] When will we learn? Are we blind? Is there a veil over our eyes that keeps us from seeing reality? Are we about to double down on what led to the current ongoing catastrophic collapse of the Catholic Church in Latin America? All of the "horizontal" values of Christianity—care for the present structures of this world and its people, making this world a better place—are essentially linked to the faith, but they are not primary. The primary commission the Lord gave to the Church is the salvation of souls and rescuing the earth's inhabitants from the eternal catastrophe of hell. What does it profit a man to save the Amazon but lose his soul?

We need to preach clearly and boldly the call to repentance and conversion, not only for environmental sins, which indeed can be real and serious, but also for sins of blasphemy, idolatry, fornication, adultery, all forms of sexual uncleanness and perversion, drunkenness, hatred, superstition, occult involvement, self-worship, worship of nature, refusal to forgive, and so forth.

It's time to tell people the truth again. It's time for bold, prophetic preaching and teaching. We are fools if we continue down these well-worn and treacherous paths which have seen the shipwreck of so many even in our lifetime. These paths, these strategies, continue to send people out on the broad way that leads to destruction and hide from them the narrow door and path that leads to real life. We can't stand by while demonic deceptions, dark blindness, and outright stupidity jeopardize the salvation of so many.

Chapter 6

IS ANYONE RESPONSIBLE?

The heart is deceitful above all things, and desperately corrupt; who can understand it? "I the LORD search the mind and try the heart, to give every man according to his ways, according to the fruit of his doings." (Jer 17:9–10)

WE ARE LIVING in a culture which often communicates that nobody is responsible and everyone is a victim and that forces beyond our control are overwhelming our will and determining our actions, so "we are not really responsible." The increasingly common pressure in youth sports to not focus on the actual outcomes of games but rather to award trophies to everyone just for participating may have some positive features to it, but not when it comes to the final outcomes of human lives. When it comes to the ferocious battle of kingdoms that we find ourselves in the midst of, there are clear-cut winners and losers, the saved and the damned. One of the background presumptions that undermines conviction about the importance of what God's Word reveals concerning salvation, including sexual morality, is that even though these things may be objectively seriously wrong, the conditions for them to be subjectively seriously wrong—and culpable—are so demanding that most people who do these things are probably not really culpable.

The statement of the Malta bishops in their response to *Amoris*

Laetitia speaks of this:

> Throughout the discernment process, we need to weigh
> the moral responsibility in particular situations, with due
> consideration to the conditioning restraints and atten-
> uating circumstances. Indeed, "factors may exist which
> limit the ability to make a decision," (AL 301) or even di-
> minish imputability or responsibility for an action. These
> include ignorance, inadvertence, violence, fear, affective
> immaturity, the persistence of certain habits, the state of
> anxiety, inordinate attachments, and other psychological
> and social factors (see AL 302; CCC 1735, 2352). As a
> result of these conditioning restraints and attenuating cir-
> cumstances, the Pope teaches that "it can no longer simply
> be said that all those in any 'irregular situation are living
> in a state of mortal sin and are deprived of sanctifying
> grace" (AL 301). "It is possible that in an objective situ-
> ation of sin—which may not be subjectively culpable, or
> fully such—a person can be living in God's grace, can love
> and can also grow in the life of grace and charity, while
> receiving the Church's help to this end" (AL 305). This
> discernment acquires significant importance since, as the
> Pope teaches, in some cases this help can include the help
> of the sacraments (see AL, note 351).

> "By thinking that everything is black and white, we some-
> times close off the way of grace and of growth, and discour-
> age paths of sanctification which give glory to God" (AL
> 305). This calls for more prudent instruction in the law of
> gradualness, (see AL 295) in order to discern the presence,
> the grace and the working of God in all situations, and
> help people approach closer to God, even when "not in a

position to understand, appreciate, or fully carry out the objective demands of the law" (AL 295). [315]

Yes, there are factors that may diminish culpability. Yes, accompanying people means working with them, discerning where God's grace is stirring in their lives, but with the goal of helping them come to the repentance and amendment of life that is necessary in order to be reconciled with the Lord and the Church and receive Communion. When I expressed my deep concern to a friend who serves the Church in Rome that it seemed like influential Church leaders were downplaying the seriousness of sexual sin, despite what Scripture and the Church teach, he shared his understanding of the situation. He confirmed that indeed sexual morality was being downplayed in an effort to appeal to today's culture, but also perhaps because the Church has "winked" at sexual sins in various Latin cultures. He also said that many leaders believe that hardly anyone is really culpable for sexual sins "because men are so weak," even though, theoretically, we believe these are grave sins. At root, it's a crisis of faith, not believing that with the help of grace, people are able to repent and change their lives.

This came to my attention in a vivid way one day while teaching a course in our STL program at Sacred Heart Major Seminary in Detroit.[316] I was conducting a seminar on the stages of spiritual growth for a class made up entirely of priests. When we were working on the concept of what Scripture says about sins that will exclude us from entering the kingdom—mortal sins—one of the priests spoke up in class and said something quite remarkable, both for its honesty and for its implications for understanding some truths about culpability.

He said to his fellow priests: "Let's face it. Sometimes we use the three conditions that are necessary to commit a mortal sin as a way to rationalize a choice we actually make to sin. We deceive ourselves into thinking that the gravely wrong action that we are doing isn't being done with sufficient reflection or full consent of the will when in fact we are actually freely choosing to do it, although with less-than-full consciousness. Although sufficient reflection and full consent can happen in an instant, we often try to cover over our truly free choice to do a bad action with rationalization and self-justification."[317]

And, of course, the controversy around the proper interpretation of *Amoris Laetitia* has put the question of objective wrongdoing accompanied by a lack of personal culpability front and center.

As Pope Francis put it and as was cited by the Maltese bishops:

Hence it can no longer simply be said that all those in any irregular situations are living in a state of mortal sin and are deprived of sanctifying grace. More is involved here than mere ignorance of the rule. A subject may know full well the rule, yet have great difficulty in understanding its inherent values, or be in a concrete situation which does not allow him or her to act differently and decide otherwise without further sin.[318]

This statement has led some cardinals, bishops, and bishops' conferences to suggest that as an outcome of pastoral counseling, couples who have divorced and remarried, without submitting the situation of their first marriage to the judgment of the Church to see if they qualify for an annulment, may be given permission to "follow their conscience" if they feel at peace about receiving Communion despite their irregular situation. Other cardinals, bishops, and bishops' conferences have concluded that these interpretations are not in harmony with the teaching of the Church or the teaching of Pope Francis's immediate predecessors.

While the focus of properly weighing "mitigating circumstances" has been almost exclusively directed to the situation of the divorced and remarried, it has been noted by various commentators that this principle can also be applied to other irregular situations, such as same-sex relationships.

As we noted in a previous chapter, this possibility has been explicitly affirmed in an interview that Cardinal Cupich gave that appeared in the *Chicago Tribune*. He made the logical point that if the objective wrong but subjective lack of culpability principle could be broadly applied to the case of the divorced and remarried, it must, of course, also be applicable to other irregular situations, such as same-sex relationships. "You can't have one particular approach for a certain group of people and not for everybody. Everyone has the ability to form their conscience well."[319]

It is not my intention in this chapter to directly address the issues as they are presented in *Amoris Laetitia* and the ensuing contradictory interpretations of it; we have already done that to some extent in earlier chapters. In this chapter, I want to explore the implications of the comment of my priest-student cited above. One of the main points I will be making is that, particularly in matters of sexual morality, deception and self-deception are easy to fall into, and this propensity needs to be taken into serious account in judging our own culpability in a particular matter or in guiding others in assessing their own culpability. Another point I will make is that, even in cases of invincible ignorance or severely diminished culpability, and whatever the gravely wrong sins that are being committed may be, the pastoral response needs to be not primarily focused on determining culpability but calling to a full life in Christ, to repentance and faith and life in the Holy Spirit. Even in cases where there may be no subjective culpability, the gravely wrong actions that may have inculpably been committed are objectively damaging to souls and bodies and nevertheless need to be turned away from and replaced with a holy way of life.

What Does the Church Teach?

There is a widespread presumption in the general atmosphere of the Church today that the conditions necessary to commit a truly culpable mortal sin are so stringent that such sins must be very rare. It's not uncommon for people to say things like this: "I've never killed anyone, so I'm ok," or, "I'm not a serial killer, or I've never committed adultery, so I'm ok." Whether we're ok or not is ultimately for God to judge, but by citing things we haven't done, we minimize those things we have done that may not even be on our radar but may be very grave, for example, not loving the Lord our God with our whole soul, mind, and heart, and our neighbor as ourself! In an insightful article, a German writer pointed out how focus on the horror of the Holocaust sometimes has the result of giving the impression that the only really horrendous sin is behind us and everything from then on is pretty minor:

> The danger of a violent hubris arises from the idea of a unique guilt. If the worst possible crime is behind us, then nothing that lies before us can ever compare. Everything that comes after Auschwitz (or colonialism, or whatever other "unique" debt may be found) has the character of a mere post-history, a *posthistoire*. This is the secret maximal permission hidden in the maxima culpa of a history without God. Nothing that we can do will ever be as terrible as the Holocaust. This relaxes our moral vigilance and introduces the idea that everything is allowed—as if there were no God.[320]

For that reason, my priest-student, in a flash of illumination, felt the need to call out himself and his fellow priests as willing participants in self-deception regarding their culpability and that of others. In this chapter, then, we will first examine what the Church actually teaches about the reality of mortal sin, as represented by the teaching of the *Catechism of the Catholic Church*, and then consider what light can be thrown on this teaching through the examination of a few of the most relevant Scriptures. Our goal is to identify some truths that can be helpful in our own lives and in our pastoral responsibilities. I will put in bold type some statements of the *Catechism* that are little known or commented on.

We find the Church's teaching on mortal sin—which sums up the moral reflection of the Church through the centuries—in sections 1857–1861 of the *Catechism*:

> For a *sin* to be *mortal*, three conditions must together be met: "Mortal sin is sin whose object is grave matter and which is also committed with full knowledge and deliberate consent."

> *Grave matter* is specified by the Ten Commandments, corresponding to the answer of Jesus to the rich young man: "Do not kill, Do not commit adultery, Do not steal, Do not bear false witness, Do not defraud, Honor your father and your mother." The gravity of sins is more or less great: murder is graver than theft. One must also take into account who is wronged: violence against parents is in itself graver than violence against a stranger.

> Mortal sin requires *full knowledge* and *complete consent*. It presupposes knowledge of the sinful character of the act, of its opposition to God's law. **It also implies a consent sufficiently deliberate to be a personal choice. Feigned ignorance and hardness of heart do not diminish, but rather increase, the voluntary character of a sin.**[321]

The *Catechism* elsewhere, when discussing the deception of the

Antichrist during the final trial of the Church, acknowledges the reality of "culpable unbelief":

> Then will the conduct of each one and the secrets of hearts be brought to light. (Mark 12:38–40; Luke 12:1–3; John 3:20–21; Rom 2:16; 1 Cor 4:5) Then will the culpable unbelief that accounted the offer of God's grace as nothing be condemned. (Matt 11:20,24; 12:41–42)[322]

The gravely wrong actions that my priest-student was referring to were actions that included full knowledge of the gravity of the sin but, because of what appears to be "self-deception," denied that a "sufficiently deliberate . . . personal choice" had been made. The example given by this priest would seem, then, to be a case of "feigned ignorance" that actually worsens the gravity of the sin. We will examine "feigned ignorance" later on in this chapter. We will also see clearly that Scripture provides many cases where the hardness of heart that results in the rejection of Jesus's teaching is clearly thought to be culpable.

CULPABILITY

> *Unintentional ignorance* can diminish or even remove the imputability of a grave offense. **But no one is deemed to be ignorant of the principles of the moral law, which are written in the conscience of every man.** The promptings of feelings and passions can also diminish the voluntary and free character of the offense, as can external pressures or pathological disorders. Sin committed through malice, by deliberate choice of evil, is the gravest.[323]

First, let me acknowledge that potential cases of inculpable ignorance regarding the commission of grave sins seem to be on the rise. For example, I have talked to young people who were shocked to discover that masturbation was considered to be a grave sin—so accepted has this become in our culture. I have also talked to married couples who were shocked to discover that contraception was considered to be a grave sin—so commonly accepted in our culture, and so little spoken of in our churches, has this become. And who can fully comprehend the horror of children who are exposed to grave forms of evil and even drawn into them at a very young age, who certainly have very diminished culpability, if any at all. It becomes understandable why some moral theologians have sometimes counseled that such apparently inculpable ignorance should not be disturbed by informing such people of the truth. I will suggest later in this chapter that this is not really a merciful approach to dealing with situations like this.

Also, it is important to note that the *Catechism* says that "no one is deemed to be ignorant of the principles of the moral law, which are written in the conscience of every man." While the implications of the moral law for masturbation and contraception may not be immediately apparent to many, nevertheless the "grave matter" specified by the ten commandments is held by the Church—and Scripture—to be given by God to every human conscience. We will examine briefly the foundation of this teaching in Romans 1 and 2.

The *Catechism* further addresses the question of culpable ignorance:

> This ignorance can often be imputed to personal responsibility. This is the case when a man "takes little trouble to find out what is true and good, or when conscience is by degrees almost blinded through the habit of committing sin" (*Gaudium et Spes* 16). In such cases, the person is culpable for the evil he commits.[324]

In my contact with many Catholics in many dioceses, I have been astounded to discover how widespread disdain for Church teaching and the teaching of Scripture has become in the name of "being an adult and making my own decisions about what seems right to me" and how little concern is evidenced to "find out what is true and good." After giving talks on some of the more challenging aspects of the teachings of Jesus, I frequently hear such comments as these: "My Jesus would never say that!" or, "That isn't what I've heard Pope Francis say!" or, "I'm supposed to follow my own conscience, and I feel fine about what I'm doing, and besides, the Church has to change with the times!" I believe that such approaches cloak a troublesome lack of fear of the Lord, of regard for the person of Jesus Christ, of a sincere desire to find the truth and submit to it, and a foolish presumption about virtually universal salvation.

The second instance in which ignorance does not excuse is an ignorance that is the result of the habit of committing sin. Many people, when they first commit an act of adultery, for instance, or who steal to support a drug habit, know perfectly well that they are sinning, but over time, begin to be indifferent to the concept of sin and can even come to justify their actions. Their sinful habit has almost obscured their consciences. Since the obscuring is a result of their own sinful choices, their ignorance does not excuse them from culpability.

What the Catechism Teaches about Mortal Sin

Mortal sin is a radical possibility of human freedom, as is love itself. It results in the loss of charity and the privation of sanctifying grace, that is, of the state of grace. **If it is not redeemed by repentance and God's forgiveness, it causes**

> **exclusion from Christ's kingdom and the eternal death**
> **of hell, for our freedom has the power to make choices**
> **for ever, with no turning back. However, although we**
> **can judge that an act is in itself a grave offense, we must**
> **entrust judgment of persons to the justice and mercy of**
> **God.**[325]

Since only God can really know the conscience of a person and their degree of culpability, and since self-deception and hardness of heart and feigned ignorance are quite common, it would be foolish for anyone entrusted with the pastoral care of such persons to presume inculpability—just as it would be foolish to presume culpability. After a time of "pastoral accompaniment," we may or may not have some idea of the degree of culpability, but in every case when people are committing objectively gravely wrong acts, they are harming themselves—and others if the acts involve others—and very well could be endangering their eternal salvation. This is why I am suggesting that the focus of our pastoral care and general concern for others should not be on determining culpability but on calling people to turn away from their gravely sinful (even if not subjectively culpable) actions. I say this with the understanding that, from time to time, it is important, particularly for priests in the confessional, to make some determination of culpability in order to discern appropriate penances or to assuage false guilt and scrupulosity.

It seems good here to underline the two important principles enunciated by this article of the *Catechism*. First of all, the sins explicitly listed in Scripture of being of such gravity to exclude persons who commit them from the kingdom of God if they don't repent (and the adumbrations of these sins as discerned by the Church in the natural law and its subsequent moral reflection) are to be clearly understood and used as a criterion for judging the objective rightness or wrongness of our own and others' actions. But secondly, again based on the witness of Scripture and Church teaching, only God in the last analysis can truly judge the degree of personal culpability involved in a particular person's actions and determine the implications for the eternal consequences in question here. So, Pope Francis's famous declaration, "Who am I to judge?" is absolutely true as it pertains to ascertaining personal culpability, as it seems he intended, but absolutely untrue if used, as it seems he clearly wasn't intending, to cast any doubt on the objective rightness or wrongness of particular actions. Pope Francis's statement was not intended to say that the previous homosexual acts that may have been committed by the person in question were not gravely wrong and did not require full repentance along with a firm purpose to never commit them again, but, unfortunately, the lack of precision at the time let his comment go "viral," and his subsequent informal clarifications never had the same impact. Let's consider now what Scripture tells us about culpability and serious sin.

THE WITNESS OF SCRIPTURE

The overall sense one gets from the Old Testament is that sin is punished—most often in a way that seems severe—and yet God is always ready to take his people back and show them compassion if they repent. Another recurring theme of the Old Testament is that when human beings culpably sin, they have a strong tendency to deny responsibility. The blame shifting in the garden, where Eve shifts the blame to the serpent and Adam blames both the woman and the Lord for his participation in the grave sin of disobedience and rebellion, is one primary example. God does not accept their excuses or claims of not being culpable and they (and all of humanity) suffer the very painful consequences. Moses is punished for striking the rock twice, an expression of distrust in the word of the Lord, and as a consequence, is forbidden to enter the Promised Land. Saul, among other failures, thinks he has a better idea than the Lord and disobeys in keeping some of the spoils of war and loses the kingship. David, specially chosen by the Lord, does great evil by committing adultery and murder and only repents when confronted by Nathan. While David is forgiven because of his sincere repentance and penance, the punishment is nevertheless severe: the death of the child and endless disunity and rebellion in his own household.

The story of Susanna and the unjust judges in the Book of Daniel portrays, in a striking manner, the corruption of conscience that can occur as one sin leads to another. The injustice of the judges' court rulings, perhaps motivated by greed, forms part of a complex of sins, involving lust and false witness, and leads ultimately to their undoing and their own deaths as punishment for their sins. I will put in bold type parts of the text that are particularly relevant to our considerations.

> They began to desire her. **And they perverted their minds and turned away their eyes from looking to Heaven or remembering righteous judgments.** (Dan 13:8–9)

This is clearly portrayed as a culpable giving in to lust and the willful suppression of their knowledge of "righteous judgments," with their death as the punishment.

The New Testament tells us that these examples, and many more, are preserved in Scripture for us as a warning:

> I want you to know, brethren, that our fathers were all under the cloud, and all passed through the sea, and all were baptized into Moses in the cloud and in the sea, and all ate the same supernatural food and all drank the same supernatural drink. For they drank from the supernatural Rock which followed them, and the Rock was Christ. Nev-

ertheless with most of them God was not pleased; for they were overthrown in the wilderness. Now these things are warnings for us, not to desire evil as they did. Do not be idolaters as some of them were; as it is written, "The people sat down to eat and drink and rose up to dance." We must not indulge in immorality as some of them did, and twenty-three thousand fell in a single day. We must not put the Lord to the test, as some of them did and were destroyed by serpents; nor grumble, as some of them did and were destroyed by the Destroyer. Now these things happened to them as a warning, but they were written down for our instruction, upon whom the end of the ages has come. Therefore let any one who thinks that he stands take heed lest he fall. (1 Cor 10:1–12)

It is unfortunately common for many people today to dismiss the Old Testament as outmoded in some of its essential moral teaching, when, in fact, it is solemnly reaffirmed in the teaching of Jesus and the Apostles and faithfully transmitted to this day in the *Catechism of the Catholic Church*.

Putting Christ to the test by flagrantly dismissing his teaching in the area of sexual morality is indeed an incredibly foolish thing to do. This is a mocking of God that will inevitably have severe consequences. Sexual immorality is punished in two ways, in the wretched consequences in this life—to which people enmeshed in these sins are often blinded—and, if unrepented, in the loss of eternal life:

Do not be deceived; God is not mocked, for whatever a man sows, that he will also reap. For he who sows to his own flesh will from the flesh reap corruption; but he who sows to the Spirit will from the Spirit reap eternal life. And let us not grow weary in well-doing, for in due season we shall reap, if we do not lose heart. (Gal 6:7–9)

Romans 1, a text we looked at earlier but which we now need to consider again in greater detail, also talks about a culpable suppression of the truth that leads to every kind of disorder, with very dire consequences. I have put parts of the text that are of particular interest in bold type, although the whole text is quite remarkable for the light it sheds on our current cultural situation, and it is well worth rereading slowly and meditating on:

> For the wrath of God is revealed from heaven against all ungodliness and wickedness of men **who by their wickedness suppress the truth.** For what can be known about God is plain to them, because **God has shown it to them.** Ever since the creation of the world his invisible nature, namely, his eternal power and deity, has been clearly perceived in the things that have been made. **So they are without excuse;** for although they knew God they did not honor him as God or give thanks to him, but **they became futile in their thinking and their senseless minds were darkened.** Claiming to be wise, they became fools, and exchanged the glory of the immortal God for images resembling mortal man or birds or animals or reptiles. **Therefore God gave them up in the lusts of their hearts to impurity, to the dishonoring of their bodies among themselves, because they exchanged the truth about God for a lie and worshiped and served the creature rather than the Creator,** who is blessed for ever! Amen. For this reason God gave them up to dishonorable passions. Their women exchanged natural relations for unnatural, and the men likewise gave up natural relations with women and were consumed with passion for one another, men com-

mitting shameless acts with men and receiving in their own persons the due penalty for their error. **And since they did not see fit to acknowledge God, God gave them up to a base mind and to improper conduct. . . .** [They are] faithless, heartless, ruthless. **Though they know God's decree that those who do such things deserve to die, they not only do them but approve those who practice them.** (Rom 1:18–32)

It's important to note how culpability is explicitly attributed to those spoken about in Romans 1. Indeed, what we have here is a relentless indictment of culpability. Similar to the case of Susanna and the elders who gave in to disordered desires and culpably suppressed the truth, Romans 1 asserts that God has revealed himself in some perceptible fashion to every human being and so no one is without culpability if this revelation is ignored or suppressed or actually rejected in favor of sinful actions. The sign of their rejection of the truth revealed by God and their refusal to worship him is their addiction to immoral behavior, characterized by homosexual activity and the approval in others of these behaviors, as well as many other wicked behaviors. Satan, the rebellious one, whose very identity is formed by rejecting the authority of God, desires to be worshipped, and he is working in our culture to require all to bow down to the purported "goodness" of these wicked behaviors. Those who place themselves above the authority of God and his revelation desperately want to be affirmed in their behavior and won't rest until they compel everyone to do so. The Roman emperors required this submission of the early Christians from time to time, and it produced thousands of Christian martyrs. There is a tremendous pressure on the Church and all her members and ministers today to blur the truth about these matters to avoid a confrontation with a culture that will not rest until they label us "enemies of the state, enemies of equality, haters."

Romans 1 and Romans 2, as we will see shortly, convey relentless indictments of the culpable suppression of the truth, that feigned ignorance and hardness of heart that the *Catechism* warns about and to which the priest-student in my class shockingly called our attention.

Romans 2 declares that people will be judged on the basis of the light that they have been given. It is the clear teaching of the Church throughout the ages, based on Scripture, that light is given to every human being, and how they respond to that light determines their eternal destinies. This is a basis for what the *Catechism* asserts in §1860: "But no one is deemed to be ignorant of the principles of the moral law, which are written in the conscience of every man." In commenting on Romans 2:15, Cardinal Ratzinger pointed out: "The whole theory of salvation through ignorance breaks apart with this verse."[326]

As familiar as this text from Romans may be, it is well worth reflecting on carefully as it is relevant to these considerations on culpability:

> **By your hard and impenitent heart you are storing up wrath** for yourself on the day of wrath when God's righteous judgment will be revealed. For he will render to every man according to his works: to those who by patience in well-doing seek for glory and honor and immortality, he will give eternal life; but **for those who are factious and do not obey the truth, but obey wickedness, there will be wrath and fury.** There will be tribulation and distress for every human being who does evil, the Jew first and also the Greek, but glory and honor and peace for every one who does good, the Jew first and also the Greek. For God shows no partiality. All who have sinned without the law will also perish without the law, and all who have sinned

under the law will be judged by the law. **For it is not the hearers of the law who are righteous before God, but the doers of the law who will be justified.** When Gentiles who have not the law do by nature what the law requires, they are a law to themselves, even though they do not have the law. They show that what the law requires is written on their hearts, while their conscience also bears witness and their conflicting thoughts accuse or perhaps excuse them on that day when, according to my gospel, God judges the secrets of men by Christ Jesus. (Rom 2:5–16)

It is important not to overlook in the texts above the supreme importance of obedience to the light that God gives to everyone, to the witness of conscience, to the universal knowability of the natural law and to the explicit Word of God. While obedience is a virtue that is widely mocked in our culture in the name of a personal freedom that often leads to deep bondage and blindness, it is essential for accessing the mercy of God. God's mercy is profound, but it must be gratefully received with faith, responded to with repentance, and lived out in obedience to the revelation of God:

Although he was a Son, he learned obedience through what he suffered; and being made perfect he became the source of eternal salvation to all who obey him. (Heb 5:8–9)

He who believes in the Son has eternal life; he who does not obey the Son shall not see life, but the wrath of God rests upon him. (John 3:36)

And we are witnesses to these things, and so is the Holy Spirit whom God has given to those who obey him. (Acts 5:32)

I think it is fair to say that the **emphasis** of the Bible is not on determining culpability or degrees of culpability but on clearly calling everyone to a life of obedience to God. There is a focus on teaching and demonstrating that committing grave sin is severely punished, both in this life and in the life to come. I would go even further and suggest that the thrust of Scripture in both the Old and New Testaments is to presume widespread culpability along with widespread self-deception, and the rationalizing, blame shifting, and justification for sins that are intrinsic to fallen human beings. This was what the priest in my class was bravely acknowledging in admitting to self-deception in supposedly not giving sufficient personal consent to certain sins. The sobering declaration in the verse above—"for those who are factious and do not obey the truth, but obey wickedness, there will be wrath and fury" (Rom 2:8)—certainly seems to indicate that "giving in" to selfish, lustful, rebellious desires risks eternal damnation if not repented from before death. The culpable suppression of the truth and of conscience mentioned in the story of Susanna and in Romans 1 would seem to be an easy enough thing to do when tempted by pride, lust, greed, or rebellion—as we frequently are.

Where there is some acknowledgement of lessened culpability in Scripture, the actual texts can sometimes be disconcerting:

> But if that servant says to himself, "My master is delayed in coming," and begins to beat the menservants and the maidservants, and to eat and drink and get drunk, the master of that servant will come on a day when he does not expect him and at an hour he does not know, and will punish him, and put him with the unfaithful. And that servant who knew his master's will, but did not make ready or act according to his will, shall receive a severe beating. But he who did not know, and did what deserved a beating,

shall receive a light beating. Every one to whom much is given, of him will much be required; and of him to whom men commit much they will demand the more. (Luke 12:45–48)

Jesus makes clear that truly invincible ignorance is excusable, but now that God has clearly revealed his will in Jesus, those who hear the teaching of Jesus are without excuse:

If I had not come and spoken to them, they would not have sin; but now they have no excuse for their sin. (John 15:22)

Even before his resurrection, Jesus knew that, even after his resurrection and the remarkable continuation of signs and wonders that would testify to his identity, many would still not believe and be culpable for their unbelief. When the rich man found himself in hell, he pleaded that someone go and warn his brothers so they would not suffer the same fate:

But Abraham said, "They have Moses and the prophets; let them hear them." And he said, "No, father Abraham; but if some one goes to them from the dead, they will repent." He said to him, "If they do not hear Moses and the prophets, neither will they be convinced if some one should rise from the dead." (Luke 16:29–31)

Paul teaches the same principle in his speech to the Athenians:

The times of ignorance God overlooked, but now he commands all men everywhere to repent, because he has fixed a day on which he will judge the world in righteousness by a man whom he has appointed, and of this he has given assurance to all men by raising him from the dead. (Acts 17:30–31)

Jesus himself, on the Cross, recognizes that some of those participating in the crucifixion didn't realize what they were doing. Some may have realized they were participating in an unjust action but not realize they were crucifying the Son of God: "And Jesus said, 'Father, forgive them; for they know not what they do'" (Luke 23:34). To what extent the people eventually recognized their need for forgiveness and accepted the offer of God's forgiveness, the Gospel is silent. To what extent they knew they were participating in an unjust execution but didn't know who was being executed, the Gospel is silent.

One very notable fact, as we look at the New Testament, is how often Jesus and the Apostles, the most perfect communicators of the Word that there ever were, are rejected, and how often this rejection is attributed to a culpable, self-chosen blindness or hardness of heart:

> The true light that enlightens every man was coming into the world. He was in the world, and the world was made through him, yet the world knew him not. He came to his own home, and his own people received him not. (John 1:9–11)

> He who believes in him is not condemned; he who does not believe is condemned already, because he has not believed in the name of the only Son of God. And this is the judgment, that the light has come into the world, and men loved darkness rather than light, because their deeds were evil. For every one who does evil hates the light, and does not come to the light, lest his deeds should be exposed. But he who does what is true comes to the light, that it may be clearly seen that his deeds have been wrought in God. (John 3:18–21)

When Stephen was boldly declaring the identity of Jesus, the response he received reveals what can be the wicked blindness and hatred of the human heart when faced with truth:

> **"You stiff-necked people, uncircumcised in heart and ears, you always resist the Holy Spirit.** As your fathers did, so do you. Which of the prophets did not your fathers persecute? And they killed those who announced beforehand the coming of the Righteous One, whom you have now betrayed and murdered, you who received the law as delivered by angels and did not keep it." **Now when they heard these things they were enraged, and they ground their teeth against him.** But he, full of the Holy Spirit, gazed into heaven and saw the glory of God, and Jesus standing at the right hand of God; and he said, "Behold, I see the heavens opened, and the Son of man standing at the right hand of God." But they cried out with a loud voice and **stopped their ears** and rushed together upon him. Then they cast him out of the city and stoned him; and the witnesses laid down their garments at the feet of a young man named Saul. And as they were stoning Stephen, he prayed, "Lord Jesus, receive my spirit." And he knelt down and cried with a loud voice, "Lord, do not hold this sin against them." And when he had said this, he fell asleep. (Acts 7:51–60)

There is much that can be said about this text. Some of the same themes we have highlighted are found here also: the reality of hard-heartedness, the refusal of those in darkness to tolerate the light, the lack of obedience while claiming to be religious, the deep hostility to the claims of Jesus. But we should note here, as many commentators have, that Stephen is recapitulating the life and death of Jesus, even to the point of praying for forgiveness for those who are killing him, as Jesus did on the Cross. God never delights in the death of the evildoer and always extends forgiveness and mercy, but mercy and forgiveness need to be humbly received in order to effect their work of justification and sanctification in the soul of a repentant believer.[327]

Deliberate Unbelief

We sometimes forget that unbelief—not believing the testimony of God himself in the person of Jesus—is one of the gravest of sins revealed in the Scriptures. As Fr. Francis Martin puts it:

> The root sin of the world is the refusal to believe in Jesus and the place he holds next to the Father as the revelation of the Father. The root sin is to reject the truth: "Whoever believes in the son has eternal life, Whoever disobeys the son will not see life but must endure God's wrath" (John 3:36).[328]

The recurring theme in Scripture of culpable unbelief and the heart's choice to take pleasure in immorality is particularly underlined as the cause for those who will perish in the deception of the last days. Deception and self-deception often work together. The external deception of the evil one and his lies, working directly in the mind and heart of the individual or through the culture of the world, are found to be attractive to the selfish desires of the flesh and are yielded to with "sufficiently deliberate" personal assent to become culpable self-deception.

It is also clear, from the regular warnings of Jesus and the Apostles against false teachers and prophets, that deception within the thought environment of the Church must be guarded against. At one point, Scripture indicates that the "doctrines of demons" will be infiltrated into the Church through "the pretensions of liars" (1 Tim 4:1–2). Who can deny that, just as in the early Church, we are again encountering demonic lies that are leading many to rebel against God and engage in immorality? As Paul VI said on one occasion, "The fog of Satan is infiltrating the Church":

> And then the lawless one will be revealed, and the Lord Jesus will slay him with the breath of his mouth and destroy him by his appearing and his coming. The coming of the lawless one by the activity of Satan will be with all power and with pretended signs and wonders, and with all wicked deception for those who are to perish, because they refused to love the truth and so be saved. Therefore God sends upon them a strong delusion, to make them believe what is false, so that all may be condemned who did not believe the truth but had pleasure in unrighteousness. (2 Thess 2:8–12)

So many of the points we have already made are repeated again, now in the context of the last days and the final separation of the human race. This is the time when the division will become apparent between those who love God and those who disdain him, when the city of God and the city of man constructed against God will be separated for all eternity. I do believe we see signs of this division and separation becoming clearer in our own time.

AUGUSTINE'S INSIGHT INTO CULPABILITY

The *Catechism* notes that there are various factors in a person's life that may reduce culpability. It states in §1860: "The promptings of feelings and passions can also diminish the voluntary and free character of the offense, as can external pressures or pathological disorders."

Even when culpability is greatly lessened in a person's current state of "addiction," we need to remember the sobering insight of St. Augustine. Augustine acknowledges that by the time he was convinced of the truth of the faith and wanted to live in accordance with it, he was actually a slave of sexual sin and not able to get free by his own willpower alone. He was "addicted" in the language of today. Some might say today that because of the habit of sin, he was not fully culpable for repeated sinning. Yet in his remarkable honesty and deep perception of the tangled workings of the human soul, he points out that he was responsible for getting to the point of addiction or slavery by a repeated number of decisions to sin made over a period of time that were freely chosen. In other words, he was culpable for having gotten to the point of helplessness. But over a long period of time and step by step, the Lord took his desire for knowing and following him as the foundation for leading him out of his addiction, until one day, in an infusion of grace, he was given the opportunity to step free from his sin, and he did. It is well worth considering at some length his own words. We have seen previously how the *Catechism* (§1791) points out how conscience can gradually and culpably be deadened through the repeated decisions to commit sin:

> I sighed after such freedom [the freedom of Victorinus to turn away from it all] but was bound not by an iron imposed by anyone else but by the iron of my own choice. The enemy had a grip on my will and so made a chain for me to hold me a prisoner. The consequence of a distorted will is passion. By servitude to passion, habit is formed, and habit to which there is no resistance becomes necessity. . . . But I was responsible for the fact that habit had become so em-

battled against me, for it was with my consent that I came to the place in which I did not wish to be.[329]

Augustine goes on to tell of the agonizing struggle to get free from sexual bondage and love of worldly success, which eventually led him to freedom:

Lord, my helper and redeemer, I will now tell the story, and confess to your name, of the way in which you delivered me from the chain of sexual desire, by which I was tightly bound, and from the slavery of worldly affairs. I went about my usual routine in a state of mental anxiety.[330]

You thrust me before my own eyes so that I should discover my iniquity and hate it. I had known it, but deceived myself, refused to admit it, and pushed it out of my mind. But at that moment the more ardent my affection for those young men of whom I was hearing, who for the soul's health had given themselves wholly to you for healing, the more was the detestation and hatred I felt for myself in comparison with them. Many years of my life had passed by—about twelve—since in my nineteenth year I had read Cicero's Hortensius, and had been stirred to a zeal for wisdom. . . . But I was an unhappy young man, wretched as at the beginning of my adolescence when I prayed you for chastity and said: "Grant me chastity and continence, but not yet." I was afraid you might hear my prayer quickly, and that you might too rapidly heal me of the disease of lust which I preferred to satisfy rather than suppress.[331]

As our class studied Augustine's remarkable analysis of deception and self-deception, of bondage and freedom, we all came to understand with greater clarity what the courageous priest-student articulated about the self-deception that can so often be involved in choosing sin at a deeper-than-conscious level, but nevertheless truly choosing it.

One area of concern that has come up periodically in the course of this book is the underlying culture of unbelief that acknowledges what Scripture says about sexual morality and other moral issues but believes that "people are weak, and can't really be expected to live in conformity with Jesus's teaching," and that to expect real holiness is unrealistic. Unfortunately, this is a deception.

When Paul asked the Lord to remove what was a very troubling "thorn in the flesh," the Lord responded:

> My grace is sufficient for you, for my power is made perfect in weakness. (2 Cor 12:9)

When Paul taught about temptation, this is what he said:

> No temptation has overtaken you that is not common to man. God is faithful, and he will not let you be tempted beyond your strength, but with the temptation will also provide the way of escape, that you may be able to endure it. (1 Cor 10:13)

And the Council of Trent solemnly taught:

> If anyone says that the commandments of God are impossible of observance even by a person justified and established in grace: let him be anathema.[332]

In the teaching that provides the context for rightly interpreting the definition, Trent explains:

> For God does not command the impossible, but by com-

manding he instructs you both to do what you can and to pray for what you cannot, and he gives you his aid to enable you.[333]

If we are trapped in sin, we must throw ourselves upon the Lord's mercy with great abandon and fervor and ask his help for deliverance. We must also, of course, do our part by avoiding the near occasions of sin, frequenting the sacraments, joining a 12 Steps group if appropriate, installing blocking software on our computer if necessary, and implementing the spiritual wisdom our tradition has, which has helped so many, like Augustine, get free from serious sin.[334]

THE CHURCH AS A FIELD HOSPITAL

But, some may ask, what about Pope Francis's emphasis on the Church as a "field hospital for the wounded," and the need to be a "welcoming" Church, a Church of mercy, and to "accompany" people in the messy complexity of their lives and relationships?

The purpose of a field hospital is to bring healing and restore the patients to active engagement in the life and mission of the Church, not to affirm them in a wounded state. The purpose of "welcoming" people to the Church is to welcome them to an encounter with the person of Christ, his truth, love, and holiness, and to draw them to deep faith, repentance, and conversion, and to embrace their baptismal identity as "missionary disciples." To accompany people is to help people, with compassion and patience, to see clearly their own situations in light of the Gospel and to take steps to bring them to true friendship with Christ, which essentially includes faithfulness to his teaching in all its dimensions.

It is not merciful to keep from people the truth about Jesus, his teaching, and their own situations. It is not merciful to allow people to deceive themselves or be deceived and not challenge the false wisdom of the world, the flesh, and the devil, which envelops the culture today.

If we are not calling people to take up their cross and die to the world, the flesh, and the allurements of the devil, we are not preaching the true Gospel. Those who preach and teach will be held to a higher standard and judged on their fidelity to delivering the "whole counsel of God" (Acts 20:27).

Only God can judge the culpability of the human heart. Our job is to call people to salvation, to righteousness, to repentance, to a life of holiness and mission. The focus of our ministry needs to be not on determining culpability but leading to holiness.

Truly, only God can judge. The time between the first and second comings of Jesus is the time to focus on proclaiming the gracious offer of mercy and forgiveness, won for us at such a price, calling all men and women everywhere to faith, repentance, and conversion. Our primary mission is not to determine culpability but to call to repentance. It is urgent that we be about the Master's business:

> The times of ignorance God overlooked, but now he commands all men everywhere to repent, because he has fixed a day on which he will judge the world in righteousness by a man whom he has appointed, and of this he has given assurance to all men by raising him from the dead. (Acts 17:30–31)

> And [he] said to them, "Thus it is written, that the Christ should suffer and on the third day rise from the dead, and that repentance and forgiveness of sins should be preached in his name to all nations, beginning from Jerusalem." (Luke 24:46–47)

We are bearers of such very good news. Mercy is available, sins can be forgiven, a new and better way of life is open to all, and best of all, if we persevere to the end, the unending glory and happiness of heavenly life will be ours.

Part II

PATHWAYS FORWARD

PART I has been devoted to analyzing the problems we are facing, the alien forces infiltrating the Church, the lack of decisive action to counter them on the part of our leadership, and the multiple areas of doctrinal and moral confusion that have left many confused and concerned. Part II is devoted to outlining pathways that, if followed, could lead us to real and deep renewal in the Church. Chapter 7 will discuss why we need to stop pretending that things are ok and that perhaps non-radical solutions might be enough to solve things. Chapter 8 will consider how very real supernatural forces are in play and how, throughout history and in our time, demonic forces are clearly certainly involved in the crisis we are experiencing. We will also consider how demonic forces often work through particular individuals and through organizations that have become instruments of the demonic. Chapter 9 will contrast the vigorous picture of bold preaching and active pastoral care we get from reading the Scriptures and the often-pastoral passivity we see today in confronting the evil that is assaulting the Church. Chapter 10 will talk about the reality of God's judgment, both in history and at the end of time, and how we are experiencing judgment right now, an urgent call to repent. Chapter 11 will consider the very specific forms repentance must take to be effective. Chapter 12 talks about specific actions every individual Christian can take to address the confusion. Chapter

13, in a sense, sums up the whole message of the book by inviting us all to understand more deeply what it is to participate in the prophetic mission of Jesus and a summons to do so, confident in the Lord's presence and protection.

Chapter 7

SEEING AND NOT SEEING

UNLESS WE FACE SQUARELY the crisis we are in, there is no hope of discerning an appropriate solution. We will not be able to respond adequately to the crisis of truth unless we Catholics—especially those with pastoral responsibilities—parents, lay leaders, priests, deacons, religious superiors, bishops—face the current situation squarely. I do not want to deny that some aspects of the Church's situation today are encouraging. The Church is blessed with many men and women of great faith and talent. In some regions, even in some entire nations, the Church is relatively healthy and vigorous. There are movements, communities, ministries, and wonderfully holy clergy and lay people who are truly bright lights in the midst of the growing darkness. However, as we have attempted to show in this book, the Church is embroiled in a crisis. Broad currents and trends inside and outside the Church are weakening it. Great masses of Catholics have not been properly evangelized, formed in the faith, and incorporated into local church bodies and are being blown about by "every wind of doctrine" and seduced by the lies of the culture. The statistics that continually show the unrelenting decline of true Catholic belief among those who identify as Catholic and who increasingly are taking on the "mind of the world" are clear evidence that something is radically deficient in the effectiveness of our pastoral strategy and in our teaching and preaching.

A statement like this may well have been true of the Catholic people in almost any time in the history of the Church, outside of the early centuries during the time of persecution. Today, however, the general lack of cohesion, unity, and commitment among Catholics leaves them vulnerable to anti-Christian forces that are worldwide in scope and growing stronger. Modern secular culture has a stronger hold on the minds of many Catholics today than does the teaching of the Church. Many of the most faithful Mass attendees and active parishioners no longer believe what the Church teaches if it conflicts with the culture. In the developing nations, the Church is under growing pressure from Islamic governments and movements, pressure from developed nations that are tying aid offers to acceptance of contraception, abortion, and gay relationships, and even more so from the pervasiveness of secularized Western culture being communicated through Western media, inundating the whole world with its corruption. The secularized developed countries are relentlessly expunging all traces of the Christian culture that once provided protection and support for the Christian life.

The gravest danger, though, is not from persecution from the outside but from infidelity, stupidity, and corruption on the inside. Catholics are cooperating with, and even welcoming, political and intellectual forces that are hostile to the Church. This has happened because many Catholics have begun to lose their grasp of and commitment to basic Christian truths. A very real corruption of basic doctrine, moral behavior, spirituality, and mission is now apparent in many places, not just in isolated instances. We have devoted the first part of this book to documenting and analyzing this, and I could have documented much, much more than I had space for.

The Church's prospects would be difficult enough if it had to contend with only a continuation of the current unhappy situation. However, the Church must also face the probability that the pressures on it will intensify and the environment it inhabits will become more hostile. Sober men and women today predict major dislocation in the world economy. Resource shortages, media manipulation, punitive social and legal measures, political terrorism, social upheaval, and even war are happening now and may well worsen later. The rapidly growing surveillance technologies that are being developed and used in a widespread way in response to the coronavirus pandemic have given governments and the major international technology organizations unprecedented power to monitor the personal lives of their citizens and decide what we have a right to say and even to believe. One country has developed the surveillance to such a point that if a suspected infected person leaves their house, the police tracking their cell phone come to arrest them.[335] Already, Christian groups are being deleted from the most popular social media channels of communication, such as Facebook, YouTube, Twitter, and Instagram, and their right to free speech and freedom of religion is being taken away because they don't go along with the secular agenda. Facebook has just recently announced that their artificial intelligence capabilities have developed to the point that they can detect quickly, and sometimes proactively, 88.8 percent of "hate speech" across hundreds of languages on a worldwide basis so they can better "protect" their viewers.[336] Many Catholics today do not have the organization, commitment, and loyalty to cope with this challenge and come out as effective witnesses to Christ.

Unless God intervenes in response to the cry of his people, large segments of the Christian population will likely continue to abandon the faith. If there is a serious intensification of hostility toward the Church, persecution, political and economic collapse, hostile ideologies, and anti-Christian governments, then these forces abetted and urged on by "powers and principalities" could well decimate a lukewarm, uncertain Church. At stake is nothing less than the continued existence of the Catholic Church in anything like its present size, strength, or geographical extension. But we may already be beyond the point where large populations of nominal Catholics can be rescued from being captured by the culture. A "remnant" Church is not beyond possibility.

Pope Benedict XVI, when he was simply "Fr. Ratzinger," gave a radio interview in 1968 that was later published as a chapter (entitled "What Will the Church Look Like in 2000?") in his book, *Faith and the Future*, published in 2009:

> From the crisis of today the Church of tomorrow will emerge—a Church that has lost much. She will become small and will have to start afresh more or less from the beginning. She will no longer be able to inhabit many of the edifices she built in prosperity. As the number of her adherents diminishes, so will she lose many of her social privileges. In contrast to an earlier age, she will be seen much more as a voluntary society, entered only by free decision. As a small society, she will make much bigger demands on the initiative of her individual members. . . . But in all of the changes at which one might guess, the Church will find her essence afresh and with full conviction in that which was always at her center: faith in the triune God, in Jesus Christ, the Son of God made man, in the presence of the Spirit until the end of the world. . . . When the trial of this sifting is past, a great power will flow from a more spiritualized and simplified Church. Men in a totally planned world will find themselves unspeakably lonely. If they have completely lost sight of God, they will feel the whole hor-

ror of their poverty. Then they will discover the little flock of believers as something wholly new. They will discover it as a hope that is meant for them, an answer for which they have always been searching in secret.

And so it seems certain to me that the Church is facing very hard times. The real crisis has scarcely begun. We will have to count on terrific upheavals . . . But I am equally certain about what will remain at the end . . . she will enjoy a fresh blossoming and be seen as man's home, where he will find life and hope beyond death.[337]

How much longer can we go on ignoring the "elephant in the living room"? Many of those Catholics who are still coming to Church occasionally, or even regularly, are coming not with the mind and heart of Christ and the Spirit of God but with the mind and heart of the world and the spirit of the age. Many priests and deacons know this, some consciously, others unconsciously, and are afraid to preach the "full Gospel" because they know their people have already rejected those parts of it that conflict with their own desires or the cultural brainwashing they have been subjected to and were ill prepared to resist. How much longer can we go through the motions of confirming young people, knowing, or trying not to know, that the majority of them see Confirmation as the last thing they are being made to do before they can stop attending Mass, in imitation oftentimes of their parents? How much longer can we keep baptizing babies when there is no reasonable hope of their being raised as Catholics, as canon law insists is necessary, in order for the sacrament not to be approached as "magic"?[338] How much longer can we keep running RCIA programs when more than half of those who complete it are no longer around after a year?[339] How much longer can we keep boasting about the large numbers of

Hispanic immigrants who are coming from Catholic cultures and now comprise almost half of all American Catholics and ignore the fact that as generation succeeds generation, fewer and fewer of these cultural Catholics remain Catholics and many who are not simply being assimilated into the secular culture are leaving for evangelical and Pentecostal churches where they find a more vigorous preaching of the Gospel and environment of faith. If we keep on with "business as usual," we will soon be almost out of business.

The first step toward dealing with the Church's situation is to face it squarely. To do so, we must remove and overcome obstacles to a clear and accurate assessment of the Church's situation.

OBSTACLES TO SEEING

When they ponder the Church's severe problems, many Catholics almost automatically declare themselves to be optimistic. Among some leaders, optimism is almost an official policy. This optimism sometimes flows from genuine Christian hope and trust in Christ's promise to be with the Church through all time. Often, however, this official optimism misunderstands both Christian hope and Christ's promise. It operates as a defense mechanism that blocks clear seeing, permitting "business as usual" while masking the radical adjustments that the actual situation and God's Word truly demand. Sometimes, optimism is rooted in the fear that if we admitted the severity of our problems, we would lose hope and despair.

Authentic Christian hope, however, is quite different than naive optimism and has nothing to fear from facing the truth squarely.

Authentic Christian hope is the confidence that Jesus's victory foreshadows the victory of those who are faithful to him (see Heb 6:17–20). Christian hope is based on the certain promises of Christ, which don't promise that the Church in a particular region will not succumb to opposing forces. Christian hope is not wishful thinking. It does not excuse negligence. We deal with our sin by acknowledging it and repenting, not by pretending it isn't there or presuming forgiveness. Refusal to face sin only makes matters worse. As the psalmist prayed:

> When I declared not my sin, my body wasted away
>> through my groaning all day long.
> For day and night thy hand was heavy upon me;
>> my strength was dried up as by the heat of summer.
> I acknowledged my sin to thee,
>> and I did not hide my iniquity;
> I said, "I will confess my transgressions to the LORD";
>> then thou didst forgive the guilt of my sin.
> Therefore let every one who is godly
>> offer prayer to thee;
> at a time of distress. (Ps 32:3–6)

What often passes for Christian hope these days is presumption. Many optimistic Christians are blind to the actual requirements for God's blessing. A false understanding of Christian hope keeps many from seeing that our situation requires profound repentance.

Christ's promise to be with the Church till the end of time has been similarly misunderstood and abused (see Matt 28:20). The Catholic Church commonly understands this promise to mean that in the final eventuality, the pope and the bishops teaching in union with him will be preserved from error when officially teaching on faith and morals, and that the true understanding of the Gospel will therefore be maintained, even if it is not effectively taught and proclaimed and even if the Church's pastoral strategy is misguided. Christ's promise does *not* mean—as many think—that the Church as we know it will be preserved. The pope and the bishops teaching in union with him will be preserved from error in their official teaching but not, of course, in their informal comments, their approach to pastoral strategy, or their statements on matters of prudential judgments. The Church that they poorly govern may well yield to massive infidelity, confusion, and decay. Indeed, this has happened to the Church before. In the fourth century, whole segments of the Church—including many bishops and priests—were led astray by Arianism, a heresy which denied the true divinity of Jesus. The heresy was so powerful that secular authority was invoked to exile Pope Liberius and the minority of other orthodox bishops.

It is also quite possible for the Church to virtually disappear from whole regions of the world where it was once powerful. This happened to the strong churches of North Africa after the time of Augustine and to the Pauline churches of Asia Minor. Nothing in Christ's promise to remain with the Church assures that large regional, national, or international expressions of the Church cannot disappear through lukewarmness, infidelity, or persecution.

Persecution can strengthen the Church, but it can also reveal and exploit its weaknesses. For example, the French Revolution first split the French Catholic Church, and then, through persecution, provoked widespread apostasy among bishops, priests, and people. One historian described the consequences of persecution this way:

> With a sound instinct those who thus sought to destroy the Church concentrated their attention upon the priests. . . . Of the eighty-five bishops of the Constitutional Church, twenty-four abdicated their office, while a further twenty-three specifically apostatized, renouncing their faith. . . . If more than half the episcopacy thus bowed to the storm, the proportion of the lower clergy who did so was probably even larger.[340]

A similar situation happened in the England of Henry VIII, where, after he declared himself the head of the English Church, dissatisfied with the pope's refusal to grant him an annulment of his first marriage so he could marry someone else, almost all the bishops abandoned their allegiance to the pope and accepted Henry and his subsequent adulterous marriages in order to avoid persecution, a shocking and shameful apostasy. Do we not already have such a split, under the surface and not out in the open, in the significant number of national bishops' conferences and individual bishops who are taking a "liberal" interpretation of *Amoris Laetitia* that is not in harmony with Scripture and tradition? And yet at the same time, we have the truly heroic accounts of the English martyrs, both lay and clerical, who refused to "bow the knee" to Henry's usurpation of Church authority and doctrine and died rather than renounce the faith. And did we not, in France, have hundreds of faithful priests who refused to submit to the atheistic revolution and were imprisoned for their refusal in prison ships docked off the coast of France, where many of them died? Thanks be to God we have such brave voices today as well.

It's time for all of us to do a real "gut check." Is our relationship with the Lord and confidence in the truth of his love and grace strong enough to resist the temptations and trials that lie ahead and are, indeed, even "at the door"? None of us can be sure of what we would do under increased pressure, but unless we are cultivating the deepest relationship with the Lord possible and practicing self-denial, the acceptance of suffering, and courage and boldness in proclaiming and living the truth now, we will not be ready for the infusion of additional grace that will be needed—and given—as the pressures increase.

God's treatment of his chosen people under the Old Covenant offers a relevant and sobering parallel. God's eternal covenant with the Hebrew people did not mean he overlooked their sin, negligence, lukewarmness, immoral behavior, corruption of worship, and accommodation to the surrounding pagan cultures. When his people failed to repent, he punished them. His chosen people suffered economic difficulty and military defeat, long-term exile, oppression at the hands of brutal powers like Assyria and Babylon, and finally the destruction of Jerusalem itself and dispersal and exile throughout the world. Many of these chastisements were specifically directed against the negligence of the leaders of the people, especially their failure to diligently uphold the Word of God and administer discipline. The Israelites were guilty of presumption about their status as God's chosen people. Their misunderstanding of his eternal covenantal promises blinded them to the facts of their infidelity. They failed to do what was necessary to correct their sins and avoid judgment.

The same psychological blocks that exist among Catholics today plagued the leaders of the Israelites. The prophet Jeremiah lamented that his people indulged in false optimism:

> Woe is me! I am undone,
>> my wound is beyond healing;
> Yet I had thought:
>> if I make light of my sickness, I can bear it. (Jer 10:19, NABRE)

By the time Jeremiah spoke these words, it was too late. The time for repentance had passed. It was time for judgment. As disaster approached, the prophet laid bare the defense that had prevented the people from seeing and responding to the situation facing Israel from within and without: "My wound is beyond healing . . . if I make light of my sickness, I can bear it.'"

The same dynamic is at work within the Church today. Many

Catholics think, "If I minimize the seriousness of these problems, I can bear them." Such an attitude is, I believe, behind much of the "Christian optimism" and even the "Catholic pride" within the Church today.

Catholics, especially Catholic leaders, have good reason to fear the problems facing the Church and to doubt their ability to cope with them. Yet a policy of minimizing problems is self-deluding. If it breeds passivity and prevents repentance and the seeking of God's will, it can be a sin that must itself be repented of.

REDUCTIONIST ANALYSIS

Self-deluding optimism often functions along with other attitudes that block a realistic assessment of the Church's condition. Optimistic Catholics and their pastors tend to look for reasons to be optimistic. They often find these reasons through modes of reductionist analysis that replace moral and spiritual considerations with secular social science.

Analyses of the Church's position become reductionist when they leave out spiritual and moral criteria and reduce problems to sociological, psychological, and aesthetic categories. For example, reductionist analysis would say that the widespread fornication, adultery, homosexual activity, and other sexual immorality among Catholics represent "a swing of the pendulum." The same attitude is sometimes expressed when it is pointed out that huge numbers of young Catholics are no longer practicing their faith and rarely, or never, go to Mass. As the saying goes, "When they get married and have children, they'll come back." Some may, but as a matter of fact, fewer and fewer are marrying and having children at all! The implication is that the pendulum will one day swing back through normal social processes. A thoroughly Christian perspective would more accurately label immorality as "sin" and would not presume that the pendulum will swing back. The social sciences rightfully try to avoid value judgments, thus they cannot detect the most important forces at work in the Church today—namely, the spiritual and moral elements involved in the interplay between the Spirit of God and the spirit of the age, the works of the flesh, and the work of evil spirits.

This kind of sociological analysis has a psychological counterpart. Disdain for authority is explained as an "understandable reaction." Rebellious behavior is "acting out." Acceptance of immorality is termed "an understandable influence of our culture's approach to sexuality." There is often value in psychological analysis, but not if it lulls Christians into the posture of the "disinterested observer" who ignores the spiritual and moral considerations that an effectively Christian response requires. One of my friends who is involved in a scholarly debate about universalism is most distressed by how many of his fellow scholars view it as just another interesting theological debate and don't realize that the salvation of souls is resting on the outcome. Comfortable indifference on matters such as the reality of heaven and hell is a sign of deep spiritual blindness.

The great danger of overreliance on sociological and psychological analyses is that they can leave the distinct impression that the Church's life is essentially deterministic, an ebb and flow of trends which we watch as passive participants. Determinism eliminates accountability and responsibility: people are held to be not really responsible or culpable for their actions, and leaders are said to be unable to lead a Church on a pendulum swing.

A reductionist tendency is also evident in the way many Christians employ aesthetic categories in their interpretation of the Church's situation. For example, many Christians cherish a certain "don't-get-too excited" serenity when pondering what to do about unfaithfulness and decay in the Church. Their priority is "balance." In this way of thinking, a response to a problem must, above all, be "balanced and proportionate," even if the problem itself represents something highly unbalanced in terms of Christian orthodoxy. Some of the problems facing the Church call for strong measures—corrective action that may well appear to be unbalanced and disproportionate to those who do not understand the spiritual and moral depths of the situation. Yet a Christian leader whose desire is to preserve an aesthetically pleasing "serenity" and "balance" will avoid them. When someone is drowning, the rescuers may appear rather intense when looked upon from the outside.

This is, unfortunately, often communicated explicitly in even the best seminaries. The attitude conveyed is "don't rock the boat," "your job is to keep unity in the parish," "don't alienate your donors," and so on. Everything should indeed be balanced and proportionate, but often the truly balanced and proportionate pastoral actions will be perceived by the "unspiritual man" and the media as "outrageous." Feigned "outrage" is a common manipulative tactic these days.

Indeed, the whole business of being a Christian who is faithful to the Gospel and who desires to do the Lord's work is neither serene nor balanced in the way these categories are often understood in the Church today. A "sense of history" is very valuable, but not if it functions to instill indifference or passivity about the need for us to take responsibility before God for how we act in *our* historical situation. St. Francis Xavier, the great Jesuit missionary to Asia, expressed something of the awfulness of this false serenity when viewed in the light of eternal truths:

> Many times I am seized with the thought of going to the
> schools of your lands [Europe] and there cry out like a man
> who has lost his mind, and especially at the University

of Paris, telling those in the Sorbonne who have a greater regard for learning than for willing so that they might dispose themselves to produce fruit with it: "How many souls fail to go to glory but instead to hell through their neglect." Would that they were as diligent in studying how much God our Lord will demand of them as they are in studying letters, and what will be expected of them for the talent which they have received; then they would be greatly moved . . . and they would say: "Lord, here I am! What would you that I should do? Send me wherever you will, and, if necessary, even to the Indians!" With how much greater consolation would they then live; and they would have great hope in the divine mercy of the hour of their death when they encounter that particular judgment which no man can escape, saying for themselves: "Lord you gave me five talents, behold, I have gained another five."[341]

We need this zealous Christian perspective today. St. Francis Xavier didn't have the added perspective that a genuine development of doctrine has given to us and believed that unless someone were actually baptized, they could not be saved, which certainly drove his urgency. Even with the development of doctrine that we now have, the situation remains urgent. We now know that it is possible for people who have never heard the Gospel, under certain conditions (inculpable ignorance of the Gospel, sincerely seeking God, living according to the light of conscience) to be saved. Nevertheless, as Vatican II teaches, "very often" these conditions aren't met and people give in to the world, the flesh, and the devil, and unless they are called to faith, repentance, and baptism, they are in grave danger of being lost, and we urgently need to preach the Gospel.[342]

And if we truly share in the mind and heart of Christ and if his Spirit dwells in us, should we not also expect to share Jesus's anger when he saw his Father's temple defiled?

> In the temple he found those who were selling oxen and sheep and pigeons, and the money-changers at their business. And making a whip of cords, he drove them all, with the sheep and oxen, out of the temple; and he poured out the coins of the money-changers and overturned their tables. And he told those who sold the pigeons, "Take these things away; you shall not make my Father's house a house of trade." His disciples remembered that it was written, "Zeal for thy house will consume me." (John 2:14–17)

Today too, the temple of God is being defiled—the very body of Christ, the people of God, the Church. Is not a false "serenity" or a false "balance" in response to this situation in itself something of a defilement?

Complacent attitudes like this are sometimes associated with sayings that we periodically hear, such as, "Beauty will save the world." This saying from one of Fyodor Dostoyevsky's characters has been repeated oftentimes by those supposing that exposing people to the beauty of the Catholic tradition in its art and music and architecture, its vestments and liturgical ceremonies, will lead them to faith. For some, I am sure that may be the case. But for the vast majority, it is not and will not be the case. The vast majority will never have a chance to access, at an elite aesthetic level, these works of beauty. As Michael O'Brien, the Catholic artist and novelist, says:

> "Beauty will save the world." This oft-quoted maxim of Dostoevsky's, derived from *The Idiot*, is widely misunderstood and misused in our times. As the author demonstrates throughout the novel, beauty alone cannot save the world. . . . The beauty that will save the world is the love of God. This love is both human and supernatural in charac-

ter, but it germinates, flowers, and comes to fruition only in a crucified heart. Only the heart united with Christ on the Cross is able to love another as himself, and as God loves him. Only such a heart can pass through the narrow gate of the Cross and live in the light of Resurrection. The good news is that this resurrection begins here and now.[343]

The one who saved the world, "had no form or comeliness that we should look at him, and no beauty that we should desire him. He was despised and rejected by men; a man of sorrows and acquainted with grief; and as one from whom men hid their faces he was despised, and we esteemed him not" (Isa 53:2–3).

Is it the crucified Christ, not our art or music or buildings, that will save the world? Yes, it is the crucified Christ, proclaimed boldly in the power of the Holy Spirit who will save the world:

> For Christ did not send me to baptize but to preach the Gospel, and not with eloquent wisdom, lest the cross of Christ be emptied of its power. For the word of the cross is folly to those who are perishing, but to us who are being saved it is the power of God. . . . Where is the wise man? Where is the scribe? Where is the debater of this age? Has not God made foolish the wisdom of the world? For since, in the wisdom of God, the world did not know God through wisdom, it pleased God through the folly of what we preach to save those who believe. (1 Cor 1:17–22)

Our response to the crisis of truth in the Church must begin with a candid look at the inner nature of our response to the situation facing the Church. Those of us who bear Christ's name should be consumed with zeal for the purity of his body, the Church, the holiness of his Name. Those of us who have some degree of responsibility for the Church must be honest about the way we view what is happening to those under our care. If our people are being misled, if they are behaving unfaithfully to God and to each other, do we slip into ways of thinking that tend to make these facts seem less painful and less serious? Worse, do we think about what is happening to the people under our care in a way that tends to lessen our own responsibility for changing the situation?

It can be difficult to discern God's will for his people and even harder to faithfully and consistently implement it in the midst of the pressures, crosscurrents, and difficulties that plague the Church today.

Nevertheless, we must not let our discernment of the real situation of the Church and God's will be lulled by a false optimism, serenity, and balance, or by our acute sensitivity to the ways social forces act on institutions and psychological dynamics operate on individuals and groups. This is not to say that sociological, psychological, aesthetic, and historical perspectives cannot be helpful in pastoral work. They can be helpful in their proper place. However, these modes of analysis are limited and subordinate. They are essentially "natural" ways of seeing and thinking. If employed exclusively or excessively, they will squeeze the spiritual and moral components out of our vision and deny us the means to make a response appropriate to the magnitude of the problem. Today, as always, the words and deeds of God are "madness" and "foolishness" in the eyes of the world.

Catholics—especially those who share in pastoral responsibility for the Church today, which in some measure is all of us—should be no less zealous for the Word and the way of God than those who preceded us. Increasingly today, the right attitude toward the corruption of faith and life that is going on in the Church is godly indignation. And godly indignation should characterize our response to it.

This means being open to more radical solutions than have yet been attempted. These solutions need to be characterized primarily by profound repentance and mighty intercession, prayer, and fasting. They need to include preaching and teaching with the fire of the Spirit, and the tedious, day by day work of doing what we can to follow Jesus more closely ourselves as his disciples. This means helping others, one by one or in groups, to do so as well, helping to facilitate a healthy remnant out of which true renewal can flow. This remnant has been prepared over many years now and is growing and being readied by the Lord to step forth with boldness and confidence to confess the Lordship of Christ in the power of the Holy Spirit, to call people to stop straddling the issue. Every reader of this book is called to be part of it!

And it has always been through remnants that God has worked to bring renewal. Remember the mustard seed, how small it is, and how it grows. Remember Elijah, who thought he was the only one who was still faithful, and the Lord told him that, no, there were actually seven thousand that hadn't gone over to false gods (see 1 Kgs 19:18). And remember that when Israel thought they were outnumbered and surrounded by their enemies, "the servant [of Elisha] said, 'Alas, my master! What shall we do?' [Elisha] said, 'Fear not, for those who are with us are more than those who are with them.' Then Elisha prayed, and said, 'O LORD, I pray thee, open his eyes that he may see.' So the LORD opened the eyes of the young man, and he saw; and behold, the mountain was full of horses and chariots of fire round about Elisha" (2 Kgs 6:15–17).

May our eyes be opened to see that we are not alone, that the remnant is small but mighty in God, and that we are surrounded by a great cloud of witnesses, not just passively looking on but interceding mightily for the victory of the Lord. And what a privilege it is to be given a role in the battle, with joy and confidence, knowing what the outcome will be.

Chapter 8

POWERS, PRINCIPALITIES, AND ORGANIZATIONS

IN ORDER TO BE ABLE to adequately respond to the crisis of truth confronting the Church today, we need to realize the significant extent to which our struggle is not just with "human weakness," "cowardice and fear," and "well-meaning mistakes" but with powers, principalities, and organized centers of hostility. Jesus and the Apostles warned about the pervasive activity of Satan, the methodology of his operations, and the desire of his heart. The "whole world is in the power of the evil one" (1 John 5:19), who "prowls around like a roaring lion, seeking some one to devour" (1 Pet 5:8). "Satan, the deceiver of the whole world" (Rev 12:9), is luring human beings to destruction and ruin, getting them to believe the ruinous lies of plausible liars who are often within the Church. His compelling motivation is a murderous hatred of God and men.

Contemporary men and women often lack this spiritual perspective. The opinion of secular society, shared by many in responsible positions of Church leadership, is that today's struggle is simply a clash of human ideas, movements, and trends. Fr. Arturo Sosa, the Superior General of the Jesuits, declaring that Satan is just a symbol and not a real spiritual power is certainly a disturbing example of this.[344] And not a word of correction from higher authority! They completely ignore the often hidden, but sometimes open, work of Satan and the evil ideologies under his control. The fact is that the influence of ideologies and trends on society and the Church is not simply a matter of "flesh and blood." It also involves an encounter with "powers and principalities" working brilliantly and deviously to bring the human race to spiritual, moral, and physical destruction (see Eph 6:12). The precise elements of evil spiritual influence often cannot be clearly distinguished from human contributions. But often they can be, and discerning them is a valuable task. The purpose of this chapter is to show clearly that the demonic element can sometimes be identified. This will help us learn how to be more discerning when intelligent people, the madness of crowds, or powerful organizations impel us to embrace ideas and causes that have as their goal separating us from the one true God. If we become more aware of this dimension, we will better understand the struggle we are engaged in and be better equipped to resist and counter it with the only weapons that can be successful, true discernment of spirits and spiritual weapons.

Much of the rest of this chapter will be devoted to a description of Satan's often hidden work in various movements in society and the Church. Of course, we must here guard against the danger of seeing Satan's activity everywhere and undervaluing the significant contribution of human sin and malice to our present situation. But in the present climate of the Church, in which Satan's reality and activity are often ignored and even denied, some attention to this reality is essential.

In a recently published comprehensive biography of Pope Benedict XVI, Peter Seewald, a longtime collaborator and author of previous book-length interviews with Pope Benedict, quotes an observation of Pope Benedict that is relevant to the spiritual discernment we are trying to carry out, not only in this chapter but throughout the book:

> One hundred years ago everybody would have considered it to be absurd to speak of a homosexual marriage. Today, one is being excommunicated by society if one opposes it. [The same applies to] abortion and to the creation of human beings in the laboratory.

> Modern society is in the middle of formulating an anti-Christian creed, and if one opposes it, one is being punished by society with excommunication. The fear of this spiritual power of the Anti-Christ is then only more than natural, and it really needs the help of prayers on the part of an entire diocese and of the Universal Church in order to resist it.[345]

Earlier, we saw Cardinal Mueller's warning about the influence of the Antichrist in what is happening in the Church and world today.

Avid supporters of Pope Francis were outraged that Pope Benedict would liken support of gay marriage to the work of the Antichrist and saw it as a direct attack on Pope Francis. This is somewhat ironic, since Pope Francis has talked about the devil more frequently than I remember any of his recent predecessors doing.

As another indicator of how many people are understanding Pope Francis's agenda, Lynda Telford, author of *Women of the Vatican: Female Power in a Male World*, told a major journal in the United Kingdom that "Benedict's doing his absolute best to sabotage all the reforms that Francis is trying to bring in."[346]

In his biography of Pope Benedict, Peter Seewald went on to ask him what he had in mind when, upon being elected pope, he asked for prayers that he may not "flee from the wolves." Benedict replied that the remark was not just simply focused on the curia but on the ascendency of powers operating in the world coming against Christ and the Church. He stated that "the real threat" comes from "the world-wide dictatorship of seemingly humanistic ideologies" with the consequence that contradicting these ideologies "means the exclusion from the basic consensus in society."[347]

Despite Cardinal Kasper being "horrified" at Cardinal Mueller's mention of the Antichrist, it is clear from Scripture and the *Catechism of the Catholic Church* that the work of the Antichrist is real and will become particularly intense during the final apostasy and the removal of the restrainer on lawlessness, just before the Second Coming of Jesus:

> Before Christ's second coming the Church must pass through a final trial that will shake the faith of many believers (Luke 18:8; Matt 24:13). The persecution that accompanies her pilgrimage on earth (cf. Luke 21:12; John 15:19–20)will unveil the "mystery of iniquity" in the form of a religious deception offering men an apparent solution to their problems at the price of apostasy from the truth. The supreme religious deception is that of the Antichrist, a pseudo-messianism by which man glorifies himself in place of God and of his Messiah come in the flesh (2 Thess 2:4–12; 1 Thess 5:2–3, 2 John 7; 1 John 2:18, 22).[348]

And how relevant to our considerations in this book is the next section of the *Catechism*:

> The Antichrist's deception already begins to take shape in the world every time the claim is made to realize within history that messianic hope which can only be realized beyond history through the eschatological judgment. The

Church has rejected even modified forms of this falsification of the kingdom to come under the name of millenarianism, especially the "intrinsically perverse" political form of a secular messianism.[349]

Will things be getting better and better as we approach the end? No:

> The Church will enter the glory of the kingdom only through this final Passover, when she will follow her Lord in his death and Resurrection (Rev 19:1–9). The kingdom will be fulfilled, then, not by a historic triumph of the Church through a progressive ascendancy, but only by God's victory over the final unleashing of evil, which will cause his Bride to come down from heaven (Rev 13:8; 20:7–10; 21:2–4). God's triumph over the revolt of evil will take the form of the Last Judgment after the final cosmic upheaval of this passing world.[350]

ARCHBISHOP SHEEN'S REMARKABLE INSIGHTS

A quite remarkable radio address by Venerable Archbishop Fulton J. Sheen in 1947 spoke about the modalities by which the Antichrist will work.[351]

Archbishop Sheen said that the devil is never more powerful than when people think he doesn't exist. He reminded us that the devil will certainly not look like a comic book devil but will be disguised as a great humanitarian. A 2011 Center for Research on the Apostolate (CARA) report found that 83 percent of Catholics thought that the devil was only a symbol.[352]

Archbishop Sheen writes:

He [the Antichrist] will write books on the new idea of God to suit the way people live; induce faith in astrology so as to make not the will but the stars responsible for sins; he will explain guilt away psychologically as inhibited eroticism, make men shrink in shame if their fellowmen say they are not broadminded and liberal; he will be so broadminded as to identify tolerance with indifference to right and wrong, truth and error; he will spread the lie that men will never be better until they make society better . . . he will foster more divorces under the disguise that another partner is "vital," he will increase love for love and decrease love for persons; he will invoke religion to destroy religion; he will even speak of Christ and say that he was the greatest man who ever lived; his mission he will say will be to liberate men from the servitudes of superstition and Fascism, which he will never define. But in the midst of all his seeming love for humanity and his glib talk of freedom and equality, **he will have one great secret which he will tell to no one; he will not believe in God.**[353]

A Pew Research report from October of 2018 reported that 33 percent of Catholics believed in astrology, 36 percent in reincarnation, and 46 percent in psychics. Additionally, 61 percent wanted the Church to permit cohabiting couples to receive Communion, 62 percent to permit those divorced and remarried who did not have an annulment to receive Communion, 46 percent to recognize gay/lesbian marriages.[354] And these numbers keep growing. The flock is being carried off by the world, the flesh, and the devil, yet the shepherds refuse to sound the alarm and cry out the impassioned cry of Peter: "Save yourself from this crooked generation" (Acts 2:40).

Archbishop Sheen continues, commenting on how the three temptations of Christ in the desert will be repeated:

The temptation to turn stones into bread as an earthly Messiah will become the temptation to sell freedom for security, as bread became a political weapon, and only those who think his way may eat. . . . [The Antichrist] wants no proclamation of immutable principles from the lofty heights of a Church, but mass organization through propaganda. . . . Opinions not truths, commentators not teachers, Gallup polls not principles, nature not grace—and to these golden calves will men toss themselves from their Christ . . . to have a new religion without a Cross, a liturgy without a world to come, a city of man without a city of God, or a politics which is a religion.

It breaks down all national boundaries, laughs down patriotism, dispenses men from piety to country . . . makes men proud not that they are Americans, French, or British, but members of a revolutionary class.[355]

Today, the Archbishop might add to his description of those under the spiritual influence of the Antichrist the revolutionary class, Silicon Valley, and the global elite.

Sheen saw the Antichrist setting up a counter-Church "which will be the ape of the Church because, he the devil, is the ape of God. It will have all the notes and characteristics of the Church, but in reverse and emptied of its divine content. It will be a mystical body of the anti-Christ that will in all externals resemble the mystical body of Christ."[356]

Archbishop Sheen foresaw people, lonely and desperate but not wanting to humble themselves and adore the one true God, flock to accept the counter-Church that promises to unite people in a world brotherhood and give meaning to their lives that they once found in the true Church. "Only those who live by faith really know what is happening in the world. The great masses without faith are unconscious of the destructive processes going on."[357] "From now on the struggle will be . . . for the souls of men."[358]

He saw a great division taking place, people dividing into two different religions as absolutes, "the God Who became man and the man who makes himself God; brothers in Christ and comrades in anti-Christ."[359]

It is good to remember that Satan inspired man's original turning from God and spurred his drive for autonomy and for knowledge apart from God. He continues to inspire the human race's rebellion against God, a rebellion visible in many contemporary forms.

THE PRIMORDIAL TEMPTATION

This primordial satanic temptation of man—to be "like God" apart from him and in opposition to him—appears again and again in the history of the development of modern thought and modern man. For example, studies of the Renaissance have shown that the desire of man at that time to be liberated from religious restraints was combined with involvement in various forms of "magic." Drawing on "esoteric knowledge" and "powers," leading Renaissance figures attempted to control their destinies and manipulate the physical world.[360]

Michael McClymond has meticulously documented how the spread of the demonic lie that everyone will be saved has sources in theologians who openly acknowledged getting insight from spiritualist experiences. As we have considered at length in Chapter 3, this is a massive deception that has led, and is leading, many astray and is a major cause of the deterioration of faith, morality, and mission in the Church today.[361]

Before I met Dr. McClymond and read his massive two-volume work on the rise of universalism and its spiritualist roots, I had reason to research the relationship between the well-known Swiss theologian Hans Urs von Balthasar and his relationship to the alleged mystic Adrienne von Speyr. Balthasar is perhaps the most influential purveyor of the hope that all be saved. He says that the following statement perfectly expresses what he is saying: it can become "infinitely improbable" that anyone can persist in resisting God's grace.[362] Because of his wide influence, I felt the need to study the sources of his views. His views have led many to presume that virtually everyone will be saved, despite the witness of Scripture, tradition, and the official teaching of the Church. I was shocked to discover that von Speyr was a major influence on the development of Balthasar's thought in this area and that she often claimed to be in direct communication with St. Ignatius, whom she asserted wanted Balthasar to leave the Jesuits, which he did on the basis of her revelations. He also claimed that, in her visions of hell, she didn't see anyone there, which supported his own lifelong leanings toward that conclusion. Some of his firsthand accounts of the unusual nature of their relationship (he wrote two books about their relationship) raise serious concerns about what spiritual influences were at work in the formulation of his theories and his hope that all will be saved.

Spiritual Influences on Balthasar's Hopeful Universalism

I'm going to quote at length from an article I've written that carefully documents what I am concerned about.[363] I am devoting more space to this because it very much relates to one of the main deceptions we are identifying and addressing in this book, the deception that it can be infinitely improbable that anyone is in hell. But it also illustrates how strange spiritual influences can infiltrate themselves into high places, through apparently very intelligent and spiritual people. In Balthasar's own words:

> As her confessor and spiritual director, I observed her interior life most closely, yet in twenty-seven years I never had the least doubt about the authentic mission that was hers. . . . I not only made some of the most difficult decisions of my life—including my leaving the Jesuit Order—following her advice, but I also strove to bring my way of looking at Christian revelation into conformity with hers. . . . Today, after her death, her work appears far more important to me than mine, and the publication of her still unpublished writings takes precedence over all personal work of my own.[364]

Balthasar openly talks about the unusual nature of their relationship—he moved in with Speyr and her second husband and lived with them for fifteen years in order to facilitate their close collaboration. Their activity seems to include what today we would call "recovered memories" and "spiritual channeling," and Balthasar offers some startling defenses of their relationship.

As her confessor, Balthasar was given the ability to

> transfer Adrienne (back) to each of the various stages of her life, in order to run through her biography. This made it possible for her to recall much of what she had forgotten. . . . At each stage, she used the language she had spoken at the time—whether as a small child, as a high-school student, or as a medical student. This transferring of Adrienne back into her past (always in conversation with me) had a further effect, which for her was quite crucial: it gave me a presence in her earlier life.[365]

Balthasar admiringly reports:

> On her countless "journeys" she was transported to places
> in the world where trouble of some kind was taking place.
> She would then be transported into the soul of, say, some-
> one who was finding it hard to make his confession, so that
> she could give him inner help. In this way she was able to
> support the dying, people being tortured and burned alive
> in concentration camps, men on battlefields and in prison,
> in fact suffering of every kind. . . . There were many mysti-
> cal phenomena in Adrienne's life—stigmata, transferences,
> the radiating of light, levitation, speaking with tongues,
> and other things of that kind but they all occurred in a to-
> tally unemphatic way. They were mere accompaniments to
> show forth the heart of the matter: what was to be passed
> on to the Church invisibly through prayer and strenuous
> penance, visibly through the dictated works. . . . Adrienne
> once told me that my mother, whom she had met in heaven
> . . . had entrusted me to her.[366]

Speyr's reports of what her heavenly revelations wanted
Balthasar to do often involved exhortations for him to trust her
more:

> Ignatius, who insisted that he (Balthasar) should be more
> communicative and give Adrienne more responsibility,
> didn't always appreciate von Balthasar's prudence and
> restraint: "Adrienne von Speyr needs trust and love, she
> hasn't received much during her life."[367]

Speyr stated that she was in constant communication with St.
Ignatius, a claim that Balthasar completely accepted. Speyr offered
to ask Ignatius questions that Balthasar wished to submit to him.

Speyr reported to Balthasar that St. Ignatius, after meeting St. John the Evangelist in heaven, had become much more Johannine in his thinking and that the community they were to found together ("our child") should therefore be Johannine. It was St. Ignatius's guidance, given through Speyr, that confirmed Balthasar in leaving the Jesuits and moving in with Speyr and her husband to carry out their common mission.

"Quite early on very quiet and gentle suggestions began to be made that the mission of St. Ignatius would perhaps be more important than remaining in the Society."[368] Speyr knew what a huge decision this was and suggested that maybe if she died, Balthasar wouldn't have to leave the Jesuits. Balthasar forbade her to die, left the Jesuits, moved in with her and her husband, and the two become more deeply entwined than ever.

Once, during a retreat that Balthasar was giving, Speyr spoke about what her role would be in it, indicating that this was revealed to her by St. Ignatius:

> He [St. Ignatius] would like Adrienne to be sent to heaven for the next few days. H.U. must do this and let Adrienne share the Exercises with him from heaven. After each conference, she must give a short commentary on how things look from there, in the light of the Trinity. With this in mind, on each occasion, H.U. should take her out of heaven for, say, a quarter of an hour and ask her questions. He can think up all kinds of questions. . . . If he wants to, H.U. can call upon SP [*Sanctus Pater* = St. Ignatius] if there is something he does not understand or wants to know. . . . She will also share in a large part of the confessions of other people. From where she is, she can go almost anywhere she thinks necessary, or where H.U. thinks she should go. H.U. has therefore a certain power over heaven, which lat-

er, when A. no longer returns, will be important for him.
. . . Anything negative, anything that does not come off,
must always be seen as a learning experience, never as an
estrangement from Father (St. Ignatius). Father is glad to
be allowed to help his children.[369]

Apparently, things that don't seem to work out as expected are
not to put in question the authenticity of the link with St. Ignatius
but are to be viewed as learning experiences.

There were two main emphases in their common work. The first
was finding a way to introduce into Catholic theology an interpretation of Scripture and doctrine, based on Speyr's descent into hell,
experiences, revelations, and theology that would allow Balthasar
to propose that it is "infinitely improbable" that any human being
will ultimately be able to resist God's salvific grace. The other main
emphasis which, in some ways, they considered the most important
fruit of their common effort was the birthing of a new secular institute to be called the Community of St. John. Speyr reported to
Balthasar her numerous communications from Mary and the saints
and the Lord himself about the importance of founding the community. At one point, when she was troubled because a Jesuit had
told her that founders need to be saints, Balthasar consoled her by
saying they wouldn't be founding a "grand order" like the Jesuits or
Franciscans and that their community will be "more modest." To
which Speyr replied, based on her revelations:

> It will become something great. It will spread out. . . . She
> prayed constantly for the "Child" and learned a great deal
> about it. She also prayed for my "inadequacy," so that I
> would be able to cooperate properly. . . . As for her spiritual
> life, she said that "the Child" and the general task always
> stood at the center of the visions . . . and "the *new parents*"

really ought to bear responsibility for the birth.[370]

The community itself has never become "something great" and has never "spread out;" it has remained very small and local.

Speyr's exhortations and prayers about Balthasar's "inadequacy" are tame compared to what Balthasar recounts of her lengthy and severe rebukes of him—for the most part for not providing enough emotional support or defending her enough from her critics. He describes this as her "relentless rebuking and training of her confessor" and recounts some truly harrowing scenes that he nevertheless seems to be abjectly grateful for.

During her first Holy Week as a Catholic, she reported that she experienced the Passion and complained that Balthasar wasn't "there" for her. This feeling that Balthasar wasn't supporting her enough intensified, and on July 11, 1941, Speyr summoned Balthasar to her office, so that she could, as he later put it, "show her contempt for me face to face." At first Speyr wouldn't say anything, knowing that it could cost their friendship, but Balthasar urged her to speak and she did,

> quietly, with a kind of ice-cold severity. It is not her voice. Someone else is speaking out of her. . . . A terrifying indictment continues for almost an hour. . . . She says she is like a young mother in a labor ward. The medical students look at her and make cynical, indecent remarks. Her husband hasn't the time. He's busy somewhere else, perhaps with another woman. . . . Finally the child arrives. He is inspected from every angle, weighed, registered. The mother nearly dies of shame. She feels violated. . . . Later she spoke about the woman's sexual role: "Carrying the child is naturally the woman's role, but the husband ought to support her and take care of her. After all, the child is his as well as hers."[371]

At other times, Speyr expresses concern about Balthasar's spiritual life and says she sees darkness settling into his soul, a lack of "total love" of God, and his "lack of prayer."[372] Yet, despite her misgivings and regular rebukes, she affirms: "If the Lord and his Mother didn't hold your hand forcefully . . . it would be very dangerous for me, because in this moment I view God entirely through you. But it would be absurd to think that you could show me another but the true God."[373] These comments warrant reflection.

The mutuality of the total trust in one another's revelations/theology/guidance is clear. Each has surrendered a critical ability and has embarked on a path of trust in the revelations and theological interpretations of the other. The fear that Speyr expresses—that Balthasar's vision of God could be false—which she quickly rejects, is worth noting. It's possible that Balthasar had to overcome similar fears in what he was receiving from Speyr, although what he expresses is only complete trust. Balthasar reports that her rebuke of his lack of support led to a conflict with his Jesuit superiors over her "which began the long and painful story of my departure from the Jesuits."[374] Forbidden to any longer go to her house, they continued meeting in his office until he left the Jesuits and moved into her house.[375]

ENLIGHTENMENT ROOTS

A significant element of the Enlightenment—that upheaval of learning and change which profoundly shaped the modern world—was an explicit rejection of God, the Church, and revelation. What Voltaire, a leading figure of the Enlightenment, said about the Church, *Ecrasez l'infame!,* probably comes close to reflecting the sentiments of Satan on the subject: "Crush the accursed thing!"

This overt hostility toward Christianity and the Church manifested itself unmistakably in the French Revolution, a revolution that became something of a prototype for the political upheavals that have characterized the modern world. Along with its hostility to Christianity, the French Revolution ushered in an idolatrous worship of "reason," a conscious and deliberate exaltation of man above God, an affirmation of absolute human autonomy. Yet this esteem for reason and autonomy was coupled with irrationality and produced something like an anti-religious religion. A "feast in honor of reason," held on November 10, 1793, in Notre Dame Cathedral in Paris, graphically illustrates the point:

> On the top of a scaffolding, placed in front of the choir, was erected a temple dedicated to philosophy, and to crown all was installed, in place of "inanimate images," an actress from the Opera, chosen for her beauty, as a "masterpiece of nature," but entitled, without very evident cause, the "Goddess of Reason."[376]

This "abomination of desolations" in a holy place focuses and symbolizes that murderous hostility toward God that constitutes the center of Satan's activity and works. His hostility is directed toward man's own destruction.

The shocking destruction of Notre Dame by fire in 2019 has been interpreted by many as both a judgment and wake-up call to the Church and the nations. While participating in a conference in France shortly after the burning of Notre Dame, a French Dominican priest pointed out that at the very top of the steeple of Notre Dame was not a cross but a rooster, proud symbol of France and the French state. It was that rooster that first fell in the conflagration. And yet as Notre Dame burned, something of the latent Catholicism in the French became manifest as thousands gathered nearby, with many praying and singing hymns in shocked awe.

THE MARXIST REVOLUTION CONTINUES

If we can see some satanic purposes being achieved in the French Revolution and still embedded today in the French nation, once lauded as the "eldest daughter of the Church" and now in massive apostasy, they are much more evident in the more recent unfolding of the Marxist revolutions, even though these revolutions have protested, like the French Revolution before them, real injustices. Marxists displayed the same opposition to God and the Church, the same conscious exaltation of man in place of God. However, they imposed their hostility more ferociously and explicitly, more systematically, and for much longer spans of time. Recent research into the life of Karl Marx has found the seeds of the wider revolution in Marx's personal life. After apparently converting to Christ while a teenager, Marx soon rejected him. Marx's miserable personal life and relationships, and the subsequent suicides of his daughters, all witness to the victory of Satan, the enemy who lies and deceives in order to bring man to ruin, death, and damnation.[377] In many ways, Marx's own life became an anti-sign of the "new man" his revolution was supposed to produce.

And the "fruits" of this devilish ideology continue to shock. How many tens of millions were killed, condemned to prison and labor camps, and forced into starvation in the effort to create a society of "equality and brotherhood" in the Soviet Union? How many thousands of priests and bishops were murdered by the Soviet Union in an effort to crush and subjugate the Russian Church, which it succeeded in doing? How many Soviet women were led to believe that aborting their babies was their duty to the state and normal birth control? How many forced abortions are carried out to this day in China?

As I write this, as we have seen, the bloody journey of Chinese communism continues to unfold, with more than a million Muslims consigned to "reeducation" camps intended to purge them of their faith. We have also seen relentless efforts to bring the Christian churches under the total control of the Communist Party and to prevent the transmission of the faith to the next generation. To live in China now is to live in the most highly developed surveillance state the world has ever seen. With ever-growing numbers of facial recognition cameras with advanced AI (artificial intelligence) capabilities, with ever more sophisticated monitoring of everyone's communications, travels, and contacts, citizens are given "social credit" scores and are rewarded and punished accordingly. The Chinese government's goal is to have six hundred million surveillance cameras operational in the next two years so that everywhere citizens go, they can be instantly recognized, tracked, and instantly looked up in a central database. If a person has a "bad social score," that is, isn't obedient to the government, they will be denied access to travel and won't be able to buy a train or plane ticket. Already in the first year of deployment, three thousand wanted criminals have been discovered and arrested. In an interview with one of the systems developers, a reporter asked if this could be used for bad purposes. The developer said it is possible.[378]

Our understanding of human history will always be inadequate unless we realize that, as Paul puts it, "we are not contending against flesh and blood, but against the principalities, against the powers" (Eph 6:12). To the solidly instructed and spiritually sensitive Christian, the role played by satanic principalities and powers in the lives of certain "great" men and "great" events is unmistakable.

Jesus identified Satan as one who is seeking to deceive and blind the human race, to direct it down paths that will lead to murder and death now, and damnation forever (see John 8:43–47). Satan accomplishes his will through human instruments, just as God does. A view of history that does not take these spiritual realities into account is of necessity partial, blind, and distorted.

DECEPTION OF THE ELITES

Sometimes we can surmise only by external signs and indications that a satanic element is at work in certain historical movements and figures. Other times, however, the evidence is fairly direct. Such a case is that of H. S. Chamberlain, a writer whose racial theories were hailed by the Nazis as the "Gospel of the Nazi movement." Chamberlain's ideas found a hearing, inspiring the people who destroyed at least six million Jews. Chamberlain openly acknowledged a significant demonic element in his life and work:

> Hypersensitive and neurotic and subject to frequent nervous breakdowns, Chamberlain was given to seeing demons who by his own account, drove him on relentlessly to seek new fields of study and get on with his prodigious writings. One vision after another forced him to change from biology to botany, to the fine arts, to music, to philosophy, to biography, to history. Once, in 1896, when he was returning from Italy, the presence of a demon became so forceful that he got off the train at Gardone, shut himself up in a hotel room for eight days, and abandoning some work on music that he had contemplated, wrote feverishly on a biological thesis until he had the germ of the theme that would dominate all of his later works: race and history.

> Whatever its blemishes, his mind had a vast sweep ranging over the fields of literature, music, biology, botany, religion, history, and politics. There was, as Jean Réal has pointed out, a profound unity of inspiration in all his published works and they had a remarkable coherence. Since he felt

himself goaded on by demons, his books (on Wagner, Goethe, Kant, Christianity and race) were written in the grip of a terrible fever, a veritable trance, a state of self-induced intoxication, so that, as he says in his autobiography, *Lebenswegt,* he was often unable to recognize them as his own work, because they surpassed his expectations.[379]

We can observe a continuum of evil. The Renaissance magus's role as a secular messiah, who attempts to control human life through knowledge and power assisted by magic, becomes full-blown in Adolf Hitler, who built his Third Reich on the foundation of Chamberlain's racial theories. The doctrines designed by demons for the blinding and destruction of the human race are successfully promulgated through a plausible liar and applauded by "great men" and "leading intellectuals" of the day. "Liberation" from divinely ordered restraints becomes slavery to the infernally evil genius who roams the world seeking for opportunities to deceive, blind, and destroy.

Also worth noting is how the most educated classes in Germany often participated eagerly in the "madness of the crowds." The German Philosophical Association, including such luminaries as Martin Heidegger, came out in full support of Hitler and his program. When I was at Notre Dame studying philosophy, Heidegger was a "god."

A major study by Yvonne Sherratt about how the intellectual elite of Germany eagerly collaborated with Hitler, reviewed in *The Catholic Thing*, is worthy of note.[380] The elite, motivated at that time, as today, by a concern for professional advancement and being "on the right side of history," saw which way the wind was blowing and positioned themselves to take advantage of it, despite the moral and intellectual compromises they would have to make.

The most prominent was Martin Heidegger, the author of *Being and Time* and one of the central figures in existentialism. After leaving a Jesuit seminary, Heidegger studied under the great phenomenologist Edmund Husserl, who arranged for him to take over his chair of philosophy at the University of Freiburg in 1928.

In May 1933, weeks after he joined the Nazi Party, Heidegger was named rector of Freiburg University and, in his inaugural address, praised National Socialism and gave the Nazi salute.

In the University newspaper in late 1933, he wrote:

> May you ceaselessly grow in courage to sacrifice yourselves for the salvation of the nation's essential being and the increase of its innermost strength in its polity.... The Führer himself and he alone is the German reality, present and future, and its law ... Heil Hitler.[381]

He issued the Baden Decree that suspended non-Aryan professors at the University. His mentor, Edmund Husserl, was a victim of that decree.

Heidegger also lobbied for the creation of a chair in race studies and genetics and advocated that "in order to preserve the health of the state questions of euthanasia should be seriously contemplated."[382]

Sherratt observes:

> Heidegger had helped glorify the Führer. He had provided the icing on the cake of Hitler's dream: for here was the intellectual Nazi superman for all to see.[383]

After the philosopher-Führer committed suicide in 1945, the philosopher-collaborators ran for cover. With the aid of university colleagues, they covered up their activities and ignored the past: "A veil of silence descended across the university halls."[384]

Heidegger never even condemned the Holocaust and "simply likened the loss of Jewish lives to the Germans killed during combat."[385] When pressed to repent, he complained "that Hitler let him down. 'Is Hitler going to apologize to me?'"[386]

Today our "leading universities" are the locus of the most amazing brainwashing in leftist ideology and the most amazing violators of academic freedom and freedom of speech. Those who hold opinions different from the reigning cultural liberalism are often not permitted to speak on campus, and when they are officially allowed, they are sometimes met by mobs that refuse to let them speak, and sometimes they are physically assaulted. Remarkable studies have been done of the political views of faculty at the leading universities as well as of journalists at the major media organizations and found that a huge percentage of both professors and journalists consider themselves liberal.[387] Freedom of speech? Academic freedom? No, only if you agree with the controlling elite.

ANGELS OF LIGHT

In light of the rapidly advancing legalization of "euthanasia," the remarkable career of Elisabeth Kübler-Ross provides another insight into how apparently very "gifted" people can themselves be misled and mislead others in what appear to be, at first, very innocent ways.

A psychiatrist, Kübler-Ross published a book in 1969, *On Death and Dying*, in which she outlined five phases of and responses to death, ranging from angry denial to ultimate acceptance. The book became immensely successful, was adopted by many Christians, and was widely used in counseling and ministry to the dying. She was named one of the eleven "women of the decade" during the seventies.

Kübler-Ross gave numerous seminars, many of which were attended and sponsored by church people. In them, often in response to questions, she would tell of her admiration for Mother Teresa and then go on to explain that her research with the dying indicated there was no "judgmental" God. Without necessarily calling into question her early research with the dying, I think it is fair to say that, over a period of time, her work tended to lead people away from orthodox Christian faith. She later acknowledged explicitly doing so.[388]

In 1979, the depth of Kübler-Ross's bondage to "spirits" became public when she declared herself to be an "immortal visionary and modern cartographer of the River Styx," and defended her deep involvement with a spiritualist group called the Church of the Facet of Divinity. A regular feature of this group's sessions was the invocation of spirits, who then were said to materialize and "minister" to the participants' various problems. (These spirits were sometimes purported to give back rubs.) Kübler-Ross bought land near this spiritualist center, naming it Shanti Nilaya (Sanskrit for "final home of peace") and made it a center for workshops on death and dying. In subsequent appearances and interviews, Kübler-Ross openly admitted that she'd had contact with "spirit guides" for nine years and that they told her that there is no such thing as damnation, judgment, or hell.[389]

At a certain point, she professed disillusionment about her heavy dependence on a particular psychic, but her non-Christian occult views remained unchanged:

> There is no such thing as good or bad. If we don't learn what we're supposed to in this life, we'll learn it in another.[390]

Participants at seminars run by Kübler-Ross often described her as "peaceful," "gentle," "wise," "like an angel." This can serve as a reminder, once again, that sometimes theories which most deeply undermine Christian truth are attractive and presented by spokespersons who appear to be "angels of light." The most diabolical and murderous "wisdom" can appear "life-enhancing" and "liberating."

We need to be alert enough today to recognize the spiritual forces at work in certain contemporary theories, spokesmen, and movements. We need to ponder God's Word of warning about angels of light and be firmly rooted in the objective truth of his Word:

> But even if we, or an angel from heaven, should preach to you a gospel contrary to that which we preached to you, let him be accursed. (Gal 1:8)

> For even Satan disguises himself as an angel of light. (2 Cor 11:14)

To be successful, deception must deceive. It must include much truth, and it must appeal to what appears noble, positive, creative, and just. Chamberlain intertwined with his demon-inspired racial theories many references to Christ and Christianity. Kübler-Ross's gentleness, peacefulness, "respect for religion," and admiration for Mother Teresa put her in an excellent position to lead people to doubt or to be silent about important aspects of God's Word to us. Someone's immense erudition can so impress us that we unconsciously completely surrender to their views, including deception smuggled in among many good things:

> Now the Sprit expressly says that in later times some will depart from the faith by giving heed to deceitful spirits and doctrines of demons, through the pretension of liars. (1 Tim 4:1–2)

It is not uncommon that a polite, reasonable desire to "purify" Christianity of its belief in the reality of the devil goes along with doing the devil's work.

A FLAWED FEMINISM

The spiritual roots of post-Christian humanism are especially evident in the origins of the modern feminist movement. Gloria Steinem, for many years the editor of the influential *Ms.* magazine, wrote that "Feminism is the path to Humanism, and it is Humanism which is the goal." Ms. Steinem went on to say: "By the year 2000 we will, I hope, raise our children to believe in human potential, not God."[391] Betty Friedan, a leading feminist and founder of the National Organization for Women, is a signer of Humanist Manifesto II, which espoused similar goals.

Certain feminists expressed intense, open hostility to the Christian view of sex and the family. Dr. Mary Jo Bane, associate director of Wellesley College Center for Research on Women, declared, "We really don't know how to raise children.... The fact that children are raised in families means there's no equality ... We must take them away from families and raise them."[392]

And aren't we hearing the same ideas today?

Another Catholic theologian's book carried the message in its title: *Beyond God the Father.* This book introduced the subject of going beyond God the Father with a somewhat incoherent mélange of references to lesbianism and the occult.[393] For many years, even after publishing this book, the theologian continued teaching at Boston College. Her books still sell well.

Some feminists rejected God and Christ and called for a return to witchcraft and the worship of pagan gods and goddesses. As one feminist document put it, "All of history must be rewritten in terms of the oppression of women. We must go back to ancient female religions."[394] The *Los Angeles Times* described one such feminist worship service:

Nearly 400 women picked different notes and held them, catching their breaths at different times so the sound droned unabated for five minutes. The eerie monotones from this congregation of sorts reverberated against the angular outside walls of the Theater of Performing Arts and filtered through clumps of tall pines on the UC Santa Cruz campus. The hymnic call was to the Goddess. Later in the day, encouraged by the beat of bongo drums, spontaneous groups of circling women danced bare breasted in scenes suggestive of frolicking wood nymphs. . . .

More than a successful university extension course, however, the event was indicative of a burgeoning spiritual dimension of the women's movement in America.[395]

Christine Downing, head of San Diego State University's religious studies department at the time, estimated that many—if not most—spiritually sensitive women in the women's movement were willing to replace the biblical God with a frankly pagan and polytheistic approach. The *Los Angeles Times* article also noted, "A Santa Cruz woman, Ebon of the Mountain, 38, said, 'Some of the women think of themselves as witches, but not all.'"[396]

As another Catholic theologian put it:

Through him [an antichristian college professor] I discovered the meaning of religious symbols not as extrinsic doctrines but as living metaphors of human existence. . . . I knew that Ba'al was a real god, the revelation of the mystery of life, the expression of the depths of being which had broken through into the lives of the people and gave them a key to the mystery of death and rebirth. . . . As for the defects of Ba'al, were they more spectacular than the defects of the biblical God or Messiah, or perhaps less so? . . .

I could not give allegiance to any "jealous god" on the level of historical particularity. . . .

I could not tell her [a nun] that my devotion to Mary was somewhat less than my devotion to some more powerful females that I knew: Isis, Athena, Artemis.[397]

Unfortunately, such profoundly anti-Christian trends did not die out with the fragmentation of the secular feminist movement into many tributaries, in their many varying degrees of radicalness. Whole orders of nuns, now dramatically declining and not attracting new members, embodied some of the more extreme views of feminism and even sympathy for the "goddess" and still do. Recent visitors to a retreat center of one of these orders were surprised to see a whole collection of esoteric and feminist literature prominently available to retreatants. To see the same spirits manifesting themselves in Rome recently, through "mother earth" and the "Pachamama" idols, was a shocking reminder that pantheism and goddess worship—long lurking about in numerous retreat houses and dying religious orders—are alive and well, even at the highest levels of the Church.

Even though there is a reasonably strong and healthy "Christian feminism" movement that attempts to integrate positive elements of feminism into a Christian worldview, oftentimes with inspiring results, the deep anti-Christian roots and hostility to the biblical sexual ethic of the original feminist movement continues to run deep in contemporary society. One of the two major political parties in the United States that used to be a "big tent," including both pro-life and pro-abortion members, has become a radical force for abortion at any stage for any reason and refuses to support any remaining pro-life members who would like to run for office. If they already hold office, this party will encourage other pro-abortion members to run against them. This party now even refuses to support caring for children born alive after a botched abortion, which can only be considered infanticide. The same party has now adopted support for gay marriage as one of its foundational positions. Catholics who traditionally valued this party for its defense of the working person are finding it hard to remain members in light of the party's radical evolution, which continues to embrace new extremes, despite the fact that alternatives are not without their significant problems.

The feminist movement attacked some genuine injustices, and some of its ongoing goals, especially those pertaining to economic injustices and the positive values of the "me too" movement, which calls out male abuse, can and should be supported by Christians. Nevertheless, the militantly anti-Christian heart of this movement, at least as revealed in many of its leaders, should make Christians extremely cautious.

The Post-Christian Assault on Life

The denial of the reality of Satan and his activities are often associated today with a wider doctrinal and moral decay. In the name of God and of life, "reasonable" people have wreaked terrible havoc on humanity. A book written by a Yale University psychiatrist asks how German physicians, "heirs to Europe's proudest medical tradition," could participate in mass slaughter and grisly human experiments in the Nazi death camps. The problem, of course, was not restricted to German doctors; as we have already noted, most of the educated professional classes in Germany were also implicated. The author of this study concludes that the German doctors participated in a self-chosen delusion:

Doctors were the embodiment of Nazi political and racial ideology in its ultimate murderous form. The killing came to be projected as a medical operation. . . . "If you have a gangrenous growth, you have to remove it." . . . If you view the Jews as death-tainted, then killing them seems to serve life. . . . *Most killing is not done out of sadism, not even most Nazi killing. . . . The murders are done around a perverted vision of life enhancement.*[398]

The Nazi Holocaust was carried out by men who believed they were "enhancing life." The similarity to today's silent holocaust of abortion is numbing. Abortion clinics, frequently located in minority population centers, were considered "essential services" in many states during the coronavirus lockdown, while churches were not.

Under the ironic ideal of "enhancing life," we are seeing the rapid adoption of hormonal and surgical intervention for those who feel they are not really their biological gender. As we have seen, those who want to "transition" to the opposite gender through mutilating treatments are now assisted by many doctors who no longer have reservations about performing surgeries or prescribing hormone therapy, even though there is no evidence that such treatments have long-term positive outcomes. Even radical gay authors are questioning the rush to perform such treatments, likening it to the "madness of crowds."[399] Someday, I think we will look back at the almost inexplicable social acceptance of such treatments based on nonexistent evidence that such treatments are helpful. We will marvel how we ever became so deluded, and we will repent for the awful mutilation enacted on even young children whose parents foolishly insisted were capable of deciding for themselves at very young ages that they should be the opposite gender.

Rebellion against God and Sexual Disorder

There is a particular link today between satanically inspired rejection of God and his Word and sexual sin and disorders. Romans 1 gives a devastating account of the downward descent into sexual confusion and disorder that flows from a rejection of God and a willful suppression of the truth that he has revealed to all mankind. The rejection of God's Word regarding sexuality and its purposes in the name of "fulfillment" not only assaults Christian values but produces a harvest which is miserable in simply human terms. In the name of "life," the dominant power of our culture brings death and disease through abortion and venereal disease, broken relationships through massive infidelity and divorce, and deep sexual confusion and psychological problems through attacks on commitment, fidelity, and the very nature and meaning of male and female.

Thomas Aquinas points out that there is a particular link between sexual disorder and the darkening of the mind, as well as a link between sexual sin and the loss of the fear of God.[400]

Planned Parenthood

Organized groups are working skillfully to push contemporary societies in this direction. Often, they enlist Church personnel to help them. The International Planned Parenthood Federation (IPPF) is one such group—and is perhaps the most effective of all on a global basis.

With international headquarters in London and local affiliates in more than 132 countries, and a significant presence in 21 others, IPPF directly influences 164 countries. In 2018, the London office facilitated 223.3 million "sexual and reproductive health services." They tend to bury their abortion statistics, but the Planned Parenthood Federation of America's 2018–2019 Annual Report claims that only 4 percent of their services for that year were abortions.[401] If that is also the case internationally, although it may well be higher, the number of abortions for the year would be about 8,932,000. The International Federation had income of $133 million in the 2018–2019 fiscal year, and its member associations had income of $264.2 million. 82 percent of their funding comes from governments, especially the United States, Canada, the United Kingdom, and the Nordic countries. Another significant part of their funding comes from private foundations such as the Bill and Melinda Gates Foundation, the David Packard and Hewlett foundations, and multinational organizations such as the UN and the WHO (World Health Organization). They use the money to fund an international network of organizers, educators, and lobbying operations to influence schools and governments to adopt policies and laws to facilitate their aims, and to reduce the shame factor in the image of abortion. They claim to have influenced 163 legal and policy changes in the last fiscal year. IPPF is dedicated to freeing sexual experience from any link with procreation or family life. It pursues an active program of promoting contraception, abortion, sterilization, and sex education, using blatantly anti-Christian materials. It often brings volunteers to assist states and local school boards in developing sex-education materials, which, if the average parent saw, they would be shocked. Children in early grades are now being taught about gender identity, gender fluidity, and being taught how to "consent" to various forms of sexual conduct.[402]

In the United States alone, Planned Parenthood affiliates operate more than six hundred "health centers" and carried out 345,672 abortions in the fiscal year ending on June 30, 2019. Their income for the fiscal year was a staggering 1638.6 million dollars.[403] Even so, when the US government offered help to small businesses during the coronavirus outbreak, Planned Parenthood asked for, and received, eighty million dollars, even though, with many more than the five-hundred-employee limit, they were clearly ineligible to receive the aid. The government is now asking for the money to be returned, and an investigation launched into whether there was outright fraud in the applications for the aid or collusion by the banks or by people in the government.[404]

Planned Parenthood affiliates target their efforts especially at the poor and at teenagers. The recent book and movie, *Unplanned*, laid bare the seamy underside of the abortion business, as management directives went out to affiliates to increase the number of abortions each year to increase income. The videos that exposed the "business" of selling body parts from aborted babies as Planned Parenthood executives sipped their glasses of wine over lunch shocked many and led to congressional investigations that went nowhere.

Margaret Sanger, the founder of Planned Parenthood, was a woman dedicated to the overthrow of Judeo-Christian morality and openly advocated and practiced premarital and extramarital sex. Sanger's followers today seldom mention some of her other beliefs. She frequented séances and wanted to weed "bad stock" out of the race by manipulating the poor into using contraceptive devices and getting them sterilized.[405] She was blatantly and thoroughly racist, but only lately has there been any acknowledgement by Planned Parenthood of their founder's shocking views on limiting minority populations.

The title of this chapter is "power, principalities, and organizations." Planned Parenthood is probably one of the most powerful international organizations, influencing governments with well-organized local activists and centers that are dedicated to completely establishing the sexual revolution as the law of the land! Many lands. But there are many other organizations as well.

THE POWER OF ORGANIZATIONS

The Gay Lobby

One of the most successful campaigns to normalize sexual immorality was that undertaken by the gay lobby. In a remarkably short period of time, the majority of Americans and Catholics went from overwhelmingly thinking that the practice of homosexuality was morally wrong to overwhelmingly approving it. How did this happen? Many people worked very hard over a long period of time to make it happen. The strategy that was adopted and succeeded was laid out in 1989 in a book entitled *After the Ball: How America Will Conquer Its Fear and Hatred of Gays in the 90's* by gay Harvard grads Marshall Kirk and Hunter Madsen.[406] It was a brilliant strategy that counseled homosexuals to "cool it in public" and only put forward the most normal and attractive people as spokespeople. They also counseled not to get into what sex acts homosexuals actually do but concentrate on "equality" and "love" and comparing their cause to the civil rights movement. They also advised seeking to exploit cracks in what used to be the united front of Christians by highlighting dissenting scholars who "reinterpret" Scripture passages that are commonly thought to forbid homosexuality.[407] They advised massive advertising campaigns featuring attractive gay people and featuring them in television and movies as much as possible. The campaign was hugely successful and goes on to this day. The pressure on corporations and states to be "gay friendly" has been likened to extortion. If companies or states were thought to discriminate against gay people, huge, gay-friendly or gay-run corporations, such as Apple, would threaten to pull out of the state, or movie studios would threaten not to film in their state.

The Southern Poverty Law Center threatens to put groups that don't embrace the LGBTQ agenda on their "hate list" and publicize it. Cowardice isn't just a problem in the Church. Corporate America regularly gives in to this bullying.[408]

The Human Rights Campaign (HRC), which is the largest LGBTQ lobbying firm in the country, regularly rates corporations for their compliance with HRC standards for "gay-friendly" policies and are publicly proud of their policies. They triumphantly announced recently that 686 of the top corporations and law firms now had a 100 percent rating. They have weaponized the "Equality Index" quite successfully.[409]

And the presence of gay propaganda in television and the movies continues to increase. The gay activist group GLAAD continues to pressure the TV industry to increase LGBTQ characters in prime-time broadcast. Their goal was to have 10 percent of all characters be LGBTQ, and they recently declared that the goal was achieved with the 2019 TV season. Their new goal is 20 percent.[410] Even Disney has begun to introduce gay characters to its "family-friendly" fare. A Disney producer apologized to the gay community for not doing more but promised that they were working on ways to increase gay representation in Disney productions in the future.[411]

Sex Education

Another organized effort to push society and the Church in the direction of secular humanistic values and lifestyle is the development and promotion of many sex education programs now required in public schools, and even adopted by some Catholic schools. Many of these programs are designed to break down the Christian approach to sex and family life; they encourage children to be open to a multitude of sexual experiences. They have children experiment in handling contraceptives and talking about their use. Despite claims of diversity, the Christian viewpoint is often excluded, and diversity comes to mean the imposition of the reigning ideology of sexuality divorced from procreation and no longer under the law of nature or of God. The issue here is not whether children should have sex education. Obviously they should. Rather, the issue is by whom, in what context, with what values, and by what methodology.[412]

There are some useful sex education curricula available that are respectful of Christian values. But many are subtly or blatantly undermining Christian belief. They seek to break down resistance to sexual activity, even among very young children. While often pretending to be "value-neutral" programs which simply help students "clarify" their values, these programs are, in fact, designed to open a wedge between the student and any authority, including the Church and parents, and to encourage them to independent action in the area of sexuality. They present various forms of sexual activity in an allegedly "neutral" way so that students can examine their feelings about them. Of course, the "value neutral" claim is often a hoax. The underlying value is relativism, the belief that truth and morality are what you make them and what you wish. And not only that, but if you don't go along with the "anything goes," "you are who you think you are," "you be you" agenda, you're on the "wrong side of history," and who wants to be on the wrong side of history!

The proponents of value-clarification programs sometimes reveal their anti-Christian presuppositions clearly. Sidney Simon, a leading developer of such value programs, once said this:

> The old "shalt nots" simply refuse to maintain relevance. . . .
> We certainly do not need more moralizing and preaching on
> the right and good values.[413]

Simon went on to say that his own value clarification system is a method by which teachers can change the values of students "without being caught."[414]

Advocates of "value-neutral" sex education often argue that the only way to overcome such problems as unwanted teenage pregnancies is to equip young people with a good knowledge of sex and of the ways to prevent pregnancy. The programs usually include outright propagation of views about sexual behavior which are contrary to Christian teaching. Many of these programs now include frequent positive presentations of homosexuality and lesbianism, bisexuality, and gender transitioning, proposing them as alternate lifestyles, which students can choose if they wish.

The claim that such "value-neutral" sex education will decrease teenage pregnancies is not supported by the facts.

The percentage of children born out of wedlock is increasing around the world, but most particularly in Western countries:

> At one extreme are some 25 countries, including China, India and most countries in North Africa and Western and Southern Asia, where the proportion of births out of wedlock is low, typically less than 1 percent. In those societies births outside of marriage carry strong social disapproval, including sanctions, penalties and punishments to the mother and father as well as stigmatization of the child. Some travel guides advise couples to pretend to be married. In striking contrast, the proportions of births outside marriage in another 25 countries mostly in Latin America, including Brazil, Chile, Costa Rica, Jamaica, Mexico and Colombia, are estimated at more than 60 percent. In another 20 countries, including Belgium, Denmark, France, Norway and Sweden, the majority of births occur outside marriage, with government assistance typically provided to single mothers.[415]

Currently in the United States, 40 percent of children are born out of wedlock, contributing to massive family breakdown, oftentimes fatherless children, and almost certain economic poverty. What's even more tragic is that about 70 percent of African American children are born out of wedlock, very often with absentee fathers.[416] Such a high incidence is not unrelated to the rise of violence and drug addiction in localities particularly affected by this breakdown. Programs that throw money at the problem without a serious look at the underlying breakdown of morality and family structure haven't worked for fifty years, but that still seems to be what is always proposed as the solution. Interesting studies have been done showing that the educated post-Christian population who most vigorously espouse the "anything goes" mentality when it comes to marriage and sexuality are the ones with the most traditional approaches to marriage and family life, while those most victimized by the mentality, who actually act on it, are the poor and uneducated.

Lacking evidence for their views, proponents of "value-neutral" sex education usually fall back on secular humanist rhetoric. They say that such programs will produce a "fuller life," a "more fulfilled and sexually integrated" personality. These claims also depend on ignoring other facts, such as the well-documented increase in the rate of impotence and other sexual dysfunction in modern society. One of the saddest things I heard recently was a newly married young man disclosing that his long-standing addiction to pornography made sexual relations with his wife almost impossible. The proponents of sexual freedom are actually making a spiritual statement and have a "vision" of human life. It is one based on a rejection of God and Scripture and a hostility to the Church, and it is not good for human beings in any way. It is truly another religion, another gospel.

What's particularly concerning today is the impression that the Vatican is now flirting with entering into alliances with organizations that are diametrically opposed to the most fundamental truths of the faith and of the very structure of reality. The

"Francis economy" initiatives and the Global Education for a New Humanism are purported to be ready to include many of the same and similar organizations and funding sources that we have identified in this chapter and throughout the book as working to undermine fundamental truths.

WE CAN'T SAY WE HAVEN'T BEEN WARNED

Dr. Armand Nicholi, a Christian psychiatrist affiliated with the Harvard Medical School, commented, years ago, on the disturbing trends he saw in our increasingly de-Christianized society, their implications for the future, and the passivity of the churches in giving effective guidance to their members. His words can rightly be called prophetic:

> The trend toward quick and easy divorce and the ever-increasing divorce rate subjects more and more children to physically and emotionally absent parents. The divorce rate has risen 700 percent in this century and continues to rise. There is now one divorce for every 1.8 marriages. Over a million children a year are involved in divorce cases and 13 million children under eighteen have one or both parents missing. . . .

> The family is also affected by the lack of impulse control in our culture today. . . . The deep moral confusion we have observed over the past decade seems to have lifted all restraint. During the past ten years, I have noticed a marked change in the type of problems that bring people to a psychiatrist. Previously, a great many came because of their inability to express impulses and feelings. Today, the majority come because of an inability to *control* their im-

pulses. (People in my field relate this lack of control to the declining influence of the father in the home.)

The steady rise of violent crime in this country most clearly demonstrates our inability to control aggression. In Boston, where more people pursue higher education than perhaps any place on earth, a murder occurs about every third day. Aggression in the home has been increasing steadily. . . .

Even more prevalent in society is the failure to control sexual impulses. The number of illegitimate births in this country continues to rise. . . . I have also noticed an increased incidence of homosexuality among young people and also much greater freedom in expressing it. . . . A home in which both parents are available to the child emotionally as well as physically has become the exception rather than the rule. . . .

What about the future? What can we expect if these trends continue? First, the quality of family life will continue to deteriorate, producing a society with a higher incidence of mental illness than ever before. Ninety-five percent of our hospital beds may be taken up by mentally ill patients.

This illness will be characterized primarily by a lack of self-control. We can expect the assassination of people in authority to be a frequent occurrence, as well as events like the sixteen-year-old girl who recently began shooting people "for the fun of it."

Crimes of violence will increase, even those within the family. . . . The suicide rate will continue to rise . . . In the past twenty years, however, the suicide rate in ten to fourteen-year-olds has tripled. We already are producing an enormous number of angry, depressed, and suicidal kids. . . .

As sexuality becomes more unlimited, more separated from family and emotional commitment, the deadening effect will cause more bizarre experimenting and widespread perversion. Jean O'Leary has written in the National Organization for Women publication that lesbianism should be taught in our schools and that school counselors should take courses "to teach a positive view of lesbianism." And a group in Boston called the Boston Boise Committee has been trying to convince the public that there is nothing "inherently wrong with sex between men and boys," to lower the age of consent to fourteen, and to change the child molestation laws to reduce legal barriers against such relationships.[417]

Dr. Nicholi pointed out that the Christian churches have been responsible for much of this disorder by their passivity, silence, and ambiguous teaching:

As a nation we appear to be more confused morally than at any time in our history, and the church has failed to give leadership. Perhaps we need to hear a little less about self-fulfillment and a little more about self-denial. Could it be that denial is the key to fulfillment? . . . The church should spell out clearly the Christian sexual ethic. The church's reluctance to speak out clearly on this issue has resulted in confusion within many homes. So many voices in our society point in opposite directions, and enormous stress falls upon the young person who has no clear guidance in this area.[418]

Finally, Dr. Nicholi pointed out the embarrassing fact that the conclusions to which even the social scientists are coming merely confirm what the Christian Church has known all along but has sometimes become too confused and compromised to teach clearly and confidently:

> Social scientists have recently been trying to clarify scientifically through large surveys what constitutes happiness and fulfillment. These studies describe the most significant prediction of fulfillment and happiness to be family relationships and love within those relationships. Yet we have known this for 2,000 years. If the scriptures are what they claim to be, "inspired by God . . . useful for teaching the faith and correcting error" . . . the comprehensive equipment for resetting the direction of a man's life and training him in good living. . . then we might expect to find in them guidelines on how to live on this planet with a sense of fulfillment.[419]

A Spiritual Perspective

We need a spiritual perspective on this aspect of the crisis of truth. How many of those that the world calls "great"—how many "great leaders," "innovative thinkers," "distinguished jurists," "university presidents," "distinguished scholars," "philanthropists," "humanitarian organizations,"—will be found, on the day of judgment, to have been instruments of Satan's purposes? How much of the world's wisdom will be revealed to have come, not from "on high," but from below, to have been satanic in its origins and its purposes? (see Jas 3:13–18). Or even from well-organized pressure groups that use skillful propaganda, intimidation, guilt, and bullying to impose their views on society? As John Paul II put it:

For then, there is revealed—with an almost implacable necessity this second alternative: only the earth, which for a certain time accepts the dominion of man, turns out to be the master in the last analysis. Then the cemetery is the place of man's final defeat. It is the place where a final and irrevocable victory of the "earth" over the whole human being, rich as he is, is manifested; the place of the dominion of the earth over him who, in his own lifetime, claimed to be its master.

These are the inexorable logical consequences of the view of the world which rejects God and reduces the whole of reality exclusively to matter. At the moment in which man, in his mind and in his heart, makes God die, he must consider that he has condemned himself to an irreversible death, that he has accepted the programme of man's death. This programme, unfortunately, and often without reflection on our part, becomes the programme of contemporary civilization.[420]

The evidence is all around us, for those who have eyes to see and ears to hear. Christian eyes and ears should be able to recognize and identify the workings of the world, the flesh, and the devil in the midst of our fallen, blinded society. It is a society, which, in the words of John Paul II, has set out on "the programme of man's death."

Many Christians today think nothing of breaking solemn commitments, wantonly expressing their urges, and threatening the human life and happiness of others—all in the name of "fulfillment" and "freedom." A deep-seated rebellion against God and a rejection of Christ and the apostolic witness in Sacred Scripture lurks behind phrases like, "I deserve to be happy," or, "I feel God accepts what I'm doing since he is so merciful," and "I need to be me."

How different are the words of Jesus:

Enter by the narrow gate; for the gate is wide and the way is easy, that leads to destruction, and those who enter by it are many. For the gate is narrow and the way is hard, that leads to life, and those who find it are few. (Matt 7:13–14)

For whoever would save his life will lose it, and whoever loses his life for my sake will find it. (Matt 16:25)

And if your hand causes you to sin, cut it off; it is better for you to enter life maimed than with two hands to go to hell, to the unquenchable fire. And if your foot causes you to sin, cut it off; it is better for you to enter life lame than with two feet to be thrown into hell. And if your eye causes you to sin, pluck it out; it is better for you to enter the kingdom of God with one eye than with two eyes to be thrown into hell. (Mark 9:43–47)

I tell you, my friends, do not fear those who kill the body, and after that have no more that they can do.... Fear him who, after he has killed, has power to cast into hell. (Luke 12:4–5)

The way to fulfillment is to live in holiness and obedience to God. We must lay down our lives, renouncing the distorted thoughts, feelings, and desires of our fallen natures in order to become new creatures. We must follow him to his Cross, so that we may follow him in his Resurrection and be found acceptable in his sight on the Day of Judgment.

It is far better to be poor and unfulfilled in the eyes of the world than to risk eternal condemnation, resulting from an unrighteous pursuit of earthly good or "fulfillment." It is far better to enter eternal life without having entered into an unrighteous second marriage, without having selfishly pursued that full expression of our potential, without purchasing that "integrated personality" at the price of obedience to God and his Word, without having "gained the whole world" but suffered the loss of our soul. Such self-denial ultimately leads to a fulfillment that passes all understanding, to a life of eternal joy and fullness of life with God and with those who have followed and obeyed him. Those who have unrighteously pursued their own fulfillment in this life will live to eternally regret it and find companions in misery, hatred, and resentment with those who have based their lives on the lies of the evil one and accepted his invitation to disaster and eternal hate.

Only in the light of eternity can we really make wise choices about how to live life in this world. Only God's Word tells us the purpose for which we have been created and the manner in which we can fulfill most fundamentally and lastingly our "potential" for life and happiness. The work of the powers, principalities, and organizations dedicated to the silencing of the Gospel and the destruction of the Church, and indeed, of the whole human race, can only be countered by Christians properly defending themselves and taking up appropriate arms to counter these forces. In the words of Scripture:

> Finally, be strong in the Lord and in the strength of his might. Put on the whole armor of God, that you may be able to stand against the wiles of the devil. For we are not contending against flesh and blood, but against the principalities, against the powers, against the world rulers of this present darkness, against the spiritual hosts of wickedness in the heavenly places. Therefore take the whole armor of God, that you may be able to withstand in the evil day, and

having done all, to stand. Stand therefore, having girded your loins with truth, and having put on the breastplate of righteousness, and having shod your feet with the equipment of the gospel of peace; above all taking the shield of faith, with which you can quench all the flaming darts of the evil one. And take the helmet of salvation, and the sword of the Spirit, which is the word of God. (Eph 6:10–17)

Yes. The powers, principalities, and the dark forces of demonic power are abroad in the land, working through plausible liars, through governments and powerful organizations, but so are Jesus, his holy angels, the whole intercessory power of the communion of saints, and the blood of the contemporary martyrs! And the truth is that the Lord only permits evil to show itself and do its damage because he has a plan to bring good out of it and defeat it and rescue his oppressed ones. Like little children, trusting in our heavenly Father, the love of Jesus, and the always present power of the Holy Spirit, we can get up each day and do, to the best of our knowledge, our Father's will for us and know that the victory belongs to the Lord, and we will see it!

Chapter 9

PASTORAL PASSIVITY: GOOD SHEPHERDS AND BAD

AN IMMENSE AMOUNT of false teaching has been propagated in the post-conciliar period by people who were, or still are, under pastoral authority. Yet, for the most part, they have not been corrected. And the "flock" has not been warned. The early Church had to deal with similar situations. The Apostles were clear about how deviations like this needed to be handled: they needed to be corrected, the Church needed to be warned not to listen to them, and sinners and heretics needed to be "admonished," even publicly, so as to warn others not to go in that direction (see 1 Tim 5:20). In the face of the stubborn refusal to repent of particularly serious sin, excommunication was insisted upon for the good of the unrepentant sinner (see 1 Cor 5:1–5)! And Christians were told by Paul not to associate with Christians who refused to repent of serious sin so as not to pollute the community and give people the impression that such unrepented sin wasn't really serious (see 1 Cor 5:9–13). And he warned those who receive the Eucharist unworthily that there can be very bad consequences, both in this life and in the life to come (see 1 Cor 11:27–32). Such leadership as we see in the Apostles is very rare today, and consequently the sickness of unbelief and immorality continues to spread in the Church and in society.

Dr. Jeffrey Mirus accurately identifies a root of the problem. Bishops are still trying to be "players" in the wider society, not recognizing that wider society couldn't care less what the bishops really think, unless it is to support what the culture thinks. He draws our attention to the guidance Paul gave to the early Church:

> "For what have I to do with judging outsiders? Is it not those inside the church whom you are to judge? God judges those outside" (1 Cor 5:12–13). If Paul says this to all the members of the church in Corinth, how much more does it apply to those set over the churches of our time? Our bishops must curtail the eagerness of their episcopal conferences to participate in national and regional debates. God judges those outside. They must, each in his own diocese, devote themselves to faith, morals and sacraments, insisting that each of their priests be a close collaborator in this work. They must provide for charitable works not through government grants but through deacons and others set aside for this purpose, attending first and foremost to the needs of the Church's own members.[421]

Today there is quite a remarkable silence regarding the areas of the truth revealed by God that are most in conflict with our culture. Hardly ever is there a clear sermon on the seriousness of sexual sin, where the sins are actually specified. Scarcely ever is there a sermon on the eternal consequences of not repenting from serious sin, not just sexual sin, but all kinds of sins. Seldom ever is there a clear sermon on the reality and eternal duration of hell and the likelihood of going there if we don't leave the "broad way" and enter on the "narrow way" of Christian discipleship. Almost never is there ex-communication for so-called "practicing Catholics" who boldly and publicly deny there is any contradiction between aggressively supporting abortion and same-sex relationships and claiming to be a good Catholic. Because of the toleration of this contradiction and the meek posture of the shepherds, what the Church really believes about these things is raising questions in people's minds about how serious these contradictions of Church teaching really are. Not only that, but there are still professors of theology, priests, and bishops who sometimes directly, and very often through studied ambiguity, lead the flock away from the living waters of Christ into accommodation with the culture. Very seldom is there ever any correction of such false teaching or deception by omission from those responsible for guarding the flock from error. Sometimes they are even affirmed and "protected" by cardinals and bishops sympathetic to their views; sometimes they are even appointed to significant Vatican positions. The refusal of the bishops to "judge" where they really have the responsibility and power to judge, to maintain solidity of doctrine, morality, and mission within the Church, and to keep trying to be a player in the secular culture, thereby remaining silent about the ever-widening chasm between the culture and what the Church really stands for, has done and continues to do grievous harm.

How are we to understand this considerable problem of pastoral passivity? In order to do so, we must take a look at the purpose of the Second Vatican Council and the confusion that followed in its wake.

Vatican II

Vatican II was an attempt by the Church to get its own house in order and to adopt a stance toward the modern world that would overcome unnecessary alienation. Pope Paul VI summed up the objectives of the Council in these terms: "to make the Church of the twentieth century ever better fitted for proclaiming the Gospel to the people of the twentieth century."[422]

To renew itself internally, the Council adopted a concept of the Church that was expressed in more biblical terms, took a concern for liturgical renewal, put Scripture front and center, encouraged lay people to consider themselves full and active members of the Church, called for renewal of priestly and religious life, and completed the interrupted work of Vatican I by affirming the important role of bishops and their co-responsibility with the pope to care for the Church. All of this was intended to make the Church better situated to carry out its mission of evangelization.

The Council moved in several ways to change the relationship of the Church with the world at large. Its Decree on Ecumenism, *Unitatis Redintegratio*, established better relations with non-Catholic Christians by trying to create a positive climate in which Christian unity might move ahead. Its Declaration on Religious Liberty, *Dignitatis Humanae*, affirmed the Church's respect for the freedom of people to choose their own religion without undue interference from civil authorities, while still affirming the unique status of the Catholic Church as the place where the fullness of the means of salvation may be found.[423] In its Declaration on the Relation of the Church to Non-Christian Religions, *Nostra Aetate*, it tried to establish more productive relations with non-Christian religions by acknowledging our special relationship with the Jewish people and the "rays of truth" and "seeds of the word" that could be found in the other non-Christian religions. The declaration also expressed a willingness to dialogue with non-Christian religions to find areas of mutual collaboration for the welfare of mankind and to establish an atmosphere in which the claims of Christ might be presented more effectively. Such collaboration between the Catholic Church and

Muslims led to some fruitful efforts years ago to impede the United Nations from pushing pro-abortion and pro-homosexuality resolutions through without opposition. In the Pastoral Constitution on the Church in the Modern World, *Gaudium et Spes*, the Council endeavored to overcome, once and for all, the Church's reputation as an enemy of "progress" and an opponent of even the good elements of modern culture and civilization, such as scientific and political progress and human, social, and economic development. It did so by forsaking unnuanced condemnations of modern culture and by affirming those elements of modern culture that are compatible with Christianity. The Council also strove to present the Church as the true friend of mankind. It portrayed the Church as the only institution in a position to care for all man's needs and to help him develop all his potentialities. At the same time, the Council made very clear in numerous references, particularly in *Gaudium et Spes* and the Decree on the Mission Activity of the Church, *Ad Gentes*, but in many other documents as well, that the Church's primary aim in the renewal it was calling for was to win again a hearing for the Gospel it was entrusted to proclaim to all mankind and to work more effectively for the incorporation of all men into Christ and his Church.

Unfortunately, there is little evidence that the Church, so far at least, except among relatively small groupings, has adequately realized the internal renewal that the Council hoped for, which was primarily a renewal in holiness. Neither has it been notably successful in the renewed affirmation of mission and evangelization that it so insistently called for, except among relatively small groupings. Despite genuine bright spots here and there, the overall fact is that the Church has been in a constant state of decline in the West since Vatican II. We need to ask what went wrong, not only to understand how we got to where we are today but also to give some guidance about how to proceed now.

In the space we have available, we can only quickly survey some of the factors that have led to the confusion that followed in the wake of the Second Vatican Council. Those interested in studying this question more thoroughly can consult the full-length studies that are available, some written right after the Council and many more added as we celebrated the fiftieth anniversary of the Council in 2012.[424]

Since the election of Pope Francis, the boldness with which proponents of going "beyond" Vatican II have felt free to speak is rather shocking. As we noted in Chapter 4, the *National Catholic Reporter* devoted a special issue on the occasion of the fiftieth anniversary of the Council to evaluating it and advocating that we need to recapture its "spirit." It is clear that the same old attacks on faith, morality, and mission are being launched again with a newfound energy.

Since theologians made such a major contribution to the Council, their status was greatly enhanced afterward. People looked to them as the "definitive" interpreters of the Council. Bishops frequently did not feel qualified to interpret the Council. Moreover, they often tended to wait for other bishops to say something first, as bishops so often do today, with some wonderful exceptions. As a result of these factors, theologians quickly became the primary interpreters of the Council.

From the very beginning of the post-conciliar period, and indeed, even during the Council itself, a small but influential group of theologians—along with some priests, lay leaders, journalists, and even a few bishops—worked to push the Council to "go farther" than it did. They were active during the Council. After the Council, they were among its most prominent interpreters, and they often interpreted it as having gone "farther" than it actually did. They influenced crucial choices in the translation of Council documents and gave a certain slant to the explanatory footnotes in the more widely used editions of these documents.[425] Some pushed the interpretation of such favorite Council documents as *Gaudium et Spes* to make openings for the "new morality" and for the narrowing of Church mission to the embrace of transitory popular social and political causes.

Interpretation of the Council was, of course, necessary. After the Council, the vast majority of Catholics did not comprehend its significance for their lives. Theologians and journalists were willing to explain what the Council meant, but they often distorted its meaning in a more "progressive" direction. The Catholic and secular presses played a crucial role in coining labels: "progressive" forces prevailed over "reactionary" ones; "liberals" influenced some documents; "conservatives" won other rounds. ("Liberals," of course, were regarded as good by most commentators and "conservatives" as bad.)

Many Catholics, including bishops, formed their understanding of the Council from the media's interpretations. In these interpretations, the Council was often presented as one more step on the progressive road, a road the Church would inevitably take, a road leading to ever-greater openness to the world and appreciation of its values. People who wanted to interpret the Council as authoritative and binding were made to feel as though they would be left behind in a few years if they did so. In order not to be left behind, they were encouraged to move "beyond" the Council. Often, they were encouraged to disregard its actual texts in favor of what was called the "spirit of Vatican II."

Of course, there is nothing intrinsically wrong with wanting to move beyond the Council if this means discussion of issues not treated by the Council, elaboration of issues the Council did not treat fully, deeper understanding and appropriation of conciliar teaching, or even the clarification of ambiguous texts in the Council. However, those wanting to move "beyond" the Council often intended to move beyond the boundaries of Christian truth and morality. They wanted to *change* Christian teaching, not merely develop or adapt it.[426] They wanted to soften the Church's teaching to be less discordant with modern culture. This is, indeed, the very explicit intention of the majority of the German Bishops' Conference as they engage in their multiyear "binding synod" which seeks to accommodate Church teaching to the secular culture. It is also "in the air" as the Australian Catholic Church embarks on their own Plenary Council.

The windows opened by Pope John XXIII and the Council allowed other spirits besides the Holy Spirit to move more freely in the Church, and after being underground for many years, they are on the move again. The "restrainer" (see 2 Thess 2:6–7) in both the Church—(the clear teaching of St. John Paul II and Pope Benedict XVI)—and the culture (Christian culture) has been removed. Many Catholics were caught up in a heady sense of freedom and new frontiers. Many theologians, as well as many "progressive" priests and lay people, began their work and theology in the Spirit but ended up "in the flesh" as victims of their own pride, rebellion, and sense of importance. Some people used the new freedom to justify the works of the flesh, giving in to both intellectual and bodily vices. Other people, slowly and almost imperceptibly, came under the domination of "the spirit of the age." Unsound theological theories were irresponsibly and widely promulgated as reliable truth to thousands of priests, religious, and lay people. Years of applying the historical-critical method to Scripture and then to conciliar definitions and magisterial teachings, "monuments" of tradition, weakened Catholics' allegiance to the teaching of Scripture and the Church. No longer sure how to interpret or whether to trust Scripture and tradition, fruits of the "hermeneutic of suspicion," the way was open for speculative theology to gain greater credence than it would have if people remained grounded in Scripture and tradition.

Along with this, many Catholics, particularly priests and religious, indulged in a certain naive and adolescent delight in "rediscovering the world and its goodness." Since many had abandoned basic truths in their theological speculation, they no longer possessed adequate criteria for judging what was appropriate and what was inappropriate. Consequently, their new freedom and openness was often indiscriminate and, frequently, overtly sinful. Infidelity to vows of celibacy and marriage commonly occurred in the name of the new "openness" to the world and "freedom" from rigid rules and doctrines. Tens of thousands of priests, sisters, and brothers abandoned their promises and vows, and countless marriages were destroyed as frustrated or discontent spouses felt newly empowered to "grab at happiness" in another relationship rather than work through the difficulties in their existing marriages. Who can begin to measure the horror and gravity of such disasters? To make things worse, some dioceses became known as "annulment mills" where virtually anyone could claim "lack of discretion" at the time of marriage and get an annulment.

One of the most notable trends in the Church, even among the leaders of the Church, was a headlong rush to embrace certain secular causes and to incorporate into the Church the latest findings of secular research. Many equated "newer" with "better," whether it meant catching up with advanced theories of biblical exegesis or social action or adapting moral theology to Marxist, Freudian, or Jungian insights. The desire to be respected by the secular world and accepted by secular experts often led to indiscriminate affirmation of their findings and adoption of their methodologies, which often were based on hidden anti-Christian presuppositions. We can see examples of this today in how frequently outspoken secular experts are invited to present at Vatican conferences, even though they are known proponents of contraception and abortion and of global alliances that seek to include the Vatican to give moral cover to their population control and "ideological colonization" goals.

Many Catholics tried to develop a "contemporary, relevant spirituality." This often meant equating doing God's will with doing what one pleased. Many people gave up prayer, self-denial, and self-discipline, further weakening their ability to discern the Spirit of God from the human spirit, the spirit of the world, or the evil spirit. The lack of clear criteria of objective truth, coupled with the abandonment of authentic spiritual life, led many to become spiritually blind. They could no longer distinguish the true from the false, the things of God from the things of the world, the flesh, and the devil. Today, we have a plethora of supposedly Catholic and Christian spirituality books and programs that are not solid, in addition to the amorphous spirituality abroad in the culture, characterized by Oprah, and in the Catholic Church by Richard Rohr. This is an issue we will discuss in greater detail in Chapter 12.

The effects of this spiritually weakened condition were noticeable as Catholics developed a preoccupation for responding to the Council on the structural level, setting up parish and diocesan councils, the proliferation of committees and consultations, all of which may be helpful, but not if detached from the foundations of the faith and the guidance of the Holy Spirit. Their efforts to set up structures that would facilitate wider consultation usually followed secular political and organizational models. These models often proved unsuitable for a spiritual organism like the Body of Christ, with its distinctive modalities of life. This, in turn, produced little spiritual, evangelistic, or even organizational fruit. In many ways, we still are mired in a structural and process-oriented approach to Church life that impedes the real release of spiritual energy.

THE ASSAULT ON AUTHORITY

Implementation of the Council also involved a concerted effort to reinterpret authority so that appropriate obedience was severely weakened. The Council, it was said, presented authority as "loving service." Those in authority were said to have an obligation to "affirm" those for whom they were responsible and, by implication, very rarely to correct, discipline, or give actual direction.[427] This reinterpretation of authority, of course, was contrary to the Council's teaching, and to common sense. At the same time, interpreters of the Council tried to intimidate those in authority so that, in practice, they would not use their authority. Bishops and other pastors were urged to adopt a passive, permissive silence as the theologians and experts went about their work of implementing the Council. Today, the intimidation of those in authority is even stronger, but it is now coming from a culture that has turned hostile to Christ and the Church and from a strong fifth column within the Church that supports the culture. The shepherds have allowed themselves to be neutered by fear of men, both within and without the church.

A Catholic theologian defined authority in this way: "Authority for a human may be defined as 'the ability to perceive and point out the good.' Authority exercises its own attractiveness and sweetly compels the human heart to its embrace."[428] Such definitions simply reduce authority to kindly advice, to be accepted or rejected as one pleases. In the end, people under this kind of authority are free to do as they please. As a result, unity is no longer possible, whether in family life or in wider Church life. When unity is no longer based on truth, it becomes amorphous and eventually includes mutually contradictory positions. If you point out logical inconsistency to people nowadays, it is not uncommon for them to say something like this: "I don't care what you say; it's what I feel, and it's my truth."

Of course, authority should be exercised in love. Decisions

should be based on good information, and there should normally be a phase in which the one in authority discusses matters with those under authority, seeking wisdom about the best path forward. But this is only part of the authentic definition and exercise of authority. A person in authority also needs to be able to correct, admonish, discipline, and, ultimately, to exclude someone from a position of responsibility or from the community itself for serious cause and as a last resort, with appropriate due process, accountability, and appeal procedures. It's ironic that virtually the only times authority is still exercised in certain places is to admonish and penalize outspokenly orthodox priests and lay people—devout and obedient people who don't operate as pressure groups—who sometimes point out that "the emperor is not wearing any clothes," while giving a pass to those whose insubordination is popular with the growing numbers of secularized Catholics and the wider culture and whose disapproval might trigger activist pressure groups.

Another pressure on pastors and parents was a post-conciliar emphasis on authority as "service." Authority, of course, is primarily service, but service of a very particular kind; it involves listening, consulting, and reaching consensus if possible, but also, when necessary, correcting, admonishing, rebuking, and making tough decisions even when there isn't consensus. Authentic Christian service is based on fidelity to the truth. To "give people what they want" is indeed to serve them very badly when it involves assenting to the obscuring of the Word of God.

The naive view of human nature implicit in these definitions of authority is typical of much of the distorted teaching that occurs in the Church today. It fails to fully take into account the depth of the Fall, just as efforts at social justice can't really succeed unless the underlying problem of sin in individuals' lives is dealt with. Concepts of the Trinity and of the Church, which inadequately envision them as a democratic society or community, fail to properly reflect the nature of God or of the Church. Such ideas contribute greatly to the foolishness that sometimes abounds today under the guise of Christianity and renewal.

This reinterpretation of authority has been accompanied by successful efforts to reward and publicize those bishops, priests, and parents who operate in harmony with this deficient concept of authority, and to punish those who do not. Too often, a new wave of "pastoral" bishops who are currently being appointed are praised in a way that conveys the impression that their main virtues reside in their ability to give good press conferences, to be popular in secular society, to present a good image, and to not be "culture warriors." "Pastoral" has often become a code word for "permissive" and "accommodating." Too often, "pastoral" bishops are contrasted with "behind-the-times" bishops who are "doctrinally" oriented and "rigid," as if there is a necessary conflict between objective truth and actual life, between the clarity of truth and the depth of compassion. And it is wonderful to see the appointment of bishops who embody both of these capacities. Unfortunately, just as in the immediate aftermath of Vatican II, there seems today to be a strong resurgence in the appointment of "pastoral" bishops who are not known for guarding the flock from error or correcting wrongdoing and who seem to be quite ready to not offend the culture even when to remain silent is to permit the flock to be misled. In many cases, bishops are being appointed who are indeed not "culture warriors," which unfortunately there were never very many of, but are rather "culture accommodators," who for various reasons don't want to confront not just the culture but the lies that the culture is forcing people to believe under threat of penalties of various kinds.

This blatant media promotion of "pastoral" bishops was and is accompanied by subtle and private intimidation. Bishops are sometimes confidentially and "caringly" told, "You don't really know much in this area, so why don't you leave it to the experts?" Parents are often told the same thing by religious educators. It is even more blatant in the public school system, where parents are often seen as an obstacle to the proper indoctrination of the students and efforts are made to keep them from discovering what is really being taught. Often, bishops' unofficial "advisors," professional public relations and communications specialists, operating with a secular mindset even though they may be "good Catholics," will shape their behavior by advising what will "look good" and what will not "look good" in the eyes of the press. They will be told how to "put out the fire" of bad publicity, oftentimes by abjectly denying the truth of the faith. Of course, forthright exercise of spiritual authority or clear biblical teaching seldom looks good to the press.[429]

Sometimes official statements issued in the name of whole episcopal conferences bear the marks of careful "public relations" staff management. On the occasion of the first direct elections for members of the European Parliament, the Bishops' Conferences of Europe issued a joint message that went to unusual lengths to avoid a direct statement of the Gospel. It even omitted specifically Christian words in a quote from John Paul II. This is a quote from the Statement of the Presidents of European Episcopal Conferences on the Future of Europe:

> Europe must establish an opportunity of economic, cultural, and spiritual development for all. The words addressed by John Paul II to the whole world, on 22 October last, still ring in our ears and it seems to us that they should be applied to Europe itself: "Open the frontiers of States, economic and political systems, the immense fields of culture, civilization and development. Do not be afraid!"[430]

The actual words of the pope are as follows:

Brothers and sisters, do not be afraid to welcome Christ and accept his power. Help the Pope and all those who wish to serve Christ and with Christ's power to serve the human person and the whole of mankind. Do not be afraid. Open wide the doors for Christ. To his saving power open the boundaries of States, economic and political systems, the vast fields of culture, civilization and development. Do not be afraid.[431]

Some of the people who would like to push the Church in a certain direction are banking heavily on the hope that the new "pastoral" bishops will move into positions of greater responsibility in the coming years. As one prominent Catholic priest said shortly after the Council, "I look forward to unbelievable changes in the next five years when some of these men move up into important positions."[432] This statement is applicable again today.

One of the Saint Gallen "mafia" who openly admitted to trying to influence the election of Pope Francis is reported to have said that if Pope Francis can have five years to lead the Church, the changes will be irrevocable.[433]

Inadequate Criteria for Pastoral Judgment

Pastoral leaders today often fail to exercise their responsibility effectively because they have inadequate models for leadership and employ inadequate criteria to judge their own work and the work of others.

Pastoral passivity is often justified as an appropriate posture for leaders of a "pluralist" Church. Indeed, pluralism in the Church can be a very good thing. The life of the Church is enriched by a certain kind of diversity in cultural expression, pastoral approach, and even theological and philosophical expression of the faith. Yet pluralism is legitimate only if it involves diverse expressions of the *one faith* as definitively interpreted by the teaching authority of the Church over the centuries. Today, calls for pluralism are often pleas to abandon the one faith. Many of those who work for the "pluralistic" Church of the future, in contrast to the "monolithic" Church of the past, are actually working for the destruction of the Church and any meaningful measure of unity of faith. Pope Paul VI called this kind of indiscriminate pluralism, the kind that lacks any clear criteria, as "corroding and ambiguous." It is indeed at work in the Church today.

Pope Francis, in *Evangelii Gaudium*, calls for a "healthy de-centralization" which, by definition, would be a good thing. But is the de-centralization that is presently occurring healthy? Is it healthy to have cardinals and bishops publicly fighting with each other? Is it healthy to have something considered serious sin on one side of the Polish-German border and, on the other side, considered to be an unduly narrow interpretation of Revelation that needs to be accommodated to changes in the culture? Is it a healthy de-centralization to have some bishops publicly warn about the serious ambiguities in Fr. James Martin's advocacy for "welcoming" the LGBTQ community and then have "higher-ups" appoint him to an official position in a Vatican department and have other bishops and the pope himself warmly welcome him to their dioceses?

Often an uncritical pluralism is combined with a conception of a pastoral leader as someone who is a "unifier." Of course, those responsible for families, parishes, and other segments of God's people need to work to unify their people. But they should not achieve unity at any price. The unity appropriate to God's people is a unity based on common adherence to Christian truth and the person of

Christ. Saying "yes" to the teaching of the Church in areas of faith and morals is to say "no" to those who undermine and challenge them. Unity is based on truth. Yet many pastoral leaders today are presiding over a "unity" which contains contradictory elements. Many pastoral leaders today are presiding over a false unity which includes parishioners who accept the teaching of Christ and the Church and those who reject it—not really a unity at all. To tolerate the corruption of Christian truth in the name of unity or pluralism is to make a mockery of the genuine function and role of pastoral authority. It is, in fact, to preside over that corroding of Christian faith which Paul VI warned about and which a growing number of cardinals and bishops continue to warn about today.

Sometimes, such corroding pluralism is tolerated because of a muddled or vague understanding of the wheat and the weeds parable or other Scripture passages that talk of problems within the Church. It is frequently said that "the Catholic Church is a church of sinners, a broad church that includes everybody; it is not a sect." Besides often incorporating an imprecise and often incoherent use of the sociological categories of "church" and "sect," such formulations are, more seriously, based on a misinterpretation of such Scripture passages. The point of such passages is often to describe actual or future situations that can never be remedied simply by human effort but can ultimately only be fully resolved by an action of God himself. The point of such passages, though, is not to counsel the advocacy of a lukewarm, passive, indifferent vision of Church life, in which the corruption of Christian truth and God's people is benignly presided over.

Such false applications of the parable have been common previously in Church history to justify a distorted approach to Church life—and St. Augustine addressed this situation squarely:

In answer to these persons I would say, first of all, that in reading testimonies of Sacred Scripture which indicate that there is presently, or foretell that there will be in the future, a mingling of good and evil persons in the Church, anyone who understands these testimonies in such a way that he supposes the diligence and severity of discipline ought to be relaxed altogether and be omitted is not taught by those same writings but is deceived by his own conjecture. The fact that Moses, the servant of God, bore most patiently that mixture of good and evil among the chosen people did not prevent him from punishing many, even with the sword. . . . In our times, when the sword has ceased to be visible in the discipline of the Church, what must be done is pointed out by degradations and excommunications.[434]

Other reasons for pastoral inadequacy are in large part psychological. Many pastors and parents are so deeply troubled by the extent of problems plaguing the Church or family that they tend to seize on any apparent positive sign as an indication that everything is really alright. This often leads to self-deception. Let us consider some of the "positive" signs that cause pastoral passivity and wishful thinking.

Sometimes, those in pastoral authority assume that evidence of someone's "good motives" somehow excuses the objective wrong he or she is doing. It is not uncommon to hear someone who is damaging the Church described as "sincere" or "nice" or "well meaning," as "someone who loves the Church," as a "man of faith," or a "prayerful man." "Sincerity" is invoked to overlook the objectively damaging results of such a person's ministry.

It is, unfortunately, all too possible to sincerely do evil. It is all too possible to show love for the Church on the affective level yet speak, teach, and act in a way that weakens the Church. It is possible to appear prayerful—even pious and devout—and yet do evil; it is also possible to appear humble and yet be proud and rebellious. It is not sufficient today to call someone a "person of faith"; it is necessary to ascertain if they are a person of *Christian* faith.

Increasingly, even mistaken sincerity seems in short supply. A complete lack of goodwill and even outright deception characterize some of what is happening in the Church today. In those areas of Church life where one expects objectivity and fairness, one frequently discovers obvious political manipulation, outright lying, and financial wrongdoing. A case in point is the Catholic Theological Society of America's manipulation of a committee it established to examine the question of the status of women in the Church and society. The Society chose as committee members only people who openly support the ordination of women. Furthermore, when the committee called in consultants, it selected scholars who were also already on record as supporting this view. The manipulation of committee appointments to guarantee a certain outcome reminds us of how the Catholic Theological Society similarly manipulated the formation of the committee it set up to do the human sexuality study which we have already analyzed at some length.[435] And as George Weigel has demonstrated in article after article, such manipulation is strongly at work in the "synodal processes" in Rome today.

Something similar seems to be happening again as the delegates and "experts" to the recent synods on youth and the Amazon were carefully selected to support the predetermined outcomes as telegraphed in the preparatory documents. It is hard to detect goodwill and sincerity in statements like the one made years ago by a young biblical scholar who praised several prominent colleagues after they had been criticized for using their scholarship to undermine faith and morals. Referring to those who raised the criticisms, he said, "If they ever knew what some of the rest of us are doing, they'd have a heart attack."[436]

A "polite and reasonable" manner of presentation often cloaks the most destructive positions. And just because a person uses Christian language doesn't mean that he is teaching sound doctrine. A person's ability to use the right Christian language is not an adequate indication of his Christian fidelity. One of the most notable ways in which the Church's faith and life is being undermined today is through the perverse twisting of Christian language to camouflage fundamentally secular and humanistic ideologies.

Another inadequate criterion for judging Christian soundness is the notion of "popularity" or "effectiveness." If, for example, large numbers of young people are responding "positively" to a certain youth leader or religious educator, pastors and parents are tempted to interpret this "success" as Christian success. Quite often, they should examine more deeply the basis of the popularity and the exact nature of the positive response. The failure to penetrate beneath the surface only assures that, sooner or later, in large measure or small, many in the flock will end up as food for wild beasts. This is, of course, not to say that successful youth ministries that are popular are not well founded, as many certainly are.

Some Church leaders and parents have become victims of the cult of feelings that has infiltrated the Church at every level. The fear of "hurting someone" has allowed many unsound programs, publications, and even institutions to obscure Christian truth. In the process, many people's prospects for eternal life have been seriously damaged.

Sometimes a false sentimentality has allowed the faith and moral lives of others to be undermined. This kind of sentimentality is exemplified in a mistaken allegiance to an old schoolmate or friend or family member. A bishop will feel reluctant, for example, to discipline a priest who went to the same school or seminary with him. A parent may withhold needed discipline because of the emotional bond with a child. The temptation to compromise Christian truth and fidelity to Jesus will only increase as the culture captures more and more of our young people. How many families today have children and grandchildren who are involved in immoral relationships and yet demand acceptance and approval of their choices? And how many parents, afraid of alienating their children, are prepared to give such approval and affirmation by their silence or outright encouragement? Often parents give in and accept the immoral behavior because "they don't want to lose their children." Our main concern for our children as Christian parents is not losing them for a limited time on this earth but losing them for all eternity out of a deluded sentimentality that makes us afraid to speak the truth in love. We need to strengthen our relationship with Christ so that when we are tempted to deny him, we will resist and be faithful to Christ and his Word rather than deny him by our cowardly and selfish acquiescence in immoral behavior. Christian parents and grandparents today have to prepare to bear the pain of children and grandchildren saying hurtful things to us and threatening to break off relationships if we refuse to approve of their immoral activity. The fact is that if we approve of their immoral activity, we are confirming them on their path to hell. We can't. Jesus warned us that there will be division in families over him, and indeed there is and will be, but we have to know where our first and greatest loyalty lies. We have to fear and love God more than we fear and love our children. And of course, to confirm them in their sin is not to love them at all.

Pope Benedict warned us:

> If the Church simply aims to avoid conflict, merely to
> ensure that no disturbances arise anywhere, then her real

message can no longer make any impact. For this message is in fact there precisely in order to conflict with our behavior, to tear man out of his life of lies and to bring clarity and truth. Truth does not come cheap. It makes demands, and it also burns.[437]

The toleration of corruption of faith or morality poisons the atmosphere of a community, large or small. It breeds the indifference and lukewarmness that allows evil to increase and others to be corrupted. Prompt and unambiguous correction and discipline produce the kind of healthy "fear of the Lord" that provides the community with a bulwark against sin (see Prov 14:26; Ps 2:11).

The consequences of weak and vacillating pastoral authority are clearly illustrated in the story of Eli and his sons, told in the First Book of Samuel. Eli and his two sons were priests in the Temple. However, the sons were corrupt; they took offerings for themselves and engaged in immoral behavior with women who had come to serve the Lord. Eli rebuked them and even pleaded with them, but he did not exercise effective discipline by actually removing them from their positions. Because of this, a prophet revealed to Eli that his sons would die, that the priesthood would be taken away from his family, and that his family and all his descendants would experience humiliation and chastisement: "I will raise up for myself a faithful priest, who shall do according to what is in my heart and in my mind" (1 Sam 2:35).

Situations similar to that of Eli and his sons are not uncommon in the life of the Church today. It is not uncommon for those with pastoral authority to give one message verbally—correction or admonishment perhaps—but then to negate it by giving another message nonverbally, by doing nothing when those corrected do not respond to the correction. The consequences of this passivity are often clearly evident in families. Parents who remain passive when children ignore their correction preside over the destruction of their own authority and perhaps the destruction of their own children.

The same is true in the wider Church. For example, the American bishops admonished and corrected the authors of the *Human Sexuality* study that we discussed previously. Yet all of the authors of the study persisted in their opinions. And all of the authors continued to teach on the faculties of Catholic seminaries and theology schools for many years afterwards. This has led many Catholics to draw the obvious conclusion that the bishops do not think they have any real authority in the matter or that they no longer believe their own teaching. They regard the bishops' correction of these scholars as only one of many theological opinions about sexual morality. The same bishops continued to ordain and hire people trained by scholars who dissented from and continued to undermine the teaching of the Church. Like parents who let children ignore correction, the bishops are in fact oftentimes presiding over, indeed subsidizing, those who are undermining their authority and misleading God's people. It is shocking to see how, over the years, almost every Jesuit university in the United States has come to the point of openly advocating dissenting views on human sexuality by approving programs and honoring scholars and others who promote positions at odds with Church teaching and by hiring radical professors in almost every department, with nary a word being said by bishops, who, while they don't directly control such universities, have the responsibility to assure their Catholic identity.

The Consequences of Pastoral Passivity

The pastoral passivity that can end up tolerating great evil often begins with very small acts of disobedience. Many people in pastoral positions fear "rocking the boat." They are reluctant to summon the personal effort that would be necessary to challenge a questionable direction. They avoid making the effort to actually become acquainted with a troubled situation. In a recent conversation with someone who works closely with bishops on a national level, we were discussing the state of Catholic education on the high school level, and he told me that most bishops don't really know what's happening in their Catholic high schools and *don't care to know.* And now we have case after case hitting the news, manifesting the division in our Church, particularly over the issue of homosexuality. Why is homosexuality coming up so often in this book? Because it is the cutting edge of the culture's attempt to subvert the Church and punish those who don't go along. We have not sought out this issue; it is being forced on us almost daily. Some bishops have told Catholic high schools to no longer employ teachers who are in "gay marriages" or others in sexual relationships that contradict Church teaching, and some have complied. Other Catholic high schools have employed such persons and have either not been corrected by their bishops or have refused to obey their bishops when corrected.

The depth to which the homosexual culture has influenced "good Catholics" is evidenced by the ferocious attacks on bishops and religious superiors who attempt to deal with faculty members in Catholic schools who are openly advocating a worldview directly contradictory to the revealed truth by living "alternative lifestyles." When the archbishop of Cincinnati ordered a Catholic high school in the archdiocese to not renew the contract of a male teacher "married" to a man, all hell broke loose. The principal apologetically said it wasn't her decision, but the archbishop insisted on it, and ten thousand people signed a petition opposing the decision that was organized by a secular far-left pressure group.[438]

When the Archdiocese of Seattle made clear to two Catholic school teachers who had entered same-sex "marriages" that continued employment would not be possible, they resigned. But then, all hell broke loose. Students staged a walkout, parents indignantly protested, state legislators weighed in, and the principal mysteriously was placed on leave. One of the state senators, a graduate of the Catholic high school, had this to say: "Institutions like the Archdiocese of Seattle are on the wrong side of history and this will be a moment they'll look back on in shame."[439]

The principal of the Jesuit high school in the archdiocese gave an interview where he said people's personal decisions should be respected and that he had never fired anyone in twenty-two years.[440]

Similar demonstrations and division within the Church occurred when the Archdiocese of Indianapolis faced a similar situation.[441] This will be repeated all over the Catholic school world. Years of lax hiring, lax oversight, and lax formation, as well as willful blindness and outright treachery, have brought us to this point.

So many of our "Catholics" have been captured by the enemy and are now enlisting in a campaign to shame and change the Church. The enemy is now well within the gates.

Religious superiors fear the unpleasant scene that may follow their denial of someone's request. A bishop fears the outraged protests that would greet his demand that a Catholic university professor submit his course outlines for a review. A parent wants to avoid the scene that would follow his request that his child inform the parent of what he is reading or where he is going. Yet small acts of pastoral passivity, laziness, and negligence have allowed very great evils to grow up and go unchecked.

As Dr. Mirus put it:

> But what is the crisis of the Church in the West today if not a crisis of those who refuse to embrace a genuine commitment to a Church that is no longer culturally dominant? So I ask again: What have we to do with judging

outsiders? Is it not those inside the church whom we are to judge? And do not our own bishops most often stand in the way of precisely that sort of judgment? And is not the Church horribly disfigured, weakened and robbed of her evangelical witness as a result?[442]

The separation of an individual, an institution, or a whole people from the will of God is often a very gradual process that has quite modest and almost imperceptible beginnings. C. S. Lewis cast light on this process in *The Screwtape Letters*. The instructor devil, Screwtape, gives the following advice to a younger devil:

> You will say that these are very small sins; and doubtless like all young tempters, you are anxious to be able to report spectacular wickedness [Auschwitz?]. But do remember, the only thing that matters is the extent to which you separate the man from the Enemy. It does not matter how small the sins are provided that their cumulative effect is to edge the man away from the Light and out into the Nothing. Murder is no better than cards if cards can do the trick. Indeed the safest road to Hell is the gradual one—the gentle slope, soft underfoot, without sudden turnings, without milestones, without signposts.[443]

The late Cardinal Basil Hume, former head of the Catholic Bishops' Conference of England and Wales, made a similar point when speaking about the situation of Christianity in Great Britain:

> The majority of people in Britain have not so much rejected God, but have rather drifted away from him and now find themselves at the mercy of fashions, forces and influences which they are not able to shape or to control.[444]

Indeed, those in positions of pastoral responsibility in the post-conciliar Church at every level have too often overlooked the significant and sometimes decisive influence and activity of the "powers" and "principalities" (Eph 6:12). The Holy Spirit has his plan for the authentic renewal of the post-conciliar Church. The "prince of this world" also has his own plan. I doubt whether the first plan can be implemented successfully unless the second plan is recognized and dealt with. As one prominent Christian put it, "The diabolical strategy is still the same . . . persecution; intellectual deception, including false teaching; and moral erosion, including sub-Christian ethical standards."[445]

Bishops, priests, ministers, religious superiors, and parents have occasionally been startled to find that their passivity has created situations over which they can no longer easily exercise any control. It is not easy for a bishop to control a whole religious order which has been allowed to become an advocacy group for secular causes and dissents on important areas of Church teaching. The membership of theologians and even some seminary professors in secular professional associations has, in some cases, meant that the Church is no longer master of its own house. Because of pastoral passivity, dissident Church members have quietly obtained the legal leverage, alliances, and popular support that they need to protect their own status in these institutions. Similar situations often develop in families.

Some dissident individuals and groups get protection directly from passive pastors. For example, a leading Catholic feminist theologian in Europe stated that "critical" Catholics, like herself, will simply go on doing what they would like to do. She cynically explained, "Rome won't excommunicate people like us as long as an important cardinal . . . is our leader."[446] This was a statement made when John Paul II was pope. She would have nothing to fear today from Rome.

The "important" German cardinals who control billions of

dollars in annual income from the Church tax have no fear of correction from Rome, which has proven rather meek in the face of blatant defiance. The fact is that manipulation and intimidation are not the only causes for pastoral passivity. Some pastors have made plainly unwise pastoral decisions in dealing with very real pastoral problems. Pastors have sometimes closed their eyes to outright false teaching, or even immorality, among those in their care because it would be difficult to deal with the situation or find a replacement for an errant teacher or pastor. Recently, in a parish close to me, concerned parishioners protested that it was inappropriate that an outspoken lesbian should be hired as youth minister. The pastor hired her anyway, apparently no longer believing what Scripture says about same-sex relationships or perhaps making the decision out of a misguided "compassion" or a desire to be "inclusive and diverse." Some bishops have knowingly allowed priests with serious personal and faith problems to pursue advanced theological training and, upon their return, placed them in sensitive pastoral positions, such as campus ministry or seminary teaching. Many bishops today are under great pressure to staff their existing institutions and keep them functioning. The fact that they can no longer find reliably Christian pastoral personnel to staff them presents a dilemma. But to overlook doctrinal and moral infidelity in order to "keep the ship going" is a very poor choice indeed.

One bishop, when asked why he was allowing incompetent and unfaithful priests to continue leading parishes, replied, "It's either bad priests or no priests. I don't have enough competent and faithful priests." Actually, there's a better choice. If necessary, have Masses in sports arenas and led by gifted and faithful priests rather than allow the faithful to be corrupted by false doctrine or disillusioned by bad leadership.

Even when pastoral leaders act, the measures they take often stop short of really dealing with the problem. They administer discipline that only hides the bad fruit. They do not lay "the axe to the root," the action often required for real cleansing and change.

For example, a number of years ago, Jesuit superiors ordered a Jesuit priest to stop his direct involvement in efforts to have women ordained as priests. He had been leading a national movement for women's ordination, in direct opposition to Christian tradition and to the clear teaching of the pope and bishops. The priest's superiors, however, assigned him to another position of influence and responsibility. The priest soon declared his intentions: "I sure won't be publicly advocating women's ordination, but I will be publicly advocating equality in the Church."[447] Such discipline did not deal with the priest's rebelliousness but only deterred him from publicly challenging the specific issue of women's ordination. Such discipline was too weak to even begin to get to the heart of the problem.

Sometimes, the consequences of pastoral passivity can engulf a whole national Church. The disarray of the Catholic Church in the Netherlands in the years immediately after Vatican II was a case in point. It led to widespread and immense infidelity to the Church's doctrinal and moral teaching and what could be called the collapse of the Catholic Church in the Netherlands. The Dutch Church has since made great strides in "righting the ship" and now has a growing number of faithful bishops and priests who are unfortunately facing a huge pastoral challenge as a result of years of pastoral passivity and outright patronage of false prophets and teachers on the part of the bishops. The lessons for bishops and others with pastoral responsibilities is clear: letting little infidelities go uncorrected today assures that larger infidelities and far more serious problems will develop tomorrow and be even more difficult to confront.

The Lord expects those whom he appoints as shepherds of the flock—whether they be fathers or mothers, priests or bishops or pope—to take effective measures to guard the flock by disciplining those who corrupt faith and morality. Pastors are not to be deterred by a close personal relationship with the erring individual. Throughout the Bible, the Lord indicates how serious it is when the shepherds are "bad" and refuse to teach clearly or discipline effectively. It is a very serious thing indeed not to protect the flock from wolves:

> Therefore, you shepherds, hear the word of the Lord: As I live, says the Lord God, because my sheep have become a prey, and my sheep have become food for all the wild beasts, since there was no shepherd; and because my shepherds have not searched for my sheep, but the shepherds have fed themselves, and have not fed my sheep; therefore, you shepherds, hear the word of the Lord: Thus says the Lord God, Behold, I am against the shepherds; and I will require my sheep at their hand, and put a stop to their feeding the sheep; no longer shall the shepherds feed themselves. I will rescue my sheep from their mouths, that they may not be food for them. (Ezek 34:7–10)

In the New Testament, Jesus and the Apostles constantly urge such vigilance over matters of faith and morality. In almost every book of the New Testament, Jesus and the Apostles continually urge the Christians and their shepherds to guard the flock against false prophets and teachers, whom Paul describes as wolves:

> Beware of false prophets, who come to you in sheep's clothing but inwardly are ravenous wolves. (Matt 7:15)

> I know that after my departure fierce wolves will come in among you, not sparing the flock; and from among your own selves will arise men speaking perverse things, to draw

away the disciples after them. Therefore be alert. (Acts 20:29–31)

Vigilance and decisive action are necessary on the part of the shepherds if the flock is to be protected from corruption and the risk of losing their salvation:

As I urged you when I was going to Macedonia, remain at Ephesus that you may charge certain persons not to teach any different doctrine, nor to occupy themselves with myths and endless genealogies which promote speculations rather than the divine training that is in faith. (1 Tim 1:3–4)

I am astonished that you are so quickly deserting him who called you in the grace of Christ and turning to a different gospel—not that there is another gospel, but there are some who trouble you and want to pervert the gospel of Christ. But even if we, or an angel from heaven, should preach to you a gospel contrary to that which we preached to you, let him be accursed. As we have said before, so now I say again, if any one is preaching to you a gospel contrary to that which you received, let him be accursed. Am I now seeking the favor of men, or of God? Or am I trying to please men? If I were still pleasing men, I should not be a servant of Christ. (Gal 1:6–10)

May we all be delivered from the pressure to please people at the expense of being disloyal to Christ!

Our modern sentimentality recoils from direct speech, from the admonition and rebuke that so often are counseled in the Scriptures. Yet by failing in this way, we recoil from true love and mercy and put at risk the eternal salvation of the wrongdoers and of those members of the community who are being corrupted by them. We often overlook the fact that one of the chief concerns of the Holy Spirit in speaking prophetically to the early Churches in the Book of Revelation was that the Churches maintain a high level of purity in their faith and morality. The Holy Spirit specifically warns the Christian people against tolerating in their midst those who hold or teach false doctrine or encourage others to immorality:

> But I have a few things against you: you have some there who hold the teaching of Balaam, who taught Balak to put a stumbling block before the sons of Israel, that they might eat food sacrificed to idols and practice immorality. So you also have some who hold the teaching of the Nicolaitans. Repent then. If not, I will come to you soon and war against them with the sword of my mouth. (Rev 2:14–16)

Those Churches that failed to maintain such discipline and to diligently exercise pastoral authority were warned in prophecy that the Lord would directly chastise their communities:

> But I have this against you, that you tolerate the woman Jezebel, who calls herself a prophetess and is teaching and beguiling my servants to practice immorality and to eat food sacrificed to idols. I gave her time to repent, but she refuses to repent of her immorality. Behold, I will throw her on a sickbed, and those who commit adultery with her I will throw into great tribulation, unless they repent of her doings; and I will strike her children dead. And all the churches shall know that I am he who searches mind and heart, and I will give to each of you as your works deserve. (Rev 2:20–23)

In short, pastoral authorities who tolerate doctrinal or moral corruption become implicated in the corruption. The Lord gave Jezebel time to repent, but when she didn't, she was plunged into intense suffering, as were those involved with her. Pastoral leaders who refused to deal with the corruption in their midst share in the responsibility for the corruption and its evil results. A little leaven leavens the whole lump.

What keeps clergy from preaching clearly in this area today? First of all, fear. Not fear of hell, not fear of God, but fear of how people will react to them, what people will say about them, and what price they may have to pay if they spoke about these things clearly. Another way of putting this is to say that the problem is self-love. This is also known as cowardice, and we should remember that the cowardly are finally banished from God's presence and consigned to the second death, hell:

> But as for the cowardly, the faithless, the polluted, as for murderers, fornicators, sorcerers, idolaters, and all liars, their lot shall be in the lake that burns with fire and brimstone, which is the second death. (Rev 21:8)

How pathetic to fear what people will think of us if we tell them the truth that could save them rather than to fear having to give an account before the judgment seat of Christ and have to give an account to him!

What keeps clergy from preaching clearly in this area today? A lack of love. How terrible not to have the courage to tell people the truth about what could save their souls! We all have to be willing to pay whatever price is needed to preach and teach clearly the truths that can save people, just as Jesus did. The servant is not above the master. We have to be willing to endure the same persecution as he did. But as the writer of Hebrews says, we have not yet had to pay the price of shedding our blood (see Heb 12:4)!

What keeps clergy from preaching clearly in this area today? A lack of faith. Many clergy and people, through corrosive "Scripture scholarship," have lost their confidence in the truth and reliability of God's Word as it comes to us in Scripture and tradition. Vatican II didn't cast us into a sea of doubt and skepticism, and we need to recover its authentic teaching. Wherever I speak, I never miss the opportunity to repeat this affirmation of the truth of the Scriptures, and I don't mind repeating it in this book:

> Therefore, since everything asserted by the inspired authors or sacred writers must be held to be asserted by the Holy Spirit, it follows that the books of Scripture must be acknowledged as teaching solidly, faithfully and without error that truth which God wanted put into sacred writings for the sake of salvation.[448]

As St. Augustine put it, "If you believe what you like in the Gospels and reject what you don't like, it is not the Gospel you believe but yourself."[449]

What keeps clergy from preaching clearly about salvation and morality today? Sometimes, unfortunately, it's their own personal sin. Sad to say, it appears that a certain number of priests have themselves become ensnared in relativistic thinking and even bondage to sexual immorality. The incidence of pornography addiction, adultery, fornication, and homosexual relationships appears to be not inconsiderable in many places, sometimes combined with embezzlement to support a sinful lifestyle. While bishops, under pressure from lawyers, journalists, and the threat of financial ruin, did indeed take significant steps toward greatly reducing incidences of sexual abuse of children, there is a strange reluctance to talk about other kinds of sexual immorality among the clergy, including those purported to be with "consenting" adults, and most particularly a reluctance to talk about homosexuality among the clergy.

This, unfortunately, has not been the first time in Church history that bishops have been negligent in dealing with an outbreak of sexual immorality among the clergy.

St. Peter Damian's struggle against the widespread tolerance of sexual immorality, particularly homosexuality, among the clergy in the eleventh century is devastatingly chronicled in the book he wrote to combat it, *The Book of Gomorrah*.[450] Just reading the chapter headings is enough to curdle one's blood. The depth of depravity and the depth of "cover-up" that sought to shield the widespread abominations is shocking. Consider it the Pennsylvania Attorney General's report of clergy sexual abuse of the eleventh century and the refusal to confront it by passive pastoral authorities:

> A certain most abominable and exceedingly disgraceful vice has grown in our region, and unless it is quickly met with the hand of strict chastisement, it is certain that the sword of divine fury is looming to attack, to the destruction of many. Alas, it is shameful to speak of it! It is shameful to relate such a disgusting scandal to sacred ears! . . . The cancer of sodomitic impurity is thus creeping through the clerical order and indeed is raging like a cruel beast within the sheepfold of Christ with the audacity of such liberty. . . . And unless the force of the Apostolic See opposes it as quickly as possible, there is no doubt that when it finally wishes for the unbridled evil to be restrained, it may not be able to halt the fury of its advance.[451]

This plague is indeed advancing with fury, threatening to overtake the Catholic Church and silence its shepherds with threats of ferocious and public opposition from within and without.

Catherine of Siena, in the fourteenth century, expressed righteous anger at the bishops in her day who were pretending they didn't see the problems or were too afraid or self-interested to bear the pain of correcting them. She details multiple aspects of corruption among the clergy, most especially concerning finances, sexual immorality, and particularly homosexual activity, so much so that she perceived that the demons were "grossed out" to see humans falling so low:

> For those who are not corrected and those who do not correct are like members beginning to rot, and if the doctor were only to apply ointment without cauterizing the wound the whole body would become fetid and corrupt. . . . So it is with prelates or with anyone else in authority. If they see the members who are their subjects rotting because of the filth of deadly sin and apply only the ointment of soft words without reproof, they will never get well. Rather, they will infect the other members with whom they form one body under their one shepherd. But if those in authority are truly good doctors to those souls, as were those glorious shepherds (speaking of the Apostles and holy bishops over the ages), they will not use ointment without the fire of reproof. And if the members are still obstinate in their evildoing, they will cut them off from the congregation so that they will not infect the whole body with the filth of deadly sin. . . .

> But those who are in authority today do not do this. In fact they pretend not to see. And do you know why? Because the root of selfish love is alive in them, and this is the source of their perverse slavish fear. They do not correct people for fear of losing their rank and position, and their material possessions.

Another reason they will not correct others is that they themselves are living in the same or greater sins.... They will never correct persons of any importance, even though they may be guilty of greater sin than more lowly people.... They will, however, correct the little people because they are sure these cannot harm them ... Such injustice comes from their wretched selfish love for themselves ... This selfishness has poisoned the whole world as well as the mystic body of holy Church and made the garden of this bride a field overgrown with putrid weeds.

Concerning the sins of homosexuality:

They get up in the morning with their minds contaminated and their bodies corrupt. After spending the night bedded down with deadly sin they go to celebrate Mass! O tabernacles of the devil! ... They come to this mystery wholly impure—and not simply with the sort of impurity and weakness to which you are all naturally inclined.... No, these wretches not only do not restrain their weakness; they make it worse by committing that cursed unnatural sin. As if they were blind and stupid, with the light of their understanding extinguished, they do not recognize what miserable filth they are wallowing in. The stench reaches even up to me, supreme Purity, and is so hateful to me that for this sin alone five cities were struck down by my divine judgment. For my divine judgment could no longer tolerate it, so despicable to me is this abominable sin. But the stench displeases not only me, as I have said, but the devils as well.... It is not its sinfulness that displeases them ... but because their nature was angelic, that nature still loathes the sight of that horrendous sin actually being committed.

Catherine goes on to specify the responsibility of those in authority for letting the virus of sexual immorality spread:

> Their own sins have left them bereft of any enthusiasm or zeal for holy justice. . . . And sometimes when they recognize that these religious are incarnate devils, they send them from one monastery to the next to those who are incarnate devils like themselves. Thus each corrupts the other. . . . Superiors are the cause of these and many other evils because they do not keep their eyes on their subjects. They give them plenty of rope and even send them out, and then pretend not to see their wretched behavior.[452]

Until bishops overcome their fear, their entanglement in their own emotional bondages to certain priests out of fear of offending a "classmate" or losing popularity among his priests or their fear of being portrayed in the press as a heartless conservative, it will be hard for our priests to stand firm and proclaim with boldness, confidence, and joy the whole truth of the Gospel. And proclaiming the whole Gospel today has to include the truth about heaven and hell and the truth about those sins which will exclude us from the kingdom unless they are repented of.[453]

A recovery of zeal for the holiness of God's house, and his glory and a recovery of the prophetic dimension of Jesus's ministry, needs to be based on a recovery of a profound fear of God. Holy fear of God leads to profound reverence and adoration and gives birth to great love for his people, and great courage and joy in proclaiming the difficult parts of the Gospel that we know are revealed to us for our salvation and eternal happiness.

Those in pastoral responsibility in the Church often display immense goodwill and exert an often heroic effort to do the best possible job. I know of no bishop and few parents who take their job lightly. I myself have pastoral responsibilities, including responsibilities as a parent. I have had to struggle and continue to struggle with many of the factors contributing to pastoral passivity that I discussed in this chapter. It is difficult to be a parent today in the increasingly pagan environment our children are exposed to, and it is difficult to be a pastor of a parish or a bishop of a diocese. I do not pretend to have all the answers or even to understand all the complexities that those entrusted with wider responsibilities have to face. Yet, as difficult as it is to face the facts of pastoral passivity and to repent of it, it must be done. I believe the welfare of God's people depends on it. If we're to move forward, this is one of the pathways that must be "made straight."

Pastoral passivity or negligence—whether in the diocese, the parish, the seminary, the family, or the worldwide church—is an invitation for the world, the flesh, and the devil to play havoc with God's people, whom he purchased at the price of his own blood. Pastoral passivity has been, and continues to be, one of the main factors contributing to the crisis of truth in the Church, and an adequate response to the crisis must include a response to it. The eternal destinies of multitudes of souls hang in the balance. May all of us, as we approach the end of our lives, be able to echo what Paul said in his farewell words to the Ephesian elders:

> And now, behold, I know that all you among whom I have gone about preaching the kingdom will see my face no more. Therefore I testify to you this day that I am innocent of the blood of all of you, for I did not shrink from declar-

ing to you the whole counsel of God. (Acts 20:25–27)

What God requires of us, he gives us the grace to accomplish. We can be confident of that.

Chapter 10

THE SIGNS OF THE TIMES: POINTING TOWARD JUDGMENT

My heart is beating wildly; I cannot keep silent; for I hear
the sound of the trumpet, the alarm of war. (Jer 4:19)

THE JUDGMENT OF GOD is expressed in many different ways.
He makes partial and preliminary judgments manifest in history and will judge all of the living and the dead at the end of time,
with the consequences being eternal reward or eternal punishment.
Within history, God judges individuals, groups, and nations, pagans and even his own people. These judgments sometimes appear
to be simply the inevitable, natural unfolding of the consequences
of unrighteousness and rebellion against God. Such is the judgment
experienced by those who turn from God and come into bondage
to lust and every kind of evil, as described in the first chapter of Romans (see Rom 1:20–25). These judgments, while in some ways the
natural consequence of infidelity, are truly judgments of God. Judges not only rule on whether someone is innocent or guilty but also
determine punishment and reward.

The dimension of judgment is an essential perspective for understanding the situation of the world and the Church today. In many ways, the world and the Church are beginning to experience the natural, inevitable consequences of numerous acts of rebellion against God. The world may be about to reap what it has sown over several centuries of progressive turning away from God and exaltation of the creature over the Creator. Significant segments of the Church, unfortunately, are to a considerable extent implicated in this turning away from God, this deafness to his Word and blindness to the signs of the times.

God has always judged his people severely for accommodating themselves to the prevailing worldly cultures. In the Old Testament, he punished them for intermarrying with pagans, for intermingling with them in a way that led to infidelity to his Word and ways, which then led to idolatry and the worship of false gods. Many in the Church today have intermingled with the contemporary culture in a way that has led them to turn away from God and his Word. Even shepherds of the flock are implicated in this corruption, and "false prophets" have told many Catholics to regard the unclean as clean and to identify the spirit of the age as the Holy Spirit. Unfaithful priests have allowed God's Word to become blurred and confused; they have not distinguished between the sacred and profane, the clean and unclean. Parents of families have timidly allowed their children to adopt the thinking and behavior of "the nations" around them, with only pleading rebukes rather than effective discipline. Many have acted like Eli in relation to his sons. Fidelity to the Lord is essential. We must never go over to the "rebels":

> Blessed is the man who makes
> the LORD his trust,
> who does not turn to the proud,
> to those who go astray after false gods! (Ps 40:4)

In the Old Covenant, God always judged this syncretistic and unfaithful accommodation to the prevailing cultures of the day. This was God's complaint against his people in this prophecy of Ezekiel:

> Thus says the Lord God: This is Jerusalem; I have set her in the center of the nations, with countries round about her. And she has wickedly rebelled against my ordinances more than the nations, and against my statutes more than the countries round about her, by rejecting my ordinances and not walking in my statutes. Therefore thus says the Lord God: Because you are more turbulent than the nations that are round about you, and have not walked in my statutes or kept my ordinances, but have acted according to the ordinances of the nations that are round about you; therefore thus says the Lord God: Behold, I, even I, am against you; and I will execute judgments in the midst of you in the sight of the nations. And because of all your abominations I will do with you what I have never yet done, and the like of which I will never do again. (Ezek 5:5–9)

Today, there is little doubt that the Church is guilty of similar accommodation. As we have seen, even whole episcopal conferences have adopted this as their goal! Some sociologists have pointed out that accommodation to the prevailing secular culture has become a dominant factor in the decline of contemporary Christian life in the Western countries. John Tracy Ellis, a distinguished historian of the American Catholic Church, years ago wrote that the chief cause of the decline of Christian life has been the assimilation of Catholics into the mainstream of American life. This has brought an emphasis on the pursuit of material success and the collapse of religious morality into an aggressive and increasingly anti-Christian secular humanism.[454]

Even Christian leaders who often expressed optimism began, decades ago, to express serious concern about the trial the Church may soon undergo. The coming judgment has been on the horizon for some time. As far back as 1979, Billy Graham reported on a conversation that he'd had with his wife:

> Ruth reminds me often that we need to be preparing the church in America to go underground, because that may be where we're headed. It may not be too long before judgment comes upon America and upon Europe, leaving us to face hostility and oppression as Christians.[455]

This warning was born out in 2020, when Franklin Graham, Billy Graham's son and the leader of Samaritan's Purse, a Christian aid organization that brings help to people all over the world, was vilified by the Speaker of the New York City Council.

Samaritan's Purse had set up a field hospital in Central Park, with trained medical personnel volunteering their services, to take care of the COVID-19 patients that were, at one point, overflowing NYC hospitals. After the virus died down, the Speaker, who self-identifies as gay, demanded that they leave:

> This group, which is led by the notoriously bigoted, hate-spewing Franklin Graham, came at a time when our city couldn't in good conscience turn away any offer of help. That time has passed. Their continued presence here is an affront to our values of inclusion, and is painful for all New Yorkers who care deeply about the LGBT+ community.[456]

Samaritan's Purse left after treating three hundred patients, and then the LGBTQ activists "cleansed" the park where the field hospital had been:

Queer flags of all stripes were on display Saturday morning, May 16, as several dozen members of Reclaim Pride, Rise and Resist, and Reverend Billy Talen's Stop Shopping Choir turned out in Central Park's East Meadow to exorcise the demons left by the hospital tents that had been established there by Franklin Graham's Samaritan's Purse.[457]

This reminds me of the sin against the Holy Spirit; Spirit-inspired compassion is now being called demonic.

The hostility to Christian witness is increasing while leaders, intimidated by the activist tactics of the few, remain silent and permit freedom of speech and religion to be suffocated. Recently Jason Evert, the well-known Catholic chastity speaker in the United States, was invited to Ireland to give a series of talks at both secular and Catholic settings. A pressure campaign was mounted by gay activists, and they all were cancelled, including those at Catholic parishes. When a bishop was asked to comment, his spokesperson said that he doesn't wish to comment on this.[458]

The same thing happened when Franklin Graham was invited to speak in the United Kingdom. Pro-LGBTQ groups rose up in "outrage" and forced his visit to be cancelled.[459]

The day after his election as pope, as John Paul II addressed the cardinals in the Sistine Chapel, he chose to interpret the sudden and unexpected death of his predecessor and his own unexpected election as warnings from God to turn to sober reflection and prayer:

> Brothers, dear sons and daughters, the recent happenings of the Church and of the world are for us all a healthy warning: how will our pontificate be? What is the destiny the Lord has assigned to his Church in the next years? What road will mankind take in this period of time as it approaches the year 2000?[460]

John Paul II viewed the time we live in as one in which there is an epic confrontation between the Gospel and the anti-Gospel, the Church and the anti-church. It is almost as if there were a prophetic, providential significance to what is unfolding before us. A few years before he was elected pope, Cardinal Wojtyla on a trip to America during United States Bicentennial, made the following comments:

> We are now standing in the face of the greatest historical confrontation humanity has gone through. I do not think that wide circles of the American society or wide circles of the Christian community realize this fully. We are now facing the final confrontation between the Church and the anti-church, between the Gospel and the anti-Gospel, between Christ and the antichrist. The confrontation lies within the plans of divine Providence; it is a trial which the whole Church . . . must take up and face courageously.[461]

When he wrote about this confrontation in his book, *A Sign of Contradiction,* he pointed us toward a text from Scripture that speaks of the final confrontation: 2 Thessalonians 2:1–12.[462]

In this text, Paul assures the Thessalonians that they have not missed the return of the Lord because two specific events need to happen before he returns. First of all, Paul says that a "great apostasy" must occur.

It is certain that we are currently experiencing a great apostasy, though only time will tell whether it is "the" great apostasy or not. We will only know that for sure when the Lord appears to put down the work of the "man of iniquity," perhaps the Antichrist, and to usher in the fullness of the kingdom and the final judgment.

What is very striking, however, is how traditionally Christian nations, one after the other, are turning away from faith and embracing an ideology actually hostile to Christ and the Church. Who would have thought that we would see Catholic Ireland so boldly repudiate eight hundred years of fidelity under persecution, undone by fifty years of prosperity and the desire to be "just like the other nations"? Who can forget the sight of tens of thousands of young people rushing into the streets of Dublin to celebrate the day that abortion became legal in Ireland,[463] and who would have imagined the related abominations that the undermining of marriage and the family, the rejection of sexual morality, and the tragic spread of gender confusion have brought in their wake? And the first statistics are now published. 6,666 abortions were performed in Ireland in the first year of its legalization.[464]

It is almost as if the devil had planted time bombs throughout the Church and nation and then pushed the button to detonate them at the most damaging moment. After the horrible exposure of the clergy sex scandals and other abusive behavior, the Irish bishops were left "tongue-tied" when aggressive secular forces began to push for dismantling the Church's influence on society, removing a restraint that had been resisting the waves of secularism that were beating against the Irish shores from their membership in the European Union.

And who can understand the rapid collapse of Catholicism in Malta, known, until very recently, as one of the most Catholic countries in the world, and its tragic apostasy that has been revealed since divorce was first legalized in 2007 and all that began to unravel in its wake.

The second event that Paul indicated needed to happen before the Lord returns is the manifestation of the "lawless one" and the removal of what "restrains" evil until that time. Who can deny that there has been a systematic stripping away of restraint after restraint on the working of evil? The widespread legalization of abortion, of euthanasia, of same-sex marriage, of "no fault" divorce, of transgenderism, of the brainwashing of the young, the open mockery of God and Christians, the "exclusion" of known Christians from "polite society," the criminalization of those who seek to oppose this deterioration, and the attempts, often "bullying," and sometimes violent, to silence those who seek to speak out on these issues.

But what is most shocking about the 2 Thessalonians 2 text is what it indicates is the fate of those who "refuse to love the truth and so be saved" (2 Thess 2:10). **They are destined to perish.** Because of the rebellion in their hearts, they will be deceived by the false signs and wonders of the evil one; they will believe his lies and so become blind to the truth. They will thus, as the just judgment of God, fall into ever deeper, perhaps almost irreversible, deception, and they will be condemned:

> The coming of the lawless one by the activity of Satan will be with all power and with pretended signs and wonders, and with all wicked deception for those who are to perish, because they refused to love the truth and so be saved. Therefore God sends upon them a strong delusion, to make them believe what is false, so that all may be condemned who did not believe the truth but had pleasure in unrighteousness. (2 Thess 2:9–12)

This, of course, is exactly what the Gospel of John says will be the case for those who don't believe Christ's word:

> He who believes in him is not condemned; he who does not believe is condemned already, because he has not believed in the name of the only Son of God. And this is the judgment, that the light has come into the world, and men loved darkness rather than light, because their deeds were evil. (John 3:18–21)

The picture that Scripture gives us of the "end times" is not of the world becoming progressively more "advanced" in what matters, but becoming increasingly more depraved, believing lies that lead to destruction. Of course, an apostasy is not something that pagans do but something that those who were once Christians do, and so these texts are talking about a repudiation of the faith by those who once had it. The decline of the Church is not just a sociological phenomenon but a profoundly spiritual one.

It is also worth noting that a remarkable convergence is occurring in the realm of what might be called prophetic vision. Although prophetic words are not, of course, at all on the same level as Scripture, tradition, and the magisterium, some of these words are worth taking note of briefly before we move on, even though we prophesy and see now only "in a mirror dimly" (1 Cor 13:12).

In the seventeenth century, a locally approved Marian apparition spoke of our times:

> Thus I make it known to you that from the end of the 19th century and shortly after the middle of the 20th century . . . the passions will erupt and there will be a total corruption of morals. . . . As for the Sacrament of matrimony, which symbolizes the union of Christ with His Church, it will be attacked and deeply profaned. Freemasonry, which will then be in power, will enact iniquitous laws with the aim of doing away with this Sacrament, making it easy for everyone to live in sin and encouraging procreation of illegitimate children born without the blessing of the Church. . . . In this supreme moment of need for the Church, the one who should speak will fall silent.[465]

In 1917, Our Lady of Fatima told the three children that the current war (World War I) would end soon but, unless there was repentance, a second and worse war would come. There wasn't repentance, and that war came. In the First World War, twenty million died; in the Second World War, an estimated fifty million died. The only request that Mary repeated at each of her apparitions was to pray the rosary every day for world peace. Since World War II, we have experienced an absolutely massive turning away from faith and the glorification and normalization of blasphemy and sin. The world is in danger. When Jacinta was dying in a Lisbon hospital, Mary appeared to her several times and repeated to her that war is a punishment for sin, that most people go to hell because of sins of the flesh, that immodest fashions would arise that would greatly offend the Lord, that many marriages were not real marriages, and that priests had to live pure lives and devote themselves to the salvation of souls.[466]

In the Japanese city of Akita, Mary appeared to a nun, who passed on this message:

> The work of the devil will infiltrate into the Church in such a way that one will see cardinals opposing cardinals, bishops against bishops. The priests who venerate me will be scorned and opposed by their confreres . . . churches and altars sacked; the Church will be full of those who accept compromises and the demon will press many priests and consecrated souls to leave the service of the Lord.[467]

This apparition was approved by the local bishop in consultation with Rome.

Sr. Lucia, the last of the three children of Fatima still alive at the time that the John Paul II Pontifical Theological Institute for Marriage and Family Sciences was being established in Rome, wrote to Cardinal Caffarra (one of the dubia cardinals) the following:

> The decisive battle between the Lord and the kingdom of

Satan will be about marriage and the family. Do not be afraid because anyone who works for the sanctity of marriage and the family will always be fought and opposed in every way, because this is the decisive issue. However, Our Lady has already crushed its head.[468]

How ironic that the Institute established by St. John Paul II and headed by Cardinal Caffarra has now been effectively turned into an instrument against marriage and the family under the leadership of Archbishop Paglia, who has hired faculty who are open dissenters to Church teaching on sexuality and marriage.

One of the most remarkable developments in the Church since Vatican II has been the great outpouring of the Holy Spirit in the charismatic renewal. This has been accompanied by a restoration of some of the gifts of the Spirit commonly at work in the early Church, including the gift of prophecy. The most tested, mature prophetic words coming from this renewal movement in the Catholic Church bring a message similar to that of the various Marian apparitions. From this unexpected direction, in a different manner and vocabulary, the Holy Spirit seems to be trying, once again, to communicate something of importance to the Church. It is a message as old as the Bible, but it is addressed *to us*, here and now, and it demands a response.

Several prophesies have been referenced repeatedly since 1975, when they were given at the end of a liturgy at St. Peter's Basilica concluding the first large international conference of the Catholic Charismatic Renewal, attended by over ten thousand people from over forty nations. At the end of the liturgy, Pope Paul VI gave his famous speech calling this renewal "an opportunity for the Church." Among the prophecies are the following:

Because I love you, I want to show you what I am doing

in the world today. I want to prepare you for what is to come. Days of darkness are coming on the world, days of tribulation. . . . Buildings that are now standing will not be standing. Supports that are there for my people now will not be there. I want you to be prepared, my people, to know only me and to cleave to me and to have me in a way deeper than ever before. I will lead you into the desert . . . I will strip you of everything that you are depending on now, so you depend just on me. A time of darkness is coming on the world, but a time of glory is coming for my church, a time of glory is coming for my people. I will pour out on you all the gifts of my spirit. I will prepare you for spiritual combat; I will prepare you for a time of evangelism that the world has never seen. . . . And when you have nothing but me, you will have everything: land, fields, homes, and brothers and sisters and love and joy and peace more than ever before. Be ready, my people, I want to prepare you.

And another:

I speak to you of the dawn of a "new age" for my church. I speak to you of a day that has not been seen before. . . . Prepare yourselves for the action that I begin now, because things that you see around you will change; the combat that you must enter now is different; it is new. You need wisdom from me that you do not yet have. You need the power of my Holy Spirit in a way that you have not possessed it; you need an understanding of my will and of the ways that I work that you do not yet have. Open your eyes, open your hearts to prepare yourselves for me and for the day that I have now begun. My church will be different; my people will be different; difficulties and trials will come upon you. The comfort that you know now will be far from you, but the comfort that you will have is the comfort of my Holy Spirit. They will send for you, to take your life, but I will support you. Come to me. Band yourselves together, around me. Prepare, for I proclaim a new day, a day of victory and of triumph for your God. Behold, it is begun.[469]

Another extraordinarily striking prophetic word, read in light of today's events, was delivered a year later, in 1976, the year we celebrated the American Bicentennial. It is so extraordinary that I will bold it. It was delivered by a respected Church leader, Fr. Michael Scanlan, T.O.R., whose leadership established Franciscan University as a premier faithful Catholic University:

Son of man, do you see that city going bankrupt? Are you willing to see all your cities going bankrupt? Are you willing to see the bankruptcy of the whole economic system you rely on now so that all money is worthless and cannot support you? Son of man, do you see the crime and lawlessness in your city streets, and towns, and institutions? Are you willing to see no law, no order, no protection for you except that which I myself will give you? Son of man, do you see the country which you love and which you are now celebrating—a country's history that you look back on with nostalgia? Are you willing to see no country—no country to call your own except those I give you as my body? Will you let me bring you life in my body and only there? Son of man, do you see those churches which you can go to so easily now? Are you ready to see them with bars across their doors, with doors nailed shut? Are you ready to base your life only on me and not on any particular struc-

ture? Are you ready to depend only on me and not on all the institutions of schools and parishes that you are working so hard to foster? Son of man, I call you to be ready for that. That is what I am telling you about. The structures are falling and changing—it is not for you to know the details now—but do not rely on them as you have been. I want you to make a deeper commitment to one another. I want you to trust one another, to build an interdependence that is based on my Spirit. It is an interdependence that is no luxury. It is absolute necessity for those who will base their lives on me and not the structures from a pagan world. I have spoken and it will take place. My word will go forth to my people. They may hear and they may not—and I will respond accordingly—but this is my word. Look about you son of man. When you see it all shut down, when you see everything removed which has been taken for granted, and when you are prepared to live without these things, then you will know what I am making ready.[470]

Several years later, in 1980, Fr. Scanlan prophesied again:

The Lord God says: "Hear my word. The time that has been marked by my blessings and gifts is being replaced now by the period to be marked by my judgment and purification. What I have not accomplished by blessings and gifts, I will accomplish by judgment and purification. My people, my church is desperately in need of this judgment. They have continued in an adulterous relationship with the spirit of the world. They are not only infected with sin, but they teach sin, pamper sin, embrace sin, dismiss sin. . . . Leadership unable to handle it . . . fragmentation, confusion throughout the ranks . . . Satan goes where he will and infects who he will. He has free access throughout my people and I will not stand for this.

My people specially blessed in this renewal are more under the spirit of the world than they are under the Spirit of my baptism. They are more determined with fear for what others will think of them, fears of failure and rejection in the world, loss of respect by neighbors and superiors and those around them, than they are determined by fear of me and fear of infidelity to my word. Therefore your situation is very, very weak. Your power is so limited. You cannot be considered at this point in the center of the battle and the conflict that is going on.

So this time is now come upon all of you—a time of judgment and purification. Sin will be called sin. Satan will be unmasked. Fidelity will be held up for what it is and should be. My faithful servants will be seen and will come together. They will not be many in number. It will be a difficult and necessary time. There will be collapse, difficulties throughout the world but—more to the issue—there will be purification and persecution among my people. You will have to choose what word you will follow and who you will respect. And in that choice what has not been accomplished by the time of blessing and gifts will be accomplished. What has not been accomplished in the baptism and the flooding of gifts of my Spirit will be accomplished in a baptism of fire. The fire will move among you and it will burn out what is chaff. The fire will move among you individually, corporately, in groups, and around the world. I will not tolerate the situation that is going on. I will not tolerate the mixture and the adulterous treating of gifts and graces and blessing with infidelity, sin, and prostitution. My time is now among you. What you need to do is to come before me in total submission to my word, in total submission to my plan. In the total submission of this hour, what you need to do is to drop the things that are your own, the things of the past. What you need to do is to see yourselves and those whom you have responsibility for in light of this hour and judgment and purification. You need to see them in that way and do for them what will best help them to stand strong and be among my faithful servants. For there will be casualties. It will not be easy, but it is necessary. It is necessary that my people be in fact my people, that my church be in fact my church and that my Spirit in fact bring forth the purity of life, purity and fidelity to the Gospel."[471]

It is clear that the Church is under judgment for multiple infidelities. Our wickedness is being exposed, our buildings are being taken away, our public image is collapsing, our money is disappearing, and our people are leaving. In some countries, there is lawlessness in the streets, and the economy is fragile. In some of our countries, mob rule or rule by the "strongest" is in the ascendency; in many of our countries, secular leaders are pandering to the mobs or are manipulated by "public opinion" and leading by seeing which way the loudest and most threatening voices are pointing. In many of our countries, powerful technological elites are more and more brazenly eliminating voices from social media that don't support their revolutionary, socialist goals. In many of our countries, journalism and the media are no longer even trying to be truthful and objective but are turning everything they report on to destroy their enemies and further their own ideological agendas. The institutions in many of our countries are falling into silence and impotence and allowing powerful anti-Christian forces to shape the path forward. The institutions and stability of many of our countries are unraveling. When will we wake up?

In Poland right now, the battle is particularly fierce. The European Union and well-funded LGBTQ activist groups, some funded by George Soros, are threatening Poland with every kind of economic punishment and moral shaming for standing firm for Christian values. Some describe it as an "ideological hurricane" threatening to break Poland's Christian culture. The conservative government and the Church are fighting a good battle, but mob rule, vicious threats, and hysterical propaganda are threatening to overwhelm the country and silence the Church and those political parties wanting to hold out for Christian values concerning marriage and family. Mobs of gay activists had to be restrained by the police from disrupting a children's religious procession.[472] If they gain power, they openly state that they are determined to indoctrinate young children in the LGBTQ ideology, which they claim is only to promote "equality." A lot is at stake in Poland, perhaps one of the last significant Catholic strongholds in Europe.

And how painful it is to hear prominent Church leaders at the highest levels saying that "God does not send chastisement." "God does not punish." The blind are leading the blind.[473] The Lord chastises those whom he loves. If the Church is being chastised so severely, what will become of those who are in open rebellion against God—the world?

> For the time has come for judgment to begin with the household of God; and if it begins with us, what will be the end of those who do not obey the gospel of God? And

> "If the righteous man is scarcely saved, where will the impious and sinner appear?"

Therefore let those who suffer according to God's will do right and entrust their souls to a faithful Creator. (1 Pet 4:17–19)

What many thought had been swept clean through the ministry of St. John Paul II and Pope Benedict seems now like the person from whom a demon had been expelled but, being empty (not filled with the Lord), seven came back. There is little room for pleading ignorance. We have eyes to see and ears to hear. We can look at the pattern of judgment established in the Old Testament, the warnings of the New Testament, the lessons of history, the current signs of the times, and the actual prophetic word being addressed to the Church and world today. What we need now is action.

The prophetic word is often conditional. If God's people hear his word and respond in repentance and restoration, sometimes the chastisement and judgment can be withheld or lessened. Sometimes, the beginning of judgment produces a repentance and turning to God that leads to restoration. But sometimes, if God's people remain blind, the whole, awful judgment must unfold:

When I shut up the heavens so that there is no rain, or command the locust to devour the land, or send pestilence among my people, if my people who are called by my name humble themselves, and pray and seek my face, and turn from their wicked ways, then I will hear from heaven, and will forgive their sin and heal their land. (2 Chr 7:13–14)

I think there is still a window open where, if enough of us pray and repent, God may spare us from more devastating correction and chastisement. One of my friends thinks that the coronavirus was like the first of the plagues of Egypt, the frogs, and if there is not repentance, additional chastisements will be sent until those of us who share in Pharaoh's hardness of heart finally surrender to the one

Lord. But if there is no repentance, the glory of the Lord eventually "leaves the temple," and there remain only judgment and captivity (see 2 Chr 7:19–22).

As C.S. Lewis said:

> Pain insists upon being attended to. God whispers to us in our pleasures, speaks in our consciences, but shouts in our pain: it is his megaphone to rouse a deaf world.[474]

So, let's pray fervently, while there is still time, that God will hear our prayers and accept our sacrifices and repentance and heal our land. And if the whole land can no longer be healed, let us pray that we, in humility, may be part of the "remnant" continuing on in his service by his grace and mercy, no matter what storms are raging, witnessing to the bright light of Christ which the darkness can never overcome and knowing that the power that is at work in us is greater than the power that is at work in the world.

Chapter 11

A TIME FOR REPENTANCE

THE SITUATION OF THE CHURCH TODAY—and of the world—is so serious that an appropriate response to it must be rooted in a profound repentance and turning back to God. We, as individuals and as a Church, must repent and turn more wholeheartedly to God and undergo his purification. Only then can we really be the powerful witness to the world that the Lord intends. Only then can we speak clearly, truthfully, courageously, powerfully, lovingly, in a way that makes clear the choice that all men and women face: the choice for or against God and the presence of his only beloved Son in our midst today. We need to ask this question of the world: Who do you say he is? But we can only ask it with confidence when we have answered it for ourselves with much greater conviction and fire than is normally manifested in our official statements. The polluted streams of water that are flowing throughout the Church need to be purified so that the waters that Ezekiel spoke about, flowing forth from the temple and bringing life wherever they flowed, may flow again in greater power and purity, not only within the Church but out into the world.

Each of us must face our individual situations and seek repentance accordingly. To some degree or another, many of us have accepted or tolerated false teaching, half-truths, and unrighteous behavior in ourselves and in those for whom we have been responsible. Because we form the body of Christ together, our lives are intertwined. We bear a corporate responsibility for our common situation. Genuine reformers have usually identified in some real sense with the "sins of the people." Personal righteousness and holiness are not sufficient in themselves for thoroughgoing reform. There is also a need for corporate repentance. Because God deals with us as individuals and as a people, we must respond on both levels.

The prayer of Nehemiah provides an example of how the individual and corporate dimensions intermingled in one reformer's prayer of repentance:

> O LORD God of heaven, the great and terrible God who keeps covenant and steadfast love with those who love him and keep his commandments; let thy ear be attentive, and thy eyes open, to hear the prayer of thy servant which I now pray before thee day and night for the people of Israel thy servants, confessing the sins of the people of Israel, which we have sinned against thee. Yea, I and my father's house have sinned. We have acted very corruptly against thee, and have not kept the commandments, the statutes, and the ordinances which thou didst command thy servant Moses. Remember the word which thou didst command thy servant Moses, saying, "If you are unfaithful, I will scatter you among the peoples; but if you return to me and keep my commandments and do them, though your dispersed be under the farthest skies, I will gather them thence and bring them to the place which I have chosen, to make my name dwell there." (Neh 1:5–9)

In order to turn back to God in individual and corporate repentance, we must first deal with the question of "blame." As we have already discussed, often today we are so concerned with ascertaining the degree of subjective culpability, or even with rationalizing by trying to convince ourselves that our culpability is only minimal when we really know otherwise, that we never properly deal with and even entirely overlook objectively wrong and unfaithful actions. The prophet Jeremiah spoke to such neglect of objective wrong:

> "To whom shall I speak and give warning,
>   that they may hear?
> Behold, their ears are closed,
>   they cannot listen;
> behold, the word of the LORD is to them an object of
>   scorn,
>   they take no pleasure in it. . . .
> For from the least to the greatest of them,
>   every one is greedy for unjust gain;
> and from prophet to priest,
>   every one deals falsely.
> They have healed the wound of my people lightly,
>   saying, 'Peace, peace,'
>   when there is no peace.
> Were they ashamed when they committed abomination?
>   No, they were not at all ashamed;
>   they did not know how to blush.
> Therefore they shall fall among those who fall;
>   at the time that I punish them, they shall be over-
>   thrown,"
>   says the LORD. (Jer 6:10, 13–15)

It is virtually impossible to ascertain the subjective degree of responsibility in many cases. The remedy is to make the question of blame a subordinate consideration, as we have argued for in Chapter 6, and leave that judgment to God. Our attention should be focused on the objective nature of actions and their objective consequences. Subjective culpability is not even a judgment that rests with men. Rather, it rests with God: "I do not even judge myself. I am not aware of anything against myself, but I am not thereby acquitted. It is the Lord who judges me" (1 Cor 4:3–4).

I believe the time has come for us to stop condoning objectively wrong behavior with excuses: "I didn't know"; "I didn't have enough training"; "Everybody was doing it and it looked like the Church had changed its teaching"; "It's difficult for me to face conflict situations, so I just went along with the tide"; "I'm not really responsible because of my weaknesses"; "I know that God is merciful, and I thought he would understand," and so on. Let us leave these questions and excuses in God's hands. It is time for us to stop investing our energies in whitewashing crumbling walls and instead to rebuild from the foundations on the basis of a wholehearted return to God and his Word:

> Because, yea, because they have misled my people, saying, "Peace," when there is no peace; and because, when the people build a wall, these prophets daub it with whitewash; say to those who daub it with whitewash that it shall fall! There will be a deluge of rain, great hailstones will fall, and a stormy wind break out; and when the wall falls, will it not be said to you, "Where is the daubing with which you daubed it?" (Ezek 13:10–12)

It is time to stop echoing the false prophets, saying "peace, peace" where there is no peace and confirming people in lives of sin, lukewarmness, and corruption:

But in the prophets of Jerusalem
    I have seen a horrible thing:
they commit adultery and walk in lies;
    they strengthen the hands of evildoers,
    so that no one turns from his wickedness;
all of them have become like Sodom to me,
    and its inhabitants like Gomorrah. . . .
Behold, I will feed them with wormwood,
    and give them poisoned water to drink;
for from the prophets of Jerusalem
    ungodliness has gone forth into all the land. . . .

They say continually to those who despise the word of the Lord, "It shall be well with you"; and to every one who stubbornly follows his own heart, they say, "No evil shall come upon you." . . .

But if they had stood in my council,
    then they would have proclaimed my words to my
    people,
and they would have turned them from their evil way,
    and from the evil of their doings. (Jer 23:14, 15b, 17,
    22)

The teaching of Scripture is that we need to accept responsibility for the wrong we have done—be it active or passive, an action or an omission—and leave questions concerning the degree of guilt or blame in God's hands. As a Church and as individuals, we need to fully face the present situation of lukewarmness and widespread infidelity and, in repentance, seek God's mercy and forgiveness. For currently our situation is under judgment:

Hear, O earth; behold, I am bringing evil upon this
people,
    the fruit of their devices,
because they have not given heed to my words;
    and as for my law, they have rejected it. . . .
Behold, I will lay before this people
    stumbling blocks against which they shall stumble;
fathers and sons together,
    neighbor and friend shall perish. . . .
Behold, a people is coming from the north country,
    a great nation is stirring from the farthest parts of the
    earth.
They lay hold on bow and spear,
    they are cruel and have no mercy,
    the sound of them is like the roaring sea;
they ride upon horses,
    set in array as a man for battle,
    against you, O daughter of Zion!
O daughter of my people, gird on sackcloth,
    and roll in ashes;
make mourning as for an only son,
    most bitter lamentation;
for suddenly the destroyer
    will come upon us. (Jer 6:19, 21–23, 26)

The fact is that millions of Catholics, men and women who are
the Church's responsibility through baptism, are living lives that are
greatly offensive to God and gravely injurious to their fellow man—
lives of adultery and fornication, greed and lust, sorcery and idolatry,
anger, hatred, jealousy, lying and cheating, murder, homosexuality,
disobedience to parents, oppression of the poor, and yes, polluting
the environment. There are many who are trying to serve both God

and money, mixing the worship of God with the invocation of evil spirits, the love of God with the hatred of men. Among those exercising pastoral responsibilities in the Church, there are parents, clergy, and bishops who are functioning as false prophets, giving assurance of innocence where there is in fact guilt; as false priests, who no longer truly teach the Word of God, no longer distinguishing between the clean and the unclean, the sacred and profane; as false shepherds, whose sin of negligence and passivity has left the flock scattered, a prey for wild beasts, who now roam at will through the dispersed flock "seeking some one to devour" (1 Pet 5:8):

> Woe to the shepherds who destroy and scatter the sheep of my pasture!" says the LORD. Therefore thus says the LORD, the God of Israel, concerning the shepherds who care for my people: "You have scattered my flock, and have driven them away, and you have not attended to them. Behold, I will attend to you for your evil doings, says the LORD. Then I will gather the remnant of my flock out of all the countries where I have driven them, and I will bring them back to their fold, and they shall be fruitful and multiply. I will set shepherds over them who will care for them, and they shall fear no more, nor be dismayed, neither shall any be missing." (Jer 23:1–4)

For us, as a Church and as individuals, the only appropriate response to this situation is thorough and deep repentance and prayer; given the wretched condition of God's people, questions of degrees of blame are secondary. We need to evaluate our situation, not by the standard of "what has always been the case" or what is the "statistical norm" but by the norm of God's Word, his standards, his criteria, as expressed clearly by the Scripture and the teaching of the Church.

By this standard, we stand greatly in need of his mercy and forgiveness, greatly in need of repentance.

Preparation for Repentance

In order not to take "the wound of my people lightly" (Jer 6:14), we need to approach repentance, as individuals and as a Church, by careful consideration of our unfaithfulness before God.

We must consider not only objectively wrong things that we have done but also the serious nature of what we have failed to do. Our omissions as well as our commissions have allowed evil to flourish and the Church to be corrupted: "Whoever knows what is right to do and fails to do it, for him it is sin" (Jas 4:17).

We need to consider not only the evil we have done but also the "good" we have done that was not the will of God. What have we done under the impulse of the "flesh," of the desires of "natural man," that were, in fact, obstacles to God's plan for his people? Sometimes, even apparently very "worthwhile" Christian activities can be done without the will of the Lord:

> Not every one who says to me, "Lord, Lord," shall enter the kingdom of heaven, but he who does the will of my Father who is in heaven. On that day many will say to me, "Lord, Lord, did we not prophesy in your name, and cast out demons in your name, and do many mighty works in your name?" And then will I declare to them, "I never knew you; depart from me, you evildoers." (Matt 7:21–23)

How much of what has been done in the name of Church "renewal" has been simply the product of man's "natural" thinking or enthusiasm—not the will of God and therefore bearing no lasting fruit, producing no life? How much apparent "service" of God has been disobedience, a manifestation of a failure to seriously seek to know God, his will, and his Word? How much of our activity has been in direct contradiction to God's will, Word, and ways?

How many times have we been "anxious and troubled about many things"—many good and useful things—while forgetting the "one thing [that is] needful" (Luke 10:41–42), namely, seriously listening to God, knowing his Word, and doing his will?

For all of this, we need to accept responsibility and ask forgiveness in the measure appropriate to each.

Let us now examine particular areas that will help us approach repentance.

Our Own Lives

Here are some questions to ask:

Have I allowed myself to be seduced by false teaching? Have I been eager to believe things to satisfy the desires of my flesh, to satisfy my "itching ears" (see 2 Tim 4:3)?

Have I been eager to believe teachers or advisors who told me what I wanted to hear?

Have I used the "freedom" of the post-conciliar Church and the resurgence of moral and doctrinal confusion in recent years as an opportunity to satisfy the lusts of the flesh?

Have I allowed myself to be formed in my thinking and acting by contemporary culture in a way that has choked off my life with God and clouded my Christian mind?

Cardinal Avery Dulles suggested that confronting ourselves with the eternal perspective can help reveal ways in which we have wrongly adopted the thinking of the world:

> Few Christians, I suppose, would say that the question of life beyond death is marginal or irrelevant . . . and yet

many seem to act as though they believed that the only salvation worth considering must be attainable in this world before death, if not by ourselves, at least by some future generation. The very exercise of asking ourselves whether we subscribe to this view can prove medicinal. Once we have explicitly reaffirmed the Christian understanding of salvation, we see the ambiguity of our previous behavior. We are alerted to the apparent implications of our silence and omission, our enthusiasms and boredoms, our approvals and disapprovals. We often find evidence of tacit heresy in our own lives and in the lives of Christians whose professed beliefs are unexceptionally orthodox.[475]

When the eternal perspective of God's Word is obscured, Christian morality, spirituality, and mission very quickly become more vulnerable to the pressure of contemporary culture. John Paul II often drew our attention to this essential eternal perspective, and in our approach to repentance, we would do well to meditate on his words:

> Christianity is a program full of life. Confronted with the daily experience of death, in which our humanity shares, it repeats tirelessly: "I believe in eternal life." In this dimension of life is found the fulfillment of man in God himself: "We know that . . . we shall be like him, for we shall see him as he is" (1 John 3:2).[476]

It is clear that Jesus does not eliminate normal concern and pursuit of daily bread and of everything that can make human life more advanced, highly civilized, more satisfying. But life passes inevitably. Jesus points out that the real meaning of our earthly existence lies in eternity, and that the whole of human history with its dramas and its joys must be seen in the perspective of eternity.[477]

Jesus, speaking of the kingdom of heaven, wishes to teach us that human existence has value only in the perspective of truth, of grace, and of the future glory. Everything must be accepted and lived with love and for love in the eschatological reality revealed by him: "Sell your possessions, and give alms; provide yourselves with purses that do not grow old, with a treasure in the heavens that does not fail" (Luke 12:33).[478]

It is repentance in the light of eternity that John Paul II modeled for us in calling for a solemn repentance for the sins of members of the Church in preparation for the dawning of the new millennium and the hoped-for new springtime for Christianity.

There are certain events of the Jubilee year of 2000 that the pope singled out for special mention. Among them is the special focus on repentance that culminated in the solemn request for pardon on March 12, 2000:

To purify our vision for the contemplation of the mystery, this Jubilee Year has been strongly marked by the *request for forgiveness*. . . . How could we forget *the moving Liturgy of 12 March 2000* in Saint Peter's Basilica, at which, looking upon our Crucified Lord, I asked forgiveness in the name of the Church for the sins of all her children? This "purification of memory" has strengthened our steps for the journey towards the future and has made us more humble and vigilant in our acceptance of the Gospel.[479]

The pope was specific in what he asked God pardon for in the name of the Church:

Let us forgive and ask forgiveness! While we praise God who, in his merciful love, has produced in the Church a wonderful harvest of holiness, missionary zeal, total dedication to Christ and neighbor, we cannot fail to recognize *the infidelities to the Gospel committed by some of our brethren*, especially during the second millennium. Let us ask pardon for the divisions which have occurred among Christians, for the violence some have used in the service of the truth and for the distrustful and hostile attitudes sometimes taken towards the followers of other religions.

Let us confess, even more, *our responsibilities as Christians for the evils of today.* We must ask ourselves what our responsibilities are regarding atheism, religious indifference, secularism, ethical relativism, the violations of the right to life, disregard for the poor in many countries.

We humbly ask forgiveness for the part which each of us has had in these evils by our own actions, thus helping to disfigure the face of the Church.[480]

The pope expressed a wish that dioceses throughout the world would similarly do an examination of conscience and conduct their own solemn liturgies of pardon; not many did.

I am happy to say, though, that in the Archdiocese of Detroit where I teach at the seminary, the archdiocese took a very serious step of repentance. In order to prepare for a major reorientation of the archdiocese, from maintenance to mission, the archbishop asked that the archdiocese do a serious examination of conscience. The archbishop and his advisors recognized that the first order of business must be repentance for ways in which we as an archdiocese had offended the Lord and harmed his people over the years. The archbishop, in the name of the archdiocese, in the presence of the former archbishop, Cardinal Adam Maida, and all the auxiliary bishops, repented for very significant sins:

For ignoring the Word of God and hiding behind policies and procedures

For cowardice in confronting the culture of death

For silence regarding human trafficking, the ravages of pornography, and many other evils

For the times we have not conducted our affairs with justice and have misused Church funds for private gain

For sloppy work, ill prepared homilies, for not giving God what is our best

For failing to protect children from sexual abuse

For not keeping the Lord's Day holy

For turning a deaf ear to the cries of the poor

For turning away from the widow and the orphan and choosing the sleek and the rich

For the times we have refused to allow African American Catholics into our parish communities

For unbelief and cowardice for failing in our prophetic mission to proclaim the fullness of the Gospel and the demands of discipleship

For substituting mere human means for the power of your Word

For not recognizing and releasing the spiritual and moral

gifts of the lay faithful and having relied overmuch on institutional means, rather than the power of the Holy Spirit

For falling prey to the lies of the Tempter and relying on worldly means to secure the spread of your Kingdom rather than on the love of Christ and the power of his cross.[481]

It is solemn, serious acts of repentance, followed by "fruits" that show the sincerity of such repentance, that we all need to undertake at every level of the Church. The repentance for clergy sexual abuse of minors is a good start, but much more is needed. What preceded the solemn repentances led by Pope John Paul II, and those that were led in my own archdiocese, was a serious examination of conscience. We need to undertake a similar examination of conscience at every level and to keep renewing it to avoid falling back into old ways and old sins. Once done is never done. There must be ongoing renewal of repentance so real changes happen and noble sentiments and statements are actually translated into concrete changes.

Additional Questions

Since morally wrong behavior often ensues when our basic grasp of Christian truth becomes uncertain and our clear, eternal perspective clouded, we must ask ourselves:

Have I done things that are morally wrong, no matter what the rationalizations, no matter who told me it was alright?

Have I led others to believe and to do wrong things by my example and my active encouragement, or by my silence and passivity?

OUR TEACHING

Besides reviewing the way we have lived our own lives, we also need to examine the faithfulness of our teaching. We teach in many ways—informally and formally, directly and through delegation to others.

Have I faithfully and fully taught the Gospel of our Lord and Savior Jesus Christ, as understood by the official teachers of the Catholic Church? Or have I taught the opinions of men as the Word of God?

Have I "affirmed" people in their pride, sense of self-sufficiency, and "autonomy," rather than leading them to submit themselves to God and his Word?

Have I presented a mixture of God's Word and the "current thinking of the academic community" which has left people confused and uncertain?

Has my own teaching, or the teaching of those I have delegated (in my children's school, in seminaries, or religious education programs) led people to forsake sin and live lives of purity and holiness, zeal and dedication? Or has my teaching subtly communicated a cynicism concerning the possibility of knowing God's Word with any certainty, and therefore the possibility of living enthusiastically and heroically?

Here it may be useful to meditate on the reflections of a small group of European bishops, who had begun to acknowledge the way in which some of the "wisdom of this world" had perhaps obscured some of their teaching:

> Many of our decisions, of our beliefs, are linked to an anthropology influenced by contemporary philosophical currents, for which the phenomenon of "secularization" has left an irreversible mark on modern man. Don't such convictions now have to be relativized by this renewal of the transcendent which reminds us that all anthropology which forgets the spiritual dimension of man is a truncated anthropology? . . . And don't we have to reconsider some of our approaches

so that our speaking about God doesn't exhaust itself simply in an abstract and rational modality which unfortunately sometimes marks our declarations and our publications?[482]

Our Spheres of Responsibility

We must also examine how we have conducted ourselves in our spheres of responsibility, which are broader than our personal lives, example, and even our teaching.

Most of us have a definite sphere of responsibility for the lives of others, beyond our personal lives and example. Parents, for example, are responsible, to a certain extent, for the lives of their children. Older children are, to some extent, responsible for the lives of younger children. Parish priests have significant responsibility for the moral and spiritual lives of their parishioners. Leaders of religious orders have considerable responsibility for the personal lives and service of those in the order. Bishops are responsible for the overall moral and spiritual health and soundness of teaching and discipline in their dioceses, and with other bishops, they share responsibility for their own regions, their countries, and the world.

Virtually all of the massive infidelity, false teaching, and moral and spiritual corruption in the years since Vatican II has taken place in situations for which others have pastoral responsibility. In many of these situations, those with the responsibility have done little to stop evil from being done or have only weakly bemoaned the situation, as Eli did with his sons, or even worse, have covered it up in a woefully misguided effort to protect the institution at the expense of the ongoing destruction of bodies and souls of children and vulnerable adults and the corrupt squandering of the offerings of the people. They have failed to exercise their responsibility and use their authority effectively; rather, they have used it to "whitewash" crumbling walls and make light of the grievous wounds being inflicted on the flock.

As we repent, we need to look closely at how we have discharged our God-given responsibility in the spheres where we have it.

As Regards People

Have I allowed people for whom I have been responsible to be exposed to false teaching?

Have I allowed those for whom I have been responsible to accept false teaching and promulgate it?

Have I been passive in the face of unrepented immorality in the lives of these people?

Have I been sufficiently in touch with the lives of those for whom I am responsible to know what they are thinking and doing and so to be able to effectively "accompany" them?

As Regards Institutions and Programs

Many of us have responsibilities for institutions, programs, or communities. These include families, schools, religious education programs, adult education programs, seminary curricula, and diocesan institutions. We need to ask ourselves some questions regarding our stewardship or guardianship over these things, too.

Have I allowed my family (seminary, diocese, etc.) to become lukewarm, lax in the faith?

Have I tolerated ambiguous teaching and moral counsel in my institution?

Have I overlooked unfaithful, disloyal belief and practice?

Have I taught clearly or arranged to have taught clearly:

—God's plan of salvation

—the Church's teaching on sexual morality

—the important differences between Christianity and the non-Christian religions

—the authority of the Scriptures, tradition, and the authentic teaching authority of the Church?

In particular, those responsible for institutions need to ask questions like these:

Have I taken the path of "least resistance" and added people to my faculty who are ambiguous in their Christian life and teaching, perhaps using the excuse that no one else was available? Have I ordained seminarians of questionable character, even if they were still dealing with moral weaknesses, contrary to the official guidelines, and ignoring that the temptations will only get stronger after ordination, when the protection of the seminary environment is no longer present?

Have I treated the continued existence of my institution and the financial support of donors as being more important than its continued faithfulness to God?

ACCOUNTABILITY BEFORE GOD

All of us need to answer to God for our care of what he has entrusted to us, be it people, institutions, our families, our students, other people, or our own lives. As we have seen, Scripture teaches clearly that each Christian needs to give an accounting before God for how he has lived his life. Scripture also says that a special accounting will be asked of those who have been given pastoral responsibility: "Let not many of you become teachers, my brethren, for you know that we who teach shall be judged with greater strictness" (James 3:1).

John Paul II manifests this awareness of accountability before the Lord in the extraordinary efforts he made to call his own diocese of Rome to conversion and holiness of life. In an address to the students and staff of the Pontifical Irish College, he spoke of this awareness of his accountability before the Lord:

Because you are living in Rome, in a diocese for which I personally must give a particular accounting to the Lord, you will understand how ardently I desire that Christ should be formed in you. (cf. Gal 4:19)[483]

We have already considered how the Lord held Eli responsible for failing to effectively discipline his sons (see 1 Sam 2:11–36). We have also seen how the Spirit admonished early Christian communities for tolerating infidelity in their midst (see Rev 3:12–23). Now let us look specifically at God's expectations concerning those who hold pastoral responsibility, particularly as this pertains to the prophetic and pastoral role, which those in authority among God's people share to some degree.

To not adequately exercise the teaching and warning function that God has given us is to run the risk of being held responsible for whatever may flow from such passivity:

Son of man, I have made you a watchman for the house of Israel; whenever you hear a word from my mouth, you shall give them warning from me. If I say to the wicked, "You shall surely die," and you give him no warning, nor speak to warn the wicked from his wicked way, in order to save his life, that wicked man shall die in his iniquity; but his blood I will require at your hand. But if you warn the wicked, and he does not turn from his wickedness, or from his wicked way, he shall die in his iniquity; but you will have saved your life. (Ezek 3:17–19)

Today, those of us who are parents, teachers, deacons, priests, bishops, religious education directors, seminary rectors, theology department chairmen, college presidents—all of us share in this "guardian" and "watchman" role. The consequence of not exercising this role effectively is to be held accountable for the evil that is done under our responsibility.

Jesus's heartfelt remark that it is better to be thrown into the sea with millstones around one's neck than to allow simple believers to be corrupted in their faith indicates how he feels about leading—or allowing others to lead—the "little ones" astray:

> Whoever receives one such child in my name receives me; but whoever causes one of these little ones who believe in me to sin, it would be better for him to have a great millstone fastened round his neck and to be drowned in the depth of the sea. (Matt 18:5–6)

While primary responsibility in these areas falls to those who have been given authority in various areas of life—namely, parents and Church leaders at all levels—there is a sense in which every Christian, simply by virtue of being a Christian, has a responsibility to challenge false teaching and immorality, even when we are not directly responsible. We have a concern for one another's welfare simply by virtue of our baptism, for Christians are brothers and sisters in Christ, and Jesus wants those who are not Christians to become our brothers and sisters in him. It is often fitting for ordinary Christians to speak directly to those involved in corruptions of the faith and to bring the matter to the attention of the appropriate authority—parents, pastors, bishops, or religious superiors. If the immediate authority does not make a satisfactory response, it is often appropriate to go to the next higher authority. At a certain point, matters like these, then, have to be left to the judgment of the appropriate authority, who in turn will have to answer to God for the situation. When exercising this basic level of responsibility simply by virtue of being a "concerned Christian," it is important to act with respect and with openness to the possibility that the situation is not being perceived correctly or that there is more to it than meets the eye. At the same time, when a real corruption of truth or life is at stake, working diligently and persistently to bring it to the attention of the people involved and to the proper authorities is a valuable service to the whole Church and to the Lord. It is a duty of love and concern for the salvation of souls to persist in addressing these situations until we have exhausted our legitimate options, with due adherence to Matthew 18:15–17.

As we come before the Lord and reflect on his Word to us, as we measure our lives and the discharge of our responsibilities against his Word, our next step is to actually turn to God in repentance. Let us now look at some of the elements involved in authentic repentance.

Receiving Forgiveness

Forgiveness must be specifically sought, not simply presumed. If we repent and acknowledge our sin to God and to those we have wronged, we can be sure that God and those who obey his Word will forgive us. All the same, this forgiveness is to be sought and received as a gift, not presumptuously.

Sorrow for Sin

As we acknowledge our sin and infidelity and turn to God to confess it and ask his forgiveness, it is appropriate for us to manifest sorrow. This is an important part of both individual and corporate repentance. In times past, when God's Word has been "rediscovered" and God's people have measured their life against it anew, their repentance has often included an appropriate manifestation of sorrow for sin and infidelity, such as fasting and weeping.

The foundation for authentic sorrow is a recognition of who it is that we have sinned against and of the consequences that have come into the world and people's lives through our infidelity. Sorrow for sin does not necessarily have to be rooted in an emotional response. We simply need to recognize that wrong has been done and that it is fitting to express sorrow for that wrong. In other words, we do not have to wait for certain emotions to well up before we can express sorrow for sin. We can simply try to express it in various ways. For most of us, feelings of sorrow will usually be a component of such expression; God's people have often given way to "mourning and weeping" as they returned to him. For example, when Ezra gathered together all the people and read to them the Word of God, they broke out into weeping because they saw how far short they had fallen in their lives as individuals and as a people (see Neh 8). On another occasion, when Ezra learned of the unfaithfulness of the people—including the leaders, who had married wives and adopted practices from the nations around them—he began to weep and mourn, praying and fasting for the people:

> While Ezra prayed and made confession, weeping and casting himself down before the house of God, a very great assembly of men, women, and children, gathered to him out of Israel; for the people wept bitterly. (Ezra 10:1)

That emotional response, though not necessary for true repentance, should be sought as a gift from God. In his *Spiritual Exercises*, St. Ignatius of Loyola instructs the retreatant before each prayer period to ask God for the grace he desires. When the retreatant is calling to mind his sins, Ignatius writes, "Here it will be to ask for growing and intense sorrow and tears for my sins."[484]

In the days of Ezra and Nehemiah, acknowledgement of sin and an expression of sorrow were essential elements of the process of restoring God's people to a close and faithful relationship with himself. Today, the same thing holds true: we have to acknowledge sin and express appropriate sorrow for our sin, individually and as a people. In cases of serious sin, recourse to the Sacrament of Reconciliation is necessary.

BEARING THE FRUITS OF REPENTANCE

When the crowds were coming to John the Baptist in an apparent show of repentance, he exhorted them to give some evidence of their change of heart in concrete actions and changes in their lives (see Matt 3:8).

This is the required expression of any true repentance: unrighteous behavior must yield to righteous behavior. Also, specific acts or reparation are often necessary if the damage occasioned by our action, or lack of action, is to be repaired. Unfortunately, I know of dioceses where there were services of repentance and healing for issues connected with the horrible sexual abuse of minors by clergy that didn't actually result in any change. Ties of friendship and institutional self-protectiveness continued to lead bishops to cover up past abusive situations. Quite unfortunately, if it weren't for lawsuits, the investigations of attorneys general, and the media, a great deal of the cover-up and abuse would still be going on. In such cases, the repentance itself was probably superficial.

REPAIRING THE DAMAGE

"They have healed the wound of my people lightly" (Jer 6:14).

Repentance must be in-depth. It must take responsibility for the wrong done and must seek to repair the damage and set things right. Just as repentance for thievery is inauthentic unless it includes restoring the stolen property, just as repentance for slander is inauthentic without effort to restore the injured party's reputation, so too must repentance toward God express itself in reparation and restitution in all its dimensions.

Where we have sowed doubt or allowed doubt to be sown, we must sow certainty. Where we have taught ambiguously or have allowed ambiguity to flourish, we must restore clarity. Where we have permitted cynicism about the things of God to grow up, we must replace it with sincerity and purity of heart. To the extent that we have allowed God's Word and ways to be distorted, neglected, or denied in our spheres of responsibility, we must see that God's Word is restored. Whether in our families, parishes, dioceses, schools, seminaries, publishing houses, religious orders—wherever our pastoral passivity or lack of courage or discipline has allowed God's Word and people to be corrupted—there must we take action so that restoration and repentance can take place. If we have recommended unsound books to our people, then we must de-recommend them. If in our institutions we have tolerated teachers who do not faithfully present God's Word as understood by the Church, we must take measures to lead them to repentance, and if unrepentant, to remove them. If we have permitted situations to become established that undermine the Christian community life of our family, our parish, our diocese, we must work to change them.

A "Firm Purpose of Amendment"

Another prerequisite for authentic repentance is what has traditionally been called a "firm purpose of amendment." This means making the resolutions and taking the steps that will ensure that the infidelity or abdication of responsibility will not recur. We must combat our weaknesses, change our circumstances, and do whatever else may be necessary so that we can faithfully fulfill our responsibility as "watchmen" and "shepherds" for ourselves and God's people.

Many of us in positions of pastoral responsibility in the Church today quite simply have not made the decisions or established the conditions that will equip us to carry out our duties in faithfulness to God. I believe that it is virtually impossible to be a responsible Christian unless we are making room in our daily lives for prayer and sound spiritual reading, for study of Christian truth, and for contact with others who also want to live fervent Christian lives and serve God faithfully. Making time for the Lord, for studying his Word, and for regular contact in a support group of other earnest Christians shows the kind of "firm purpose of amendment" that genuine repentance calls for.

These activities need to be complemented by a decision to remove from our lives those contacts and situations that lead us to become lukewarm and unfaithful in the service of God. All of us need to discern where the work of the world, the flesh, and the devil have led us to sin and infidelity. Then, we must take measures to renounce the specific works of the devil, crucify the flesh, and become crucified to the world so as to live fully for God. The atmosphere of worldliness, sensuality, and cynicism that often pervades many, even in leadership positions in the Church today, needs to be renounced. An atmosphere of godliness, purity, and love for God must reign in its place.

C. S. Lewis put his finger on the kind of "separation" from the world that is required if a Christian is to be faithful to God and truly able to serve the world as God intends:

> Every attentive reader of the Psalms will have noticed that they speak to us severely not merely about doing evil ourselves but about something else. In 26:4 the good man is not only free from "vanity" (falsehood) but has not even "dwelled with," been on intimate terms with, those who are "vain." He has "hated them" (5).... In 50:18, God blames a

man not for being a thief but for "consenting to" a thief.....
Not because we are "too good" for them. In a sense because
we are not good enough. We are not good enough to cope
with all the temptations, not clever enough to cope with all
the problems, which an evening spent in such society produces. The temptation is to condone, to connive at; by our
words, looks and laughter, to "consent." . . . "Lead us not
into temptation" often means, among other things, "Deny
me those gratifying invitations, those highly interesting
contacts, that participation in the brilliant movements of
our age, which I so often, at such risk, desire."[485]

Oftentimes, the lack of real Christian community in the
Church today, the absence of real Christian support, the absence
of true Christian friendship, and the personal isolation of many of
those in leadership positions foster a vulnerability to temptation
and infidelity that must be faced and changed. We need to with-
stand the pressure of the culture which pushes us into ever-deeper
isolation through "virtual reality," "virtual relations," social media,
electronic "breaking news," and various alerts that further occupy
our hearts and minds, day and night, and keep us from the communion with the Lord and each other that is so essential to genuine
Christian life. Seeking appropriate Christian support is essential for
anyone who wants to live as a faithful servant of Christ today and
may be an essential fruit, for many of us, of authentic repentance.

In conclusion, I'd like to suggest that those of us involved in
"pastoring" at some level, whether the family, parish, school, or
diocese, go through the various steps outlined in this chapter and
do a collective examination of conscience. Do it in a spirit of humility, brotherly love, patience, and compassion, as well as courage.
Be honest; don't be afraid. However deep the infidelity, laziness,
or fear that the Holy Spirit may reveal, the Lord has a remedy; the

Lord has healing and reconciliation at the ready. Identify specific infidelities; identify specific fears; identify specific obstacles and deficiencies. Repent when appropriate, and then determine what steps need to be taken to repair the damage and what measures need to be put in place so the same sins don't happen again. The Lord is a merciful God and is so ready to meet our genuine repentance with an outpouring of his love and mercy. This searching examination of conscience, which will lead to true repentance and amendment of life, is critical, not just for our personal lives and accountability before the Lord but for the future of the Church and the salvation of souls. Repentance isn't a negative thing; it's extremely positive. In Acts 11:18, Peter describes repentance as "unto life," and so it is.

Chapter 12

A Time for Action

Since repentance involves a change of mind as well as a change of heart, it will inevitably affect our plans and goals, our life and action. I would like to sketch some of the elements of a sound foundation for action that is pleasing to God. Obviously, an adequate discussion of this subject would fill a book. Consequently, I intend the following remarks to serve not as a comprehensive treatment but as a starting point or reference point for reflection and action.

Based on the Truth

A main thrust of this book has been that the truth of the Gospel must be clearly grasped, lived, and proclaimed so that healthy Christian life may exist and grow. Therefore, a firm and clear grasp of Christian truth must be the basis of our relationship with God and with those we are trying to serve. One of the great weaknesses of both the pre- and post-Vatican II Church has been a widespread tendency to presume that Catholics already understand and are trying to live the fundamentals of the faith. Many millions do not, as survey after survey makes abundantly clear. A recent Pew study indicated that only 26 percent of Catholics under age forty believe in the Real Presence of Jesus in the Eucharist.[486] As a result, many houses have been built on sand, with no sure foundation of Christian truth, as is evidenced by how easily so many millions of Catholics are being passively swept along with the culture.

The basic truths of creation, sin, and forgiveness, the sacrifice of Christ on the Cross, the Resurrection, the gift of the Holy Spirit, the Church, the Sacraments, the Second Coming, and the final judgment should never be presupposed, even in ourselves. They must be solidly built into and constantly renewed in our own lives and the lives of those for whom we have responsibility.

In the Power of the Holy Spirit

There has been a tendency in the Catholic Church for the Christian truths to be intellectually held and perhaps accurately expressed, but not adequately incarnated in life or action. Often this has been due to what Spanish bishop, Juan Hervas, one of the founders of the Cursillo Movement, called the "minimalist corruption of the Gospel." By this, Bishop Hervas meant the tendency in practice to ask less of Catholics than what the Gospel asks and to offer less than what the Gospel offers. This has resulted in the widespread practice of a "lukewarm" Catholicism, one that is extremely vulnerable to deception and seduction. Scripture makes it clear that God does not look kindly on a lukewarm Christianity: "I know your works: you are neither cold nor hot. Would that you were cold or hot! So, because you are lukewarm, and neither cold nor hot, I will spew you out of my mouth" (Rev 3:15–16).

"Normal" Christianity must ask of people all that the Gospel asks: total commitment. It must offer all that the Gospel offers: most especially, for our purposes here, the gift of the Holy Spirit, which brings Christian truth to life, generates Christian experience, and motivates and guides Christian action, indeed, makes possible the "new evangelization." Christian truth is meant to bring life, to cause the release of the power of the Holy Spirit in the lives of Christians. Unless this happens, Christianity is subnormal.

LED BY THE SPIRIT

"All who are led by the Spirit of God are sons of God" (Rom 8:14).

While the firm and clear foundations of Christian truth and the empowering of the Holy Spirit are essential to any adequate vision of Christianity, the *guiding* action of the Holy Spirit is uniquely important. Only the Spirit of God knows the depths of God, the depths of our own soul, and the real situation of the world and guides us along the only truly wise course for individuals, the family, the parish, the diocese, the religious order, and the universal Church. Seeking God directly for his guidance and developing a sensitivity to the leading of the Holy Spirit is crucial for adequate Christian life and action today. Scripture calls the person "foolish" who doesn't seek God—and it is a very bad thing to be called a "fool" by the inspired Word of God.

One of the great sins we need to acknowledge and confess is our neglect of actively seeking God's guidance for the situations we face as individuals and as a people. One of our great problems as a Church is that we have too many "natural" men and women—be they liberals or conservatives, pragmatists or intellectuals, educated or uneducated—and not enough men and women who are "spiritual" men and women led by the Spirit in their life and work. This failure to submit our plans to God's Word and to the leading of his Spirit is one of the main causes for the emptiness and lack of fruit of so much "renewal." Scripture urges us and assures us: "If any of you lacks wisdom, let him ask God, who gives to all men generously and without reproaching, and it will be given him" (Jas 1:5). Sometimes, when I'm puzzling over something connected with the faith, I all of a sudden recall this verse and realize I have been trying to figure something out by myself and neglecting the generous offer of God to give us wisdom if we lack it. I quickly acknowledge my lack and ask God for wisdom, and quite often the "answer" to what I was puzzling over comes very soon indeed. Dr. Coggan, the former archbishop of Canterbury, adverted to this in a sermon: "Some of us have almost given up believing that God still speaks to the Church. May God forgive us."[487] Unfortunately, the subsequent path of the Anglican Church since Dr. Coggan uttered these words indicates that they were definitely not heeded. May we heed them before it is too late.

Ever-Deepening Union with God

It is clear that Scripture and our spiritual tradition, particularly the wisdom of the Doctors of the Church in the area of spirituality, teach us that the fruitfulness of our life and work depends on the degree to which we have been "transformed in Christ." I intentionally single out Doctors of the Church, in whom we find the depth of our spiritual tradition.[488] There is much spurious spirituality being promulgated in the Church today. But life is short and Catholics need to drink at the wells of the best and truest sources of Catholic spirituality—not the brackish waters of "pop" spirituality. "New Age" spiritualty has been gaining ground for a long time, and many Catholics are being victimized by it. Practitioners of it are being led away from the true God into syncretistic and spiritually dangerous beliefs and practices, including self-worship, nature worship, and pantheism. Sometimes "New Age" spiritual masters, even though they may use Christian language and even speak of Mary, explicitly acknowledge being under the control of "spirit guides." One of the main messages of the "spirit guides" is almost always that "there is no judgment, no hell" and nothing to fear.

At the same time, St. Francis of Assisi has become something of the patron saint of the environmentalist movement and pops up in New Age spirituality, along with Mary, from time to time, as do angels. After many years of chiefly being known as a friendly person to animals, and having his image on many birdbaths, he now has become an ecologist. The real Francis is quite different, and there is no question that the burning heart of his life and message was for sinners to be reconciled to God and that if he were here to preach today, he would be brutally rejected by many of those who are currently "adopting" him for their causes. Of course, the same would be true if Jesus himself were here today. Obviously, he is here today, in his Church, but he is strangely silent now on what would offend the culture.

I've listed some more of St. Francis's sayings and writings that reveal the heart of his mission:[489]

> If we observe what we have promised him, we shall certainly receive what he has promised to us. The pleasures of this world pass quickly away, but the punishment which follows them is eternal. The sufferings of this world are trifling, but the glory of the life to come is without bounds.[490]

In the words of St. Bonaventure, St. Francis was:

> A sharp sword all on fire, zeal for the salvation of others pierced the depths of Francis' heart in his burning love. . . . If he saw a soul redeemed with the Precious Blood of Jesus Christ being stained with sin, he would be overcome with sorrow, and weep so compassionately that he seemed to travail over them continually, like a mother in Christ.[491]

He realized he was sent by God to win for Christ the souls which the Devil was trying to snatch away. . . . He became a herald of the Gospel and he went about the towns and villages, preaching the Kingdom of God "not in such words as human wisdom teaches, but in words taught him by the Spirit" (1 Cor 2:13).[492]

And a recurring theme, a stanza from the famous *Canticle of the Sun*:

Woe to those who die in mortal sin, Blessed are those whom death will find in Your most holy will, for the second death shall do them no harm.[493]

And no matter where or when or how a man dies in the guilt of sin without doing penance and satisfaction, if he is able to perform some act of satisfaction and does not, the devil snatches up his soul from his body with so much anguish and tribulation that no one can know it unless he has experienced it. Worms eat the body. And so they have lost body and soul in this passing world, and both will go down to hell where they will be tormented without end.[494]

And he was so bold as to write a *Letter to the Rulers of the People*, calling them to repentance, given the shortness of life and each man's approaching death. He warns:

And when the day of death does come, everything which they think they have will be taken from them. And the wiser and more powerful they may have been in this world, so much greater will be the punishments they will endure in hell.[495]

Unfortunately, one of the most popular Catholic teachers of

spirituality today is a Franciscan priest, Fr. Richard Rohr, who leads his followers into a spiritual fog. It is rather shocking to find that Fr. Richard Rohr's book *The Universal Christ*[496] has been the number one bestseller in Christology on Amazon for more than a year since its publication, and as of this writing, it was still number 3 in both Christology and Christian Ethics. One of the many celebrity endorsers of the book (including Melinda Gates, among many others), Bono,[497] of U2 musical fame, has this to say about the book on its Amazon listing:

> Rohr sees Christ everywhere, and not just in people. He reminds us that the first incarnation of God is in Creation itself, and he tells us that "God loves things by becoming them." Just for that sentence, and there are many more, I cannot put this book down.[498]

What was called "creation spirituality" in the 1980s, when the then-Dominican priest Fr. Matthew Fox was a very influential teacher of "spirituality," is back. Matthew Fox is now an Episcopal priest who calls himself a post-denominational priest and is described like this in his "About the Author" section on Amazon:

> Matthew Fox is an internationally acclaimed theologian and spiritual maverick who has spent the last forty years revolutionizing Christian theology, taking on patriarchal religion, and advocating for a creation-centered spirituality of compassion and justice and re-sacralizing of the earth. He has written more than thirty books, which have sold over 1.5 million copies in fifty-nine languages.

> Originally a Catholic priest, Fox was silenced for a year and then expelled from the Dominican order, to which he

had belonged for thirty-four years, by Cardinal Ratzinger for teaching liberation theology and creation spirituality. Fox currently serves as an Episcopal priest, after he received what he calls "religious asylum" from the Episcopal Church. With exciting results he has worked with young people to create the Cosmic Mass to revitalize worship by bringing elements of rave and other post-modern art forms to the western liturgical tradition.[499]

The Franciscan priest Richard Rohr is carrying on the tradition, and his books are in many Catholic retreat houses and convents, and they are read widely by many clerics, nuns, and lay people.

Michael McClymond, the professor of theology at Saint Louis University who wrote the monumental two-volume study of universalism that we referred to in an earlier chapter, was so shocked by Rohr's latest book—and that it was so wildly popular among Catholics—that he wrote an in-depth review analyzing its heretical Christology and pantheistic spirituality:

> The problem with Rohr isn't just that he has adopted certain theologically debatable positions. It's that the indispensable, all-transforming, holy mystery of the gospel—the Word become flesh (John 1:14)—is not even there. In its place is emptiness. If Jesus's human body vanished, as Rohr tells us, and its diffusive beams scattered everywhere, then there is nothing left to worship except the universe itself. Or perhaps the conclusion is that one worships one's own Christ-nature? It's hard to see how worshiping the universe or worshiping oneself is any different from worshiping nothing, in a shadowy sort of pious nihilism.[500]

Rohr publishes a daily meditation that goes to over three hundred thousand online readers. In one of his meditations from Tuesday, October 22, 2019, he shared this:

> Today I share thoughts from Episcopal priest and CAC
> [Rohr's Center for Action and Contemplation] faculty
> member Cynthia Bourgeault on an important question,
> "What does the Bible say about sexual orientation?" For
> the record, I couldn't agree more with her response, so I
> will allow her words to stand on their own. I hope you will
> take them to heart.[501]

She says:

> Like most other critically thinking Christians, I see the
> Bible as a symphony (sometimes a cacophony!) of divinely
> inspired human voices bearing witness to an astonishing
> evolutionary development in our human understanding of
> God (or God's self-disclosure as we grow mature enough
> to begin to comprehend it, another way of saying the same
> thing).[502]

Bourgeault says, "I am compelled by my Christianity to refrain
from any behaviors or judgments which arrogantly demean the dignity of another human being or cause them to lose hope."[503] While
that statement is true in the abstract, the context in which she affirms it strongly suggests that she means we've evolved to the point
of being able to see that it would be demeaning to others if we were
to claim that homosexual behavior, or indeed any form of sexual
behavior, is intrinsically wrong.

Faulty Christology leads to faulty spirituality and then to ratio-
nalized immorality. When you make up your own Christ and pick
and choose from the Bible what you "agree with" and are continually "evolving" in your understanding, it is easy to justify almost
anything by way of personal morality and simply to make it up as

you go along. The Vatican has issued two important documents in recent years pointing out the dangers in "new age" spirituality.[504]

Another celebrity influenced by Rohr is Oprah. At a sold-out positive thinking rally at the Barclays Center in Brooklyn, Oprah and Michelle Obama presided over a "you can be great" pep rally, with lots of opportunity to sign up for Weight Watchers, get massages, and get in harmony with the elements of the earth. *The Washington Post* gave an account of it:

> They filled out self-assessments of their mood, relationships and health. They meditated to the tune of sound bowls played by a blond woman in a traffic-cone-orange suit. They cheered for New York City police officers who participate in Weight Watchers. They listened to a "Transformation Talk" by "Girl, Wash Your Face" author Rachel Hollis, . . . which eventually segued into a pep talk about how every woman is capable of greatness. . . .
>
> So, how does one make one's visions come true?
>
> A dance party, to start. Daybreaker's Radha Agrawal began the day by leading an energetic one to the tune of songs such as Adele's "Rolling in the Deep," telling the audience that when they "awaken our seven energy centers, this is how our vision manifests." Okay. And, by the way, our energy centers? Each one is a color of the rainbow. (Number six, indigo: "This is our third eye, our intuition.") The colors, projected across giant screens, flashed upon the exuberant faces of thousands of middle-aged women shaking their hips.[505]

When people lose their grounding in Scripture and tradition, they are adrift, vulnerable to be pushed along by whatever mish-mash of spirituality and positive thinking and new age superstition they run into. It is very sad to see so many people drifting away into nonsense, making up their own religion and morality, when the "solid food" of Scripture and tradition goes unplumbed.

One of *The Washington Post* writers recently published an essay entitled, "When we come to the end of our strength, the universe will hold us."[506]

I'm sorry to say that I don't think the universe is thinking of holding anyone.

As John of the Cross points out with devastating accuracy and precision, the disorders in our heart, unless they are healed and purified by the action of the one true God, will leave us enslaved to our passions and unable to think clearly, decide wisely, and live in a way worthy of our dignity as bearers of the image of God. It is essential for a healthy Church of the future to be grounded in the profound wisdom of our spiritual tradition, especially the wisdom of the Doctors of the Church in the area of spirituality.[507]

As John says:

Let those, then, who are singularly active, who think they can win the world with their preaching and exterior works, observe here that they would profit the Church and please God much more, not to mention the good example they would give, were they to spend at least half of this time with God in prayer, even though they might not have reached a prayer as sublime as this. They would then certainly accomplish more, and with less labor, by one work than they otherwise would by a thousand. For through their prayer they would merit this result, and themselves be spiritually strengthened. Without prayer they would do a great deal of hammering but accomplish little, and sometimes nothing, and even at times cause harm. . . .

> However much they may appear to achieve externally, they
> will in substance be accomplishing nothing; it is beyond
> doubt that good works can be performed only by the pow-
> er of God.[508]

Bernard of Clairvaux makes a similar point, claiming that someone who is not living under the Lordship of Christ, in true communion with him, should not exercise authority in the Church:

> One who has not been admitted to this room should never
> take charge of others. This wine should be the inspiring
> influence in the lives of those who bear authority. . . . Your
> desire is venal if you hanker to rule over others without the
> will to serve them; your ambition is unprincipled if you
> would hold men in subjection without concern for their
> salvation. I have also named this the room of grace . . . be-
> cause grace is especially found here in its fullness.[509]

Sr. Emmanuel from Medjugorje, in a recent newsletter, cited an incident from the life of St. John Vianney, the Cure of Ars, which makes this point strongly:

> Saint John Mary Vianney, the Cure of Ars, had a true heart
> of a shepherd and lived in constant prayer and sacrifice, to
> the point of heroism. In doing so, he snatched many souls
> from Satan's hands and brought them back to the path
> of salvation. But in his fury against the Saint, the enemy
> let slip these words: "If there were only three like you in
> France, I would not be able to set foot there!" That makes
> things perfectly clear. . . . What reduces the enemy to im-
> potence are neither the weapons of the world, nor endless

political discussions, nor petitions born of anger, nor violence, nor the plans for control devised by the powerful leaders in our nations, nor even indifference....What saves us from the dangers of death that threaten us today more than ever before, is the man who prays, fasts and above all does everything for the love of Love. For Love bears the name of the living God, Love is God!

In other words, let us be clear: **what will save us is the holiness** of all who have understood what an extraordinary destiny awaits us, already here on earth with divine peace in our hearts, and then with God in eternity. The "elite" and the "powerful" are like everyone else, they will die one day, perhaps even tomorrow, and their plans will die with them; so why be afraid of them? If two more saints like the Cure of Ars would have been enough to kick Satan out of my country, then here is the true power, the immense power of holiness!510

Realistic Attitudes toward "the World"

One of the most notable sources of confusion in the life and mission of the Church in recent years has been an unclear, sometimes confused, and often naive attitude toward the world. This stems from an erroneous reaction to the fundamental pastoral thrust of the Second Vatican Council—the important and worthwhile attempt to overcome an excessively negative attitude toward the world in order to regain a hearing for the Church in an increasingly secularized society. Handled with skill and understanding, as, for example, in the ministry of John Paul II and others, this "opening to the world" has had a good effect. Elsewhere, however, it has resulted in disastrous confusion, frequent infidelity, and an abundance of negative results.

A naive "love of the world" often overlooks the reality of the fallen world's hostility to God, the work of the evil one, and the lusts of the flesh. It can result in the acceptance and encouragement of profoundly anti-Christian values, attitudes, practices, and beliefs in the lives of many Christians. Future action for the Church must take into account the whole Word of God concerning the world. It must take into account the profound practical implications of Scripture texts like the following:

> Do not love the world or the things in the world. If any one loves the world, love for the Father is not in him. For all that is in the world, the lust of the flesh and the lust of the eyes and the pride of life, is not of the Father but is of the world. And the world passes away, and the lust of it; but he who does the will of God abides for ever. (1 John 2:15–17)

Can anyone deny any longer that the world, in this sense, is rising up, unrestrained by the weak and disappearing vestiges of Christian culture and enabled by the cowardice and passivity of many of our leaders, with ferocious hatred and overwhelming worldly power to crush the preaching of the Gospel, to muffle the clear sound of the trumpet that would have called people to battle, and to leave people unmoored and swept along the broad way that is clearly leading to destruction?

THE DESIRE TO BE ACCEPTED BY THE WORLD

A naive and uncritical love for the world often goes with a deep desire to please the world, to be well thought of and accepted by it. Christians, of course, want the world to recognize the good things the Lord has done in them and so to reveal Christ to the world. However, this very desire has sometimes led them to so want to please the world and be accepted by it that they have, consciously or unconsciously, grown silent about the things which would offend the world. Most profoundly offensive, of course, is the word and work of God centered in the Cross and Resurrection of Jesus Christ and in his absolute claims to sovereignty and the complete loyalty and submission of every human being on the face of the earth. In practice, this desire to please and be accepted has sometimes led to an emphasis on what Christians and non-Christians have in common that chokes off the "offensive" proclamation of the Gospel, with its absolute claims on the life of every human being and its summons to be joined to Jesus Christ or to suffer the consequences of judgment.

This desire to be accepted by the world has profoundly affected the attitudes of many in the Church. In some Church leaders, the desire to lecture at a prestigious secular university, to attend a UN conference, or to be invited into a social media conversation by popular cultural figures or institutions—as long as we don't offend by calling clearly to repentance—has too often been accompanied by a silence about the central message of the Christian Gospel.

In forming our pastoral approach to the family and the Church, we need to take into account the profound truth of the "offensiveness" of the Gospel to the "natural" man:

> For since, in the wisdom of God, the world did not know God through wisdom, it pleased God through the folly of what we preach to save those who believe.... When I came to you, brethren, I did not come proclaiming to you the testimony of God in lofty words or wisdom. For I decided to know nothing among you except Jesus Christ and him crucified.... My speech and my message were not in plausible words of wisdom, but in demonstration of the Spirit and power, that your faith might not rest in the wisdom of

men but in the power of God. (1 Cor 1:21; 2:1–2, 4)

FIXATION ON A PASSING HISTORICAL MOMENT

One of the goals of the Second Vatican Council was to help the Church develop a fresh approach to modern realities that would make its mission of evangelization more effective. The pastoral strategy of the Church had, in some ways, become fixated in stances taken at the time of the Reformation, the French Revolution, and the "age of revolution" in Europe. The realities engendered by these historical events needed to be taken into account in the Church's pastoral strategy, but ensuing events demanded consideration, too. The Council was an attempt to do this.

Today, however, almost sixty years after the Council, we face the danger of staying fixated too long on another particular historical moment—the actual moment during which the Council formed its pastoral strategy. Just as the Church itself is always in need of renewal, so also is its pastoral strategy.

As early as in his second encyclical, just fifteen years after the Council, John Paul II pointed out that Vatican II alluded to dangers in modern culture and society that have only grown much clearer and more menacing since then:

> In the span of the fifteen years since the end of the Second Vatican Council, has this picture of tensions and threats that mark our epoch become less disquieting? It seems not. On the contrary, the tensions and threats that in the Council document seem only to be outlined and not to manifest in depth all the dangers hidden within them have revealed themselves more clearly in the space of these years; they have in a different way confirmed that danger, and do not

permit us to cherish the illusions of the past.[511]

Another danger is the Church's propensity for disastrous "time lags"—its habit of responding to yesterday's problems today when today's problems are of quite a different sort.

Today, many Christian directives for the right ordering of society are not at all what the Spirit of God would lead his people to do. The most "relevant" action taken by God's people in the days just before the flood of judgment broke on the ancient world was the painstaking construction of the ark by Noah—an action that met with the hostility and ridicule of his fellow citizens. Are we not again in a time in God's plan when judgment approaches and one of the greatest services the Church can render the human race is to raise once again, loud and clear, the cry of the Apostles: "Save yourselves from this crooked generation" (Acts 2:40)? We are blessed in Southeast Michigan to have a strong Catholic network of many ministries and apostolates, and one of these is Ave Maria Communications. It provides much Catholic radio programming to EWTN, and many other stations as well. The founder and president, Al Kresta, has coined a slogan for their work that sums up well the priority for us today: "Build the Church, Bless the Nation." The bishops are often trying to influence "public policy," while the politicians quite accurately note that hardly anyone follows the bishops anymore or trusts them. The first order of business for today needs to be reform, repentance, and rebuilding the basic fabric of Catholic life before the Church can be again the "salt and light" it used to be when it was saltier and brighter.

INTERCESSION

All of us are expected to take responsibility for a certain sphere; if we go beyond this area, we become what the Scriptures refer to as a "busybody" (see 2 Thess 3:11). Nevertheless, in addition to our sphere of responsibility, we all share a common responsibility for the Church as a whole. This duty is most appropriately fulfilled through intercessory prayer.

As we repent for our individual sins and turn back to God, we also need to beseech God on behalf of the whole Church, asking him to have mercy on us, to forgive us our sins, and to restore us to strength and wholeness as a Church through a new outpouring of his Spirit and the raising up of wise and prophetic leadership.

Pope St. Paul VI viewed intercession for the coming of the Holy Spirit as a key to solving the Church's crisis that was exploding in his day:

> The Church itself is being engulfed and shaken by this tidal wave of change, for however much men may be committed to the Church, they are deeply affected by the climate of the world. They run the risk of becoming confused, bewildered and alarmed, and this is a state of affairs which strikes at the very roots of the Church. It drives many people to adopt the most outlandish views. They imagine that the Church should abdicate its proper role, and adopt an entirely new and unprecedented mode of existence. . . . An effective remedy is needed if all these dangers, which are prevalent in many quarters, are to be obviated, and We believe that such a remedy is to be found in an increased self-awareness on the part of the Church. The Church must get a clearer idea of what it really is in the mind of Jesus Christ as recorded and preserved in Sacred Scripture and in Apostolic Tradition, and interpreted and explained by the tradition of the Church under the inspiration and guidance of the Holy Spirit. Provided we implore the aid of the Spirit and show Him a ready obedience, He will

certainly never fail to redeem Christ's promise: "But the Paraclete, the Holy Ghost, whom the Father will send in my name, he will teach you all things and bring all things to your mind, whatsoever I shall have said to you."[512]

Paul VI thought that the hopes of John XXIII for the Second Vatican Council could really be fulfilled only through the experience of a new Pentecost. We have seen signs of this new Pentecost in a number of spiritual renewal movements following the Council, most notably and literally in the charismatic renewal. And it is noteworthy that perhaps the most widely utilized and effective evangelization going on in the Church today—movements and programs such as Catholic Alpha, ChristLife, and Encounter Ministries—all place strong emphasis on the need for every Catholic to experience the release of the power of the Holy Spirit in their lives, even though they don't consider themselves members of a particular movement dedicated to such. If the Church is to be truly equipped to carry out its mission in the world, it seems that a greater and deeper outpouring of the Spirit is needed—and not just among a few or on the periphery. As Paul VI said:

One must also recognize a prophetic intuition on the part of our predecessor John XXIII, who envisaged a kind of new Pentecost as a fruit of the Council. We too have wished to place ourself in the same perspective and in the same attitude of expectation. Not that Pentecost has ever ceased to be an actuality during the whole history of the Church, but so great are the needs and perils of the present age, so vast the horizon of mankind drawn towards world coexistence and powerless to achieve it, that there is no salvation for it except in a new outpouring of the gift of God. Let Him come, then, the Creating Spirit, to renew the face of the earth![513]

Praying for the outpouring of the Spirit is one necessary focus of intercessory prayer. Another is praying against the work of the evil one.

Our battle is not simply against "flesh and blood" but against "powers" and "principalities" (see Eph 6:12). Unless we take this seriously, we will be neglecting the only weapons that are effective in this spiritual combat. St. John Paul II pointed out that only with God's grace is it possible to deal effectively with the "prince of this world."

> Does man have within himself the strength to face with his own forces the snares of evil, selfishness and—let us say so clearly—the disintegrating snares of the "prince of this world," who is always active to give man, first, a false sense of his autonomy, and then to bring him, through failure, to the abyss of despair? . . . Entrust yourselves to the grace of the Lord who cries within us and for us: courage!

> Victory over the world will be Christ's. Do you want to take his side and face with him this battle of love, animated by invincible hope and courageous fortitude?

> You will not be alone; the Pope is with you. He loves you and blesses you.[514]

Perhaps more than any other recent pope, Pope Francis has drawn our attention to the contemporary working of the evil one, while at the same time calling on the charismatic renewal movement to help the whole Church to experience "baptism in the Spirit."[515]

Intercessory prayer, focused on specific situations to overturn and block the work of the evil one, is one way of contributing to the spiritual combat in which we are all caught up. The Rosary has a special place in this.

Appropriate Action

Another important response to the circumstances in which we find ourselves is appropriate action in response to the widespread undermining of God's Word.

In recent years, too many of us at every level in the Church have allowed God's Word to be undermined in our midst by our passivity or, perhaps, fearfulness. As we turn back to God as a people, many of us will be required to speak out or take action in our particular spheres of responsibility.

The basic principle of our action must be that we will not stand by as God and his Word are dishonored in our midst, and his people, our brothers and sisters, are misled. This means also that we must be loyal to our brothers and sisters who may be unjustly attacked for speaking the truth in love. Yes, with wisdom, but not giving in to fear or cowardice or self-love, we must be willing to stand with our brothers and sisters, in godly loyalty, and not allow them to be "thrown under the bus," without our protest and protection. In order to be effective and fruitful, our action—whether to protect those being misled or to stand with those courageously resisting evil and falsehood—must at the same time be loving, humble, wise, righteous, and courageous.

Our action must be loving, as we heed the scriptural exhortation to "speak the truth in love" (Eph 4:15). Desiring only what is good for people, we should be sure that our admonishment, encouragement, correction, or invitation is rooted in our sincere love for them.

Our concern for the truth must be precisely that—a concern for the truth and not a desire to prove someone wrong. This attitude of humility will generally mean that we will present our concerns to the appropriate people in such a manner as this: "My experience of your teaching is . . ."; "The parishioners I talk to seem to be taking some ideas from your preaching that perhaps you don't intend, namely . . ."; "People have told me that they are interpreting your advice and counsel this way . . . Are you aware of this?"; "Do you realize that by seeming to endorse your children's (immoral) relationships, you are giving them the impression that what they are doing is fine, which actually is endangering their eternal salvation?"

We should not presume that others are guilty of bad motives or conscious intention to undermine God's Word. In some situations, those who are doing the damage may not be aware of the results of their actions. On the other hand, as we have seen, some people involved in undermining the truth seem to be very aware of what they are doing and are consciously intent on this course. They may be completely sincere, in the sense that they sincerely believe that the Church needs to soften certain teachings in order to get along better in the current culture. Or they may sincerely believe that such teachings are wrong. But the fact is that we are not authorized to add or take away anything from what God reveals to us in Sacred Scripture:

> I warn everyone who hears the words of the prophecy of this book: if any one adds to them, God will add to him the plagues described in this book, and if any one takes away from the words of the book of this prophecy, God will take away his share in the tree of life and in the holy city, which are described in this book. (Rev 22:18–19)

And as Jesus himself said:

> Think not that I have come to abolish the law and the prophets; I have come not to abolish them but to fulfil them. For truly, I say to you, till heaven and earth pass away, not an iota, not a dot, will pass from the law until all is accomplished. Whoever then relaxes one of the least of

these commandments and teaches men so, shall be called least in the kingdom of heaven; but he who does them and teaches them shall be called great in the kingdom of heaven. For I tell you, unless your righteousness exceeds that of the scribes and Pharisees, you will never enter the kingdom of heaven. (Matt 5:17–20)

Our action must be humble in that we are not speaking out or taking action from a position of "self-righteousness" or a "holier-than-thou" stance, but out of love and obedience—love for God and his people and obedience to his Word and the promptings of his Spirit. We do not speak and act because we enjoy confrontation but because we *must* speak out and act in order to be faithful to God and his Word, to our relationship with our brothers and sisters in Christ, and to God's beloved creatures who are not yet brothers and sisters in Christ. We must not, by our silence or cowardice, confirm someone else in sin or serious error, or we may, in effect, be denying Christ.

Our action must also be humble, for we may not be right in our interpretation of a particular situation. We may, indeed, see only one side of a situation and not have an adequate grasp of all the relevant factors. We need to have the humility to be ready to discover this and to repent when we have misinterpreted a situation. For example, we may sometimes wrongly blame persons in authority who may not be to blame but were not able to defend themselves without inappropriately revealing confidences.

Our action must also be wise. We must seek God for guidance to answer many questions. When should we speak and act, and when should we remain silent? What has he given us responsibility for, and what is the responsibility of others? When should we act alone, and when should we consult others? When do we know enough about a situation, and when is more study needed? These can be difficult questions. God gives his Holy Spirit to guide us if we seek him.

A good part of wisdom is acting within our immediate sphere of responsibility. It is there that we have the greatest authority and clearest responsibility. On the other hand, all of us have some measure of responsibility to express our concern when fundamental issues are at stake, even though we may have little authority and can only express our concern to those who have responsibility, knowing that they may not choose to act.

Another part of wisdom is to act and speak according to the gifts and abilities God has given us. Not all of us are equally well equipped to deal with every situation. Sometimes, our best contribution may be to pray for God to equip someone to deal with a situation that we are not able to.

Wisdom also means acting in a way appropriate to the situation. Often, we should deliberately encourage what is good. For example, a word of encouragement after a sound homily or an expression of support for a pastor trying to establish a sound religious education program may be much more useful in a particular situation than denouncing things that are problematic but not on the same level of seriousness. It may be appropriate to write a letter to the diocesan newspaper about a public issue. On the other hand, when a private matter comes to our attention, private discussion with those directly involved will usually be in order. Sometimes, we should withdraw our financial support from activities which do not clearly support the truth and authority of God's Word. In such cases, we should look for worthy, God-centered activities more deserving of our financial support.

Wisdom means making sure that all of our resources—time, talent, and money—are working for the Lord and his Word and not against it and that we are encouraging others to do the same.

Our action must also be righteous. Normally, we should approach those directly involved in an activity which appears to be undermining God's Word before discussing the matter with a wider group of people or higher authority. The procedure for handling such difficulties is described in Matthew 18. Righteousness also means taking reasonable precautions against being rash in our judgments or loose in our talk. We should never unfairly damage someone's reputation. Nevertheless, it is entirely fitting for publicly taught and published material which undermines God's Word to be identified for what it is. Also, since the bishop is fully responsible for the soundness of all the teaching, preaching, and pastoral counsel in his diocese, it may be entirely appropriate to inform him of our concern at an early stage.

Our action must also be courageous. It must be said again that the dominant background of the crisis of truth that I addressed forty years ago was the silence and passivity of so many in the face of a massive undermining of God's Word. That silence and passivity remains a huge obstacle today as we see the unexpected resurgence of a crisis of truth. We need courage to act, to overcome our natural inclinations to "not rock the boat" or to "let someone else do it." We need to have the courage to run the risk of being wrong and to readily acknowledge our mistake if we are wrong. We need to have the courage to run the risk of encountering the opposition and perhaps persecution and defamation that we almost certainly will encounter if we speak out and take appropriate action. But we still need to act. Only by courageous action will the cloud of darkness now choking the lives of many be dispelled and replaced with the life-giving light of Christ and his Word. As one Catholic observer of the contemporary scene many years ago remarked:

> Genuine religious believers—as distinct from those for whom church membership is mainly a matter of habit—will be forced more and more to define precisely what the important differences are between themselves and non-be-

lievers. They may well have to accustom themselves to living in ways which the world around them will find strange and bizarre and which will require almost heroic decisions. The day may be coming once again when, as Christ foretold, those who persecute his followers will think they are doing something virtuous.[516]

Or, in the words of John Paul II:

It is less possible than ever today to stop at a Christian faith that is superficial or of a sociological type; times, as you well know, have changed. . . . It is necessary to arrive at the clear and certain conviction of the truth of one's Christian faith, namely, in the first place, the historicity and divinity of Christ and the mission of the Church willed and founded by him.

When one is really convinced that Jesus is the Word Incarnate and is still present in the Church, then one accepts his "word" completely, because it is a divine word which does not deceive, which does not contradict itself, and which gives us the true and only meaning of life and eternity. He alone, in fact, has "words of eternal life." He alone is the way, the truth and the life! . . . Jesus is not an idea, a sentiment, a memory! Jesus is a "person," always alive and present with us! . . . To seek, love and bear witness to Jesus! This is your commitment; these are the instructions I leave you![517]

It is the eternal perspective—the biblical worldview—which we receive from a knowledge of the basic truths of the Gospel that gives us courage in times of difficulty.[518]

The Christian must live in the perspective of eternity. Sometimes, just being a Christian is an offense to people; indeed, this is becoming the case ever more as time goes on. "The very sight of him is a burden to us" is becoming more and more the affective state of aggressive unbelievers:

> Let us lie in wait for the righteous man,
> because he is inconvenient to us and opposes our actions;
> he reproaches us for sins against the law,
> and accuses us of sins against our training.
> He professes to have knowledge of God,
> and calls himself a child of the Lord.
> He became to us a reproof of our thoughts;
> the very sight of him is a burden to us,
> because his manner of life is unlike that of others,
> and his ways are strange.
> We are considered by him as something base,
> and he avoids our ways as unclean;
> he calls the last end of the righteous happy,
> and boasts that God is his father.
> Let us see if his words are true,
> and let us test what will happen at the end of his life;
> for if the righteous man is God's son, he will help him,
> and will deliver him from the hand of his adversaries.
> Let us test him with insult and torture,
> that we may find out how gentle he is,
> and make trial of his forbearance.
> Let us condemn him to a shameful death,
> for, according to what he says, he will be protected.
>
> Thus they reasoned, but they were led astray,
> for their wickedness blinded them,
> and they did not know the secret purposes of God,

nor hope for the wages of holiness,
nor discern the prize for blameless souls;
for God created man for incorruption,
and made him in the image of his own eternity,
but through the devil's envy death entered the world,
and those who belong to his party experience it.
(Wis 2:12–24)

But Jesus has told us about this in advance, so when it happens, we need not be dismayed. His promise to be with us until the end of the age is certain and true. His promise of the Holy Spirit, who will lead us into all truth and inspire us with what to say when we are in situations of oppression and persecution, is certain and true. In fact, Jesus says that when we see these things begin to happen, we should look up and rejoice, for the fullness of our redemption is close at hand. But while we continue to trust him and abide in him and let his Word abide in us, we need to continue to work while the light lasts, for the night is coming in which no one then will be able to work. What work is most important to undertake right now? First and foremost, the work of believing in the One who has been sent to us by the Father. And then the work of telling people the truth about him and God's plan for the salvation of the human race. What a privilege!

The Inexhaustible Riches of Jesus: Participating in the Prophetic Mission of Jesus

SCRIPTURE TELLS US that there are inexhaustible riches in Jesus. Yes, so rich is the person of Jesus that we will never be able to fully plumb the depths. Yet, at various times in our lives and in the life of the Church, the Holy Spirit highlights certain dimensions of Jesus that are important for us personally or for the challenges the Church is facing at a certain time. I think the time has come for us, as individuals and as the community of the Church, to explore more deeply the important reality of Jesus the prophet. The whole book has pointed toward a recovery of the "whole Gospel," proclaimed with confidence and power, with a special emphasis on those revealed truths that are absolutely essential but under fierce attack today. In order to rise to the challenge of our culture and our time in history, we need to recover a deeper appreciation for Jesus as prophet. This is not just for theological or academic purposes. It is so that we can participate more fully with Jesus in his ongoing mission, which is essentially prophetic.

The Church's theological tradition has commonly taught that all the baptized participate in the priestly, prophetic, and kingly ministry of Jesus himself:

> Jesus Christ is the one whom the Father anointed with the Holy Spirit and established as priest, prophet, and king. The whole People of God participates in these three offices of Christ and bears the responsibilities for mission and service that flow from them.[519]

> "The holy People of God shares also in Christ's *prophetic* office," above all in the supernatural sense of faith that belongs to the whole People, lay and clergy, when it "unfailingly adheres to this faith . . . once for all delivered to the saints," (LG 12; cf. Jude 3) and when it deepens its understanding and becomes Christ's witness in the midst of this world.[520]

> Christ . . . fulfills this prophetic office, not only by the hierarchy . . . but also by the laity. He accordingly both establishes them as witnesses and provides them with the sense of the faith [*sensus fidei*] and the grace of the word. (LG §35)[521]

While true and important, these formulations don't really penetrate the deep meaning of Jesus's prophetic identity, and therefore, our prophetic identity. As we progress in this chapter, I believe we will discover things about who Jesus is that we perhaps never saw so clearly before, and therefore be better able to more deeply participate with him in his prophetic ministry, which he desires to be ours as well.

We know that the priestly dimension of Jesus's ministry was

most intensely exercised in his offering of himself as a sacrifice for our sins on Calvary and now in its re-presentation in the Eucharist and our participation in his sufferings. We know that his kingly ministry will be most fully exercised when he returns in glory, as the true king, to judge the living and the dead and is now exercised through those rightly established in authority in the Church. But during the entire course of Jesus's earthly ministry, his primary "function" and primary identity, both in how others perceived him as well as how he identified himself, was that of prophet.

A prophet is zealous for the holiness of the Father's house. A prophet is single-mindedly focused on the eternal consequences of believing or not believing the Word of God. A prophet knows that in each person's response or lack of response to the Word of God rests their eternal destinies, blessing or curse, heaven or hell.

Sometimes, we think that it is particularly the deacon's, priest's, or bishop's configuration to the prophetic mind and heart of Jesus that is very important for the Church, since they are officially charged with proclaiming the Word, and so it is. But this configuration is not just a matter of giving sound teaching and preaching well-crafted and orthodox homilies that aren't too long. It is so much more than that and gets to the heart of our actual union with Jesus, our actual knowledge and love of him. And while clerics have a particular call to participate deeply in the prophetic mission of Jesus, all of us do as well.

When we examine the prophetic ministry of Jesus, we will see "virtues in action" that are particularly needed to confront the cultural and ecclesial situations we are facing today. We will see remarkable courage, the freedom to speak the truth even when it will be rejected, and zeal for his Father's house and for his mission "to seek and to save the lost" (Luke 19:10).

THE PROPHETIC MINISTRY OF JESUS

First of all, it must be said that Jesus's prophetic ministry was not a minor aspect of his ministry.[522] When he asked his disciples whom people said he was, they replied, "Some say John the Baptist, others say Elijah, and others Jeremiah or one of the prophets" (Matt 16:13–14). People weren't saying he was the new David or the new Solomon or the new Aaron—they perceived him as a prophet, probably because of his bold and direct speech and freedom from the fear of offending people (showing no partiality to anyone; see Acts 10:34; 11:12), as well as his signs and wonders. When Jesus raised the widow's son from the dead at Nain, the people responded like this: "Fear seized them all; and they glorified God, saying, 'A great prophet has arisen among us!' and 'God has visited his people!'" (Luke 7:16). One way of getting to know better the prophetic nature of Jesus's ministry would be to meditate on the character and mission of John the Baptist, Elijah, and Jeremiah. This is how people who encountered him most frequently perceived him.

And one of the characteristics of true prophets is that they are frequently driven "outside the camp" as Jesus was and as he predicted his followers would be also:

So Jesus also suffered outside the gate in order to sanctify the people through his own blood. Therefore let us go forth to him outside the camp, bearing abuse for him. For here we have no lasting city, but we seek the city which is to come. (Heb 13:12–14)

Sr. Wendy Beckett brings the point home in a pertinent way:

For most, their enthusiastic acclamation of Jesus as Messiah disguises from them their repudiation of what that messiahship means. As soon as it involves not just death but degradation, to be driven "outside the camp bearing His reproach" (Heb 13:13), they reject Him. They cannot believe that holiness is without beauty and majesty.[523]

Jesus applied the designation of prophet to himself in his encounter with the people of his hostile native place. After these people, scandalized by his ordinariness ("Is this not Joseph's son?" [Luke 4:22]) became angry that he wouldn't do miracles for them, Jesus compared his situation to that of Elijah and Elisha, who only did miracles for a relatively few people (only one widow in Zarephath, and only one leper, Naaman the Syrian, respectively):

> "Truly, I say to you, no prophet is acceptable in his own country." . . . When they heard this, all in the synagogue were filled with wrath. And they rose up and put him out of the city, and led him to the brow of the hill on which their city was built, that they might throw him down headlong. (Luke 4:24, 28–29)

Jesus also self-identified as a prophet in response to the warning of the Pharisees that Herod was out to kill him:

> And he said to them, "Go and tell that fox, 'Behold, I cast out demons and perform cures today and tomorrow, and the third day I finish my course. Nevertheless I must go on my way today and tomorrow and the day following; for it cannot be that a prophet should perish away from Jerusalem.'" (Luke 13:32–33)

And on the road to Emmaus, when the disciples were explaining to Jesus (!) what had recently happened, they explained it like this: "Concerning Jesus of Nazareth, who was a prophet mighty in deed and word before God and all the people" (Luke 24:19).

Jesus didn't speak like scholars and theologians; he spoke with remarkable authority (see Matt 7:28–29; Luke 4:32). Jesus didn't try to win friends and influence people by softening his message. He didn't avoid necessary conflict (see John 8:31–57). He was willing for people to walk away rather than compromise the truth (see John 6:60–67). He didn't come to work out a modus vivendi with the ruling authorities of either the religion or the state. He wasn't at all interested in being a "player" among the secular and religious ruling elite. He wasn't about improving the temporal structures of the world. He made very clear that his kingdom is not of this world. He didn't try to preserve the reputation of the institution or of its unworthy leaders but insisted on interior righteousness as well as exterior conformity to the law (see Matt 23). He was totally focused on his mission to "seek and to save the lost" (Luke 19:10). His kingdom wasn't of this world, but he knew his disciples needed to learn how to be in it, but not of it (see John 17:14–18). He knew it would take total sacrifice, even to the death, and bluntly upbraided Peter when he tried to dissuade him from it (see Matt 16:23; Mark 8:33). He set his face toward Jerusalem, knowing what would happen to him there. When his disciples attempted to characterize what drove Jesus, they harkened back to the prophet Elijah, applying his zeal to Jesus. "I have been very jealous for the LORD, the God of hosts" (1 Kgs 19:10; see also Ps 69:9):

> In the temple he found those who were selling oxen and sheep and pigeons, and the money-changers at their business. And making a whip of cords, he drove them all, with the sheep and oxen, out of the temple; and he poured out the coins of the money-changers and overturned their tables. And he told those who sold the pigeons, "Take these things away; you shall not make my Father's house a house of trade." His disciples remembered that it was written,

"Zeal for thy house will consume me." (John 2:14–17)

He wouldn't tolerate desecration of his Father's house. Nor would he tolerate causing little ones (children, disciples, believers, the new temple of God) to be scandalized and fall:

> Whoever receives one such child in my name receives me; but whoever causes one of these little ones who believe in me to sin, it would be better for him to have a great millstone fastened round his neck and to be drowned in the depth of the sea. Woe to the world for temptations to sin! For it is necessary that temptations come, but woe to the man by whom the temptation comes! (Matt 18:5–7; see also Luke 17:2)

Serious sin is such a grave offense to God and so endangers people's eternal salvation that Jesus urges that the most extreme measures necessary to avoid sin, and damnation, be taken:

> And if your hand or your foot causes you to sin, cut it off and throw it from you; it is better for you to enter life maimed or lame than with two hands or two feet to be thrown into the eternal fire. And if your eye causes you to sin, pluck it out and throw it from you; it is better for you to enter life with one eye than with two eyes to be thrown into the hell of fire. (Matt 18:8–9)

He was especially angered, as were the Old Testament prophets, by religious leadership that was corrupt, unfaithful, and spiritually blind. Jesus was dead serious about his mission and message. He wept; he shouted; he rebuked; he insulted; he condemned; he admonished; he warned and urged with passion. He longed for "fire" to be kindled on the earth (see Luke 12:49). He almost always challenged people to make a decision to believe in him, to follow him, to obey him—or not. He frequently pointed out the eternal consequences of people's choices in relationship to him. He asked for total commitment and gave it in return. Peter Kreeft's characterization of the encounter with the real Jesus as "Jesus shock" is very apt. Jesus lived in the light of what he knew of the coming judgment and of the certain and eternal division of the human race into the saved and the lost, based on their response to him and the grace of God. He was a man on a mission, single-mindedly advancing it every day, continually warning people about the eternal consequences if they rejected the "rescue mission" he was undertaking. As Jesus asked on one occasion: "Do you take offense at this?" (John 6:61).[524]

How different from the pastoral approach of most of those in leadership in the Church today, and, indeed, how different from the currently prevailing pastoral approach of the entire post-Vatican II Church.

As Jeffrey Mirus points out:

> In the course of Western history (and Western history only, apparently), the Catholic Church became for a period of time highly influential spiritually, culturally, socially and politically. But that is not at all the normal state of affairs for the Church Christ founded, as is amply illustrated by nearly all of Our Lord's cautions, beginning with "Blessed are you when men hate you, and when they exclude you and revile you, and cast out your name as evil, on account of the Son of man!" (Luke 6:22). Typically this "blessedness" comes about only when Christians bear witness against the dominant culture (worldly power). If this "blessedness" is consistently lacking, either a particular culture is for the moment enjoying a remarkable commitment to Christianity (as does happen on rare occasions) or *something is*

seriously broken in the prophetic witness of the Church.[525]

It is very much worth paying attention to more of what Dr. Mirus is saying:

> The problem in the West is that the time of respect for the Church is long past, but churchmen in the West have never quite gotten used to it. The default position is to stave off ecclesiastical suffering at the hands of an ungrateful culture by three more or less reflexive stratagems:
>
> 1. Emphasize and speak out strongly on prudential issues on which the dominant culture advocates a policy which is at least superficially compatible with Catholic principles (common episcopal positions on immigration and the environment are two excellent contemporary examples— which, of course, renders them not wrong but convenient);
>
> 2. Substitute personal affirmation for moral teaching when dealing with absolute moral issues on which the dominant culture is dead set against Christ and the Church; and
>
> 3. Maintain good relations with the secular authorities so as not to sacrifice the "good standing" and the illusion of traction which Western bishops grew up thinking they would have.
>
> If the prevailing patterns were not so spiritually tragic, they would be comedic, for they are at least farcical. Nobody in the dominant culture of the West today has the slightest use for bishops except for the purpose of continuing to shape and restrict the Church more easily according to the purposes of the reigning secular elites. The Church manifestly cannot get stronger unless or until bishops

wean themselves from the illusion that they are players in the shaping of the larger culture. I call this an illusion because it is created by the acceptance bishops gain if they behave in ways that make them useful to this same larger culture.[526]

Of course, focusing on our configuration to the prophetic dimension of Jesus and his prophetic words, actions, and emotions doesn't give us a complete picture of Jesus, but that's not the purpose of this chapter.[527] I'd now like to identify some of the important virtues or character traits that we find in Jesus's prophetic identity.

I am thinking of virtues like fear of the Lord; zeal for the holiness of God and his house; zeal for the salvation of souls; righteous anger at those who would cause little ones (disciples, believers) to be scandalized; courage in confronting the powerful with the truth of their situation and a call to repentance; boldness in proclaiming the message without compromise; and a contemplative intensity informed by knowledge of the shortness of life, the impending judgment, and the one thing necessary. In keeping with the limits of this chapter, I'd like to primarily focus on this complex of virtues under the primary heading of the virtue of zeal.

Zeal is created through a confluence of knowledge and love and results in a single-hearted desire to take every opportunity to foster the salvation of souls[528] and the honor and glory of God.

Regularly in the Liturgy, the Church prays for zeal:

O Lord, through our Easter celebrations, renew your people in zeal to speak and live the Gospel, that the Church may truly be a living sacrament of salvation for all peoples, through Christ our Lord. Amen. (Friday of the Easter Octave)

St. Thomas Aquinas argues that zeal arises from the intensity of love:

> For it is evident that the more intensely a power tends to anything, the more vigorously it withstands opposition or resistance . . . an intense love seeks to remove everything that opposes it. . . . In this respect a man is said to be zealous on behalf of his friend, when he makes a point of repelling whatever may be said or done against the friend's good. In this way, too, a man is said to be zealous on God's behalf, when he endeavors, to the best of his means, to repel whatever is contrary to the honor or will of God; according to 1 Kings 19:14: "With zeal I have been zealous for the Lord of hosts." Again on the words of John 2:17: "The zeal of your house has eaten me up."[529]

Godly zeal, of course, is not simply a blind energy or enthusiasm; it must be enlightened by wisdom and form part of a constellation of virtues that together go to make a mature and balanced character, according to the current vision of priestly formation.

As St. Paul said in relation to the zealous Jews of his time, perhaps reflecting back on his own zeal as a Pharisee, "They have a zeal for God, but it is not enlightened" (Rom 10:2). Nevertheless, I think zeal is a virtue that is often lacking in the response I see being made to the persistent call of the Church to a new evangelization and to Pope Francis's call to form missionary disciples. Unfortunately, zeal is often lacking in the response of many priests and bishops to the horrendous crisis we are currently involved in. The desire to protect the institution and its ministers at the expense of grievous damage to those wounded by the sexual immorality of priests and bishops shows a remarkable lack of zeal. The zeal of Elijah was clearly a virtue that permeated his whole being—including a contemplative knowledge of the holiness of God, the gravity of infidelity to God, and the God-given impulse to speak a prophetic word into the situation and the courage to do so, despite the likelihood of serious opposition.

One indeed might say that zeal is a necessary component of our participation in the prophetic ministry of Jesus and one that is uniquely needed for evangelization and missionary discipleship today.

INTELLECTUAL FOUNDATIONS OF ZEAL

Knowledge is needed as a foundation for zeal. Knowledge of the holiness of God, knowledge of the purpose of creation (union with God), knowledge of the gravity and horror of sin, knowledge of the just punishment for unrepented serious sin (eternal separation from God), knowledge of the stupendous act of love in Creation, Redemption, and participation in Trinitarian life for all eternity. Clear theological (rational) understanding of these realities is essential, but so is an affective/contemplative appropriation in ever-deepening ways. St. Paul's exhortation to Timothy to "think over what I say, for the Lord will grant you understanding in everything" (2 Tim 2:7) reveals the expected interplay between rational thought on the basis of objective knowledge illumined by an action of God.[530]

Why bother to evangelize? Because the eternal destinies—heaven or hell—of many millions of our fellow Catholics,[531] not to mention many millions of countless others, are hanging in the balance. Christianity is not just an optional enrichment possibility for human life but a message that truly is a matter of life or death, heaven or hell. If a priest truly loves his people and those who are called to be his people, he's going to be dedicated to their salvation and pay the price that St. John Vianney, the patron saint of priests, was willing to pay: much personal interaction where they were living and working ("the smell of the sheep" as Pope Francis puts it), much prayer and fasting for the salvation of his flock, and repeated clear preaching and teaching about the "last things."[532] If we love sons and daughters, aunts and uncles, cousins and neighbors, we are not just going to be concerned about their job situations, their health situations, or their marriage situations—as important as these are for our journey on earth—but our primary concern needs to be about their relationship with God and their eternal salvation.

SPIRITUAL FOUNDATIONS OF ZEAL

Knowledge of the words of Jesus and the Apostles, knowledge of what is taught in the *Catechism of the Catholic Church*, is not enough, as we know, to fuel zeal. There needs to be a contemplative infusion of both love and knowledge that ignites a living flame of love and prophetic zeal. Besides a clear theological understanding of the truth about heaven and hell, salvation and damnation, a contemplative knowledge of these truths is needed; this will infuse a flame of pastoral charity that will give sustained energy to fervent preaching, teaching, and governing actions, as well as priestly sacrifice, both in the Liturgy and in personal sacrifice. I would like now to draw our attention to examples of such contemplative infusion and the results in pastoral charity and zeal.

St. Francis Xavier

The Spiritual Exercises of St. Ignatius often are the occasion for such infused contemplation to be experienced, prepared for by prayerful mediation on Jesus and his teaching. The missionary zeal that can be borne is witnessed to by St. Francis's famous words wondering how his fellow students could calmly go about their studies when souls were perishing. The zeal for the salvation of souls that fueled his missionary endeavors was born in his heart through contemplative graces received through the Exercises. From his letter of January 15, 1544:

> Many times I am seized with the thought of going to the schools of your lands [Europe] and there cry out like a man who has lost his mind . . . "how many souls fail to go to glory but instead to hell through their neglect."[533]

But not every experience of the exercises produces this zeal. No method can guarantee a contemplative infusion. As John of the Cross would say, we can only dispose ourselves for such an infusion; only God can graciously grant it, but he wants to.[534]

St. Jacinta

One of the most remarkable infusions of contemplative insight into the truths of our faith regarding heaven and hell happened to the three children at Fatima.

There are so many aspects of the Fatima events that evidence the contemplative infusion of significant graces that produced zeal in the three children, but the one that I want to focus on is the apparition of Mary to the children on July 13, 1917. Mary opened her hands, and the earth seemed to open beneath the children, and they saw a horrifying vision of hell with damned souls in agony and demons in hideous shapes. Terrified, they looked to Mary, and this is what she said to them:

> You have seen hell where the souls of poor sinners go. To save them, God wishes to establish in the world devotion to my Immaculate Heart. If what I say to you is done, many souls will be saved and there will be peace.[535]

After showing them the reality of hell, she taught them this prayer to say after each decade of the rosary:

O my Jesus, forgive us, save us from the fire of hell. Lead all souls to heaven, especially those most in need of mercy.[536]

On August 19th, Mary told them:

Pray, pray very much and make sacrifices for sinners; for many souls go to hell because there are none to sacrifice themselves and to pray for them.[537]

The vision and Mary's words deeply impacted their souls, and they fervently responded to her request.

Part of the message of Fatima is not just the words and deeds of Mary but the response of the children to them. They responded with a totally fervent, wholehearted focus on the salvation of souls. Their whole way of life, each and every day, was focused on prayer and sacrifice for the conversion of sinners. It reminds me of Jesus's words: "Unless you turn and become like children, you will never enter the kingdom of heaven" (Matt 18:3).

We all need contemplative experiences like Francis Xavier, and the children of Fatima had to illumine their souls. We need the words of Jesus, Mary, and the saints to be indelibly impressed on our souls. Meditating on the Word of God on the eternal consequences of rejecting Jesus and refusing to repent of serious sin can be the occasion for such a contemplative insight and increase of zealous love necessary to be activated as missionary disciples.[538]

THE NEW PENTECOST

There's a fascinating comment that Peter makes, as recorded in Acts 11, where he is defending his decision to baptize Gentiles after the

Holy Spirit had fallen on them in response to Peter's preaching the kerygma to them, a message that an angel had told them would be "a message by which you will be saved, you and all your household" (Acts 11:14):

> As I began to speak, the Holy Spirit fell upon them just as on us at the beginning. And I remembered the word of the Lord, how he said, "John baptized with water, but you shall be baptized with the Holy Spirit." If then God gave the same gift to them as he gave to us when we believed in the Lord Jesus Christ, who was I that I could withstand God?" When they heard this they were silenced. And they glorified God, saying, "Then to the Gentiles also God has granted repentance unto life." (Acts 11:15–18)

There are many rich insights that could be commented on in these few verses, but the comment that I want to draw our attention to now is Peter's words, "when we believed in the Lord Jesus Christ." Did Peter and the other disciples first believe in the Lord only after receiving the outpouring of the Holy Spirit at Pentecost? Yes and no. They believed before, but not with enough knowledge or love to stay with Jesus in his Passion, to not deny him under social pressure, and to venture freely in the streets of Jerusalem, even after his resurrection. And even on the day of the Ascension, they were still wondering if Jesus was about to take over Jerusalem and rule there as king. The Apostles really didn't "get it" or "get Jesus" until after the outpouring of the Holy Spirit. They didn't have the certainty of faith or the profound, affective, rational, contemplative experience of faith and its implications until after the Holy Spirit fell.

Let's look at one more text before drawing some conclusions:

> Then he opened their minds to understand the scriptures, and said to them, "Thus it is written, that the Christ should

suffer and on the third day rise from the dead, and that repentance and forgiveness of sins should be preached in his name to all nations, beginning from Jerusalem. You are witnesses of these things. And behold, I send the promise of my Father upon you; but stay in the city, until you are clothed with power from on high." (Luke 24:45–49)

Before Pentecost, the disciples had the best explanation of Scripture anyone ever had; they had the best spiritual direction, character formation, and pastoral supervision, but they were sorely lacking prophetic zeal. They were "well formed" but weren't ready to be missionary disciples. It wasn't until after Pentecost that they got it.

When we take a look at these, we must admire the prophetic/rational wisdom of every pope from St. John XXXIII up to and including Pope Francis, who have fervently prayed for, and exhorted us to pray for, a new Pentecost for the Church. Orthodoxy isn't enough, however essential it is; correct Liturgy is not enough, however essential it is; chastity isn't enough, however essential it is. What is needed in addition is the power of the Holy Spirit to bring all these wonderful dimensions of Catholic life into a living flame of love that urges on all of us with prophetic zeal.

Isn't it this contemplative experience of God's presence, power, truthfulness, and love that Paul insisted needed to be at the foundation of all faith?

I was with you in weakness and in much fear and trembling; and my speech and my message were not in plausible words of wisdom, but in demonstration of the Spirit and power, that your faith might not rest in the wisdom of men but in the power of God. (1 Cor 2:3–5)

We need to build into all our catechetical and religious education programs opportunities for the participants to appropriate this truth and to fervently desire and pray for an outpouring of the Holy Spirit. We need the Holy Spirit!

This contemplative/charismatic experience of the Spirit is not supposed to be the pinnacle of the Christian life, but its foundation (baptism in the Spirit is considered by most biblical scholars to signify full incorporation into the life of Christ and the Church—focused sacramentally in the sacraments of Christian initiation). Having this experiential foundation provides a "memory" that is extremely helpful for the arduous work of the spiritual journey, including all its stages of purification, detachment, and dark nights. It doesn't replace the need for the traditional spiritual wisdom and pastoral supervision but is an experiential foundation that is of great help, a "memory" that continues to encourage perseverance.

While contemplative prayer and meditation can often be means of igniting prophetic zeal, it can also be ignited through various "renewal experiences" that can broadly be grouped under the heading of "new Pentecost." Every post-conciliar pope has fervently called for a "new Pentecost" to come to the Church to ignite zeal for holiness and evangelization. Many contemporary renewal movements have responded to this call and are providing means and methods which enable those who participate in them to experience both the contemplative and charismatic graces of a renewal of baptismal and confirmation graces, a "new Pentecost."

We simply cannot carry out the mission without boldly praying for a new Pentecost and courageously removing any limits on what the Holy Spirit is permitted to do. We must not be timid about asking the Holy Spirit to "fall on us." May the Holy Spirit "fall on us" (see Acts 8:14–19; 10:44–48; 11:15–18; 19:1–7; 2 Tim 1:6–7) and ignite the fire of prophetic zeal in us all![539]

CHARACTER AND VIRTUE

I'd like to make clear that prophetic zeal needs the framework of other virtues in order to operate properly. Prophetic zeal that is not founded on a solid character with all the virtues needed to support it and guide it in wisdom is dangerous. Basic virtues like reliability, truthfulness, humility, fortitude, perseverance, the ability to deny oneself regularly, brotherly love, and compassion are all essential for the proper operation of prophetic zeal. Yet there are some virtues that are commonly lacking and need to be emphasized today. For example, courage is particularly important and is notably evident in the ministry of Jesus. Courage to speak the truth, even when one knows it may not be readily accepted or may even be vigorously opposed. Determination to preach the Gospel "in season and out of season, when it's convenient and inconvenient" is an important character trait. We all need to overcome our desire to be accepted and to "please men" when it would mean displeasing God. All of us need to be decidedly in the place where we fear God more than man and are able to speak and act accordingly. In the proper emphasis in the Church on the role of obedience to God-established authority, it is important that we not snuff out the appropriate adult maturity to respectfully disagree with authority and to speak the truth to it:

> In accord with the knowledge, competence, and preeminence which they possess, [lay people] have the right and even at times a duty to manifest to the sacred pastors their opinion on matters which pertain to the good of the Church, and they have a right to make their opinion known to the other Christian faithful, with due regard to the integrity of faith and morals and reverence toward their pastors, and with consideration for the common good and the dignity of persons.[540]

If laypeople have this right and responsibility, so much more do the ordained have it. A lot of the sickness in the Church today can be traced to a lack of these virtues.[541]

Spiritual Warfare

We need to take into account that the biblical worldview includes a vivid revelation of the spiritual warfare that characterizes life on earth. If we were to really "get" what Ephesians 6:10–20 implies for daily Christian life, we would certainly be approaching our own salvation with appropriate "fear and trembling." There is a spiritual war going on, and it is being conducted in the soul of every believer, in every parish and diocese, in the worldwide Church and in the culture at large. If we are not aware that there is a war going on, our Christian life will tend to descend into tepidity and lukewarmness. If we are in pastoral authority, the sacrificial zeal of John Vianney will seem strange and irrelevant.

Just consider one element of the spiritual armor that Paul considers so essential for the believer: the shield of faith which is able to quench "all the flaming darts of the evil one" (Eph 6:16).

None of us are living in a neutral environment. All day long, the symbiotic work of the influence of the world culture, the drives of our disordered desires, and the direct temptations of the devil are at play in each person's soul. And yet how many of us, and how many of those we have some responsibility for, are defenseless against these temptations! The shield of faith is composed of faith and complete trust in Jesus and knowledge of the objective content of the faith. So many of our people don't trust him or know him, and so many don't know his Word, which is the foundation of true discernment and resistance to evil. There is a vicious war going on, and if people aren't actively equipped with the spiritual armor, not just the shield of faith, they are likely to be captured or even enlisted in the enemy's campaign.

In order to equip our families, parishes, and dioceses for the situation they are really facing, we need to be vigorous in our teaching and preaching, including the correction of error, admonishment of public sinners, and confrontation with the "wolves" that both Jesus and the Apostles prophesy will be a problem that emerges from within the Church in false teachers and prophets. The good shepherd has to protect his flock, face down the wolves, and not tolerate a "jezebel" in the midst of the flock. Too often the wolves are welcomed, and even given pastoral assignments, and people are afraid to confront "jezebel," thereby allowing the flock to be misled.

The prophetic participation in Jesus's ministry also has to include the deeds that back up the words. We have so many nice words and nice documents in the Church today, but very little implementation and action.

Paul's exhortations in the Pastoral Epistles to his pastoral collaborators and subordinates would make a good guide for all of us, whatever our level of pastoral responsibility. But are we able to "receive" his exhortations, given the psychological conditioning we are undergoing to not vigorously resist evil? Are we leading those we are responsible for as Paul urges Timothy to lead in difficult times?

> I charge you in the presence of God and of Christ Jesus who is to judge the living and the dead, and by his appearing and his kingdom: preach the word, be urgent in season and out of season, convince, rebuke, and exhort, be unfailing in patience and in teaching. For the time is coming when people will not endure sound teaching, but having itching ears they will accumulate for themselves teachers to suit their own likings, and will turn away from listening

to the truth and wander into myths. As for you, always be steady, endure suffering, do the work of an evangelist, fulfil your ministry. (2 Tim 4:1–5)

Unfortunately, as we have already considered, it seems like our culture is profoundly shaping the choices of what texts priests choose to preach on in the cycle of readings. Almost always, the challenging texts are ignored, and the shorter readings that often drop the challenges are chosen. The fear of people's reactions, unfortunately, often guides the ministry of priests. So unlike the ministry of Jesus!

And again, as we have noted, what are we to make of Paul's admonition? "Rebuke them in the presence of all, so that the rest may stand in fear" (1 Tim 5:20).

Is anybody being reprimanded publicly? Is anyone afraid to sin?

What a fix we have gotten into, where so many "Catholic" politicians are modeling a false Catholicism that promotes abortion and homosexuality and have been so feebly corrected by the bishops. It makes lay people wonder if the bishops really believe what they teach, so little is discipline and admonition exercised against publicly dissenting Catholics. But then we often face the same challenges in our own families today as well.

The few bishops and priests who dare to admonish public sinners are vilified by the press and unfortunately almost always left to "hang out to dry" by the lack of support from their fellow priests and bishops. This has got to change. It is shameful.

Sometimes, the admonition may need to be done formally and authoritatively, as the many exhortations in the Pastoral Epistles to command things indicate. But sometimes, the admonition may be done informally and gently:

And the Lord's servant must not be quarrelsome but kindly to everyone, an apt teacher, forbearing, correcting his opponents with gentleness. God may perhaps grant that they will repent and come to know the truth, and they may escape from the snare of the devil, after being captured by him to do his will. (2 Tim 2:24–26)

All dimensions of continuing education, of evangelization and catechesis, work together, of course. Participation in the prophetic mission of Jesus brings with it a zeal and a fervor that will inform every part of our vocations. Concern for the salvation for souls that contains within it zeal and fervor will be willing to get up in the middle of the night to help the dying, will be diligent to make sure those in nursing homes are cared for, will be available for confession at convenient hours for people, will be fervent in preaching, will tell the truth to people in counseling, will prepare for the sacraments in a way that leads to conversion, will reach out to the "lost" knowing that many are truly "lost," will be a witness by our life and our words, in our family and work and neighborhoods. Participating in the prophetic zeal of Jesus will also keep us alive to the big truth: that the mission of the Church, and of all of us, is nothing less than the salvation of souls. Our big action step going forward? We need to tell people the truth, with love, with fervor, with humility.

But we also need to see clearly and anticipate that truth not only unites; it divides. Truth unites those who adhere to it and divides its followers from those who reject it, and missionary disciples must not let fear of a negative response prevent them from proclaiming the truth.

In every generation, a faithful presentation of Jesus shows him to be "a sign that is spoken against" (Luke 2:3), a "stumbling block" (1 Cor 1:23; see also 1 Pet 2:8), the occasion for the "fall and rising of many" (Luke 2:34). Jesus came both to unite and to divide the human race. God's will is for all to be saved, but many reject God's will. Those who do so, if they die unrepentant, will be forever divided from God and from those who obey God.

Maintaining the scriptural standards of faith and morality in the Church today, in every field of its work and life, is a solemn responsibility, not easily fulfilled yet severely judged. The salvation of the world depends on it being faithfully carried out. The pain of disunity is less than the pain of infidelity.

As I have tried to make clear in this book, after years of what appeared to be the resolution of the post-Vatican II crisis of truth and a time of relative doctrinal peace, there has now been a vigorous resurgence of a similar crisis, this time characterized by polluted streams flowing into and out of Rome itself and the rise of a hostile culture that has thrown off all restraint in its repudiation of faith, morality, and mission. This crisis affects the very foundations of faith, the core of the Gospel message of salvation and redemption. The time has come for the "sword of the Spirit, which is the word of God" (Eph 6:17), to do its work. "Sharper than any two-edged sword" (Heb 4:12), the Word of Truth must be proclaimed and responded to. As that happens, there will be division; in our own hearts, the sword of the Spirit will divide true from false, the unclean from the clean; the same will happen in our families, our parishes, our seminaries, our dioceses, our ecumenical relationships. It's time to stop straddling the issue. Painful decisions have to be made if we are to be loyal to Christ.

In commenting on the shocking warnings of Jesus about division in our most intimate family relationships concerning him, the actor Jim Caviezel, who has emerged as a fearless preacher of the Gospel, had this to say in a recent interview:

> The world at its best can only like you because love comes from God. Do you want to be liked by many or loved by One?[542]

There is a need for us to be "made clean" (John 15:3) once again, sanctified in truth (see John 17:17) through the powerful ministry of the Word of God, proclaimed in its purity and power. Then will we be restored to that relationship with God and with one another which will truly and authentically reveal to the world that Jesus has come from the Father, that he contains within himself the words of life, that he is indeed the very door to heaven, the bread that has come down from heaven to feed the deepest hunger of the world.

As Jesus is proclaimed and the Word of Truth is announced in the power of the Holy Spirit, those who respond will experience a new and profound unity and peace. Those who persist in disobedience, however, will suffer division, hostility, and war. The hostility directed against God's followers will grow deeper and fiercer. Yet, at the same time, the light, power, and glory of his body will grow brighter and more powerful. What has wrongly been kept separate will be joined together. What has wrongly been united will be separated. We will see the truth of Ignatius's description of humanity as two distinct races with eternally diverging destinies, serving under two very different lords. Every man and woman will choose one of these two opposing forces. Those who have rallied to the banner of Christ[543] will be more certain about who they are and what they are working for, and so perhaps will some of those who have rallied to the banner of Satan, although many will remain in deep deception, thinking they are "serving God" but, in actuality, are opposing him.

Scripture uses the image of two women to describe the two groupings of people that will exist at the Lord's coming. One is a harlot, the "whore of Babylon"—rebellious, insubmissive, proud, and lustful, perpetrator of all foul things, seducer of the ungodly, persecutor of Christ and his Body, "drunk with the blood of the saints" (Rev 17:6; see also Rev 17, 18). The other, a bride, stands pure and radiant, ready to meet her bridegroom who is Christ the

Lord (see Rev 21). She is an image of the Church, purified and made holy, fulfilling the promise and prayer of Mary, who is herself the image and foreshadowing of our destiny, the one whose offspring, promised long ago in Genesis, was to crush the head of Satan. And he has. And he will.

In the years ahead, all of our personal decisions will contribute to the outcome of what is unfolding in the Church and the world. Developments of great consequence rest on our fidelity, on our courage, on our obedience to Christ our Lord, to his Word and his Church.

A FINAL APPEAL

I would like to end this book by making an appeal. I would like to ask laymen and laywomen, men and women religious, deacons, priests, and bishops to join me in asking God to deliver us from fear of men and fill us with the grace of the Holy Spirit. Let's ask God to set us aflame that we may all become "apostles of the last days," filled with zeal for the holiness of God's house, filled with love for our fellow human beings, filled with fire to preach the Gospel with our lives and words, ready to accept and suffer opposition, more concerned to be faithful to Jesus than to be popular among people. I know that as we fervently ask God to deliver us from fear of men and fill us with the prophetic Spirit of his Son, he will do so. And as we rise up with a new boldness and courage, more and more under the control of the Spirit, others will be inspired to join us. Together, we can be used by God like the Maccabees of old to rally the fearful, fanning the dying embers of faith into strong flames and allowing Jesus to be more and more our Lord, and Lord of his Church.

He is with us! He is risen! And he's the same, yesterday, today, and forever! He will come again in glory! He will wipe away every tear; he will heal every wound; he will turn every sorrow and suffering into joy; he will redeem the time; he will purify our souls and give us risen bodies so we become capable of a level of life, eternal life, that the world only dimly longs for, in a glass darkly foreshadowed in the ancient dreams and contemporary myths of immortal superheroes:

> For the LORD will comfort Zion;
>> he will comfort all her waste places,
> and will make her wilderness like Eden,
>> her desert like the garden of the LORD;
> joy and gladness will be found in her,
>> thanksgiving and the voice of song. (Isa 51:3)

> Fear not, little flock, for it is your Father's good pleasure to give you the kingdom. (Luke 12:32)

> Let not your hearts be troubled; believe in God, believe also in me. In my Father's house are many rooms; if it were not so, would I have told you that I go to prepare a place for you? And when I go and prepare a place for you, I will come again and will take you to myself, that where I am you may be also. (John 14:1–3)

And in a very real way, we are already there; we have already passed from death to life:

> If then you have been raised with Christ, seek the things that are above, where Christ is seated at the right hand of God. Set your minds on things that are above, not on things that are on earth. For **you** have died, and **your** life is hidden with Christ in God. When Christ who is our life appears, then **you** also will appear with him in glory. (Col 3:1–4)

Let us go forward, together, without fear, walking in the paths he is showing us, trusting in him and looking to him for all that we need. Let us repeat frequently, in quiet attentiveness, the profound prayer: Jesus, I trust in you.

And then cry out in radiant joy: Maranatha! Come Lord Jesus! Come!

Endnotes

Introduction

[1] See www.renewalministries.net.

[2] Besides its weekly airings on EWTN, we post each week's new episode on the Renewal Ministries YouTube Channel: https://www.youtube.com/channel/UCamEooO2x92YRiL-UNWiONQ.

[3] www.renewalministries.net/shop/product/a_crisis_of_truth_pdf

[4] While I was at Princeton, my academic advisor was Richard Rorty, one of the most famous and radical philosophical skeptics in recent times. I never had him for class, but he was a very kind and supportive advisor and nominated me for the Chancellor Bamford Fellowship so I could continue my studies toward the doctorate. I went to Princeton because one of the world's leading Nietzsche scholars was there. I did my senior thesis at Notre Dame on Plato and Nietzsche, contrasting their diverging thirsts for the Absolute.

[5] Years later, Fr. Scanlan was awarded the highest honor of his branch of the Franciscan order as a Master of Theology.

[6] Msgr. Pope posts his blog on the Archdiocese of Washington, D.C. website frequently: http://blog.adw.org. His articles can be accessed at www.osv.com.

[7] Dr. Hahn did a video interview with me after one of his summer conferences for priests where he talked with me about the impact of *A Crisis of Truth*: See St. Paul Center, "A Conversation between Scott Hahn and Ralph Martin," YouTube video, July 30, 2019, https://www.youtube.com/watch?v=i-IAM-4fsM0Q&t=543s. Dr. Hahn's St. Paul Center for Biblical Theology is a rich resource for Scripture studies, videos, and much else: https://stpaul-center.com/.

8 Karim Schelkens and Jürgen Mettepenningen, *Godfried Danneels: Biographie* (Antwerp: Uitgeverij Polis, 2015); Austen Ivereigh, *The Great Reformer: Francis and the Making of a Radical Pope* (United Kingdom: Picador Paper, 2015).

9 Edward Pentin, "Cardinal Danneels Admits to Being Part of 'Mafia' Club Opposed to Benedict XVI," *National Catholic Register*, September 24, 2015, https://www.ncregister.com/blog/edward-pentin/cardinal-danneels-part-of-mafia-club-opposed-to-benedict-xvi. For another account of the Saint Gallen influence, see R.R. Reno, "Church Strife Under Pope Francis," *First Things* (November 2019): 65–67.

10 Gaia Pianigiani, "Godfried Danneels, Liberal Cardinal Tainted by Sex Scandal, Dies at 85," *New York Times*, March 14, 2019, https://www.nytimes.com/2019/03/24/obituaries/godfried-danneels-dead.html.

11 The original version can be accessed at our website: www.renewalministries.net.

CHAPTER 1

12 Various organizations have been established to track the current persecution of Christians, and they all report increasing persecution. See Solene Tadie, "Persistent Persecution," *National Catholic Register*, February 16–29, 2020. See also the US Government agency tracking religious persecution and freedom of religion around the world annual report as of 2020, United States Commission on International Religious Freedom: https://www.uscirf.gov/sites/default/files/USCIRF%202020%20Annual%20Report_42720_new_0.pdf.

13 See Pope Francis, *Amoris Laetitia* (2016).

14 See Michael W. Chapman, "Pope Francis: 'There Is No Hell,'" *CNSNews*, March 29, 2018, https://www.cnsnews.com/blog/michael-w-chapman/pope-francis-there-no-hell.

15 Peter M. J. Stravinskas, "Symposium on Priesthood 'Renews' Failed Revolution of the Sixties and Seventies," *The Catholic World Report*, January 7, 2020, https://www.catholicworldreport.com/2020/01/07/symposium-on-priesthood-renews-failed-revolution-of-the-sixties-and-seventies/.

[16] "Bishop McElroy: Abortion and Climate Change Both Crucial, Voters Must Be Prudent," *The Catholic World Report*, February 7, 2020, https://www. catholicworldreport.com/2020/02/07/bishop-mcelroy-abortion-and-climate-change-both-crucial-voters-must-be-prudent/.

[17] Cardinal Ratzinger, Homily in Mass Before Conclave, April 19, 2005, https:// zenit.org/articles/cardinal-ratzinger-s-homily-in-mass-before-conclave/.

[18] The dense summaries of de Lubac's scholarship that follow can be found in their full form in Henri de Lubac, *The Drama of Atheist Humanism* (San Francisco: Ignatius Press, 1995). I am indebted to Joey McCoy for these references to de Lubac's book.

[19] De Lubac, *The Drama of Atheist Humanism*, 136.

[20] De Lubac, *The Drama of Atheist Humanism*, 29–30.

[21] De Lubac, *The Drama of Atheist Humanism*, 41.

[22] "Full Transcript of Pope's In-Flight Press Remarks Released," *Catholic News Agency*, August 5, 2013, https://www.catholicnewsagency.com/news/full-transcript-of-popes-in-flight-press-remarks-released.

[23] As most Catholics know, it isn't the unchosen homosexual inclination or temptation that is sinful but the doing of homosexual acts or purposeful indulgence in homosexual fantasy. This distinction should always be born in mind when homosexuality is spoken about in this book. It isn't the inclination, it's the acting on it that is sinful.

[24] See J. D. Flynn, "US Bishops: Pope Francis Talks Fr. James Martin, Euthanasia, at Private Meeting, *Catholic News Agency*, February 20, 2020, https:// www.catholicnewsagency.com/news/us-bishops-pope-francis-talks-fr-james-martin-euthanasia-at-private-meeting-46135._

[25] See Edward Pentin, *The Rigging of a Vatican Synod: An Investigation into Alleged Manipulation at the Extraordinary Synod on the Family* (San Francisco: Ignatius Press, 2015).

[26] A good article on the theological background for the German bishops' push to accommodate with the culture is that by Msgr. Hans Feitchtinger, a former official of the Congregation for the Doctrine of the Faith currently serving in the Archdiocese of Ottawa, Canada. See Msgr. Hans Feitchtinger,

"Rahner's Ghost," *Crisis Magazine*, November 15, 2019, https://www.crisis-magazine.com/2019/rahners-ghost.

[27] Bishop Scott McCaig, a young Canadian bishop, has published a pastoral letter that provides an orthodox interpretation of *Amoris Laetitia* yet is pastorally sensitive. See Lianne Laurence, "Canada's Military Bishop Reaffirms Catholic Teaching on Marriage in Amoris Laetitia Guidelines," *LifeSite News*, March 15, 2017, https://www.lifesitenews.com/news/canadas-military-bishop-reaffirms-catholic-teaching-on-marriage-in-amoris-l.

[28] Edward Pentin, "Cardinal Müller Issues 'Manifesto of Faith,'" *National Catholic Register*, February 8, 2019, https://www.ncregister.com/blog/edward-pentin/cardinal-mueller-issues-manifesto-of-faith. I was so impressed with Cardinal Mueller's *Manifesto* that we published in it in our monthly newsletter and then decided to publish our own manifesto as well. See Ralph Martin, "Our Manifesto: A Look Forward," September 2019, https://www.renewalministries.net/wp-content/uploads/2020/03/september_2019_newsletter_web_final2-1.pdf.

[29] John Paul II, *Reconciliatio et Paenitentia* (1984), §26.

[30] "Cardinal Kasper Says Mueller's Manifesto Spreads 'Confusion and Division,'" *The Catholic World Report*, February 10, 2019, https://www.catholicworldreport.com/2019/02/10/cardinal-kasper-says-muellers-manifesto-spreads-confusion-and-division/.

[31] Cardinal Willem Jacobus Eijk, "Cardinal Eijk: Pope Francis Needed to Give Clarity on Intercommunion," *National Catholic Register*, May 7, 2018, https://www.ncregister.com/blog/edward-pentin/cardinal-eijk-pope-needed-to-give-clarity-to-german-bishops-on-intercommuni. For a much fuller and very informative interview with Cardinal Eijk, see Jeanne Smits, "Dutch Cardinal Willem Eijk Answers Questions on Crisis in Church, Loss of Faith," *LifeSite News*, May 15, 2019, https://www.lifesitenews.com/news/dutch-cardinal-willem-eijk-answers-questions-on-crisis-in-church-loss-of-faith.

[32] George Weigel, "The 'Historic' Amazon Synod, Revisited," *First Things* (April 29, 2020), https://www.firstthings.com/web-exclusives/2020/04/the-historic-amazonian-synod-revisited.

33 See William Kilpatrick, "Tumult in the Church: Is the Confusion Intentional?" *The Catholic World Report*, December 6, 2019, https://www.catholicworldreport.com/2019/12/06/tumult-in-the-church-is-the-confusion-intentional/.

34 Pope Francis, A Document on Human Fraternity for World Peace and Living Together, February 4, 2019, (at http://w2.vatican.va/content/francesco/en/travels/2019/outside/documents/papa-francesco_20190204_documento-fratellanza-umana.html). A truly disturbing video produced by the Vatican shows Pope Francis saying that even though we think differently, as members of different world religions, we are all children of God; we are all believers and need to engage in dialogue and work together. The editing shows adherents of different religions with symbols of their worship all proclaiming that they believe in love. The video gives the distinct impression that we are all really the same, pursuing our different ways to the same God. See Rome Reports in English, "This Innovative 'Video of the Pope' Is Causing a Sensation," YouTube video, January 6, 2016, https://www.youtube.com/watch?v=vI0tiN88ldE. See also William Kilpatrick's insightful and fact-based article, "Pope Francis Doesn't Understand Islam," *Crisis Magazine*, September 25, 2019, https://www.crisismagazine.com/2019/pope-francis-doesnt-understand-islam.

35 See Edward Pentin, "Full Text and Explanatory Notes of Cardinals' Questions on 'Amoris Laetitia,'" *National Catholic Register*, November 14, 2016, https://www.ncregister.com/blog/edward-pentin/full-text-and-explanatory-notes-of-cardinals-questions-on-amoris-laetitia.

36 Pope John Paul II, *Familiaris Consortio* (1981), §84.

37 See Solène Tadié, "JPII Institute VP Warns: 'More Here at Stake Than Just an Institution's Survival,'" Ave Maria Radio, August 8, 2019, https://avemariaradio.net/jpii-institute-vp-warns-stake-just-institutions-survival/. For a discussion of the views of some of the moral theologians being appointed to key positions, see E. Christian Brugger, "A New Assault on 'Humanae Vitae' Begins," *National Catholic Register*, February 27, 2018, https://www.ncregister.com/blog/guest-blogger/a-new-assault-on-humanae-vitae-begins. See also

Edward Pentin, "New JPII Institute Professors Question Church Orthodoxy on Homosexuality, Contraception," *National Catholic Register*, September 13, 2019, https://www.ncregister.com/blog/edward-pentin/new-jpii-professors-have-made-controversial-statements-on-homosexuality-and.

[38] Matthew Cullinan Hoffman, "Vatican Archbishop Featured in Homoerotic Painting He Commissioned," *LifeSite News*, March 3, 2017, https://www.lifesitenews.com/news/leading-vatican-archbishop-featured-in-homoerotic-painting-he-commissioned.

[39] George Weigel, "The Vandals Sack Rome . . . Again," *The Catholic World Report*, July 29, 2019, https://www.catholicworldreport.com/2019/07/29/the-vandals-sack-rome-again/.

[40] Fr. Paul Mankowski has written a number of excellent analyses about why the cover-up went on as long as it did. See Paul Mankowski, S.J., "Address to the Confraternity of Catholic Clergy," July 13, 2003, http://www.bishop-accountability.org/news/2003_07_15_Mankowski_WhatWent.htm. For an excellent historical study on how, for much of its history, the Church dealt very strictly with homosexual activity and on how changes in canon law in the last century and increasingly broad applications of the "Pontifical Secret" led to the cover-ups, see Keiran Tapsell, "Canon Law on Sexual Abuse through the Ages," https://www.catholicsforrenewal.org/Documents%20 2016/CanonLawOnChildAbuseThruTheAges.pdf?fbclid=IwAR2Oms-DUqEppap_nYgovN-5jeOBEhycj9qTnGwezhB8RBZIJtpIoVBBMYa0. For an extremely comprehensive bibliography on resources that cast light on the clergy sex abuse crisis, see Fr. Thomas P. Doyle, *Bibliography of Selected Sources Related to Clergy Sexual Abuse, Ecclesiastical Politics, Theology and Church History*, revised November 3, 2014, http://votf.org/Doyle/DoyleBibliography110314.pdf. To access a database that records clergy sex abuse cases, see "Database Publicly Accused Priests in the United States," BishopAccountability.org, accessed June 14, 2020, http://www.bishop-accountability.org/priestdb/PriestDBbylastName-K.html.

[41] See "Testimony by His Excellency Carlo Maria Viganò, Titular Archbishop of Ulpiana," August 22, 2018, https://www.documentcloud.org/docu-

ments/4786599-Testimony-by-Archbishop-Carlo-Maria-Vigan%C3%B2. html.

[42] An excellent article by J. D. Flynn points out the danger that the lack of accountability and lengthy "stonewalling" about the matter is causing to the Catholic people.

[43] See Cindy Wooden, "Legionaries Report 'Chain of Abuse' as Victims Went on to Abuse Others," *Catholic News Service*, December 23, 2019, https:// www.catholicnews.com/services/englishnews/2019/legionaries-report-chain-of-abuse-as-victims-went-on-to-abuse-others.cfm.

[44] See Joshua J. McElwee, "Honduran Bishop Serving as Deputy to Cardinal Rodriguez Resigns after Abuse Regulations," *National Catholic Reporter*, July 20, 2018, https://www.ncronline.org/news/accountability/honduran-bishop-serving-deputy-cardinal-rodriguez-resigns-after-abuse. See also Edward Pentin, "Former Seminarians Allege Grave Sexual Misconduct by Honduran Bishop Pineda," *National Catholic Register*, March 4, 2018, https://www.ncregister.com/daily-news/former-seminarians-allege-grave-sexual-misconduct-by-honduran-bishop-pineda.

[45] McElwee, "Honduran Bishop Serving as Deputy to Cardinal Rodriguez."

[46] See Francis X. Rocca, "Vatican Uses Donations for the Poor to Plug Its Budget Deficit," *The Wall Street Journal*, December 11, 2019, https://www.wsj.com/articles/vatican-uses-donations-for-the-poor-to-plug-its-budget-deficit-11576075764.

[47] Nicole Winfield, "Vatican Removes Financial Watchdog Head as Scandal Continues," *Crux*, April 15, 2020, https://cruxnow.com/vatican/2020/04/vatican-removes-financial-watchdog-head-as-scandal-continues/. See also John L. Allen, "Sooner or Later, Pope Francis Will Have to Face the Perplexities of Reform," *Crux*, May 3, 2020, https://cruxnow.com/news-analysis/2020/05/sooner-or-later-pope-francis-will-have-to-face-the-malaise-of-reform/. For the latest Vatican attempt to avoid directly answering financial questions, see Phil Lawler, "Still No Transparency in Vatican Financial Investigations," *Catholic Culture*, May 5, 2020, https:// www.catholicculture.org/commentary/still-no-transparency-in-vatican-fi-

nancial-investigations/. See also Phil Lawler, "Quick Hits: More Vatican Financial Woes; and When Will Churches Reopen," *Catholic Culture*, May 12, 2020, https://www.catholicculture.org/commentary/quick-hits-more-vatican-financial-woes-and-when-will-churches-reopen/; and Phil Lawler, "The Vatican's Financial Bait-and-Switch," *Catholic Culture*, December 18, 2019, https://www.catholicculture.org/commentary/vaticans-financial-bait-and-switch/.

48 John L. Allen, "Down the Barrel of $158 Million Gun, Vatican Reform Is Coming . . . But What Kind?" *Crux*, May 13, 2020, https://cruxnow.com/news-analysis/2020/05/down-the-barrel-of-158-million-gun-vatican-reform-is-coming-but-what-kind/. It continues and gets worse; see Phil Lawler, "Vatican Finances: The Fox in the Henhouse," *Catholic Culture*, May 14, 2020, https://www.catholicculture.org/commentary/vatican-finances-fox-in-henhouse/.

49 In my travels, I often get the opportunity to speak at various diocesan convocations for all their priests or priest study days, and often enough I hear from Vicars for Clergy about all the "messes" they are having to clean up, including multiple instances of embezzlement to support illicit sexual relationships. See "Connecticut Priest Convicted of Embezzling $1 Million Dies of Cancer," *Catholic News Agency*, August 25, 2009, https://www.catholicnewsagency.com/news/connecticut_priest_convicted_of_embezzling_1_million_dies_of_cancer. See also: "Priest with Secret Marriage Pleas Guilty to Half-Million-Dollar Embezzlement," *Catholic News Agency*, October 29, 2007, https://www.catholicnewsagency.com/news/priest_with_secret_marriage_pleas_guilty_to_halfmilliondollar_embezzlement; David Hennessey, "Ex-Greenwich Priest Headed to Prison," *Greenwich Time*, July 23, 2012, https://www.greenwichtime.com/news/article/Ex-Greenwich-priest-headed-to-prison-3728222.php; Megan Banta, "Rev. Jonathan Wehrle Embezzlement Case Began Nearly 2 Years Ago. Here's Why It's Taking So Long," *Lansing Street Journal*, March 13, 2019, https://www.lansingstatejournal.com/story/news/local/2019/03/13/jonathan-wehrle-embezzlement-catholic-diocese-of-lansing/3102461002/. And

this is not a problem limited to the United States. The gay prostitute in Italy who published photos of all the clergy and bishops who had paid him for sex shocked everyone, for a while. See Barbie Latza Nadeau, "Confessions of the Vatican's Favorite Male Escort," *Daily Beast*, March 6, 2018, https://www.thedailybeast.com/confessions-of-the-vaticans-favorite-male-escort. And unfortunately, concubinage is widespread in Africa, Latin America, and other places as well. See John R. Quinn, "Considerations for a Church in Crisis," *America Magazine*, May 27, 2002, https://www.americamagazine.org/issue/374/article/considerations-church-crisis.

50 "'The Culture Wars Are Real,' Cardinal Pell Says in New Interview," *The Catholic World Report*, April 14, 2020, https://www.catholicworldreport.com/2020/04/14/the-culture-wars-are-real-cardinal-pell-says-in-new-interview/.

51 Inés San Martín, "Argentine Bishop Accused of Sexual Misconduct Returns to Work at Vatican Central Bank," *Crux*, June 13, 2020, https://cruxnow.com/vatican/2020/06/argentine-bishop-accused-of-sexual-misconduct-returns-to-work-at-vatican-central-bank/.

Chapter 2

52 See, for example, Richard Bauckham, *Jesus and the Eyewitnesses: The Gospels as Eyewitness Testimony* (Grand Rapids: Eerdmans Publishers, 2008).

53 See Benedict XVI, *Verbum Domini* (2010); Benedict XVI's *Jesus of Nazareth*, three volumes covering the entire life of Christ from the infancy narratives to the resurrection, published from 2008 to 2012 by Ignatius Press. On pastoral and spiritual sensitivity, see Mary Healy and Peter Williamson, eds., *Catholic Commentary on Sacred Scripture*, published by Baker Academic.

54 See Denis Farkasfalvy, *Inspiration and Interpretation: A Theological Introduction to Sacred Scripture* (Washington, D.C.: Catholic University of America Press, 2010); William M. Wright IV and Francis Martin, *Encountering the Living God in Scripture: Theological and Philosophical Principles for Interpretation* (Grand Rapids: Baker Academic, 2019); Scott Hahn, ed., *Letter &*

Spirit Vol. 6: For the Sake of Our Salvation: The Truth and Humility of God's Word (Steubenville, OH: Emmaus Road Publishing, 2010). The St. Paul Center for Biblical Theology, under Scott Hahn's direction, has contributed an immense amount to the recovery of Sacred Scripture as the inspired Word of God for millions of Catholics. See www.stpaulcenter.com. For a commentary series that incorporates the best of orthodox Scripture scholarship with pastoral and spiritual sensitivity, see Mary Healy and Peter Williamson, *Catholic Commentary on Sacred Scripture.*

55 Andrea Gagliarducci, "Pope Francis: A Church 200 Years Out of Date," *MondayVatican*, July 27, 2015, http://www.mondayvatican.com/vatican/pope-francis-a-church-200-years-out-of-date.

56 "Marriage and Divorce. The General of the Jesuits: "Jesus Too Must Be Reinterpreted," February 22, 2017, http://magister.blogautore.espresso.repubblica.it/2017/02/22/marriage-and-divorce-the-general-of-the-jesuits-jesus-too-must-be-reinterpreted/.

57 After Fr. Sosa's 2017 statement about the devil being a symbol, a spokesman said he actually believes what the Church teaches—although his understanding about how loosely doctrine can be interpreted in the above-referenced interview leads one to wonder how seriously one could take a statement of fidelity. Even after his spokesperson's statements, he repeated his views about the symbolic nature of the devil, as is clear in this article: "Jesuit Superior General: Satan Is a 'Symbolic Reality,'" *The Catholic World Report*, August 21, 2019, https://www.catholicworldreport.com/2019/08/21/jesuit-superior-general-satan-is-a-symbolic-reality/.

58 Fr. Martin's contribution is the comment, "Interesting," which seems to be a sly way of expressing support without taking responsibility for the direct questioning of Scripture. The original comments of Fr. Rohr on the quote are in this article: Fr. Richard Rohr, "A Deeper Tenor," *Center for Action and Contemplation*, October 23, 2019, https://cac.org/a-deeper-tenor-2019-10-23/.

59 My colleague, Eduardo Echeverria, has written an excellent response to Fr. Martin's attempt to insinuate that slavery and homosexuality are parallel, and just as we came to understand slavery as unjust, we should come to un-

derstand the practice of homosexuality as normal. Dr. Echeverria describes how the Church distinguishes between culturally conditioned commands and those that are enduringly valid and discusses the issue of slavery in contrast to homosexuality in brilliant detail in this article: "No, @JamesMartin-SJ, the Analogy between Slavery and Homosexuality Does Not Hold," *The Catholic World Report*, October 29, 2019, https://www.catholicworldreport.com/2019/10/26/no-jamesmartinsj-the-analogy-between-slavery-and-homosexuality-does-not-hold/.

60 An excellent article surveying the history of Catholic thought on homosexuality and surveying the huge literature on it is that of Paul Gondreau, a professor at Providence College in Rhode Island. See Paul Gondreau, "Jesus and Paul on the Meaning and Purpose of Human Sexuality," *Nova et Vetera* 18, no. 2 (2020): 461–503. He does a particularly excellent job of addressing the "revisionist" readings of the biblical texts that seek to justify homosexuality and showing their substantial flaws.

61 Msgr. Charles Pope has done an excellent job analyzing the omissions and presenting reasonable interpretations of these psalms. See "Abbreviated Breviary? Pondering Omissions from the Current Breviary," *Community in Mission* (blog), January 12, 2020, http://blog.adw.org/2020/01/abbreviated-breviary-pondering-the-psalms-and-verses-omitted-in-the-current-breviary/.

62 For a detailed discussion of the differences between the two texts, see Matthew Hoffman's article, "Vatican's New Special Mass for Pandemic Doesn't Mention God's Wrath, Unlike Original," *LifeSite News*, April 7, 2020, https://www.lifesitenews.com/news/vatican-creates-special-mass-for-pandemic-that-unlike-original-doesnt-mention-gods-wrath.

63 Edward Pentin has written a balanced article on the document. See Edward Pentin, "Pontifical Biblical Commission Asks, 'What Is Man?'" *National Catholic Register*, December 19, 2019, https://www.ncregister.com/blog/edward-pentin/pontifical-biblical-commission-asks-what-is-man. The quotes from the document are from his translation. As of this writing, the document itself is not available on the Vatican website and has not been translated into English. People close to the situation in Rome have told me

that Pentin's translation is accurate and his article balanced. In his article, Pentin didn't draw any conclusions. The conclusions stated are my own.

[64] John Paul II, *Catechesi Tradendae* (1979), §30.

[65] I was named by Pope Benedict XVI as a theological consultant to the synod and gained a lot of insight from the experience.

[66] Thomas Aquinas, *Commentary On Ephesians*, excerpt on Eph 6:13–17; trans. Francis Martin, unpublished manuscript.

[67] An excellent source for the responsible, scholarly based interpretation of Scripture with solid application to our lives is the *Catholic Commentary on Sacred Scripture*, edited by Mary Healy and Peter Williamson, colleagues of mine at Sacred Heart Major Seminary in Detroit.

[68] Robert Cardinal Sarah, *The Day Is Now Far Spent* (San Francisco: Ignatius Press, 2019), chap. 3.

[69] Paul VI, *Dei Verbum* (1965), §11.

[70] Joseph Ratzinger, *Pilgrim Fellowship of Faith: The Church as Communion*, ed. Stephan Otto Horn and Vinzenz Pfnur, trans. Henry Taylor (San Francisco: Ignatius Press, 2003), 146.

[71] The word translated "immorality" here should actually be translated "sexual immorality" and will be in the forthcoming revision of the NAB New Testament translation underway at this time.

[72] Cardinal Sarah, *The Day Is Now Far Spent*, 47.

[73] "Cardinal Carlo Martini Says Church '200 Years Behind,'" *BBC News*, September 20, 2012, https://www.bbc.com/news/world-europe-19451439.

[74] See Christopher Lamb, "From Zero to 2020 in 83 Years: Pope Puts His Foot Down," *The Tablet*, December 22, 2019, https://www.thetablet.co.uk/news/12311/from-zero-to-2020-in-83-years-pope-puts-his-foot-down.

[75] George Weigel, "The Martini Curve Revisited," *The Catholic World Report*, January 8, 2020, https://www.catholicworldreport.com/2020/01/08/the-martini-curve-revisited/.

[76] See John Henry Newman, *An Essay on the Development of Christian Doctrine*, (Notre Dame, IN: University of Notre Dame Press, 1989).

[77] Applying the principles developed by John Henry Newman to discern what

is a true development of doctrine and what is a corruption would be a useful exercise in evaluating some of the speculative theology that appears to reverse the clear teaching of Jesus and the Apostles as interpreted by the Church throughout the centuries. It is, however, beyond the scope of this book. Michael Sharkey and Thomas Weinandy, eds., *International Theological Commission*, vol. 2, *Texts and Documents, 1986–2007* (San Francisco: Ignatius Press, 2009), 52, has distilled seven principles from Newman's work. This study was published *in forma specifica*, which means that not only the principle ideas are accepted but the entire text, including the wording. It indicates a consensus on the present state of the question, not necessarily that all of the approximately thirty members are in exact agreement on the issue.

[78] See Eduardo Echeverria, *Revelation, History and Truth: A Hermeneutics of Dogma* (New York: Peter Lang, 2017).

[79] Eduardo Echeverria, "Standing at the Crossroads: the Church and the Legacy of Vatican II," in *Global Perspectives on the New Evangelization*, ed. Cavadini and Wallenfang, vol. 3 (Eugene, OR: Pickwick Publications, forthcoming).

[80] Such false views of development of doctrine are appearing even in Vatican publications. See the insightful essay by Eduardo Echeverria responding to Sergio Centofanti's recent essay for Vatican News, which claims "it is necessary to follow the Spirit, rather than the strict letter." As Dr. Echeverria states: "This opposition could not be further from the truth." "The Spirit Versus the Letter: Responding to a False View of Doctrinal Development," *The Catholic World Report*, November 4, 2019, https://www.catholicworldreport.com/2019/11/04/the-spirit-versus-the-letter-responding-to-a-false-view-of-doctrinal-development/. For a good academic treatment of the attempt to sort out what authentic development of doctrine might mean in the light of the modernist challenge, see Guy Mansini, "The Historicity of Dogma and Common Sense: Ambroise Gardeil, Reginald Garrigou-Lagrange, Yves Congar, and the Modern Magisterium," *Nova et Vetera* 18, no. 1 (2020): 111–138. See also Guy Mansini's article, "Experience and Discourse, Revelation and Dogma in Catholic Modernism," *Nova et Vetera* 17, no. 4 (2019): 1119–1143.

81 "Pope Francis 'Breaks Catholic Traditions Whenever He Wants,'" *California Catholic Daily*, August 15, 2018, https://cal-catholic.com/pope-francis-breaks-catholic-traditions-whenever-he-wants/.

82 See Fr. Raymond De Souza, "'Imbergoglios' Keep Snaring the Pope?" *National Catholic Register*, February 16–29. Others have raised serious concerns about how Francis's supporters speak of him as being a "transformative force" not subject to ordinary expectations, e.g., responding to serious concerns such as those raised by many of the cardinals. See James Kalb, "The Pope as Supreme Being," *Crisis Magazine*, October 3, 2018, https://www.crisismagazine.com/2018/the-pope-as-supreme-being.

83 Faustina Kowalska, *Diary: Divine Mercy in My Soul*, (Stockbridge: Marians of the Immaculate Conception, 1996), no. 153.

CHAPTER 3

84 The Catholic theological tradition understands God's will to save all men as contingent on their willingness to be saved, humbling themselves and coming to faith and repentance and persevering in virtue until the end. The technical theological language for this is the "antecedent" and "consequent" aspects of God's will concerning salvation. See my discussion of this in Ralph Martin, *Will Many Be Saved? What Vatican II Actually Teaches and Its Implications for the New Evangelization* (Grand Rapids: Eerdmans Publishing, 2012), 161–164.

85 St. Thomas Aquinas, in *ST* III, q. 46, a. 11, comments on the significance of this separation of the human race that was manifested at the crucifixion itself, citing Chrysostom, Jerome, Pope Leo, Augustine, Hilary, and Bede. Thomas's citation of Augustine will give a sense of these patristic commentaries: "The very cross, if thou mark it well, was a judgment-seat: for the judge being set in the midst, the one who believed was delivered, the other who mocked Him was condemned. Already He has signified what He shall do to the quick and the dead, some He will set on His right, others on His left hand." (Augustine, Jo. vii. 36). *The Summa Theologiae of St. Thom-*

as *Aquinas*, trans. the Fathers of the English Dominican Province, rev. ed. (London: Burns Oats and Washbourne, 1920).

[86] This paragraph has been taken from my book: *Will Many Be Saved?*

[87] *The Didache*, Chapter 1, http://www.earlychristianwritings.com/text/didache-roberts.html.

[88] Peter Kreeft, *Jesus Shock* (Houston: Wellspring Publishers, 2012).

[89] Richard Bauckham has given a good, short treatment of the historical development of universalism in an essay of his, "Universalism: A Historical Survey," *Themelios* 4, no. 2 (January 1979): 48.

[90] See Augustine DiNoia, *The Diversity of Religions: A Christian Perspective* (Washington, D.C.: Catholic University of America Press, 1992).

[91] I've written an extensive exposition and critique of Rahner's theory in Chapter 5 of my book, *Will Many Be Saved?*, 93–128.

[92] See my chapter on von Balthasar in *Will Many Be Saved?*, 129–190.

[93] John R. Sachs, "Current Eschatology: Universal Salvation and the Problem of Hell," *Theological Studies* 52 (1991): 252–253.

[94] See David Bentley Hart, *That All Shall Be Saved: Heaven, Hell, and Universal Salvation* (New Haven: Yale University Press, 2019).

[95] Michael McClymond, "Opiate of the Theologians," *First Things* (December 2019), https://www.firstthings.com/article/2019/12/opiate-of-the-theologians.

[96] Francis, *Amoris Laetitia*, §297.

[97] Many theologians were very concerned about the possible implications of Pope Francis's statement. Two of them, distinguished Catholic scholars John Finnis of Oxford and Germain Grisez, one of the greatest moral theologians of the past century, jointly wrote a lengthy letter to the pope outlining their concerns (the final section raises concerns about universalism) and asking him to clarify the ambiguity of his statements. See John Finnis and Germain Grisez, "Misuse of *Amoris Laetitia*," *First Things* (December 9, 2016), https://www.firstthings.com/web-exclusives/2016/12/an-open-letter-to-pope-francis, 25–34. The pope never replied. Dr. John Bergsma, Scripture professor at Franciscan University of Steubenville, wrote a series of articles

entitled, *Will Everyone Go to Heaven?*, which addresses the question of universalism in a very effective manner. See "Will Everyone Go to Heaven? Part I & II," *Brown Pelican*, August 13–14, 2019, http://brownpelicanla.com/will-everyone-go-to-heaven-part-i-ii-by-john-bergsma/.

[98] See Matt 26:24; Mark 14:21. See also John 6:70, where Jesus calls Judas a devil and John 17:12, where Jesus calls him the "son of perdition." As John Paul II points out in *Crossing the Threshold of Hope*, (New York: Knopf, 1995), 186, the Church doesn't claim to know for certain the fate of Judas.

[99] See Pope Francis, Homily of the Wednesday of Holy Week, 2020 (at https://www.vaticannews.va/en/pope-francis/mass-casa-santa-marta/2020-04/pope-francis-mass-santa-marta-judas-exploitation-trafficking-bet.html).

[100] Michael McClymond, *The Devil's Redemption: A New History and Interpretation of Christian Universalism*, 2 vols. (Grand Rapids, MI: Baker Academic, 2018), 84.

[101] See McClymond, *The Devil's Redemption*. See also the article by Dr. McClymond addressing various aspects of universalism and responding to the recent book by David Bentley Hart: Michael McClymond, "Will All Be Saved?" *Credo* 9, no. 4 (2019), https://credomag.com/magazine_issue/will-all-be-saved/. See also the essay by Dr. Michael Pakaluk, professor at the Catholic University of America, in response to Hart's book: "Theological Fraud," *First Things* (February 6, 2020), https://www.firstthings.com/web-exclusives/2020/02/theological-fraud.

[102] I was so impressed with the book that I wrote a long review/essay of it. For anyone who doesn't have the time or the interest to read the two-volume work, I wrote a very detailed account of the argument of the book in an accessible style. See "Review: The Devil's Redemption," *Homiletic & Pastoral Review*, November 25, 2019, https://www.hprweb.com/2019/11/review-the-devils-redemption/.

[103] Fr. Frederick Faber, *Notes on Doctrinal and Spiritual Subjects*, Sermon given on the Fourth Sunday in Lent, 1863, the second-to-last time Father Faber preached. Quoted in Tom Mulahy, "Three Grand Helps in the Spiritual Battle for Our Souls," *Catholic Strength,* March 12, 2019, at https://catho-

licstrength.com/2019/03/12/three-grand-helps-in-the-spiritual-battle-for-our-souls/.

[104] Just as over a period of decades a body of teaching that came to be known as the Church's "social teaching" developed, so too we are seeing a body of teaching develop concerning the Church's teaching on evangelization. Pope Francis's *Evangelii Gaudium* is a significant contribution to this literature, although it focuses more on attitudinal and spiritual obstacles to evangelization rather than doctrinal. There also seems to be a shift in Pope Francis's concerns from an early concern with encouraging evangelization to a later concern in warning against proselytism, which has not yet been clearly defined, as of this writing, by him but has been understood by some to include an encouragement to silent witness and not explicit proclamation or efforts to bring people to conversion.

[105] Congregation for the Doctrine of the Faith, *Doctrinal Note on Some Aspects of Evangelization* (2007), §3.

[106] See Martin, *Will Many Be Saved?* See also John Paul II, *The Mission of the Redeemer* (Boston: Pauline Books and Media, 2015); Ralph Martin, *The Urgency of the New Evangelization: Answering the Call* (Huntington, IN: Our Sunday Visitor, 2013). See also my chapters: "Ad Gentes," in *The Reception of Vatican II*, ed. Matthew L. Lamb and Matthew Levering (New York: Oxford University Press, 2017), 266–291; "The Pastoral Strategy of Vatican II: Time for an Adjustment?" in *The Second Vatican Council: Celebrating Its Achievements and the Future*, ed. Gavin D'Costa and Emma Jane Harris (London: Bloomsbury Academic, 2013), 137–163. See also my articles on related topics: "Will Many Be Saved? What Vatican II Actually Teaches and Its Implications for the New Evangelization: A Response to Some Criticism," *Eschatology* (2014):175–215; "The Pastoral Strategy of Vatican II: Time for an Adjustment?" *Josephinum Journal of Theology* 19, no. 1 (Winter/Spring 2012): 70–90; "Doctrinal Clarity for the New Evangelization: The Importance of Lumen Gentium 16," *Fellowship of Catholic Scholars Quarterly* (Fall 2011): 9–17. I am drawing from these previously published works for this section of the chapter.

[107] He was the Dominican priest, Fr. Robert Christian, O.P., who, after teaching for many years in Rome, was named auxiliary bishop for the Archdiocese of San Francisco but died not too long after he was appointed.

[108] It also has received strong endorsements from quite a number of cardinals, bishops, and theologians.

[109] See Second Vatican Council, *Lumen Gentium: Dogmatic Constitution on the Church*, trans. Austin Flannery (Collegeville, MN: Liturgical Press, 1996), §16.

[110] See Second Vatican Council, *Ad Gentes* (1965), §7; Second Vatican Council, *Gaudium et Spes* (1973), §22.

[111] The following footnote is inserted here as part of the Council text: "Cfr. Epist. S.S.C.S. Officii ad Archiep. Boston.: Denz. 3869-72." The reference to the *Letter of the Holy Office to the Archbishop of Boston*, which offers doctrinal clarifications on the issues raised by Fr. Leonard Feeney in his strict interpretation of *Extra Ecclesiam Nulla Sallus* provides important insight to the proper understanding of the text as we will see.

[112] The following footnote is inserted here by the Council Fathers as backing for this text: "See Eusebius of Caesarea, *Praeparatio Evangelica*, I, 1: PG 21, 28 AB." Joseph Ratzinger, "La Mission d'Après Les Autres Textes Conciliaires," in *Vatican II: L'Activité Missionnaire de l'Église* (Paris: Cerf, 1967), 129, note 11, indicates that this reference to Eusebius does not really support the point being made, but, of course, the point can be supported in other ways: "The reason for this allusion is not very clear, since in this work Eusebius, in treating of the non-Christian religions, has another emphasis than our text: Eusebius underlines the aberrations of the pagan myths and the insufficiency of Greek philosophy; he shows that Christians are right in neglecting these in order to turn to the sacred writings of the Hebrews which constitute the true 'preparation for the Gospel.'" (La raison de cette allusion n'est pas très claire, car dans cet ourvrage l'orientation d'Eusèbe, par rapport aux religions non chrétiennes, est tout autre que dans notre texte: Eusèbe signale les égarements des mythes païens et l'insuffisane de la philosophie grecque; il montre que les chrétiens voint juste en les négligeant pour se tourner vers

les liveres saints des Hébreux qui constituent las véritable 'préparation évangélique.) The Sources Chrétiennes translation of this text, *La Préparation Évangélique: Livre* I, trans. Jean Sirinelli et Édouard des Places (Paris: Cerf, 1974), 97–105, shows that Eusebius, in the chapter cited, only mentions the non-Christian religions and philosophies as being in dire need of conversion. He speaks of them as representing a piety that is "lying and aberrant," (*mensongère et aberrante*) and cites the Scripture that speaks of "exterminating all the gods of the nations" and making them "prostrate before Him."

[113] Vatican II, *Lumen Gentium*, §16.

[114] The Walter Abbott translation that appeared in 1966 translates the Latin phrase as "But rather often." The commonly used Flannery translation of the Council documents translates the Latin *at saepius* as "very often." Other English translations use "but often" (the translation of the National Catholic Welfare Conference, the precursor of the National Council of Catholic Bishops, contained in: *The Sixteen Documents of Vatican II* [Boston: Pauline Books and Media, 1999]). The Vatican website translation also uses "but often." The English translation (by Clarence Gallagher) of *Lumen Gentium* in Norman Tanner's two-volume collection of the *Decrees of the Ecumenical Councils* (Washington, D.C.: Georgetown University Press, 1990) uses "more often, however." The French translation of the text that Congar collaborated on translates *at saepius* as "mais trop souvent." *L'Église de Vatican II*, Tome I, Texte Latin et Traduction, P.-Th. Camelot (Paris: Cerf, 1966). The Vatican website French translation uses "bien souvent." The Italian translation on the Vatican website is "ma molto spesso." The Spanish translation on the Vatican website is "pero con mucha frecuencia."

[115] Rob Bell's *Love Wins: A Book About Heaven, Hell, and the Fate of Every Person Who Ever Lived* (San Francisco: Harper, 2011) is perhaps the best known of the popular evangelical books adopting stances similar to Balthasar's regarding the possibility of eternal separation from God.

[116] Avery Dulles, "Current Theological Obstacles to Evangelization," in Steven Boguslawski and Ralph Martin, *The New Evangelization: Overcoming the Obstacles* (New York: Paulist Press, 2008), 19–20.

[117] Avery Dulles, "The Population of Hell," *First Things* 133 (May 2003): 37.

[118] Decrees of the Council of Trent, Session 6, "Decree on Justification," Chapter 15, in Tanner, *Decrees of the Ecumenical Councils*, 677.

[119] Decrees of the Council of Trent, Session 6, "Decree on Justification," Chapter 16, in Tanner, *Decrees of the Ecumenical Councils*, 678.

[120] John Paul II, *Reconciliatio et Paenitentia*, §17.

[121] See "Some Current Questions in Eschatology," in Michael Sharkey and Thomas Weinandy, ed., *International Theological Commission: Texts and Documents 1986-2007*, vol. 2 (San Francisco: Ignatius Press, 2009), 85–91. The widespread belief in "second chances" in the form of various theories of reincarnation caused the ITC to devote substantial attention to this issue in their document on eschatology.

[122] Ratzinger, *Pilgrim Fellowship of Faith*, 146.

[123] Ratzinger, *Pilgrim Fellowship of Faith*, 89.

[124] Dulles, "The Population of Hell," 36.

[125] When the ITC in the document on eschatology, "Some Current Questions in Eschatology," 90–91, attempts to assess the efficacy of the universal offer of salvation, it cautiously says that it has "ample efficacy." It then warns: "But, since hell is a genuine possibility for every person, it is not right—although today this is something which is forgotten in the preaching at exequies—to treat salvation as a kind of quasi-automatic consequence. . . . The Christian ought to be aware of the brevity of life since he knows we have one life only. As we 'all sin . . . in many ways' (Jas 3:2) and since there often was sin in our past lives, we must 'use the present opportunity to the full' (Eph 5:16) and, throwing off every encumbrance and the sin that all too readily restricts us, run with resolution the race that lies ahead of us, our eyes fixed on Jesus, the pioneer and perfector of faith' (Heb 12:1–2). 'We have not here a lasting city, but seek one that is to come' (Heb 13:14). The Christian then as an alien and a pilgrim (cf. 1 Pet 2:11) hurries in holiness of life to his own country (cf. Heb 11:14), where he will be with the Lord (cf. 1 Thes 4:17)."

[126] Kevin Flannery, S.J., "How to Think About Hell," *New Blackfriars* 72, no. 854 (November 1991): 477.

[127] Fr. Thomas Weinandy, a member of the Pontifical Theological Commission, has published several articles demonstrating how clearly and definitively the reality of hell is taught in Scripture, tradition, and the *Catechism of the Catholic Church*. He directly addresses the difficulties that are raised by universalists concerning the doctrine of hell and demonstrates how well founded the doctrine is and how it is completely compatible with God's love for everyone he has created. See Fr. Thomas Weinandy, "God and Hell," *The Catholic Thing*, March 15, 2020, https://www.thecatholicthing.org/2020/03/15/god-and-hell/. See also his article, "God and Hell (Part Two)," *The Catholic Thing*, March 21, 2020, https://www.thecatholicthing.org/2020/03/21/god-and-hell-part-two. See also Dr. John Grondelski's article "Hell Is Real. People Really Go There. Why Modern Man Can't Understand This . . ." *National Catholic Register*, November 29, 2019, https://www.ncregister.com/blog/grondelski/why-modern-man-cant-understand-hell. See also Fr. Gabriel Amorth, until recently Rome's diocesan exorcist: "Hell—real time risk for the obstinate," *Legatus*, November 2019, 34. And Fr. Chad Ripperger, "Reflecting on the last things," *Legatus*, November 2019, 32. The American Bishop, Joseph Strickland of Tyler, Texas, has also periodically published elements of a manifesto of the foundations of the faith reaffirming many of the same truths that Cardinal Mueller did in his Manifesto. See "Bishops Applaud Cardinal Müller for 'Prophetic' Manifesto of Faith," *LifeSite News*, February 11, 2019, https://www.lifesitenews.com/blogs/bishops-applaud-cardinal-mueller-for-prophetic-manifesto-of-faith.

[128] James O'Connor, "Von Balthasar and Salvation," *Homiletic and Pastoral Review* 54, no. 10 (July 1989): 20.

[129] Sometimes it is claimed, despite the consistent witness of Scripture and tradition to the reality and finality of the two ultimate destinations, that we are seeing a "development of doctrine" moving to a different position. Bishop Barron, in a review of my book *Will Many Be Saved?*, claimed that a phrase in Pope Benedict XVI's Encyclical *Spe Salvi* was evidence of such a development and not to go along with it would make someone a "dissenter." In my response to Bishop Barron, I pointed out that the rules for interpret-

ing magisterial statements published by the magisterium would in no way consider this apparently casual phrase an authoritative teaching, intending to develop doctrine. See *Ad Tuendam Fidem* and the Doctrinal Commentary that accompanied this document. The phrase in question was Benedict "supposing" that the majority of people go to purgatory. A supposition or a passing comment isn't an authoritative teaching and needs to be weighed in relationship to the whole of Scripture and tradition and the *Catechism of the Catholic Church*, which Benedict actually goes on to quote later on in the document. For an excellent treatment of authentic development of doctrine, see Echeverria, *Revelation, History, and Truth*. See also his article "The Spirit Versus the Letter."

Doctrine can develop, but it can never take on a different meaning than it originally had. As St. John Henry Newman said in one of his writings: "The many can never become the few." See my exchange with Bishop Barron: Ralph Martin, "Comments by Dr. Ralph Martin on Fr. Barron's Review of *Will Many Be Saved?*" December 7, 2012, https://www.renewalministries. net/wp-content/uploads/2020/04/Comments-by-Dr.-Ralph-Martin-on-Fr-Robert-Barrons-Review-of-Will-Many-Be-Saved.pdf?e112bd&e112bd.

[130] Roberto J. De La Noval, "Divine Drama or Divine Disclosure? Hell, Universalism, and a Parting of the Ways," *Modern Theology* 36, no. 1.

[131] Vatican II, *Lumen Gentium*, §14.

CHAPTER 4

[132] I gave a talk to several thousand people in Toronto about the contemporary relevance of the Fatima message that has been warmly received. Available as a DVD and CD from Renewal Ministries: www.renewalministries.net.

[133] All the above quotes and information are contained in an article and a moving video, available here, if it hasn't been taken down by the growing censorship of pro-life testimonies and what will be perceived as "conservative" views: Kelsey Bolar, "She Wrote Fake News for Cosmopolitan and Now Regrets Misleading Women on Feminism," *The Daily Signal*, May 26,

2020, https://www.dailysignal.com/2020/05/26/she-wrote-fake-news-for-cosmopolitan-and-now-regrets-misleading-women-on-feminism/.

[134] Calvin Freiburger, "TikTok Deletes Priest's Video Explaining Why Christians Shouldn't Support 'Pride' Month," *LifeSite News*, June 8, 2020, https://www.lifesitenews.com/news/tiktok-deletes-priests-video-explaining-why-christians-shouldnt-support-pride-month.

[135] I've written a short article that describes this and similar situations in some detail. See "Believing and Praying," *Homiletic and Pastoral Review*, January 1, 2019, https://www.hprweb.com/2019/01/believing-and-praying/.

[136] See our website: www.renewalministries.net.

[137] Christine Firer Hinze, "Lay Voices Need to Counter Crisis of Credibility on Sexual Teaching," *National Catholic Reporter*, October 11, 2012.

[138] Jorge A. Aquino, "The Choice before the Next Generation," *National Catholic Reporter*, Oct 11, 2012.

[139] Francis, *Amoris Laetitia*, §305.

[140] Francis, *Amoris Laetitia*, footnote no. 351.

[141] See E. Christian Brugger, "The Catholic Conscience, the Argentine Bishops, and 'Amoris Laetitia,'" *The Catholic World Report*, September 20, 2016, https://www.catholicworldreport.com/2016/09/20/the-catholic-conscience-the-argentine-bishops-and-amoris-laetitia/. See also Mariusz Biliniewicz, "*Veritatis Splendor* and the Universal Call to Holiness," *Nova et Vetera* 18, no. 1 (2020): 237–254. And in the same issue, Helenka Mannering, "*Veritatis Splendor* and the Rupture between Faith and Morals," 279–294; and also, Christian Stephens, "Catholic or Utopian? Two Irreconcilable Views about Moral 'Ideals,'" 295–312.

[142] See Edward Pentin, "The Pope's Endorsement of Argentina's Amoris Guidelines: What It Means," *National Catholic Register*, December 13, 2017, https://www.ncregister.com/daily-news/the-popes-endorsement-of-argentinas-amoris-guidelines-what-it-means.

[143] "Buenos Aires Bishops' Guidelines on Amoris Laetitia: Full Text," *Catholic Voices Comment*, September 18, 2016, https://cvcomment.org/2016/09/18/buenos-aires-bishops-guidelines-on-amoris-laetitia-full-text/.

[144] See Richard A. Spinello, "Cardinal Cupich Misreads Vatican II on Conscience," *Crisis*, February 19, 2018, https://www.crisismagazine.com/2018/cardinal-cupich-misreads-vatican-ii-conscience. See also Manya Brachear Pashman and Angie Leventis Lourgos, "Cupich: Pope's Document on Sex, Marriage, Family Life a 'Game Changer,'" April 9, 2016, *The Chicago Tribune*, http://www.chicagotribune.com/news/local/breaking/ct-pope-catholics-divorce-met-20160408-story.html.

[145] See "German Bishops Commit to 'Newly Assessing' Catholic Doctrine on Homosexuality and Sexual Morality," *The Catholic World Report*, December 12, 2019, https://www.catholicworldreport.com/2019/12/12/german-bishops-commit-to-newly-assessing-catholic-doctrine-on-homosexuality-and-sexual-morality/.

[146] See "Pro-Abortion Argentina President Receives Holy Communion along with Mistress at Vatican," *LifeSite News*, February 3, 2020, https://www.lifesitenews.com/blogs/pro-abortion-argentina-president-receives-holy-communion-along-with-mistress-at-vatican. See also "Vatican Official Claims Canon Law Required Giving Communion to Argentine President," *National Catholic Register*, February 10, 2020, https://www.newsbreak.com/news/0O6MBIIX/vatican-official-claims-canon-law-required-giving-communion-to-argentine-president.

[147] "If, as a result of the process of discernment, undertaken with 'humility, discretion and love for the Church and her teaching, in a sincere search for God's will and a desire to make a more perfect response to it' (AL 300), a separated or divorced person who is living in a new relationship manages, with an informed and enlightened conscience, to acknowledge and believe that he or she are at peace with God, he or she cannot be precluded from participating in the sacraments of Reconciliation and the Eucharist (see AL, notes 336 and 351)." Archdiocese of Malta and the Diocese of Gozo, "Criteria for the Application of Chapter VIII of Amoris Laetitia" (at http://ms.maltadiocese.org/WEBSITE/2017/PRESS%20RELEASES/Norms%20for%20the%20Application%20of%20Chapter%20VIII%20of%20AL.pdf).

[148] See Edward Pentin, "Pope Francis Thanks Maltese Bishops for 'Amoris La-

etitia' Guidelines," *National Catholic Register*, April 6, 2017, https://www.ncregister.com/blog/edward-pentin/pope-francis-thanks-maltese-bishops-for-amoris-laetitia-guidelines.

[149] See Francisco Pedro, "Casais divorciados já comungam na diocese de Leiria-Fátima," *Jornal de Notícias*, January 10, 2020, https://www.jn.pt/nacional/casais-divorciados-ja-comungam-na-diocese-de-leiria-fatima-11693838.html. The original article is in Portuguese and was translated by a staff member. For the couples' testimony, see "A viver o segundo casamento, 'Deus tornou-se ainda mais forte nas nossas vidas,'" *Diocese Leiria-Fatima*, June 9, 2019, https://leiria-fatima.pt/noticias/a-viver-o-segundo-casamento-deus-tornou-se-ainda-mais-forte-nas-nossas-vidas/. For an English-language article, see Jeanne Smits, "Portuguese Cardinal Allows Divorced and 'Remarried' Catholics to Receive Communion," *LifeSite News*, February 5, 2020, https://www.lifesitenews.com/news/portuguese-cardinal-allows-divorced-and-remarried-catholics-to-receive-communion.

[150] As we noted previously, the Catholic tradition understands the "except for unchastity" phrase to be referring to marriages within too close a degree of relationship or to be permitting divorce in the case of adultery, but not remarriage, in effect abolishing the divorce legislation of Moses and replacing it with God's original intention of life-long fidelity. Cardinal Mueller has written the best account of the history of this issue throughout the centuries that I know of: See "Testimony to the Power of Grace" (at http://www.vatican.va/roman_curia/congregations/cfaith/muller/rc_con_cfaith_20131023_divorziati-risposati-sacramenti_en.html). *The New York Times* wrote a somewhat perceptive article on the tension between Pope Francis and Cardinal Mueller. See Jason Horowitz, "Pope Francis Ousts Powerful Conservative Cardinal," July 1, 2017, https://www.nytimes.com/2017/07/01/world/europe/vatican-pope-doctrine-mueller.html.

[151] Edward Pentin, "'Doctrinal Anarchy' as Bishops' Conflicting Positions on Amoris Laetitia Show," *National Catholic Register*, June 17, 2017, https://www.ncregister.com/blog/edward-pentin/doctrinal-anarchy-as-bishops-conflicting-positions-on-amoris-laetitia-. Cardinal Mueller has done a

heroic job in attempting to give an orthodox interpretation to what Pope Francis says and publishes, but lately his efforts are beginning to fray and it is getting harder and harder to do. In an interesting article on hermeneutics and the papacy by Julie Yost, "A Paper Church," *First Things* (November 2019), 12–14, she says: "Conservative papalists struggle to regularize his verbal output with their notions of the privilege of infallibility. ('What did he say?' Peter can't say that. Ergo, he meant something other than what he said.) A few years in, one commentator was reduced to presenting the Holy Father as a practitioner of Straussian esoteric writing who sneaks subversive conservative messages into apparently progressive texts. St. John Henry Newman eventually saw that not every problem in ecclesiology can be solved by squinting hard at documents, an exercise that too often is both elitist and delusional. Catholics who do not wish to see their Church become exoterically Protestant should acknowledge with Newman that papalism pursued too far dictates piety to the person of the pope at the expense of the tradition he nominally secures."

[152] See Michelle Boorstein, "Catholic University Presidents Host Leading LGBT Advocate Rev. James Martin," *The Washington Post*, February 2, 2020, https://www.washingtonpost.com/local/social-issues/catholic-university-presidents-host-leading-lgbt-advocate-rev-james-martin/2020/02/02/89b-d832c-45fa-11ea-bc78-8a18f7afcee7_story.html.

[153] Archbishop Chaput, "Father James Martin and Catholic Belief," *Catholic Philly*, September 19, 2019, https://catholicphilly.com/2019/09/archbishop-chaput-column/father-james-martin-and-catholic-belief/. Fr. Martin responded to Archbishop Chaput's article, and Archbishop Chaput briefly replied to his response. The responses added nothing new to the argument. See Father James Martin, "Fr. Martin Responds to Archbishop's Chaput's Critique," *Catholic Philly*, September 19, 2019, https://catholicphilly.com/2019/09/commentaries/fr-martin-responds-to-archbishop-chaputs-critique/. Paul Mankowski has written an excellent analysis of Fr. Martin's book, *Building a Bridge*: "Pontifex Minimus," *First Things* (August 2017), https://www.firstthings.com/article/2017/08/pontifex-minimus.

[154] An article in *First Things* by J. D. Flynn points out that not challenging Church teaching is not the same thing as believing it and teaching it, and that promoting defining people by their sexual appetites (the use of the LGBTQ identities) is not consonant with the Catholic understanding of the human person. See J. D. Flynn, "More Than Our Appetites," *First Things* (February 18, 2020), https://www.firstthings.com/web-exclusives/2020/02/more-than-our-appetites.

[155] Msgr. Pope has clearly but sensitively written an excellent article explaining why Scripture and the Church warn against the active practice of homosexuality and geared towards Catholics who have imbibed the views of the culture on this issue. See "Turning Back the Tide: One Pastor's Attempt to Assert the Biblical Teaching on Homosexuality in an Age of Confusion," *Community in Mission* (blog), March 31, 2011, http://blog.adw.org/2011/03/turning-back-the-tide-one-pastors-attempt-to-assert-the-biblical-teaching-on-homosexuality-in-an-age-of-confusion/.

[156] See David Cooke, "Ban on Conversion Threatens Churches," *Campaign Life Coalition* (blog), December 15, 2019, https://www.campaignlifecoalition.com/clc-blog&id=95.

[157] See Jamie Wareham, "Switzerland Criminalizes Homophobia with Large Majority in National Referendum," *Forbes*, February 9, 2020, https://www.forbes.com/sites/jamiewareham/2020/02/09/switzerland-criminalizes-homophobia-with-large-majority-in-national-referendum. See also Jeanne Smits, "Switzerland Votes to Criminalize 'Homophobia,'" *LifeSite News*, February 10, 2020, https://www.lifesitenews.com/news/switzerland-votes-to-criminalize-homophobia.

[158] C. C. Pecknold, "Why Is J. K. Rowling Being Denounced? Because She Said No to a Lie," *The Catholic Herald*, December 20, 2019.

[159] R. R. Reno, "While we're at it," *First Things* (November 2019), 71.

[160] John Paul II, Angelus, Sunday April 1, 1979, https://w2.vatican.va/content/john-paul-ii/en/angelus/1979/documents/hf_jp-ii_ang_19790401.html.

[161] See Douglas Murray, *The Madness of Crowds: Gender, Race and Identity*, (London: Bloomsbury Continuum, 2019).

[162] Murray, *Madness of Crowds*, 56–57.

[163] Murray, *Madness of Crowds*, 245.

[164] "What We Believe," *Black Lives Matter*, accessed June 9, 2020, https://blacklivesmatter.com/what-we-believe/.

[165] Fr. Dwight Longenecker, "Rationalism, Irrational Rage and Revolution," *Fr. Dwight Longenecker* (blog), June 8, 2020, https://dwightlongenecker.com/relativism-irrational-rage-and-revolution/.

[166] Sidewinder77, "Michael Crichton on Environmentalism as a Religion," YouTube video, December 25, 2006, https://www.youtube.com/watch?v=V-v9OSxTy1aU.

[167] Michael McClymond, "Querying Queer Theory: Gender Expression and Transgender Identity in Manifold Perspective," in *Human Sexuality and the Holy Spirit: Spirit-Empowered Perspectives*, eds. Wonsuk Ma and Kathaleen Reid-Martinez (Tulsa: ORU Press, 2019), 51–95.

[168] See "Office for Catechseis," *Diocese of Springfield in Illinois*, accessed April 22, 2020, https://www.dio.org/catechesis.

[169] Msgr. Charles Pope, "Pete Buttigieg Is Wrong—God Still Forbids All Homosexual Acts," *National Catholic Register*, May 16, 2019, https://www.ncregister.com/blog/msgr-pope/pete-buttigieg-is-wrong-god-still-forbids-all-homosexual-acts.

[170] Ralph Martin, *A Crisis of Truth: The Attack on Faith, Morality, and Mission in the Catholic Church* (Ann Arbor: Servant Books, 1982).

[171] See Anthony Kosnik, William Carroll, Agnes Cunningham, Ronald Modras, and James Schutte, *Human Sexuality: New Directions in American Catholic Thought* (New York: Paulist Press, 1977).

[172] Kosnik et al., *Human Sexuality*, 92–94.

[173] Kosnik et al., *Human Sexuality*, 151–152.

[174] Martin, *A Crisis of Truth*, 118–119.

[175] See Congregation for the Doctrine of the Faith, "Letter to Archbishop John R. Quinn, President of the National Conference of Catholic Bishops in the U.S.A." (at http://www.vatican.va/roman_curia/congregations/cfaith/documents/rc_con_cfaith_doc_19790713_mons-quinn_en.html).

176 See "LA REC: Very Young Children Should Be Allowed to Transition from One Gender to Another," *Sons of St. Joseph* (blog), March 21, 2018, https://josephsciambra.com/la-rec-very-young-children-should-be-allowed-to-transition-from-one-gender-to-another/.

177 See "Gay Priest Who Painted 'Sodomite Christ' to Exhibit Artwork at 2020 LA REC," *Sons of St. Joseph* (blog), February 8, 2020, https://josephsciambra.com/gay-priest-who-painted-sodomite-christ-to-exhibit-artwork-at-2020-la-rec/.

178 R. R. Reno, *First Things* (February 2020), 66–67.

179 While almost all of the Jesuit universities in the United States have explicitly embraced the current "values of the world," with their emphasis on diversity irrespective of truth and their elevation of progressive causes, environmentalism, and accommodation to the sexual revolution both in theory and practice, many other Catholic universities have done the same. Since I am a graduate of Notre Dame, people often ask me what the situation there is. Good news and bad news. The good news is that there is a network of solid Catholic professors, chaplains, and students who effectively support each other in the faith. The bad news is that there are considerable numbers of faculty and students who are not orthodox Catholics and who often oppose the Church on key issues. And then a large number of "privileged" cultural Catholics for whom football, making money, drinking, and sex are unfortunately the dominant values. Just reading *Notre Dame Magazine* in almost any issue over the last forty years shows this mix. In a given issue, one can read good articles about professors and solid research going on at the university, along with articles by alumni casually talking about their divorces and affairs, in a completely value-free way and articles expressing great angst about the world we are leaving to our children and the environmental catastrophes awaiting us.

180 R. R. Reno, *First Things* (February 2020), 66.

181 Nancy Flory, "Texas Teacher Defends Drag Queen Class: Parents 'Should Not Have the Final Say' and 'Don't Know What's Best for Their Children,'" *The Stream*, November 16, 2019, https://stream.org/texas-teacher-defends-

A CHURCH IN CRISIS

drag-queen-class-parents-should-not-have-the-final-say-and-dont-know-whats-best-for-their-children/.

[182] The "hierarchy of truths" is a theological concept that asserts that all truths are true, so to speak, but some are more fundamental than others. In the properly hierarchy of truths, for example, the Trinity and the Incarnation would be considered more fundamental than, for example, the Marian dogmas, although the Marian dogmas would be considered equally true, just not as fundamental in the structure of theology. In the "moral hierarchy of truths" the debate around the "seamless garment" or pro-life issues takes its place. The prevailing opinion has been that the intentional killing of human beings has a higher place on the hierarchy of truths than issues such as global warming, whose ultimate effects and extent are yet to be seen, and should "win the day" in making political decisions.

[183] Robert Barron, *To Light a Fire on the Earth: Proclaiming the Gospel in a Secular Age* (New York: Image Books, 2017), 135.

[184] See most particularly the final chapter of *Will Many Be Saved?* "The Pastoral Strategy of Vatican II: Time for an Adjustment?" 191–208.

[185] John Paul II, *Novo Millennio Ineunte* (2001), §57.

[186] See Rodney Stark, *The Rise of Christianity: How the Obscure, Marginal Jesus Movement Became the Dominant Religious Force in the Western World in a Few Centuries* (San Francisco: HarperCollins, 1997).

[187] Stark, *The Rise of Christianity*, 95–128.

[188] N. T. Wright, *Paul: A Biography* (New York: Harper Collins, 2018), 217–218. I am grateful to Paul Gondreau for drawing this text to my attention.

[189] Tom Gjelten, "Pope Benedict Breaks 6-Year Silence to Comment on Clergy Sex Abuse Scandal," *National Public Radio*, April 11, 2019, https://www.npr.org/2019/04/11/712409110/pope-benedict-breaks-6-year-silence-to-comment-on-clergy-sex-abuse-scandal.

[190] See Joshua J. McElwee, "German Theologians Blast Benedict's Letter as 'Failed and Improper' Account of Abuse Crisis, *National Catholic Reporter*, April 16, 2019, https://www.ncronline.org/news/theology/german-theologians-blast-benedicts-letter-failed-and-improper-account-abuse-crisis.

191 "Theologians Condemn Pope Benedict's Letter on Abuse Crisis on German Bishops' Website," *LifeSite News*, April 16, 2019, www.lifesitenews.com/blogs/theologians-condemn-pope-benedicts-letter-on-abuse-crisis-on-german-bishops-website.

192 See George Weigel, "'Wittenberg' In Synodal Slow Motion," *First Things* (March 25, 2020), https://www.firstthings.com/web-exclusives/2020/03/wittenberg-in-synodal-slow-motion#print.

193 See "Record Numbers Leave Church in Munich Archdiocese," *The Catholic World Report*, May 26, 2020, https://www.catholicworldreport.com/2020/05/26/record-numbers-leave-church-in-munich-archdiocese/. In 2019, 272,771 Catholics de-registered: see "Catholic Church in Germany Lost a Record Number of Members Last Year," *Catholic News Agency*, June 26, 2020, https://www.catholicnewsagency.com/news/catholic-church-in-germany-lost-a-record-number-of-members-last-year-36747. A recent survey revealed that 30 percent of German Catholics are thinking of leaving the Church: see "Survey Finds 30% of German Catholics Are Considering Leaving the Church," *Catholic News Agency*, July 9, 2020, https://www.catholicnewsagency.com/news/survey-finds-30-of-german-catholics-are-considering-leaving-church-73824.

194 See "German Cardinal Criticized for Voicing 'Synodal Way' Concerns," *National Catholic Register*, February 16–29, 2020.

195 See Chico Harlan, "German Bishops Want to Modernize the Church. Are They Getting Too Far Ahead of Pope Francis?" *The Washington Post*, November 1, 2019.

196 See "New Head of German Bishops Was Behind Document Defending Contraception, Masturbation, Homosexuality," *LifeSite News*, March 3, 2020, https://www.lifesitenews.com/news/new-head-of-german-bishops-was-be-hind-document-defending-contraception-masturbation-homosexuality.

197 "In Easter Interview, German Bishops' Head Calls for Changing Church Teaching on Homosexuality," *LifeSite News*, April 20, 2020, https://www.lifesitenews.com/news/in-easter-interview-german-bish-ops-head-calls-for-changing-church-teaching-on-homosexuality.

198 Martin Bürger, "Austrian Bishops Commission Book Calling Same-Sex Relationships 'Images of God's Goodness,'" *LifeSite News*, May 26, 2020, https://www.lifesitenews.com/news/austrian-bishops-commission-book-calling-same-sex-relationships-image-of-gods-goodness. The original German language interview can be accessed here: Josef Wallner, "Mehr als ein normaler Segen," *KirchenZeitung*, April 28, 2020, https://www.kirchenzeitung.at/site/themen/gesellschaftsoziales/mehr-als-ein-normaler-segen.

199 Dorothy Cummings McLean, "Ukrainian Bishops Fraternally Correct German Bishops for Abandoning Catholic Sexual Morality," *LifeSite News*, February 10, 2020, https://www.lifesitenews.com/news/ukrainian-bishops-fraternally-correct-german-bishops-for-abandoning-catholic-sexual-morality; also see the head of the Ukrainian Bishops' Commission's explanation of why they corrected the German Bishops: Krystian Kratiuk, "Ukrainian Priest Defends Fraternal Correction of German Bishops' Liberal 'Synodal Path,'" *LifeSite News*, February 11, 2020, https://www.lifesitenews.com/opinion/ukrainian-priest-defends-fraternal-correction-of-german-bishops-liberal-synodal-path.

200 Krystian Kratiuk, "Ukrainian Priest Defends Fraternal Correction."

201 In Matthew's Gospel, there is a phrase added ("except for unchastity" [Matt 19:9]). See endnote 153 for a comment on this addition.

202 Fr. Andrew Apostoli, C.F.R., *Fatima for Today: The Urgent Marian Message of Hope* (San Francisco: Ignatius Press, 2010), 145.

203 In my opinion, the most reasonable understanding about whom to fear is that it's both the devil, who can deceive us and lead us to hell, and God, who can judge unrepentant wrongdoing and condemn us to hell. A fear of hell, while disdained today as a motivation for turning to God, is not disdained by some of the greatest saints and spiritual writers in the history of the Church, not to mention Jesus himself. While the goal is perfect love, the fear of hell has often been the necessary start for many.

204 Robert Bellarmine, "On the Ascent of the Mind to God," quoted in The Liturgy of the Hours, Office of Readings, September 17, 4:1412. I am grateful to Msgr. Andrew McLean Cummings for drawing my attention to this quote.

205 See Ralph Martin, "'I Haven't Killed Anyone!' What Serious Sins Will Exclude Us from the Kingdom of God?" *Homiletic and Pastoral Review,* November 21, 2013, https://www.hprweb.com/2013/11/i-havent-killed-anyone-what-serious-sins-will-exclude-us-from-the-kingdom-of-god/.

CHAPTER 5

206 Congregation for the Doctrine of the Faith, Instruction on Certain Aspects of the "Theology of Liberation" (1984), http://www.vatican.va/roman_curia/congregations/cfaith/documents/rc_con_cfaith_doc_19840806_theology-liberation_en.html; Instruction on Christian Freedom and Liberation (1986), http://www.vatican.va/roman_curia/congregations/cfaith/documents/rc_con_cfaith_doc_19860322_freedom-liberation_en.html.

207 Ambrose Evans-Pritchard, "Liberation Theology Is Back as Pope Francis Holds Capitalism to Account," *The Telegraph,* January 8, 2014, https://www.telegraph.co.uk/finance/comment/ambroseevans_pritchard/10559802/Liberation-Theology-is-back-as-Pope-Francis-holds-capitalism-to-account.html.

208 Dorothy Cummings McLean and Matthew Cullinan Hoffman, "Laicized Priest Who Helped Engineer Amazon Synod Claims Coronavirus Is Mother Earth's Revenge," *LifeSite News,* March 20, 2020, https://www.lifesitenews.com/news/laicized-priest-who-helped-engineer-amazon-synod-claims-coronavirus-is-mother-earths-revenge.

209 See Leonardo Boff, "As origens do Coronavirus," *A Terra é Redonda,* March 14, 2020, https://aterraeredonda.com.br/coronavirus-uma-reacao-e-represalia-de-gaia/.

210 Edward Pentin, "Holy See and UN Too Close for Comfort?" *National Catholic Register,* February 16–29, 2020.

211 See Paul Bois, "Pope Francis Invites Political Leaders to Sign 'Global Pact,'" *The Daily Wire,* September 16, 2019, https://www.dailywire.com/news/pope-francis-invites-political-leaders-sign-global-paul-bois.

212 See Andrea Gagliarducci, "Pope Francis: A Church 200 Years Out of Date," *Monday Vatican,* July 27, 2015, http://www.mondayvatican.com/vatican/

pope-francis-a-church-200-years-out-of-date. A thoughtful article by James Kalb raises serious issues about the wisdom or coherence of uniting the Church so closely to the secular global project, James Kalb, "What are the "Deep State" and "Deep Church?" Catholic World Report, July 8, 2020, https://www.catholicworldreport.com/2020/07/08/what-are-the-deep-state-and-deep-church/.

[213] "Vatican Official Praises China for Witness to Catholic Social Teaching," *Catholic News Agency*, February 6, 2018, https://www.catholicnewsagency.com/news/vatican-official-praises-china-for-witness-to-catholic-social-teaching-21595.

[214] See Paul Kengor, "Cardinal Marx Is 'Impressed'with Karl Marx," *Crisis*, May 10, 2018, https://www.crisismagazine.com/2018/cardinal-marx-impressed-karl-marx.

[215] See Diane Montagna, "Vatican Hosts Youth Conference with Pro-Abortion UN Activists," *LifeSite News*, November 8, 2019, https://www.lifesitenews.com/news/vatican-hosts-youth-conference-with-pro-abortion-un-activists.

[216] See Linda Bordoni, "Vatican Event Paves the Way to Global Compact on Education," *Vatican News*, February, 2020, https://www.vaticannews.va/en/vatican-city/news/2020-02/global-compact-education-vatican-seminar.html.

[217] See Paul Bois, "Pope Francis Invites Political Leaders," *The Daily Wire*, September 16, 2019, https://www.dailywire.com/news/pope-francis-invites-political-leaders-sign-global-paul-bois.

[218] See Christina Deardurff, "Giving a Soul to the Economy of Tomorrow," *Inside the Vatican*, March 2020, 20–21.

[219] See Phil Lawler, "US Bishops Must Address Charges of Catholic Relief Services Collaborating with Evil," *LifeSite News*, March 27, 2020, https://www.lifesitenews.com/opinion/us-bishops-must-address-charges-of-catholic-relief-services-collaborating-with-evil. For more on the difficulties of not having our witness muted when we work with aggressively secular agencies, see Germain Grisez, "The Church Betrayed?" *The Catholic World Report*, April 17, 2011, https://www.catholicworldreport.com/2011/04/17/the-church-betrayed/; and Germain Grisez, "Difficult Moral Questions,"

The Way of the Lord Jesus, accessed June 13, 2020, http://www.twotlj. org/G-3-87.html. See also Phil Lawler, "A New Campaign to Reform the CCHD," *Catholic Culture*, October 30, 2009, https://www.catholicculture. org/commentary/new-campaign-to-reform-cchd/; Phil Lawler, "The Time Is Now for the Reform of the CCHD," *Catholic Culture*, August 26, 2010, https://www.catholicculture.org/commentary/time-is-now-for-reform-cchd/; and Phil Lawler, "Draining the CCHD Swamp," *Catholic Culture*, November 27, 2017, https://www.catholicculture.org/commentary/draining-cchd-swamp/. A similarly troubling episode involved the complicity of the Knights of Malta facilitating "aid" which included contraception, leading to a shake-up in the leadership of the order and Pope Francis appointing someone who supported the alleged perpetrators. The control of a large sum of German money was also linked to the case.

[220] See Michael Hichborn, "Violence Erupts as More Catholic-Funded Groups Call for Defunding of Police," *Lepanto Institute*, July 14, 2020, https://www. lepantoin.org/violence-erupts-as-more-catholic-funded-groups-call-for-defunding-of-police/.

[221] For a good analysis of how money is moved from Rome to Malta to London in shady investments, see Ed Condon, "London to Malta via Rome: Following the Money in Vatican Financial Scandals," *Catholic News Agency*, February 19, 2020, https://www.catholicworldreport.com/2020/02/19/london-to-malta-via-rome-following-the-money-in-vatican-financial-scandals/.

[222] See Phil Lawler, "Here's How to End the CCHD Scandals," *Catholic Culture*, December 9, 2019, https://www.catholicculture.org/commentary/heres-how-to-end-cchd-scandals/.

[223] See Doug Mainwaring, "US Bishop Calls for Investigation after Report Links Catholic Relief Services to Condom Promotion," *LifeSite News*, March 4, 2020, https://www.lifesitenews.com/news/us-bishop-calls-for-investigation-after-report-links-catholic-relief-services-to-condom-promotion.

[224] See Jeffrey Sachs, "With 7 Billion on Earth, a Huge Task before Us," *CNN*, October 21, 2011, https://www.cnn.com/2011/10/17/opinion/sachs-global-population/index.html.

[225] See Edward Pentin, "Population Control Advocate Jeffrey Sachs Attacks Trump Administration at Vatican Gathering," *National Catholic Register*, February 6, 2020, https://www.ncregister.com/blog/edward-pentin/sachs-at-vatican.

[226] "Full George Soros 60 Minutes Interview Dec. 20, 1998 (unedited)," YouTube video, March 17, 2018, https://www.youtube.com/watch?v=AiqHiQYuoOs.

[227] "Remarks Delivered at the World Economic Forum," *George Soros*, January 23, 2020, https://www.georgesoros.com/2020/01/23/remarks-delivered-at-the-world-economic-forum-3/.

[228] Andrew Ross Sorkin, "George Soros Has Enemies. He's Fine with That," *New York Times*, October 25, 2019, https://www.nytimes.com/2019/10/25/business/dealbook/george-soros-interview.html.

[229] See the Open Society Foundations website: https://www.opensocietyfoundations.org/, accessed 4/7/2020. See also www.georgesoros.com for a description of other activities separate from the Open Society Foundation.

[230] Gregor Peter Schmitz, "The Crisis of a Lifetime," *Project Syndicate*, May 11, 2020, https://www.project-syndicate.org/onpoint/the-crisis-of-a-lifetime-by-george-soros-and-gregor-peter-schmitz-2020-05.

[231] See Astead W. Herndon, "George Soros Foundation Pours $220 Million into Racial Equality Push," *New York Times*, July 13, 2020, https://www.nytimes.com/2020/07/13/us/politics/george-soros-racial-justice-organizations.html.

[232] Dr. Maike Hickson, "Professor Hans Joachim Schellnhuber: A Rap Sheet," *Catholicism.org*, July 15, 2015, https://Catholicism.org/professor-hans-joachim-schellnhuber-a-rap-sheet.html.

[233] See di Sandro Magister, "In the Year of 'Laudato Si' It's Party Time for Everyone, except 'My Lord,'" *L'Espresso*, May 25, 2020, http://magister.blogautore.espresso.repubblica.it/2020/05/25/in-the-year-of-%E2%80%9Claudato-si%E2%80%99%E2%80%9D-it%E2%80%99s-party-time-for-everyone-except-for-%E2%80%9Cmy-lord%E2%80%9D/.

[234] See Dorothy Cummings McLean, "One World Government Needed to

Cope with Covid-19, says former British PM, https://www.lifesitenews. com/news/one-world-government-needed-to-cope-with-covid-19-says-former-british-pm. A similar call for a global government entity with "teeth," was made quite recently by the Secretary General of the United Nations, Antonio Guterres: "In the 21st century, Governments are no longer the only political and power reality. And we need an effective multilateralism that can function as an instrument of global governance where it is needed. The problem is not that multilateralism is not up to the challenges the world faces. The problem is that today's multilateralism lacks scale, ambition and teeth," Antonio Guterres, "Opening remarks to the Press on the launch of the UN Comprehensive Response to COVID-19," United Nations Secretary General, June 25, 2020, https://www.un.org/sg/en/content/sg/speeches/2020-06-25/remarks-press-launch-of-un-comprehensive-response-covid-19.

[235] "Clinton: 'Never Waste a Good Crisis,'" *Independent*, March 6, 2009, https://www.independent.co.uk/news/world/americas/clinton-never-waste-a-good-crisis-1638844.html.

[236] "Appeal for the Church and the World to Catholics and All People of Good Will," *Veritas Liberabit Vos*, May 8, 2020, https://veritasliberabitvos.info/appeal/.

[237] Andrew Willard Jones, "Catholic Ironies," *First Things* (November 2019): 47.

[238] See Erin O'Donnell, "The Risks of Homeschooling," *Harvard Magazine*, May–June 2020, https://harvardmagazine.com/2020/05/right-now-risks-homeschooling. See also a longer article by the same professor: Elizabeth Bartholet, "Homeschooling: Parent Rights Absolutism vs. Child Rights to Education & Protection," *Arizona Law Review* 62, no. 1 (2020), https://arizonalawreview.org/homeschooling-parent-rights-absolutism-vs-child-rights-to-education-protection/. For a commentary on this professor's views, see Katie Jay and Sarah Campbell, "Harvard Attack on Homeschooling Has Nothing to Do with Children's Best Interests," *The Federalist*, April 27, 2020, https://thefederalist.com/2020/04/27/harvard-attack-on-homeschooling-has-nothing-to-do-with-childrens-best-interests/.

[239] See the Facebook announcement of the "oversight board" at https://www.oversightboard.com/. For an analysis of its predominantly radical left, pro-abortion membership, see Doug Mainwaring, "Conservatives Denounce Facebook's New 'Oversight Board' for Judging 'Free Expression,'" *LifeSite News*, May 7, 2020, https://www.lifesitenews.com/news/conservatives-denounce-facebooks-new-oversight-board-for-judgckerber-free-expression.

[240] R. R. Reno, "Failed Leaders," *First Things* (December 2019): 62.

[241] Michael McClymond, "Opiate of the Theologians," *First Things* (December 2019), https://www.firstthings.com/article/2019/12/opiate-of-the-theologians.

[242] Pete Baklinski, "Vatican 'Climate Change' Light Show: More Than Meets the Eye," *LifeSite News*, December 15, 2015, https://www.lifesitenews.com/news/vatican-climate-change-light-show-more-than-meets-the-eye.

[243] Baklinski, "Vatican 'Climate Change' Light Show."

[244] See "Vatican Mounts Giant Statue of Demon Moloch at Roman Colosseum Entrance," *The European Union Times*, November 8, 2019, https://www.eutimes.net/2019/11/vatican-mounts-giant-statue-of-demon-moloch-at-roman-colosseum-entrance/. This article documents the installation of the statue of Moloch and speculates that this couldn't have happened without Vatican approval, but it offers no substantiation of that point.

[245] The first document sent to all the world's bishops and others was formerly called the *lineamenta* but is now called "the preparatory document." After the world's bishops and others responded, the next document prepared was "the working document," and then after the synod, "the final document," and then the post-synodal apostolic exhortation, *Querida Amazonia*. All are available at www.vatican.va. All have the same "flavor" and, in my judgment, consistently subordinate the core purpose of evangelization to its secondary implications, in the name of "integral environmental conversion."

[246] Synod of Bishops, Special Assembly for the Pan-Amazonian Region, "Final Document of the Synod on the Amazon" (2019), §27.

[247] "Cardinal Czerny: Love the Amazon and Its People to Save the Planet," *Vati-*

can News, February 12, 2020, https://www.vaticannews.va/en/vatican-city/news/2020-02/cardinal-czerny-amazon-pope-francis-exhortation.print.html.

[248] See Francis, *Querida Amazonia*, §63–65.

[249] See "Mons. Fernández pidió no reducir 'Querida Amazonía' a «pequeñeces eclesiásticas»," *Arzobispado de La Plata*, February 13, 2020, https://www.arzolap.org.ar/mons-fernandez-no-reducir-querida-amazonia-a-pequeneces-eclesiasticas/.

[250] "Pope Francis Approves New Bishops' Body to Remake Regional Church with 'Amazonian Face,'" *LifeSite News*, April 8, 2020, https://www.lifesitenews.com/blogs/pope-francis-approves-new-bishops-body-to-remake-regional-church-with-amazonian-face. See also "Repam-Generalsekretär: Lockerung für Zölibat wird kommen," *Katholisch.de*, February 16, 2020, https://www.katholisch.de/artikel/24546-repam-generalsekretaer-lockerung-fuer-zoelibat-wird-kommen.

[251] Mvenner, "The Pandemic May Accelerate Changes to the Church and Priesthood Too," *Catholic Network*, May 11, 2020, https://catholicnetwork.us/2020/05/11/the-pandemic-may-accelerate-changes-to-the-church-and-priesthood-too/.

[252] Massimo Faggioli, "The Limits of a Pontificate (Part II)," *La Croix International*, April 15, 2020, https://international.la-croix.com/news/the-limits-of-a-pontificate-part-ii/12179.

[253] See Massimo Faggioli, "The Limits of a Pontificate (Part I)," *La Croix International*, April 14, 2020, https://international.la-croix.com/news/the-limits-of-a-pontificate-part-i/12170. See also, Faggioli, "The Limits of a Pontificate (Part II)."

[254] This thrust is not new. It, in fact, has become deeply embedded in many of the missionary orders, whose primary focus is no longer conversion but "human development." Consider almost any issue of the Maryknoll, Jesuit Mission Publications, or Catholic Near East Welfare Association, and it is exceedingly rare to find any of the missionary efforts actually aiming at primary evangelization. For example, the lead article in the most recent CNE-

WA publication *One* is: "Confronting Climate Change in India." The next lead article is "Lifting Children out of Poverty in Ethiopia." Good things, but not the primary mission that Christ entrusted to the Church! See: *One,* Spring 2020.

[255] Synod of Bishops, "The Final Document," §81. Fr. Dwight Longenecker has written an insightful article: see "The Earth is not my Mother... Here's why," *Fr. Dwight Longenecker* (blog), November 7, 2019, https://dwightlongenecker.com/the-earth-is-not-my-mother-heres-why/. See also Dwight Longenecker, "Introducing the New Threat: Global Neo-Paganism," *Fr. Dwight Longenecker* (blog), November 15, 2019, https://dwightlongenecker.com/introducing-the-new-threat-global-neo-paganism/. He defines paganism like this, as a very simple creed that can be summed up as: "'Do what you will.' The pagan not only does what he wills, but his religion is an attempt to get the gods to do what he wills. . . . Paganism is simply the attempt of mankind to get the gods to do their will. It is the old, old temptation. 'You can be like God!'" See also the "Statement by Evangelicals and Catholics together: The Gift of Children," which points out that sexual immorality and nature worship are both identified as idolatry and strongly condemned by the Bible. Such idolatry allows someone to fulfill the innate need to "worship," but to do so on his own terms, making an idol ultimately, of the self. See "The Gift of Children," *First Things* (November 2019), https://www.firstthings.com/article/2019/11/the-gift-of-children.

[256] George Weigel, "There's a Pony in Here Somewhere: A Post-Synodal Reflection," *Ethics and Public Policy Center,* October 28, 2019, https://eppc.org/publications/theres-a-pony-in-here-somewhere-a-post-synodal-reflection/.

[257] Weigel, "There's a Pony in Here Somewhere."

[258] Francis, *Querida Amazonia,* §7.

[259] See Francis, *Querida Amazonia,* §84, where Pope Francis once again contrasts a "set of rules" with mercy. We certainly need to accept people where they are and not "straightaway" impose rules, but unless we get to the rules at the appropriate time (the ten commandments are really important rules that Jesus not only affirms but asks for a higher interior transformation and

makes clear that serious violations will endanger our salvation), language like this, I believe, will normally be interpreted by many priests as qualifying for the "pastoral compassion" of *Amoris Laetitia* that seems to say that people in a state of habitual serious sin don't have to repent before receiving communion, the concern expressed above by Msgr. Bux and many others. See also §90, where the formation of priests "must be preeminently pastoral and favor the development of priestly mercy." Yes, it can be properly understood, but not easily, and not easily in light of the "paradigm shift" from requiring repentance to not requiring repentance before receiving the Eucharist.

260 See Charles Lewis, "After 13,000 Deaths in Four Years, Canada Set to Make Euthanasia Even Easier," *National Catholic Register*, March 6, 2020, https://www.ncregister.com/blog/guest-blogger/canada-euthanasia. See "Euthanasia Deaths Increase in Belgium by 27% Every Year," *Evangelical Focus*, January 19, 2018, https://evangelicalfocus.com/lifetech/3194/Euthanasia_rising_in_Belgium_statistics. See also Christopher de Bellaigue, "Death on Demand: Has Euthanasia Gone Too Far?" *The Guardian*, January 18, 2019, https://www.theguardian.com/news/2019/jan/18/death-on-demand-has-euthanasia-gone-too-far-netherlands-assisted-dying. While we don't have the space in this book to consider the growing push towards "transhumanism," the desire to indefinitely prolong human life through technology with no reference to the transcendent, it is worth noting that a number of very insightful articles are being published that lay bare the underlying presuppositions of this push. See, for example, Bernard N. Schumacher, "The Desire for Immortality at the Dawn of the Third Millennium: The Anthropological Stakes," *Nova et Vetera* 17, no. 4 (2019): 1221–1241.

261 See "An Unholy Alliance: The UN, Soros, and the Francis Papacy, by Elizabeth Yore," *Brown Pelican*, February 21, 2017, http://brownpelicanla.com/an-unholy-alliance-the-un-soros-and-the-francis-papacy-by-elizabeth-yore-video/.

262 For an account of someone who "innocently" got involved in Amazonian indigenous religion, see: Edward Pentin, "How an Amazon Pagan Rite Brought 48 years of Demonic Torment, Until Christ Freed Me," *National*

Catholic Register, October 18, 2019, https://www.ncregister.com/blog/edward-pentin/amazon.

263 See Dorothy Cummings McLean, "Cardinal Müller Warns 'Hundreds of Thousands' Will Leave the Church over Pachamama Idolatry," *LifeSite News*, November 25, 2019, https://www.lifesitenews.com/news/cardinal-mueller-warns-hundreds-of-thousands-will-leave-church-over-pachamama-idolatry.

264 See "Cardinal Warns Church about Slipping into Idolatry of 'Mother Earth . . . Gaia' Worship," *LifeSite News*, February 21, 2020, https://www.lifesitenews.com/blogs/cardinal-warns-church-about-slipping-into-idolatry-of-mother-earth...gaia-worship.

265 "Fr. Mitch Pacwa Denounces Idol Worship at Amazon Synod," *Church Pop*, November 9, 2019, https://churchpop.com/2019/11/09/fr-mitch-pacwa-denounces-idol-worship-at-amazon-synod-were-not-stupid-this-is-an-idol/.

266 "Italian Bishops' Agency Published Prayer to Pachamama," *Catholic Culture*, October 29, 2019, https:www.catholicculture.org/news/headlines/index.cfm?storyid=43919; see also Jeanne Smits, "Italian Bishops' Mission Org Publishes 'Prayer to Pachamama' in Official Booklet," *LifeSite News*, October 29, 2019, https://www.lifesitenews.com/news/italian-bishops-mission-org-publishes-prayer-to-pachamama-in-official-booklet.

267 "Fr. Mitch Pacwa Denounces Idol Worship," *Church Pop*.

268 An employee of the Italian Bishops' newspaper *Avvenire*, Luciano Moia, just published a book entitled *The Church and Homosexuality: An investigation in the Light of Pope Francis' Magisterium*. In it, he argues that Pope Francis has given an opening to reevaluating same-sex relationships. He also commends Archbishop Carlo Redaelli of Gorizia for not "judging" two Boy Scout leaders in a homosexual relationship but rather asking people to reflect on it. See Martin Bürger, "Italian Bishops' Employee Uses Pope Francis' Teaching to Call on Church to Accept Homosexuality," *LifeSite News*, June 15, 2020, https://www.lifesitenews.com/news/italian-bishops-employee-uses-pope-francis-teaching-to-call-on-church-to-accept-homosexuality.

269 Reported in *First Things* (November 2019), 70.

270 Msgr. Charles Pope, "Pray for a Miracle—An Initial Reaction to the Close

of the Synod," *National Catholic Register*, October 28, 2019, https://www.ncregister.com/blog/msgr-pope/pray.

[271] Edward Pentin, "Full Text of Father Weinhardy's Letter to Pope Francis," *National Catholic Register*, November 1, 2017, https://www.ncregister.com/blog/edward-pentin/full-text-of-father-weinandys-letter-to-pope-francis.

[272] Pentin, "Full Text of Father Weinhardy's Letter."

[273] For a good summary of Fr. Weinandy's Letter to Pope Francis and the full text of the letter, see Pentin, "Full Text of Father Weinhardy's Letter."

[274] See "Pope Francis' In-Flight Press Conference: Full Text," *Vatican News*, September 10, 2019, https://www.vaticannews.va/en/pope/news/2019-09/pope-francis-inflight-press-conference-full-text.html.

[275] "Pope Francis' In-Flight Press Conference."

[276] Peter Herbeck, *St. Francis Used Words!* (Renewal Ministries, 2014). I am grateful to my colleague Peter Herbeck for his research on St. Francis.

[277] Personal communication from Peter Burak. April 30, 2020.

[278] Francesca Merlo, "Pope's Video Message to National Catholic Youth Conference," *Vatican News*, November 22, 2019, https://www.vaticannews.va/en/pope/news/2019-11/pope-francis-video-message-young-people-national-youth.html.

[279] Pope Francis, "Dialogo Del Santo Padre Francesco Con Gli Studenti," December 20, 2019, http://www.vatican.va/content/francesco/it/speeches/2019/december/documents/papa-francesco_20191220_visita-liceo-albertelli.html. Translation provided by Gary Seromik.

[280] See Robin Gomes, "Pope to Japanese Bishops: Witness to the Gospel and Protect Life," *Vatican News*, November 23, 2019, https://www.vaticannews.va/en/pope/news/2019-11/pope-francis-apostolic-visit-japan-bishops-message.html.

[281] See Pontifical Council for Inter-Religious Dialogue, "Dialogue and Proclamation" (1991).

[282] John L. Allen, "On Pope's Asia Swing, Doctrinal Tension Is the Dog That's Not Barking," *Crux*, November 20, 2019, https://cruxnow.com/analysis/2019/11/on-popes-asia-swing-doctrinal-tension-is-the-dog-thats-not-barking/.

[283] Paul VI, *Evangelii Nuntiandi* (1975), §22.

[284] John Paul II, *Redemptoris Missio* (1990), §46.

[285] John Paul II, *Novo Millennio Ineunte*, §40.

[286] John Paul II, *Novo Millennio Ineunte*, §58.

[287] Pope Francis has often said that his favorite evangelization document is Pope Paul VI's *Evangelii Nuntiandi*. But in his evolution from *Evangelii Gaudium*, published in 2013, to his more recent attacks on "proselytism," a quite different note is being sounded. Sandro Magister, the Italian Vatican commentator, has pointed out the growing disparity between *Evangelii Nuntiandi* and the direction Pope Francis is moving in. See Sandro Magister, "Il papa tanto amato da Bergoglio è anche il suo critico più severo," *L'Espresso*, November 24, 2019, http://magister.blogautore.espresso.repubblica.it/2019/11/24/il-papa-tanto-amato-da-bergoglio-e-anche-il-suo-critico-piu-severo/.

[288] Bishop Robert Barron, "Spending Time with My Spiritual Father," *Word on Fire*, January 28, 2020, https://www.wordonfire.org/resources/article/spending-time-with-my-spiritual-father/26427/.

[289] Martin Bürger, "Pope Francis Tells Chinese Catholics to be 'Good Citizens,' Not Engage in 'Proselytism,'" *LifeSite News*, March 6, 2020, https://www.lifesitenews.com/news/pope-tells-chinese-catholics-to-be-good-citizens-as-persecution-intensifies.

[290] "At Mass, Pope Francis Says 'Faith Is Social, It Is for Everyone: "Go into the Whole World and Proclaim the Gospel to Every Creature,"'" *Catholic News World*, April 25, 2020, http://www.catholicnewsworld.com/2020/04/at-mass-pope-francis-says-faith-is.html.

[291] Eduardo Echeverria, "The Idiosyncratic Pope Francis," *The Catholic Thing*, November 25, 2019, https://www.thecatholicthing.org/2019/11/25/the-idiosyncratic-pope-francis/.

[292] Echeverria, "The Idiosyncratic Pope Francis." See also Eduardo Echeverria, "Making Sense of Pope Francis on Faith, Evangelization, and Proselytizing (Part I)," *Catholic World Report*, February 1, 2020, https://www.catholicworldreport.com/2020/02/01/making-sense-of-pope-francis-on-faith-evangelization-and-proselytizing/; and "Making Sense of

Pope Francis on Faith, Evangelization, and Proselytizing (Part II)," *Catholic World Report*, February 5, 2020, https://www.catholicworldreport.com/2020/02/05/making-sense-of-pope-francis-on-faith-evangelization-and-proselytizing-part-ii/.

[293] Martín Lasarte, "The Three Diseases that Sterilize the Evangelization of the Amazon," *Free Republic*, October 12, 2019, https://www.freerepublic.com/focus/f-religion/3785644/posts.

[294] "A Document on Human Fraternity for World Peace and Living Together" (2019), http://www.vatican.va/content/francesco/en/travels/2019/outside/documents/papa-francesco_20190204_documento-fratellanza-umana.html.

[295] See Courtney Mares, "In Naples, Pope Francis Calls for Theological Dialogue with Islam, Judaism," *Catholic News Agency*, June 21, 2019, https://www.catholicnewsagency.com/news/in-naples-pope-francis-calls-for-theological-dialogue-with-islam-judaism-43531.

[296] See Brian McCall, "Bishop Schneider Appeals to Pope Francis: Publicly Correct Abu Dhabi Statement," *Catholic Family News*, May 8, 2019, https://catholicfamilynews.com/blog/2019/05/08/bishop-schneider-appeals-to-pope-francis-publicly-correct-abu-dhabi-statement/.

[297] See Fr. Thomas Reese, S.J., "Pope Francis Remakes the American Hierarchy, One Bishop at a Time," *Religious News Services*, January 28, 2020, https://religionnews.com/2020/01/28/pope-francis-remakes-the-american-hierarchy-one-bishop-at-a-time/. "With Chaput's retirement, the conservative bishops in the U.S. have lost their intellectual leader and the American Church has reached a turning point. Chaput and Cardinal Francis George of Chicago, who died in 2015, had been the most forceful conservative voices in the American hierarchy for a generation. With both of them gone, we will see a more pastoral vision of Catholicism promoted by the bishops."

[298] "Chinese Bishop Says Catholics Must Put 'Love for Homeland' First," *Catholic News Agency*, December 3, 2019, https://www.catholicnewsagency.com/news/chinese-bishop-says-catholics-must-put-love-for-homeland-first-53789.

[299] John Burger, "New Chinese Law Will Require Churches to Promote 'the Val-

ues of Socialism,'" *Aleteia*, January 1, 2020, https://aleteia.org/2020/01/01/new-chinese-law-will-require-churches-to-promote-the-values-of-socialism/.

[300] "Underground Catholics Ignore China's Religion Rules Amid Dangers," *Catholic San Francisco*, February 3, 2020, https://catholic-sf.org/news/underground-catholics-ignore-chinas-religion-rules-amid-dangers.

[301] See "Churches in China Must Preach 'Patriotism' to Reopen After Coronavirus," *National Catholic Register*, June 5, 2020, https://www.ncregister.com/daily-news/churches-in-china-must-preach-patriotism-to-reopen-after-coronavirus.

[302] See "Cardinal Zen: 'Parolin Is Manipulating the Holy Father' on China Deal," *Catholic World Report*, December 4, 2019, https://www.catholicworldreport.com/2019/12/04/cardinal-zen-parolin-is-manipulating-the-holy-father-on-china-deal/.

[303] See Paul Mozer and Ian Johnson, "China Sentences Wang Yi, Christian Pastor, to 9 Years in Prison," *New York Times*, December 39, 2019, https://www.nytimes.com/2019/12/30/world/asia/china-wang-yi-christian-sentence.html.

[304] See "Chinese Campaigns to Control Christianity Worsened in 2019, Watchdog Says," *The Catholic World Report*, March 10, 2020, https://www.catholicworldreport.com/2020/03/10/chinese-campaigns-to-control-christianity-worsened-in-2019-watchdog-says/.

[305] Robert Royal, "The Vatican's China Syndrome," *The Catholic Thing*, December 2, 2019, https://www.thecatholicthing.org/2019/12/02/the-vaticans-china-syndrome/.

[306] George Weigel, "Doubling Down on a Bad Deal," *First Things* (March 11, 2020), https://www.firstthings.com/web-exclusives/2020/03/doubling-down-on-a-bad-deal.

[307] Zhang, Feng, "People on Social Welfare Ordered to Worship CCP, Not God," Bitter Winter, July 16, 2020, https://bitterwinter.org/people-on-social-welfare-ordered-to-worship-ccp-not-god/ accessed 7/26/2020.

[308] See Andrew Jacobs, "Xinjiang Seethes Under Chinese Crackdown," *New York Times*, January 2, 2016, https://www.nytimes.com/2016/01/03/world/asia/xinjiang-seethes-under-chinese-crackdown.html; see also Aus-

tin Ramzy and Chris Buckley, "'Absolutely No Mercy': Leaked Files Expose How China Organized Mass Detentions of Muslims," *New York Times*, November 16, 2019, https://www.nytimes.com/interactive/2019/11/16/world/asia/china-xinjiang-documents.html.

309 In an essay describing this surprising trend, Jonathan van Maren gives an account of what is clearly now a surprising trend among avowed atheists. Jonathan van Maren, "Atheists in Praise of Christianity," *The Stream*, May 19, 2020, https://stream.org/atheists-in-praise-of-christianity/. Tom Holland's book is *Dominion: How the Christian Revolution Remade the World* (New York: Basic Books, 2019). He is an award-winning historian of ancient cultures.

310 Van Maren, "Atheists in Praise of Christianity."

311 Van Maren, "Atheists in Praise of Christianity."

312 Van Maren, "Atheists in Praise of Christianity."

313 "Evangélicos en Brasil: un fenómeno imparable que suma vínculos con el poder y transforma la política y la cultura," *Clarín*, March 5, 2020, https://www.clarin.com/mundo/evangelicos-brasil-fenomeno-imparable-suma-vinculos-poder-transforma-politica-cultura_0_F4YF8pzF.html, translation courtesy of Fr. Iván Pertiné, director of the Saint John Society and one of our STL students at Sacred Heart Major Seminary in Detroit; and Joseph Piper, one of the Society's seminarians. See also Eduardo Campos Lima, "As Evangelicals Gain, Catholics on Verge of Losing Marjority in Brazil, *National Catholic Reporter*, February 5, 2020, https://www.ncronline.org/news/parish/evangelicals-gain-catholics-verge-losing-majority-brazil.

314 In some of my earlier writings, I made greater use of statistics to try to awaken my readers to the seriousness of the Church's decline in almost everything that can be measured statistically. Now, my sense is that almost everybody knows we're in deep trouble, and if the trends continue in Europe, North America, South America, and Oceania, we will in coming years be a very small flock indeed. For those who would like a little statistical distress, the Center for Applied Research in the Apostolate (CARA) has extensive databases, updated continually, of almost every statistic one could want about

the state of the Church in the United States as well as selected other countries and for the global church. See https://cara.georgetown.edu/. Google Church statistics, birth rates, etc., for any developed countries and you will see the unrelenting negative downtrends. For an example, see di Sandro Magister, "Churches Ever Emptier. Two Shocking Surveys in the United States and Italy," *L'Espresso*, November 22, 2019, http://magister.blogautore. espresso.repubblica.it/2019/11/22/churches-ever-emptier-two-shocking-surveys-in-the-united-states-and-italy/.

CHAPTER 6

[315] Archdiocese of Malta and the Diocese of Gozo, "Criteria for the Application of Chapter VIII of Amoris Laetitia," nos. 7–8.

[316] Our seminary is privileged to grant a Pontifical Degree through the Angelicum University in Rome, the License in Sacred Theology, with a focus on the New Evangelization, with a combination of online courses and short summer residencies, geared for priests. See our website: www.shms.edu. Much of this chapter was previously published as an article: See Ralph Martin, "Considering Culpability," *Homiletic and Pastoral Review*, June 28, 2017, https://www.hprweb.com/2017/06/considering-culpability/.

[317] For a worthwhile consideration of what constitutes sufficient reflection, see Germain Grisez, "What Is Needed for Sufficient Reflection?" *The Way of the Lord Jesus*, accessed June 16, 2020, http://www.twotlj.org/G-1-17-A.html.

[318] Francis, *Amoris Laetitia*, §301.

[319] Manya Brachear Pashman and Angie Leventis Lourgos, "Cupich: Pope's Document on Sex, Marriage, Family Life a 'Game Changer'" April 9, 2016, *The Chicago Tribune*, http://www.chicagotribune.com/news/local/breaking/ct-pope-catholics-divorce-met-20160408-story.html.

[320] Andreas Lombard, "The Vanity of Guilt," *First Things* (November 2019), 25–31.

[321] *The Catechism of the Catholic Church*, §1857–1859.

[322] *CCC* §678.

[323] *CCC* §1860.

[324] *CCC* §1791.

[325] *CCC* §1861.

[326] Ratzinger, "Conscience and Truth," presented at 10th Workshop for Bishops, February 1991, Dallas, Texas, accessed April 8, 2020, https://www.ewtn.com/catholicism/library/conscience-and-truth-2468.

[327] For a treatment of some misunderstandings about the meaning of mercy, see my book, *The Urgency of the New Evangelization: Answering the Call* (Huntington, IN: Our Sunday Visitor, 2013), 75–95.

[328] Francis Martin, "The Spirit of the Lord Is upon Me: The Role of the Holy Spirit in the Work of Evangelization," in *The New Evangelization: Overcoming the Obstacles*, ed. Steven Boguslawski and Ralph Martin (New York: Paulist Press, 2008), 72–73. See also 74–76.

[329] St. Augustine, *Confessions*, trans. Henry Chadwick (Oxford: Oxford University Press, 1992), bk. VIII, nos. 10–11.

[330] Augustine, *Confessions*, bk. VIII, no. 13.

[331] Augustine, *Confessions*, bk. VIII, nos. 16, 17.

[332] Council of Trent, "Decree Concerning Justification," Session 6, Canon 18.

[333] Council of Trent, "Decree Concerning Justification," Session 6, chap. 11.

[334] See chapters 1–8, Ralph Martin, *The Fulfillment of All Desire: A Guidebook for the Journey to God Based on the Wisdom of the Saints* (Steubenville, OH: Emmaus Road, 2006).

CHAPTER 7

[335] See Isobel Asher Hamilton, "Compulsory Selfies and Contact-Tracing," *Business Insider*, April 14, 2020, https://www.businessinsider.com/countries-tracking-citizens-phones-coronavirus-2020-3.

[336] "AI Advances to Better Detect Hate Speech, *Facebook AI*, May 12, 2020 https://ai.facebook.com/blog/ai-advances-to-better-detect-hate-speech. Within their worldwide network of live monitors Project Veritas, through hidden cameras and whistleblowers, has documented pervasive violation of

Facebook's alleged political neutrality as moderators gleefully and aggressively eliminated conservative posts and favored radical left posts, some of which were manifestly hate speech, but because it was in favor of the "right cause," exceptions were made for them, "Facebook Content Moderator: 'If Someone is Wearing a MAGA Hat, I Am Going to Delete Them for Terrorism,'" Project Veritas, June 23, 2020, https://www.projectveritas.com/news/facebook-content-moderator-if-someone-is-wearing-a-maga-hat-i-am-going-to/.

[337] The original 1969 radio speech is transcribed in this article: Richard Heilman, "Father Joseph Ratzinger's 1969 Prediction: What the Church Will Look Like in 2020," *Roman Catholic Man*, April 10, 2020, https://www.romancatholicman.com/father-joseph-ratzingers-1969-prediction-church-will-look-like-2000/. The radio speech later appeared as a chapter in a book published by Ignatius Press in 2009. See Joseph Ratzinger, *Faith and the Future* (San Francisco: Ignatius Press, 2009).

[338] See my article "The Post-Christendom Sacramental Crisis and the Wisdom of Thomas Aquinas," *Nova et Vetera* 11, no. 1 (2013): 57–75. This article is available at https://www.renewalministries.net/wp-content/uploads/2020/04/The-Post-Christendom-Sacramental-Crisis-The-Wisdom-of-Thomas-Aquinas.pdf.

[339] There's debate about how many of them are just going to other parishes, have moved, or were simply not deeply converted enough or convinced enough about the truth of the faith in order to persevere through the normal difficulties that accompany the "seed" that falls on all kinds of different soils. No definitive studies have yet been done to provide a truly factual answer to this question.

[340] E. E. Y. Hales, *The Catholic Church in the Modern World* (New York: Image Books, 1960), 45–46.

[341] Georg Schurhammer, S.J., *Francis Xavier: His Life and His Times*, vol. 2, *India 1541–1545* (Rome: Jesuit Historical Institute, 1977), 407–408.

[342] See Vatican II, *Lumen Gentium*, §16. See the extended discussion on this in Chapter 3.

343 Michael O'Brian, "Will Beauty Save the World?" *Dappled Things* (blog), accessed May 13, 2020, https://dappledthings.org/4266/will-beauty-save-the-world/.

CHAPTER 8

344 Later on, under fire, a spokesman for Fr. Sosa said he believed what the Church believes. "Jesuit Superior General: Satan Is a 'Symbolic Reality,'" *Catholic News Agency*, August 21, 2019, https://www.catholicnewsagency. com/news/jesuit-superior-satan-is-a-symbolic-reality-60691. But then afterwards, he again claimed the devil is symbolic structure.

345 *Lifesite News* obtained an advance copy of the book, which is the basis for the article linked here and the direct quotes from the book. The link contains the page from the German original from which the English translation is taken. Maike Hickson, "Pope Benedict Links Dominance of 'Homosexual Marriage . . . Abortion' to Spiritual Power of 'Anti-Christ,'" *Lifesite News*, May 1, 2020, https://www.lifesitenews.com/news/pope-benedict-links-dominance-of-homosexual-marriage...abortion-to-spiritual-power-of-anti-christ.

346 Clive Hammond, "Pope Benedict 'Doing Absolute Best to Sabotage Francis' amid Gay Marriage-Antichrist Row," *Express*, May 6, 2020, https://www. express.co.uk/news/world/1278091/christian-news-pope-benedict-pope-francis-gay-marriage-row-antichrist-catholic-church-spt.

347 Hickson, "Pope Benedict Links Dominance of 'Homosexual Marriage.'"

348 *CCC* §675.

349 *CCC* §676.

350 *CCC* §677.

351 See Joseph Pronechen, "Fulton Sheen's Clear Warning about the Anti-Christ," *National Catholic Register*, February 10, 2019, https://www. ncregister.com/blog/joseph-pronechen/fulton-sheens-view-of-the-antichrist. See also Joseph Pronechen, "Did Fulton Sheen Prophesy about These Times?" *National Catholic Register*, September 20, 2019, https://www. ncregister.com/blog/joseph-pronechen/did-fulton-sheen-prophecy-about-

these-times. The original recording, remastered for better sound quality, is found here: "The Antichrist: Signs of Our Times by Vulnerable Fulton Sheen," *Virgo Sacrata*, accessed May 2, 2020, https://www.virgosacrata.com/antichrist-signs-of-our-times.html. The quotations from the Register's article have been verified from the original recording; a transcript of which is also included in the link above.

[352] See Pronechen, "Fulton Sheen's Clear Warning about the Anti-Christ.

[353] Emphasis added by me.

[354] See Pronechen, "Fulton Sheen's Clear Warning about the Anti-Christ."

[355] Pronechen, "Fulton Sheen's Clear Warning about the Anti-Christ."

[356] Pronechen, "Fulton Sheen's Clear Warning about the Anti-Christ."

[357] Pronechen, "Did Fulton Sheen Prophesy about These Times?"

[358] Pronechen, "Fulton Sheen's Clear Warning about the Anti-Christ."

[359] Pronechen, "Fulton Sheen's Clear Warning about the Anti-Christ."

[360] See, for example, Stephan A. McKnight, "The Renaissance Magus and the Modern Messiah," *Religious Studies Review* (April 1979): 81.

[361] McClymond, *The Devil's Redemption*. I was going to recommend specific chapters in this two-volume work that deal with the esoteric/occult influences, but significant references surface throughout both volumes. If you look at the index, you can pick out what particular chapters might be most relevant to your interests in terms of historical period, denominational influences, etc.

[362] See Martin, *Will Many Be Saved?*, 139.

[363] All of the quotations, and some of the commentary, for this chapter can be found in Ralph Martin, "Balthasar and Speyr: First Steps in a Discernment of Spirits," *Angelicum* 91, no. 2 (2014): 273–301. This article, which traces the influence of Speyr on Balthasar and his thought, was published in *Angelicum*, the theological journal of the Pontifical University of St. Thomas Aquinas in Rome. It's also available at the EBSCO host research database. The conclusions from this article are totally based on Balthasar's own published descriptions of what happened in the relationship and how important it was for him.

[364] H. Balthasar, *First Glance at Adrienne von Speyr*, trans. A. Lawry and S. Englund (San Francisco: Ignatius Press, 1981), 13.

[365] H. Balthasar, *Our Task: A Report and a Plan*, trans. J. Saward (San Francisco: Ignatius Press, 1994), 14.

[366] Balthasar, *Our Task*, 70, 72–73.

[367] J. Roten, "The Two Halves of the Moon," in *Hans Urs von Balthasar: His Life and Work*, ed. D. Schindler (San Francisco: Ignatius Press, 1991), 73.

[368] Balthasar, *Our Task*, 19.

[369] Balthasar, *First Glance*, 185–186.

[370] Balthasar, *Our Task*, 50–51, 54.

[371] Balthasar, *Our Task*, 77–79.

[372] Roten, "The Two Halves," 70.

[373] Roten, "The Two Halves," 82.

[374] Balthasar, *Our Task*, 79.

[375] This account of Balthasar's testimony about his relationship with Speyr and her immense influence on his theological views and personal life decisions is perhaps shocking enough to lead some to wonder if it is accurate and balanced. I can only remind readers to remember that it is all based on Balthasar's published testimony in the two books he wrote about their relationship—and encourage them to read the whole article cited above, which contains additional information that is as equally shocking as what could fit in this chapter.

[376] Hales, *The Catholic Church in the Modern World*, 43–44.

[377] Two biographies of Marx are Robert Payne, *Marx* (New York: Simon and Schuster, 1968); and Saul Padover, *Karl Marx: An Intimate Biography* (New York: McGraw-Hill, 1977).

[378] See VICE News, "How China Tracks Everyone," YouTube video, December 23, 2019, https://www.youtube.com/watch?v=CLo3e1Pak-Y. This is a very informative short video about the rapid development of surveillance technology in China and is based on interviews with those developing it.

[379] William Shirer, *The Rise and Fall of the Third Reich: A History of Nazi Germany* (New York: Fawcett, 1978), 153–154.

[380] See "Hitler's Philosophical Enablers," *The Catholic Thing*, June 12, 2013, https://www.thecatholicthing.org/2013/06/12/hitlers-philosophical-enablers/.

[381] H. Ott, *Martin Heidegger: A Political Life*, trans. A. Blunden (London: HarperCollins, 1993), 164.

[382] S. Müller-Doohm, *Adorno: A Biography*, trans. R. Livingstone (Cambridge: Polity Press, 2005), 18–19.

[383] Yvonne Sherratt, *Hitler's Philosophers* (New Haven, CT: Yale University Press, 2013), 126.

[384] Sherratt, *Hitler's Philosophers*, 241.

[385] Sherratt, *Hitler's Philosophers*, 248.

[386] Sherratt, *Hitler's Philosophers*, 249. See also the article by Judith Wolfe, "Philosophical Myths of the End," *Nova et Vetera* 18, no. 1 (2020): 55–66, which contains more astounding quotes from German philosophers and their support for Hitler and hyper German nationalism.

[387] See "Are Liberal Viewpoints Over-Represented on College Campuses?" *Forbes*, September 19, 2020, https://www.forbes.com/sites/quora/2019/09/19/are-liberal-viewpoints-over-represented-on-college-campuses/#5eb-d40e23ed5. See also Cass R. Sunstein, "The Problem with All Those Liberal Professors," *Bloomberg*, September 17, 2018, https://www.bloomberg.com/opinion/articles/2018-09-17/colleges-have-way-too-many-liberal-professors. And also "The Liberal Media: Every Poll Shows Journalists Are More Liberal than the American Public—And the Public Knows It," *Media Research Center*, accessed June 11, 2020, https://www.mrc.org/special-reports/liberal-mediaevery-poll-shows-journalists-are-more-liberal-american-public-%E2%80%94-and.

[388] Kübler-Ross now admits to having contact with "spiritual guides" as early as a few years after the publication of *On Death and Dying: What the Dying Have to Teach Doctors, Nurses, Clergy, and Their Own Families* (New York: Macmillan, 1969), and claims now never to have believed orthodox Christian doctrine on the reality of sin, the need for redemption, and the reality of judgment, eternal reward, and punishment. The first published statements

in this direction appeared in connection with her introduction to Raymond Moody's book, *Life After Life* (Covington, GA: Mockingbird Books, 1975), and in comments in her book *Death: the Final Stages of Growth* (Englewood Cliffs, New Jersey: Prentice Hall, 1975). In informal remarks in lectures, she was more open about her occult involvement. See the review of her work up until 1977 in *Spiritual Counterfeits Project Journal* (April 1977): 7–8. An article in *Time* (European ed., November 12, 1979, 55) brought the whole situation to public notice from the point of view of some of her collaborators, and she subsequently was even more open in public lectures about her views on spirituality and reincarnation (*Orlando Sentinel-Star* [February 19, 1981], B16), and spoke quite openly about her occult involvement for formal publication in her 1981 interview for *Playboy* (May 1981, 69–106). The Spiritual Counterfeits Project article gives a good analysis of the whole "thanatology" movement and its threads to Christian truth and life. See also Tal Brooke, *The Other Side of Death: Does Death Seal Your Destiny?* (Wheaton, IL: Tyndale House, 1979) for one Christian analysis of the death studies movement.

[389] See Marcia Seligson, "Interview with Elizabeth Kübler-Ross," *Playboy*, May 1981, 94.

[390] Quoted in Joan Saunders Wixon, "Explaining Death, After Death and the Living," *Ann Arbor News*, September 4, 1981.

[391] Angela Howard and Sasha Renaé, eds., *Reaction to the Modern Women's Movement, 1963 to the Present* (New York: Garland Publishing, 1997), 153.

[392] Howard and Renaé, *Reaction*, 153.

[393] See Mary Daly, *Beyond God the Father: Towards a Philosophy of Women's Liberation*, rev. ed. (Boston: Beacon Press, 1993).

[394] John Dart, "Spiritual Aspect Emerges in Women's Movement," *Los Angeles Times*, April 10, 1978.

[395] Dart, "Spiritual Aspect Emerges in Women's Movement."

[396] Dart, "Spiritual Aspect Emerges in Women's Movement."

[397] Rosemary Reuther, in Gregory Baum, *Journeys: The Impact of Personal Experience on Religious Thought* (New York: Paulist Press, 1976), 41, 43, 45.

Fr. Gregory Baum later left the priesthood and married a woman, but by the end of his life had entered a homosexual relationship. He continues to be hailed as a hero of the spirit of Vatican II by previously influential Vatican spokesperson Fr. Thomas Rosica.

[398] Robert J. Lifton, quoted in *Time* (European ed.), June 25, 1979, p. 33. Italics added.

[399] See Murray, *The Madness of Crowds*.

[400] See *ST* II-II, q. 153, a. 5, "whether the daughters of lust are fittingly reckoned." Thomas details eight daughters of the capital sin of lust. See ST II-II, q. 141, a.1, obj. 3. See also where Thomas points out that fear of God can keep one from fornication, but fornication destroys the appropriate fear of God. The two cannot coexist. Thanks to Michael McClymond for drawing my attention to these texts. See also the popular article, "The Daughters of Lust: 5 Questions on How They Pervert the Soul," *Catholic Culture*, accessed May 1, 2020, https://www.catholicculture.org/culture/library/view.cfm?recnum=11548. This article also includes material from Gregory the Great on the same topic.

[401] See "Annual Report 2018–2019," *Planned Parenthood*, https://www.plannedparenthood.org/uploads/filer_public/2e/da/2eda3f50-82aa-4ddb-acce-c2854c4ea80b/2018-2019_annual_report.pdf.

[402] See Martin Bürger, "New Sex Ed Teaches New Jersey Minors about Sodomy and How to Consent to It," *LifeSite News*, June 8, 2020, https://www.lifesitenews.com/news/new-sex-ed-teaches-new-jersey-minors-about-sodomy-and-how-to-consent-to-it. Another article that documents the efforts teachers make to keep parents ignorant about what they are teaching and how widespread it is: https://thefederalist.com/2020/07/28/speaker-most-parents-have-no-idea-their-kids-schools-are-pushing-insane-transgender-ideology/.

[403] See "Annual Report 2018–2019," *Planned Parenthood*. See also "Our Results," *International Planned Parenthood Federation*, accessed May 12, 2020, https://www.ippf.org/our-results.

[404] See Calvin Freiburger, "Feds Demand Planned Parenthood Return $80 Mil-

lion in Ill-Gotten COVID-19 Aid," *LifeSite News*, May 21, 2020, https://
www.lifesitenews.com/news/feds-demand-planned-parenthood-return-80-
million-in-ill-gotten-covid-19-aid.

405 Two particularly helpful sources are Lawrence Lader, *The Margaret Sanger
Story and the Fight for Birth Control* (Westport, CT: Greenwood Press,
1975); and *Margaret Sanger: An Autobiography* (New York: Dover Publications, 1971).

406 See Marshall Kirk and Hunter Madsen, *After the Ball: How America Will
Conquer Its Fear and Hatred of Gays in the 90's* (New Haven: Plume, 1989).

407 I again want to recommend an excellent article surveying the history of
Catholic thought on homosexuality and surveying the huge literature on
it. Paul Gondreau, "Jesus and Paul on the Meaning and Purpose of Human
Sexuality," *Nova et Vetera* 18, no. 2 (2020): 461–503. He does a particularly
excellent job of addressing the "revisionist" readings of the biblical texts that
seek to justify homosexuality and showing their substantial flaws.

408 See the Southern Poverty Law Center website: https://www.splcenter.org/
hate-map.

409 See John Stonestreet and Maria Baer, "From Equality Indexes to SOGI
Laws, the LGBTQ Movement Marches on," *Breakpoint*, February 20, 2020,
"https://www.breakpoint.org/from-equality-indexes-to-sogi-laws-the-
lgbtq-movement-marches-on/.

410 R. R. Reno, "Thirty Years at First Things," *First Things* (February 2020):
67–68.

411 See Doug Mainwaring, "Disney Introduces 'Gay Dad' Couple to Kids in
Reboot of Duck Tales," *LifeSite News*, April 14, 2020, https://www.lifesite-
news.com/news/disney-introduces-gay-dad-couple-to-kids-in-reboot-of-
ducktales.

412 See Josh McDowell and Bob Hostetler, *The New Tolerance: How a Cultural
Movement Threatens to Destroy You, Your Faith, and Your Children* (Wheaton, IL: Tyndale House Publishers, 1998).

413 Planned Parenthood, "Sex Education and Mental Health Report," vol. 10,
no. 1, Winter 1980, 9.

[414] Planned Parenthood, "Sex Education and Mental Health Report," 9.

[415] Joseph Chamie, "Out-of-Wedlock Births Rise Worldwide," *YaleGlobal*, March 16, 2017, https://yaleglobal.yale.edu/content/out-wedlock-births-rise-worldwide.

[416] See Roger Clegg, "Percentage of Births to Unmarried Women," *Center for Equal Opportunity*, February 26, 2020, http://www.ceousa.org/issues/1354-percentage-of-births-to-unmarried-women.

[417] Dr. Armand Nicholi, "The Fractured Family: Following It into the Future," *Christianity Today*, May 25, 1979, 11, 12.

[418] Nicholi, "The Fractured Family: Following It into the Future," 15.

[419] Nicholi, "The Fractured Family: Following It into the Future," 15.

[420] John Paul II, Homily at Campo Verano, November 1, 1979, *L'Osservatore Romano*, December 3, 1979, 14.

Chapter 9

[421] Jeffrey Mirus, "Bishops and the Secular Order: Seek First the Kingdom of God," *Catholic Culture*, May 22, 2020, https://www.catholicculture.org/commentary/bishops-and-secular-order-seek-ye-first-kingdom-god/.

[422] Paul VI, *Evangelii Nuntiandi*, §2.

[423] Bishop Athanasius Schneider, the auxiliary bishop of St. Mary in Astana, Kazakhstan, has been a leader of responsible conservative bishops who are asking Pope Francis to please clarify ambiguous statements of his that they believe are leading Catholics astray. Bishop Schneider has sometimes been viewed as "against" Vatican II, but that is not the case. In his recent book, *Christus Vincit*, while talking about admitted abuses following the Council, he narrows down to only three texts (in all of the sixteen actual documents) he thinks are problematic but could be interpreted in an orthodox way. "Of course, the majority of the texts of the Second Vatican Council present no rupture and are clearly in continuity with the constant tradition of the Church. There are a few expressions we are all aware of, however, and we need to clarify them. . . . Perhaps future popes could simply name the

ambiguous phrases in the Council texts—thanks be to God there are not so many," and give an orthodox interpretation. The texts that Bishop Schneider is concerned about pertain to an assessment of non-Christian religions, religious liberty, and ecumenism. Bishop Athanasius Schneider, *Christus Vincit: Christ's Triumph Over the Darkness of the Age* (New York: Angelico Press, 2019), 185–186.

[424] One of the most insightful early analyses of what went wrong in the interpretation of the Council was James Hitchcock's *Catholicism and Modernity* (New York: Seabury Press, 1979). Since then, there has been a deluge of books on Vatican II. For an extensive bibliography of such works, see Martin, *Will Many Be Saved?*, 289–305.

[425] See, for example, the discussion of Rahner's interpretations of the Council in Martin, *Will Many Be Saved*, 121–128.

[426] It should be noted again that the traditional understanding of "development of doctrine" as articulated by patristic sources, such as St. Vincent of Lérins, and by modern thinkers, such as Cardinal Newman, considers authentic development to be just that: a development of what is in some real sense already there, in a way which doesn't deny the truthfulness or reliability of what is already there. In addition to the recent work by my colleague Eduardo Echeverria on this issue, which we have cited already, some of the early attempts to communicate a correct understanding of the development of doctrine were Paul VI's *Ecclesiam Suam* and "Credo of the People of God," as well as *Mysterium Ecclesiae,* issued by the Congregation for the Doctrine of the Faith.

[427] There is a remarkable scene in Alessandro Manzoni's famous novel, *The Betrothed*, in which the holy Cardinal Federigo strongly but compassionately rebukes and admonishes one of his priests, Don Abbondio, for giving in to fear, cowardice, and the desire to please a powerful person, causing great harm to two of his parishioners. It is an amazing scene of pastoral encounter that provides deep food for thought. There are many editions and translations of the novel. The chapters that contain this exchange are chapters 25 and 26.

[428] Edward J. Foye, "Reviews," *National Catholic Register*, November 23, 1979.

[429] I recounted an egregious example of this in Chapter 4.

[430] "Declaration of the Bishops of the European Community," *L'Osservatore Romano*, May 21, 1979, 10.

[431] John Paul II, Address of October 22, 1978, *L'Osservatore Romano*, November 2, 1978, 12.

[432] Martin, *A Crisis of Truth*, 176.

[433] See Edward Pentin, "Cardinal Danneels Admits to Being Part of 'Mafia' Club Opposed to Benedict XVI," *National Catholic Register*, September 24, 2015, https://www.ncregister.com/blog/edward-pentin/cardinal-danneels-part-of-mafia-club-opposed-to-benedict-xvi. See also Maike Hickson, "Pope Benedict's Biographer: Leftist Cardinal Tried to Stop Ratzinger's 2005 Papal Election," *LifeSite News*, May 1, 2020, https://www.lifesitenews.com/blogs/pope-benedicts-biographer-leftist-cardinal-tried-to-stop-ratzingers-2005-papal-election.

[434] St. Augustine, "Faith and Works," 1737a, in *Faith of Our Fathers*, vol. 3, trans. William A. Jurgens (Collegeville, MN: Liturgical Press, 1979), 78–79.

[435] See, for example, John Sheets, "The C.T.S.A. and the Ordination of Women," *Communio* (Winter 1978), 387. "How does the Catholic Theological Society of America expect professional respect when it leads a task force with people who have the same opinions on the subject, and who call in consultants who share these opinions? . . . Has the CTSA ceased to be a body of professional scholars interested in the serious investigation of the truth, or has it become a politicized advocacy group? Every serious body of scholars realizes that the truth is not served by simply turning up the volume, hoping to drown out other points of view."

[436] Fr. John Meier, quoted by Joan Beifuss in *National Catholic Reporter*, February 22, 1980, 20.

[437] Benedict XVI, "Christ the Burning Fire," *Catholic Education Resource Center*, accessed May 20, 2020, https://www.catholiceducation.org/en/religion-and-philosophy/spiritual-life/christ-the-burning-fire.html.

[438] See Matthew Wright, "Cincinnati Archdiocese Fires English Educator Who

Has Been Teaching for More Than TWO DECADES," *DailyMail*, April 30, 2020, https://www.dailymail.co.uk/news/article-8274665/Ohio-catholic-school-fires-gay-teacher-parents-expressed-concern-married.html.

[439] Joel Connelly, "Protest at Catholic Archdiocese over Ouster of Gay Kennedy High Teachers," *Seattle Pi*, February 18, 2020, https://www.seattlepi.com/local/politics/article/Protest-at-Catholic-Archdiocese-over-ouster-of-15065024.php.

[440] See "Catholic School Facing Protests for Allegedly Forcing Gay Teachers out of Their Jobs," *CBS News*, February 18, 2020, https://www.cbsnews.com/news/kennedy-catholic-high-school-protests-washington-allegedly-firing-teachers-for-being-gay/. See also Kevin Molly, "Protests Erupt After Catholic High School Forces Two LGBTQ Teachers to Resign," *New Ways Ministry* (blog), February 20, 2020, https://www.newwaysministry.org/2020/02/20/students-and-parents-protest-after-lgbtq-teachers-resign-from-kennedy-catholic-high-school/.

[441] See Patti Armstrong, "A Tale of Two Schools: Brebeuf and Cathedral, "*National Catholic Register*, July 12, 2019, https://www.ncregister.com/blog/armstrong/a-tale-of-two-schools-brebeuf-and-cathedral.

[442] Mirus, "Bishops and the Secular Order: Seek First the Kingdom of God."

[443] C. S. Lewis, *The Screwtape Letters* (New York: Macmillan, 1961), 56.

[444] Cardinal Hume, "Address to Friends of Newman," *Briefing*, November 2, 1979, 5.

[445] Billy Graham, "The Seven Churches of Asia," *Christianity Today*, November 17, 1978, 20.

[446] Catharina Halkes, quoted in *National Catholic Reporter*, January 18, 1980, 15.

[447] *National Catholic Reporter*, January 18, 1980, 3.

[448] Paul VI, *Dei Verbum*, §11. For a fine selection of scholarly essays on the question of the inspiration and inerrancy of Scripture see *Letter and Spirit*, ed. Scott Hahn, vol. 6, *For the Sake of Our Salvation: The Truth and Humility of God's Word* (Steubenville, OH: Emmaus Road, 2010).

[449] Augustine, *Contra Faustum*, 17:3.

[450] Peter Damian, *The Book of Gomorrah and St. Peter Damian's Struggle Against*

Ecclesiastical Authority, trans. Matthew Cullinan Hoffman (New Braunfels, TX: Ite ad Thomam Books and Media, 2015)

451 Damian, *The Book of Gomorrah*, 81–82.

452 Catherine of Siena, *The Dialogue*, trans. Suzanne Noffke, O.P. (New York: Paulist Press, 1980), 224, 234–241.

453 Other books written by saints that contain remarkable wisdom about how to be a good leader are St. Gregory the Great's *The Book of Pastoral Care* (sixth century); and St. Bernard of Clairvaux's *Five Books on Consideration: Advice to a Pope* (twelfth century). Both are available in various editions. A sample from Gregory: "Whence it is necessary for the ruler of souls to distinguish with vigilant care between virtues and vices, lest . . . in remitting what he ought to have smitten he draw on those that are under him to eternal punishment" (II.9); "For indeed to give sleep to the eyes is to cease from earnestness, so as to neglect altogether the care of our subordinates. But the eyelids slumber when our thoughts, weighed down by sloth, connive at what they know ought to be reproved in subordinates" (III:5). Gregory the Great, "Pastoral Rule," in *Nicene and Post-Nicene Fathers*, vol. 12, ed. Philip Schaff and Henry Wace (Buffalo, NY: Christian Literature Publishing Co., 1895).

CHAPTER 10

454 Msgr. John Tracy Ellis, "American Catholics in 1979: Certain Signs of the Times," Address at the Dinner on the 150th Anniversary of *The Pilot*, Boston, Massachusetts, September 12, 1979, 3.

455 Billy Graham, "The Seven Churches of Asia," *Christianity Today*, November 17, 1978, 22.

456 Nick Duffy, "Homophobe Franklin Graham Told to 'Pack up His Tents and Leave New York' after Exploiting Hospital for Cruel Anti-LGBT+ Agenda," *Pink New*, May 4, 2020, https://www.pinknews.co.uk/2020/05/04/franklin-graham-new-york-city-coronavirus-tent-hospital-central-park-homophobia-samaritans-purse/.

457 Donna Aceto, "Franklin Graham's Send-Off: Cleaning Up After a False

Samaritan," *Gay City News*, May 17, 2020, https://www.gaycitynews.com/franklin-grahams-send-off-cleaning-up-after-a-false-samaritan/.

⁴⁵⁸ See Sarah Mac Donald, "Chastity Campaigner Banned over LGBT Comments," *The Tablet*, January 15, 2020, https://www.thetablet.co.uk/news/12385/chastity-campaigner-banned-over-lgbt-comments.

⁴⁵⁹ Andrew Mark Miller, "Franklin Graham Banned from Speaking in UK for Opposing Homosexuality," *Washington Examiner*, February 7, 2020, https://www.washingtonexaminer.com/news/franklin-graham-banned-from-speaking-in-uk-for-opposing-homosexuality.

⁴⁶⁰ John Paul II, Urbi et Orbi of October 17, 1978, *L'Osservatore Romano*, October 26, 1978, 4.

⁴⁶¹ Archbishop Viganò, Address of Apostolic Nuntio Archbishop Vigano, November 11, 2013 (at http://www.usccb.org/about/leadership/usccb-general-assembly/2013-november-meeting/nuncio-address-2013.cfm). See also my booklet, *The Final Confrontation*, which comments on this prophetic sense and how it applies to our day.

⁴⁶² Karol Wojtyla, *Sign of Contradiction*, (New York: Seabury Press, 1979), 34–35.

⁴⁶³ And the first results are in: 6,666 babies were aborted in Ireland in 2019, "6,666 Unborn Irish Children Killed by Abortion in 2019," Society for the Protection of Unborn Children, June 30, 2020, https://www.spuc.org.uk/News/ID/384456/6666-unborn-Irish-children-killed-by-abortion-in-2019.

⁴⁶⁴ See "6,666 Unborn Irish Children Killed by Abortion in 2019," *Society for the Protection of Unborn Children*, June 30, 2020, https://www.spuc.org.uk/News/ID/384456/6666-unborn-Irish-children-killed-by-abortion-in-2019.

⁴⁶⁵ Fr. Linus Clovis, "The Final Battle between Our Lord and the Reign of Satan Will Be over Marriage and the Family," *Voice of the Family*, September 11, 2019, https://voiceofthefamily.com/the-final-battle-between-our-lord-and-the-reign-of-satan-will-be-over-marriage-and-the-family/.

⁴⁶⁶ See Fr. Andrew Apostoli, C.F.R., *Fatima for Today: The Urgent Marian Mes-*

sage of Hope (San Francisco: Ignatius Press, 2010), 145.

[467] Joseph Pronechen, "Our Lady of Akita, Japan, and Today's Crisis," *National Catholic Register*, September 13, 2018, https://www.ncregister.com/blog/joseph-pronechen/at-akita-our-lady-gave-dire-warnings-on-todays-crisis.

[468] Diane Montagna, "Fatima Visionary to Cardinal: 'Final Battle between God and Satan Will Be over Marriage and Family,'" *Aleteia*, January 17, 2017, https://aleteia.org/2017/01/17/fatima-visionary-to-cardinal-final-battle-between-god-and-satan-will-be-over-marriage-and-family/. For an overall account of the Marian apparitions of the nineteenth and twentieth centuries, see Joseph A. Pelletier, A.A., *The Immaculate Heart of Mary* (Worchester, MA: Assumption, 1976).

[469] "Prophecies Given at St. Peter's Basilica during the Closing Eucharist on Pentecost Monday," May 1975, http://renewalministries.net/files/freeliterature/Prophecies_Pentecost_Monday.pdf.

[470] "Prophecies Given at St. Peter's Basilica during the Closing Eucharist on Pentecost Monday." I also recorded a nineteen-minute video commenting on this prophesy, which has been spread around the world and viewed by many thousands. See Renewal Ministries, "Fr. Michael Scanlan's Amazing Prophecy An Urgent Message for Today," YouTube video, June 9, 2020, https://www.youtube.com/watch?v=2XnxThW3wq0.

[471] Prophecy delivered by Fr. Michael Scanlan, T.O.R., at the National Advisory Meeting of the Catholic Charismatic Renewal, January 13, 1980. For those interested in fuller acquaintance with the prophetic word emerging in this renewal movement, see the May 1980 issue of *New Covenant*. In an unpublished paper, "St. Paul's Letters to the Corinthians: A Word to a Community," Fr. Francis Martin points out how an apparent lack of "proportion" in a prophetic word can be understood: "How is it possible to call a community to repentance? What is intended by such a call? The basic presupposition in such a situation is that once described by Abraham Heschel as: "Few are guilty, all are responsible." Or, as Paul approvingly quotes Menander as saying: "Evil company corrupts good manners" (1 Cor 15:33). In sociological terms, we might say that general attitudes of complicity in wrongdoing have

reached such a stage that the community is more and more responsible for the guilt of some of its members. These people are acting at variance with the will and word of God. They find it easier and easier to act in such a way, because the atmosphere in which they move is tolerant of such behavior. In such a situation, it is not rare for someone sent by God to hit upon certain key events in the life of the community—some of which may appear to be a bit trivial, or at least blown out of proportion. However, what a true prophet sees at this moment is what historians would call a "paradigmatic event": that is, an incident in which there is a certain coming together of component factors in a way which at once distills and illustrates the tone or tenor of a group." Such a moment was the Pachamama worship service in the Vatican.

[472] See Polish websites https://www.pch24.pl/; and also https://en.ordoiuris. pl/. See also the warning by Archbishop Marek Jedraszewski of Cracow, who warns against the new Marxism of the LGBTQ pressure groups. See UATV English, "Rainbow Rally in Support of LGBT Rights in Poland," YouTube video, May 8, 2019, https://www.youtube.com/watch?v=8JZCBtSC9jI.

[473] See Dorothy Cummings McLean, "Shepherds Who Deny God Sends Chastisement Are 'Immersed in Atheism': Catholic Historian," *Lifesite News*, May 21, 2020, https://www.lifesitenews.com/news/shepherds-who-deny-god-sends-chastisement-are-immersed-in-atheism-catholic-historian. When so many Church leaders are silent or tepid in their response to the chastisement of the current plague, it is ironic that people like the wrestling champion Hulk Hogan (see @HulkHogan, April 1 and April 6, 2020 tweets) and the celebrity Kourtney Kardashian are calling for repentance as a response to their millions of followers. See Melissa Roberto, "Kourtney Kardashian Shares Bible Passage Suggesting God Would Punish Evil World with an 'Epidemic,'" *Fox News*, March 19, 2020, https://www.foxnews.com/entertainment/kourtney-kardashian-bible-passage-god-punish-evil-world-epidemic-coronavirus.

[474] C. S. Lewis, *The Problem of Pain* (San Francisco: HarperCollins, 2001), 91.

CHAPTER 11

[475] Avery Dulles, S.J., "Unmasking Secret Infidelities: Hartford and the Future of Ecumenism," in *Against the World For the World: The Hartford Appeal and the Future of the American Religion*, ed. Peter Berger and Richard Neuhaus (New York: Seabury Press, 1976), 59–60.

[476] John Paul II, Homily of November 1, 1979, *L'Osservatore Romano*, December 3, 1979, 14.

[477] John Paul II, Mass for Italian Solidarity Center, *L'Osservatore Romano*, August 20, 1979, 3.

[478] John Paul II, Mass for Religious Sisters, *L'Osservatore Romano*, August 27, 1979, 3.

[479] John Paul II, *Novo Millenio Ineunte*, §6.

[480] John Paul II, Homily for "Day of Pardon," March 12, 2000 (at http://www.vatican.va/content/john-paul-ii/en/homilies/2000/documents/hf_jp-ii_hom_20000312_pardon.html).

[481] Archbishop Allen Vigneron, Mass for Pardon, October 7, 2016. This is just a partial list of a very comprehensive and beautiful solemn Liturgy of Repentance.

[482] "An Evaluation by the Episcopal Sub-Group Studying the Charismatic Renewal Presented to the Secretariat Général; de l'Episcopat de France," *Circulaire*, February 15, 1979, 2.

[483] John Paul II, Address to the Pontifical Irish College, January 13, 1980, *L'Osservatore Romano*, February 4, 1980, 5.

[484] Spiritual Exercise no. 55, in *Ignatius of Loyola: Spiritual Exercises and Selected Works*, ed. George E. Ganss (Mahwah, NJ: Paulist, 1991), 139.

[485] C. S. Lewis, *Reflections on the Psalms* (New York: Harcourt, Brace & World, 1958), 66, 72, 74.

CHAPTER 12

[486] See Gregory A. Smith, "Just One-Third of U.S. Catholics Agree with Their

Church that Eucharist Is Body, Blood of Christ," *Pew Research*, August 5, 2019, https://www.pewresearch.org/fact-tank/2019/08/05/transubstanti-ation-eucharist-u-s-catholics/.

487 Michael Harper, *Beauty or Ashes? The Ashe Lecture 1979* (Hounslow, England: Hounslow Printing, 1979), 6.

488 This is not to deny that there is much sound contemporary Catholic spiritual writing. Fr. Thomas Dubay, Fr. Donald Haggerty, Fr. Jacques Philippe, and many others are rich sources.

489 As noted earlier, my friend and the vice president of Renewal Ministries, Peter Herbeck, has written a booklet, *St. Francis Used Words!* that has been one of our bestsellers. It contains many of the sayings and writings that we are citing here with source references. I am grateful to Peter for his research on this important topic. Some of his research on St. Francis was also referenced in Chapter 5.

490 Brother Ugolino, *Little Flowers of St. Francis of Assisi*, trans. Arthur Livingston (Grand Rapids, MI: Christians Classics Ethereal Library, 1930), chap. 18.

491 St. Bonaventure, "Minor Life of St. Francis," in *St. Francis of Assisi Writings and Early Biographies: English Omnibus of the Sources for the Life of St. Francis* (Chicago: Franciscan Press, 1991), Chapter 3, no. 8.

492 Bonaventure, "Minor Life of St. Francis," Chapter 2, no. 5.

493 *Canticle of the Sun.*

494 St. Francis of Assisi, "Letter to the Rulers of the People," *St. Francis of Assisi Writings and Early Biographies: English Omnibus of the Sources for the Life of St. Francis* (Chicago: Franciscan Press, 1991) 115–116.

495 Francis of Assisi, "Letter to the Rulers of the People," 115–116.

496 See Richard Rohr, *The Universal Christ: How a Forgotten Reality Can Change Everything We See, Hope For, and Believe* (New York: Convergent Books, 2019).

497 Bono actively encouraged Ireland to vote to legalize abortion. A few months after this, he was received warmly by Pope Francis in an audience. See Hannah Brockhaus, "Pope Francis Meets Bono," *Catholic News Agency*, September 19, 2018, https://www.catholicnewsagency.com/news/pope-

francis-meets-bono-44083.

498 "The Universal Christ: How a Forgotten Reality Can Change Everything We See, Hope For, and Believe," *Amazon*, accessed May 19, 2020, https://www.amazon.com/Universal-Christ-Forgotten-Reality-Everything/dp/1524762091/.

499 See "About the Author" in "Confessions, Revised and Updated: The Making of a Postdenominational Priest," *Amazon*, accessed May 7, 2020, https://www.amazon.com/Confessions-Revised-Updated-Making-Postdenominational-ebook/dp/B00TNBOHHY. See also the article by Richard Bauckham, "The New Age Theology of Matthew Fox: A Christian Theological Response," *Anvil* 13 (1996): 115–126.

500 Michael McClymond, "'Everything Is Christ'—and Other Muddled Messages from Richard Rohr," *The Gospel Coalition*, September 16, 2019, https://www.theGospelcoalition.org/reviews/universal-christ-richard-rohr/. See also the article, Douglas Farrow, "The Pachamama Rohrs," *Catholic World Report*, November 17, 2019, https://www.catholicworldreport.com/2019/11/17/the-pachamama-rohrs/.

501 Fr. Richard Rohr, "Final Court of Appeal," *Center for Action and Contemplation*, October 22, 2019, https://cac.org/final-court-of-appeal-2019-10-22/.

502 Rohr, "Final Court of Appeal."

503 Rohr, "Final Court of Appeal."

504 See Congregation for the Doctrine of the Faith, Letter to the Bishops of the Catholic Church on Some Aspects of Christian Meditation, October 15, 1989, http://www.vatican.va/roman_curia/congregations/cfaith/documents/rc_con_cfaith_doc_19891015_meditazione-cristiana_en.html. See also Pontifical Council for Culture and Pontifical Council for Interreligious Dialogue, Jesus Christ, the Bearer of the Water of Life, February 3, 2003, http://www.vatican.va/roman_curia/pontifical_councils/interelg/documents/rc_pc_interelg_doc_20030203_new-age_en.html.

505 Maura Judkis, "Greetings from the Alternate Universe Where Oprah and Michelle Obama Are Running for President," *The Washington Post*, February 12, 2020, https://www.washingtonpost.com/lifestyle/style/greetings-from-

the-alternate-universe-where-oprah-and-michelle-obama-are-running-for-president/2020/02/12/54d05d18-4ba1-11ea-b721-9f4cdc90bc1c_story.html.

506 Michael Gerson, "When We Come to the End of Our Strength, the Universe Will Hold Us," *Washington Post*, March 23, 2020, https://www.washingtonpost.com/opinions/can-all-this-silence-help-us-live-a-better-life/2020/03/23/264cd788-6d3d-11ea-a3ec-70d7479d83f0_story.html.

507 This wisdom has been extremely helpful in my own life. I spent ten years synthesizing the wisdom of the main doctors of the Church that focus on the spiritual journey in order to make this wisdom available to the average Catholic in clear, understandable, and readable form. See Ralph Martin, *The Fulfillment of All Desire: A Guidebook for the Journey to God Based on the Wisdom of the Saints* (Steubenville, OH: Emmaus Road, 2006). Also available in kindle, audible, CD albums, Spanish, and many other languages.

508 John of the Cross, "The Spiritual Canticle," in *The Collected Works of St. John of the Cross*, translated by Kieran Kavanaugh, O.C.D., and Otilio Rodriguez, O.C.D. (Washington, D.C.: ICS Publications, 1991), 29.3.

509 Bernard of Clairvaux, *On the Song of Songs*, vol. 2, trans. Killian J. Walsh, (Collegeville, MN, 1971), 23.7.

510 Sr. Emmanuel, "Letter to My Friends," May 16, 2020, https://sremmanuel.org/newsletter/letter-to-my-friends-n5/.

511 John Paul II, *Dives in Misericordia* (1980), §10.

512 Paul VI, *Ecclesiam Suam* (1964), §26.

513 Paul VI, *Gaudete in Domino* (1975), §7.

514 John Paul II, Address of November 15, 1978, *L'Osservatore Romano*, November 23, 1978.

515 See "Pope Tells Priests: Run Life in the Spirit Courses," *Catholic Charismatic Renewal*, accessed May 19, 2020, http://www.ccr.org.uk/articles/pope-tells-priests-run-life-in-the-spirit-courses/.

516 James Hitchcock, "The Secular Sickness," *Columbia*, July 1979, 11.

517 John Paul II, General Audience of November 8, 1978, *L'Osservatore Romano*, November 16, 1978.

[518] See Martin, *The Fulfillment of All Desire*, chap. 4.

CHAPTER 13

[519] *CCC* §783.

[520] *CCC* §785.

[521] Vatican II, *Lumen Gentium*, §35.

[522] Some of the material in this chapter first took shape as an academic paper I delivered at a theological symposium for seminary educators hosted by the Institute for Priestly Formation, based in Omaha, Nebraska. It was published in that form in a collection of such essays. See Ralph Martin, "The Priestly Sharing in the Prophetic Mission of Jesus: Its Implications for the Formation of 'Missionary Disciples' According to the New *Ratio Fundamentalis*," in *Priestly Formation and Integrative Healing*, ed. Deacon James Keating (Omaha, NE: Institute for Priestly Formation, 2019), 23–44. The Institute then asked me to expand the original essay into a booklet length publication, which they published in the spring of 2020. See Ralph Martin, *Priest as Prophet: Priestly Participation in the Prophetic Ministry of Jesus* (Omaha: Institute for Priestly Formation, 2020). I would recommend giving a copy of the booklet, *Priest as Prophet*, to priests that you know. It is available from The Institute for Priestly Formation (priestlyformation.org) or from Renewal Ministries (renewalministries.net).

[523] Sr. Wendy Beckett, *Spiritual Letters* (London: Bloomsbury Publishers, 2013), 19.

[524] I've personally been going through another round of "Jesus shock" as some young men in our office who are reaching out to young adults and I are going through a Bible study focusing on what Jesus and the Apostles say about the eternal consequences of refusing to believe in Jesus or repent of sin. We're shocked at how frequent and clear such references are. For example, when we completed Matthew's Gospel, we found sixty-three instances of Jesus, talking, either explicitly or implicitly about the eternal consequences that rest on our acceptance or rejection of his words and deeds.

[525] Dr. Jeffrey Mirus, "Bishops and the Secular Order: Seek First the Kingdom of God," *Catholic Culture*, May 22, 2020, https://www.catholicculture.org/commentary/bishops-and-secular-order-seek-ye-first-kingdom-god/.

[526] Mirus, "Bishops and the Secular Order: Seek First the Kingdom of God."

[527] At the same time, it is hard to overemphasize the prophetic nature of Jesus's mission. In fact, a respected Dominican scholar has written a convincing book claiming that the parallels between the prophet Elijah and Jesus are key to understanding his ministry. Paul Hinnebusch, O.P., *Jesus, The New Elijah* (Ann Arbor, MI: Servant Books, 1978).

[528] I use the term "salvation of souls" in full cognizance of contemporary theological anthropology that emphasizes the salvation of the whole person, but the fact remains that the soul is separated from the body at death and at that moment is judged, either saved or lost, only at the final judgment to be reunited with its body at the general resurrection.

[529] *ST* I-II, q. 28, a. 4. I am grateful to Msgr. Daniel Trapp, Spiritual Director of the Theologate at Sacred Heart Major Seminary for reading an earlier draft of this chapter and suggesting the reference to St. Thomas.

[530] I would like to emphasize again, as I have done periodically through this book, one intellectual/theological deception that undermines zeal for holiness, evangelization, and the sacrifice of priestly vocations, which if corrected would serve to increase appropriate zeal. Theological ambivalence about whether hell could be a realistic outcome for people removes one major intellectual component that fueled Jesus's zeal. In fact, I would say that it is Jesus's profound vision of what is at stake for every human being—heaven or hell—that was a primary motivator not only of his prophetic/evangelistic zeal but of the whole plan of salvation. As you recall, I devoted all of Chapter 3 to this issue.

[531] Even though incorporated into the Church, one who does not, however, persevere in charity is not saved. He remains indeed in the bosom of the Church, but "in body," not "in heart." All children of the Church should nevertheless remember that their exalted condition results not from their own merits but from the grace of Christ. If they fail to respond in thought,

word, and deed to that grace, not only shall they not be saved, but they shall be the more severely judged. See Vatican II, *Lumen Gentium*, §14.

[532] See Msgr. John Cihak, "Saint John Vianney's Pastoral Plan," *Courageous Priest*, http://www.courageouspriest.com/father-john-cihak-saint-john-vianneys-pastoral-plan.

[533] Georg Schurhammer, S.J., *Francis Xavier, His Life and His Times*, vol. 2 (Chicago: Loyola Press, 1980), 407. See p. 160 for a fuller excerpt from Francis's letter.

[534] In my own experience of the exercises, two eight-day retreats and one thirty-day retreat, the key meditation on hell was guided by a demythologizing meditation by Rahner that was ineffective.

[535] Joseph Pronechen, "On July 13, 1917, Our Lady of Fatima Showed a Vision of Hell and Taught Us How to Avoid It," *National Catholic Register*, July 13, 2017, https://www.ncregister.com/blog/joseph-pronechen/fatima-july-13-apparition-ways-to-overcome-a-frightening-vision.

[536] Pronechen, "On July 13, 1917, Our Lady of Fatima Showed a Vision of Hell and Taught Us How to Avoid It."

[537] Donna-Marie Cooper O'Boyle, *Our Lady of Fatima: 100 Years of Stories, Prayers, and Devotions* (Cincinnati, OH: Servant, 2017), 76.

[538] And it is no accident that, not many years later, Jesus commanded an angel to take St. Faustina on a tour of hell "so that no soul may find an excuse by saying there is no hell, or that nobody has ever been there, and so no one can say what it is like" (Faustina Kowalska, *Diary of Saint Maria Faustina Kowalska: Divine Mercy in My Soul* [Stockbridge, MA: Marian Press, 1987], no. 741). Faustina's vision is terrifying and is very similar to that of Catherine of Siena's over six hundred years ago and to what Mary showed the children at Fatima. The deception that God is so merciful that no one will be lost, which has gripped the Church in a haze of indifferentism, was intended to be blocked by the vision of hell given to the children at Fatima and to St. Faustina and the many specific revelations contained in her diary that indicate that if there is no response to mercy with faith and repentance, many will perish, and that in fact, many are perishing. See *Diary of Saint Maria*

Faustina Kowalska, nos. 153, 635, 741, 965, 1396.

[539] See the chapter in my book, "A New Pentecost for the New Evangelization," *The Urgency of the New Evangelization*, 37–57. See also the seven-part DVD series developed by Renewal Ministries, *As by A New Pentecost*. This series is available for free as a download on the Renewal Ministries YouTube Channel and for purchase as a DVD set on the Renewal Ministries website. It leads participants through a series of talks and spiritual exercises with the goal of facilitating a greater outpouring of the Holy Spirit in each of the participants lives. See also the major academic work analyzing the practice of Christian initiation in the early Church, with particular attention to the experience of the Spirit and the release of charisms. Kilian McDonnell, O.S.B., and George Montague, S.M., *Christian Initiation and Baptism in the Holy Spirit: Evidence from the First Eight Centuries,* (Collegeville, MN: Michael Glazier Books, 1991).

[540] *CCC* §907.

[541] In my STL class in the summer of 2018, with thirty priests from all over the country, the question of the "McCarrick" scandal came up, and we had a lively discussion. I discussed this at some length in Chapter 6. When I suggested that the code of silence needed to be broken and people need to start speaking up when they know sexual immorality is going on, the priests surprised me. "You can't possibly understand as a layman what fear we live in." I was astounded. And this was the general consensus of the class, diocesan and religious, North American and international. They told me that they were afraid of what their superiors could do to them if they spoke up. "We could be transferred to an isolated rural parish; bad things could be put in our 'files' to be used later; we could be shunned by our fellow priests; our bishop would never favor us again; we wouldn't get the assignment that really matched our gifts," etc. These priests, for the most part, were living in a species of fear. I told them I thought they needed an infusion of simple human courage and a good dose of the fear of the Lord so they would fear God more than man. "For God did not give us a spirit of timidity but a spirit of power and love and self-control" (2 Tim 1:7). There is a culture of "cover-up," of silence,

of complacency, and quite frankly, of cowardice, that has deeply informed many of our priests and is operating strongly in forming future priests. There is an "infantilism" that has been bred in grown men, who are unable to relate as fellow human beings, brothers in Christ, in a healthy way to authority. There is a tremendous fear of conflict. Human formation needs to take this into account and help people to become accustomed to speaking the truth in love to one another and to those they serve and those they serve under.

[542] Doug Mainwaring, "Jim Caviezel: Passion of the Christ Sequel 'Will Be a Masterpiece,'" *LifeSite News*, March 25, 2020, https://www.lifesitenews.com/news/jim-caviezel-passion-of-the-christ-sequel-will-be-a-masterpiece.

[543] St. Ignatius of Loyola's meditation in the *Spiritual Exercises* on the "Two standards," the standard or banner of the devil or of Christ and the need to make a definitive choice between the two is a very important part of the *Spiritual Exercises*.

More From Ralph Martin
& Renewal Ministries

Now that you've finished *A Church in Crisis: Pathways Forward*, connect with Ralph and Renewal Ministries to continue the discussion!

- **Subscribe to our YouTube Channel**, where Renewal Ministries' President Ralph Martin shares weekly videos offering a faith-filled perspective on what's happening in the world today.

  » **www.YouTube.com/renewalministriesrm**

- **Sign up for Renewal Ministries' free monthly newsletter**, which includes a letter from Ralph, as well as ongoing commentary on the "signs of the times," food for spiritual growth, and inspiring stories of what God is doing around the world.

  » **www.renewalministries.net/newsletter**

- **Check out our website** to learn more about our outreach to younger generations, our mission work in more than forty countries, and more!

  » **www.renewalministries.net**

- **Read Ralph's best-selling book** *The Fulfillment of All Desire: A Guidebook for the Journey to God Based on the Wisdom of the Saints.*

  » **Available at stpaulcenter.com/emmaus-road-publishing and wherever books are sold.**